Praise for Baseball For Dummies

"There may not be anyone alive who knows more about baseball than Joe Morgan."

— Bob Costas, NBC Sports Broadcaster

"Whether you are a first-day fan or a lifetime fan of baseball as I am, everyone can learn something from *Baseball For Dummies.* 'Little Joe' is truly Big Joe with this book."

— Chris Berman, ESPN Sports Broadcaster

"What Joe Morgan doesn't know about baseball is simply not worth knowing."

— Jon Miller, ESPN Baseball Commentator

"Joe Morgan knows baseball. In fact, he was one of the most intelligent players to ever play the game."

— Sparky Anderson, three-time World Series winning manager

"Joe Morgan could hit singles, doubles, triples and home runs. This book is a grand slam."

— Pete Rose, 1975 World Series Most Valuable Player, Cincinnati Reds

"*Baseball For Dummies* brings out the kid in every reader. A terrific book for people of all ages."

— Fred Opper, Coach of Fordham University

"NBC's Joe Morgan again showed himself a rare bird: an ex-jock with savvy and the ability to communicate it."

— *People Magazine*

TM

References for the Rest of Us!™

Baseball For Dummies®

Quick Reference Card

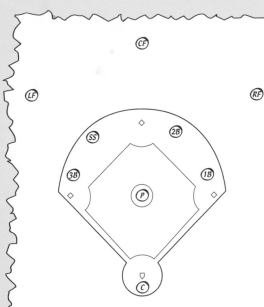

The positions

Abbreviation	Player
P	Pitcher
C	Catcher
1B	First baseman
2B	Second baseman
3B	Third baseman
SS	Shortstop
LF	Left fielder
CF	Center fielder
RF	Right fielder

Getting on base

✔ You hit a fair ball that is not caught by a fielder before it touches the ground.

✔ You hit a fair ball that touches the ground and is caught by a fielder whose throw fails to beat you to a base.

✔ The umpire calls four pitches out of the strike zone during your at-bat.

✔ A pitch in the strike zone hits you without first touching your bat.

✔ The catcher obstructs your swing.

✔ You hit a fair ball beyond the playing field (for a home run).

✔ You hit a fair, catchable ball, but the fielder drops the ball, throws it away, and so on.

✔ A third strike skips past the catcher and you beat the throw to first.

Getting out

✔ A fielder catches your fair or foul ball before it touches the ground (unless it is a *foul tip* to the catcher with less than two strikes).

✔ You hit a foul tip that is caught by the catcher for strike three.

✔ After hitting the ball, you or first base is tagged before you touch the base.

✔ The umpire calls three strikes during your at-bat (whether you swing or not).

✔ A ball that you hit fair hits your bat a second time while you are in fair territory.

✔ While running outside the foul lines, you obstruct a fielder's throw.

✔ You hit the ball with one or both feet outside the batter's box or step from one batter's box to another while the pitcher winds up.

✔ You obstruct the catcher from fielding or throwing.

...For Dummies: Bestselling Book Series for Beginners

Baseball For Dummies®

The playing field

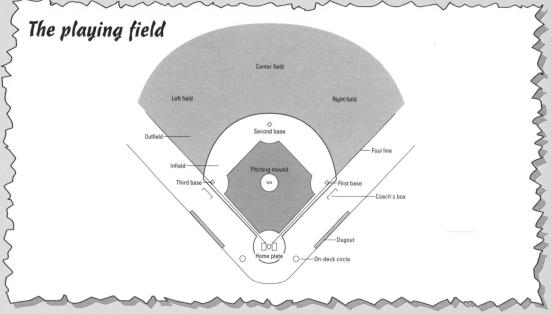

Center field

Left field

Right field

Outfield

Second base

Foul line

Infield

Pitching mound

Third base

First base

Coach's box

Dugout

Home plate

On-deck circle

Getting out on the basepaths

- ✔ If you are on the same base with a team-mate when the ball is alive (the second runner is out).

- ✔ If you pass a preceding runner on the basepaths.

- ✔ If you miss a base and the defense notices it.

- ✔ If a fielder tags you with a ball that is alive while you are off the base (however, no one can tag you out if you overrun first base provided you return immediately to that bag without making a turn towards second).

- ✔ If your teammate hits a ball that touches you in fair territory without it first touching or passing any fielder except the pitcher.

- ✔ If, in the judgment of the umpire, you hinder a fielder from making a play.

- ✔ If a batted ball forces you to advance to another base and the fielder possessing the ball tags that base before you reach it.

Major league baseball "mosts"

Most Games Played: 3,562, Pete Rose (1963–86)

Most Career Home Runs: 755, Henry Aaron (1954–76)

Most Home Runs in a Season: 61, Roger Maris (1961)

Most Career Runs Batted In: 2,297, Henry Aaron (1954–76)

Most Career Hits: 4,256, Pete Rose (1963–86)

Most Consecutive Games Batting Safely: 56, Joe DiMaggio (1941)

Most Stolen Bases in a Season: 130, Rickey Henderson (1982)

Most Career Wins: 511, Cy Young (1890–1911)

Most Career Strikeouts: 5,714, Nolan Ryan (1966–93)

Most Strikeouts in a Season: 383, Nolan Ryan (1973)

Most Strikeouts in a Game: 20, Roger Clemens (1986, 1996)

Most No-Hitters Pitched: 7, Nolan Ryan

Most Consecutive Games Played: 2,478 (and counting), Cal Ripken (1982 through 1997)

...For Dummies: Bestselling Book Series for Beginners

BASEBALL FOR DUMMIES®

by Joe Morgan

with Richard Lally

Foreword by Sparky Anderson

IDG Books Worldwide, Inc.
An International Data Group Company

Foster City, CA ♦ Chicago, IL ♦ Indianapolis, IN ♦ Southlake, TX

Baseball For Dummies ®

Published by
IDG Books Worldwide, Inc.
An International Data Group Company
919 E. Hillsdale Blvd.
Suite 400
Foster City, CA 94404
www.idgbooks.com (IDG Books Worldwide Web site)
www.dummies.com (Dummies Press Web site)

Library of Congress Catalog Card No.: 98-070137

ISBN: 0-7645-5085-3

Printed in the United States of America

10 9 8 7 6 5 4 3 2 1

1DD/SV/QS/ZY/IN

Distributed in the United States by IDG Books Worldwide, Inc.

Distributed by Macmillan Canada for Canada; by Transworld Publishers Limited in the United Kingdom; by IDG Norge Books for Norway; by IDG Sweden Books for Sweden; by Woodslane Pty. Ltd. for Australia; by Woodslane Enterprises Ltd. for New Zealand; by Longman Singapore Publishers Ltd. for Singapore, Malaysia, Thailand, and Indonesia; by Simron Pty. Ltd. for South Africa; by Toppan Company Ltd. for Japan; by Distribuidora Cuspide for Argentina; by Livraria Cultura for Brazil; by Ediciencia S.A. for Ecuador; by Addison-Wesley Publishing Company for Korea; by Ediciones ZETA S.C.R. Ltda. for Peru; by WS Computer Publishing Corporation, Inc., for the Philippines; by Unalis Corporation for Taiwan; by Contemporanea de Ediciones for Venezuela; by Computer Book & Magazine Store for Puerto Rico; by Express Computer Distributors for the Caribbean and West Indies. Authorized Sales Agent: Anthony Rudkin Associates for the Middle East and North Africa.

For general information on IDG Books Worldwide's books in the U.S., please call our Consumer Customer Service department at 800-762-2974. For reseller information, including discounts and premium sales, please call our Reseller Customer Service department at 800-434-3422.

For information on where to purchase IDG Books Worldwide's books outside the U.S., please contact our International Sales department at 650-655-3200 or fax 650-655-3295.

For information on foreign language translations, please contact our Foreign & Subsidiary Rights department at 650-655-3021 or fax 650-655-3281.

For sales inquiries and special prices for bulk quantities, please contact our Sales department at 650-655-3200 or write to the address above.

For information on using IDG Books Worldwide's books in the classroom or for ordering examination copies, please contact our Educational Sales department at 800-434-2086 or fax 817-251-8174.

For press review copies, author interviews, or other publicity information, please contact our Public Relations department at 650-655-3000 or fax 650-655-3299.

For authorization to photocopy items for corporate, personal, or educational use, please contact Copyright Clearance Center, 222 Rosewood Drive, Danvers, MA 01923, or fax 978-750-4470.

is a trademark under exclusive license to IDG Books Worldwide, Inc., from International Data Group, Inc.

About the Authors

Joe Morgan, one of six children born to Mr. and Mrs. Leonard (Ollie) Morgan, moved from Bohnam, Texas to Oakland at the age of 10 in 1954. His principal residence has been in the East Bay Area since that time. Joe was an active participant in sports and social programs at the Brookfield Community Center. He continued his education in the Peralta College District, attending Merritt College from 1961 to 1963, graduating with honors and an AA Degree. He also attended California State University at Hayward, earning a BS in Physical Education. Again, both scholastic and athletic honors were accorded him. Entering the ranks of professional baseball in 1963, Joe signed with the Houston Colt 45's. He participated with their farm club for approximately two seasons and became a regular player for the Astros in 1964. He was named National League Rookie of the Year in 1965, and his exceptional performance continued with the Astros until 1972 when he was traded to the Cincinnati Reds. He continued to be a dominant factor in the ranks of professional baseball throughout his career. Honors accorded him during this period are numerous. These honors include Most Valuable Player in the 1972 All-Star Game; Most Valuable Player in the National League in 1975 and 1976; recipient of the Commissioner's Award in 1976 for most votes by the fans for the All-Star Game; and recipient of the Comeback Player of the Year award in 1982. Before ending his career in 1984, Joe had established a new career home-run record for a second baseman; played in a record 92 consecutive games without an error (by a second baseman); played in four World Series, winning two championships; played in seven League Championship Series; and established an All-Star record by playing in seven consecutive games with a hit. In addition, he won five Gold Glove Awards, played in ten All-Star Games, and recorded 692 stolen bases. These honors are indicative of his great abilities. He was elected to the National Baseball Hall of Fame in 1990 on the first ballot.

Richard Lally's articles and columns on baseball, politics, boxing, business, the arts, and general sports have appeared in prestigious publications throughout the world. He is the author or co-author of sixteen books, including the baseball autobiography *The Wrong Stuff* written with Boston Red Sox pitching ace Bill Lee. The book enjoyed a long run on best-seller lists in the U.S. and Canada and was selected as part of *Total Baseball's* Ultimate Baseball Library.

ABOUT IDG BOOKS WORLDWIDE

Welcome to the world of IDG Books Worldwide.

IDG Books Worldwide, Inc., is a subsidiary of International Data Group, the world's largest publisher of computer-related information and the leading global provider of information services on information technology. IDG was founded more than 25 years ago and now employs more than 8,500 people worldwide. IDG publishes more than 275 computer publications in over 75 countries (see listing below). More than 60 million people read one or more IDG publications each month.

Launched in 1990, IDG Books Worldwide is today the #1 publisher of best-selling computer books in the United States. We are proud to have received eight awards from the Computer Press Association in recognition of editorial excellence and three from *Computer Currents'* First Annual Readers' Choice Awards. Our best-selling *...For Dummies®* series has more than 30 million copies in print with translations in 30 languages. IDG Books Worldwide, through a joint venture with IDG's Hi-Tech Beijing, became the first U.S. publisher to publish a computer book in the People's Republic of China. In record time, IDG Books Worldwide has become the first choice for millions of readers around the world who want to learn how to better manage their businesses.

Our mission is simple: Every one of our books is designed to bring extra value and skill-building instructions to the reader. Our books are written by experts who understand and care about our readers. The knowledge base of our editorial staff comes from years of experience in publishing, education, and journalism — experience we use to produce books for the '90s. In short, we care about books, so we attract the best people. We devote special attention to details such as audience, interior design, use of icons, and illustrations. And because we use an efficient process of authoring, editing, and desktop publishing our books electronically, we can spend more time ensuring superior content and spend less time on the technicalities of making books.

You can count on our commitment to deliver high-quality books at competitive prices on topics you want to read about. At IDG Books Worldwide, we continue in the IDG tradition of delivering quality for more than 25 years. You'll find no better book on a subject than one from IDG Books Worldwide.

John Kilcullen
CEO
IDG Books Worldwide, Inc.

Steven Berkowitz
President and Publisher
IDG Books Worldwide, Inc.

Eighth Annual Computer Press Awards ≥1992

Ninth Annual Computer Press Awards ≥1993

Tenth Annual Computer Press Awards ≥1994

Eleventh Annual Computer Press Awards ≥1995

IDG Books Worldwide, Inc., is a subsidiary of International Data Group, the world's largest publisher of computer-related information and the leading global provider of information services on information technology. International Data Group publishes over 275 computer publications in over 75 countries. Sixty million people read one or more International Data Group publications each month. International Data Group's publications include: **ARGENTINA:** Buyer's Guide, Computerworld Argentina, PC World Argentina; **AUSTRALIA:** Australian Macworld, Australian PC World, Australian Reseller News, Computerworld, IT Casebook, Network World, Publish, Webmaster; **AUSTRIA:** Computerwelt Osterreich, Networks Austria, PC Tip Austria; **BANGLADESH:** PC World Bangladesh; **BELARUS:** PC World Belarus; **BELGIUM:** Data News, **BRAZIL:** Annuário de Informática, Computerworld, Connections, Macworld, PC Player, PC World, Publish, Reseller News, Supergamepower; **BULGARIA:** Computerworld Bulgaria, Network World Bulgaria, PC & MacWorld Bulgaria; **CANADA:** CIO Canada, Client/Server World, ComputerWorld Canada, InfoWorld Canada, NetworkWorld Canada, WebWorld; **CHILE:** Computerworld Chile, PC World Chile; **COLOMBIA:** Computerworld Colombia, PC World Colombia; **COSTA RICA:** PC World Centro America; **THE CZECH AND SLOVAK REPUBLICS:** Computerworld Czechoslovakia, Macworld Czech Republic, PC World Czechoslovakia; **DENMARK:** Communications World Danmark, Computerworld Danmark, Macworld Danmark, PC World Danmark, Techworld Danmark; **DOMINICAN REPUBLIC:** PC World Republica Dominicana; **ECUADOR:** PC World Ecuador; **EGYPT:** Computerworld Middle East, PC World Middle East; **EL SALVADOR:** PC World Centro America; **FINLAND:** MikroPC, Tietoverkko, Tietoviikko; **FRANCE:** Distributique, Hebdo, Info PC, Le Monde Informatique, Macworld, Reseaux & Telecoms, WebMaster France; **GERMANY:** Computer Partner, Computerwoche, Computerwoche Extra, Computerwoche FOCUS, Global Online, Macwelt, PC Welt; **GREECE:** Amiga Computing, GamePro Greece, Multimedia World; **GUATEMALA:** PC World Centro America; **HONDURAS:** PC World Centro America; **HONG KONG:** Computerworld Hong Kong, PC World Hong Kong, Publish in Asia; **HUNGARY:** ABCD CD-ROM, Computerworld Szamitastechnika, Internetto online Magazine, PC World Hungary, PC-X Magazin Hungary; **ICELAND:** Tolvuheimur PC World Island; **INDIA:** Information Communications World, Information Systems Computerworld, PC World India, Publish in Asia; **INDONESIA:** InfoKomputer PC World, Komputek Computerworld, Publish in Asia; **IRELAND:** ComputerScope, PC Live!; **ISRAEL:** Macworld Israel, People & Computers/Computerworld; **ITALY:** Computerworld Italia, Macworld Italia, Networking Italia, PC World Italia; **JAPAN:** DTP World, Macworld Japan, Nikkei Personal Computing, OS/2 World Japan, SunWorld Japan, Windows NT World, Windows World Japan; **KENYA:** PC World East African; **KOREA:** Hi-Tech Information, Macworld Korea, PC World Korea; **MACEDONIA:** PC World Macedonia; **MALAYSIA:** Computerworld Malaysia, PC World Malaysia, Publish in Asia; **MALTA:** PC World Malta; **MEXICO:** Computerworld Mexico, PC World Mexico, **MYANMAR:** PC World Myanmar; **NETHERLANDS:** Computer! Totaal, LAN Internetworking Magazine, LAN World Buyers Guide, Macworld Netherlands, Net, WebWereld; **NEW ZEALAND:** Absolute Beginners Guide and Plain & Simple Series, Computer Buyer, Computer Industry Directory, Computerworld New Zealand, MTB, Network World, PC World New Zealand; **NICARAGUA:** PC World Centro America; **NORWAY:** Computerworld Norge, CW Rapport, Datamagasinet, Financial Rapport, Kursguide Norge, Macworld Norge, Multimediaworld Norge, PC World Ekspress Norge, PC World Nettverk, PC World Norge, PC World ProduktGuide Norge; **PAKISTAN:** Computerworld Pakistan; **PANAMA:** PC World Panama; **PEOPLE'S REPUBLIC OF CHINA:** China Computer Users, China Computerworld, China InfoWorld, China Telecom World Weekly, Computer & Communication, Electronic Design China, Electronics Today, Electronics Weekly, Game Software, PC World China, Popular Computer Week, Software Weekly, Software World, Telecom World; **PERU:** Computerworld Peru, PC World Profesional Peru, PC World SoHo Peru; **PHILIPPINES:** Click!, Computerworld Philippines, PC World Philippines, Publish in Asia; **POLAND:** Computerworld Poland, Computerworld Special Report Poland, Cyber, Macworld Poland, Networld Poland, PC World Komputer; **PORTUGAL:** Cerebro/PC World, Computerworld/Correio Informático, Dealer World Portugal, Mac*In/PC*In Portugal, Multimedia World; **PUERTO RICO:** PC World Puerto Rico; **ROMANIA:** Computerworld Romania, PC World Romania, Telecom Romania; **RUSSIA:** Computerworld Russia, Mir PK, Publish, Seti; **SINGAPORE:** Computerworld Singapore, PC World Singapore, Publish in Asia; **SLOVENIA:** Monitor; **SOUTH AFRICA:** Computing SA, Network World SA, Software World SA; **SPAIN:** Communicaciones World España, Computerworld España, Dealer World España, Macworld España, PC World España; **SRI LANKA:** Infolink PC World; **SWEDEN:** CAP&Design, Computer Sweden, Corporate Computing Sweden, Internetworld Sweden, it.branschen, Macworld Sweden, MaxiData Sweden, MikroDatorn, Nätverk & Kommunikation, PC World Sweden, PCaktiv, Windows World Sweden; **SWITZERLAND:** Computerworld Schweiz, Macworld Schweiz, PCtip; **TAIWAN:** Computerworld Taiwan, Macworld Taiwan, NEW ViSiON/Publish, PC World Taiwan, Windows World Taiwan; **THAILAND:** Publish in Asia, Thai Computerworld; **TURKEY:** Computerworld Turkiye, Macworld Turkiye, Network World Turkiye, PC World Turkiye; **UKRAINE:** Computerworld Kiev, Multimedia World Ukraine, PC World Ukraine; **UNITED KINGDOM:** Acorn User UK, Amiga Action UK, Amiga Computing UK, Apple Talk UK, Computing, Macworld, Parents and Computers UK, PC Advisor, PC Home, PSX Pro, The WEB; **UNITED STATES:** Cable in the Classroom, CIO Magazine, Computerworld, DOS World, Federal Computer Week, GamePro Magazine, InfoWorld, I-Way, Macworld, Network World, PC Games, PC World, Publish, Video Event, THE WEB Magazine, and WebMaster; online webzines: JavaWorld, NetscapeWorld, and SunWorld Online; **URUGUAY:** InfoWorld Uruguay; **VENEZUELA:** Computerworld Venezuela, PC World Venezuela; and **VIETNAM:** PC World Vietnam.   3/24/97

Dedication

Joe Morgan: To the Morgan family for their support and sacrifices when I was a player and their love that keeps me motivated today. Lisa, Angela, Ashley, Kelly — Dad loves you.

Richard Lally: To the SGI and the great desire for kosen-rufu.

Author's Acknowledgments

Joe Morgan: I want to thank all of my former teammates who were part of my learning experience about the greatest game in the world. What are friends for? They are there when you need a favor. Thank you Johnny Bench, Ken Caminiti, Bob Gibson, Ken Griffey, Sr., Barry Larkin, Bill Lee, Willie McCovey. A special thanks to the man who taught me the real philosophy of managing, the great Sparky Anderson. The Cincinnati Reds 1976 team was the greatest team ever. Richard, you are a great partner. The Wild Bunch would have cleaned up Dodge City easier than Doc and the Earp brothers. Thanks to IMG and IDG Books Worldwide, Inc.; your staffs do a great job. Your turn, Richard.

Richard Lally: I want to first thank my partner, Joe Morgan, for bringing the same dedication and intelligence to this project that he brought to the field in every game he played. Mr. Morgan is Hall of Fame in everything he does as well as being a grand fellow with great taste in westerns (and remember, JM, if you ever want to take on Johnny Ringo and the Clantons, I'm your Huckleberry). Joe's assistant, Lolita Aulston, kept us on track and on schedule. The staff at IDG could not have been more supportive: Stacy Collins, Kevin Thornton, and our meticulous editor Bill Helling made this project a pleasant task; Darren Meiss provided invaluable help on anything asked of him. Mark Reiter, our agent at IMG/Bach Literary, was a driving force behind the book. His encouragement and vision were constant sources of inspiration. Mark's assistant, Sara Falkenberry, kept the lines of communication open and was extraordinarily patient (I tend to call a lot). I could never properly express my gratitude to Julian Bach. From the time I gave him my first manuscript, the skipper at IMG/Bach has been my most enthusiastic ally. And we all want to give special thanks to Ann Torrago, who kept the checks coming regularly.

We did not have a staff of researchers, but whenever data proved elusive, I was always able to turn to one of my gang of Usual Suspects: Billy Altman, Bill Shannon, Jordan Sprechman, Bill Daughtry, and John Collett (Our Man in the Ballparks). Mr. Shannon, a walking baseball database, also double-checked our work to cut out any glitches. Bob Gibson, Rusty Staub, Bill Lee, Sparky Anderson, Johnny Bench, Willie McCovey, Barry Larkin, Ken Caminiti, and Ken Griffey, Sr., our "all-star" team of advisors, could not have been more generous with their time and insights.

Every writer should be blessed with the friends and relatives who have encouraged me, many of them from the first time I picked up a pen. I thank and love them all: My brothers Joseph and Sean, my father Richard, and my late mother, Anne, who instilled in me my love for baseball; the late Brother Leo Richard who taught me to dream in wide-screen Technicolor; the estimable Nat the Cat for her smokey voice and Barbara Stanwyck eyes; Barbara Bauer who nurtured my love of the written word; Al and Cathy Lombardo, Victor and Ellen Kiam, Joyce Altman (who doesn't seem to mind when her husband Billy and I spend hours on the phone talking about this great game), Alan and Maralice Flusser; Richard and Jessie Erlanger, Karl and Margrid Durr, Alecks, Michaela and Rasmus Budny, Robert Moss, Florence Stone, and W. Michael Gillespie; and the staff at Q Bistro in Forest Hills whose port and curried red snapper helped me keep body and soul intact throughout this project.

Publisher's Acknowledgments

We're proud of this book; please register your comments through our IDG Books Worldwide Online Registration Form located at http://my2cents.dummies.com.

Some of the people who helped bring this book to market include the following:

Acquisitions, Development, and Editorial

Project Editor: Bill Helling

Acquisitions Editor: Stacy S. Collins

Senior Copy Editor: Joe Jansen

Technical Editors: Bill Shannon, Gene Oliveri

Editorial Manager: Elaine Brush

Editorial Assistant: Paul E. Kuzmic

Production

Associate Project Coordinator: Karen York

Layout and Graphics: Linda M. Boyer, Maridee V. Ennis, Todd Klemme, Jane E. Martin, Anna Rohrer, Deirdre Smith, Lou Boudreau, Angela F. Hunckler, Brent Savage

Special Art: Precision Graphics

Proofreaders: Christine Berman, Kelli Botta, Melissa D. Buddendeck, Michelle Croninger, Rachel Garvey, Rebecca Senninger, Janet M. Withers

Indexer: Steve Rath

Special Help

Darren Meiss (Editorial Assistant), Maureen F. Kelly (Editorial Coordinator), Allison Solomon (Administrative Assistant)

General and Administrative

IDG Books Worldwide, Inc.: John Kilcullen, CEO; Steven Berkowitz, President and Publisher

IDG Books Technology Publishing: Brenda McLaughlin, Senior Vice President and Group Publisher

Dummies Technology Press and Dummies Editorial: Diane Graves Steele, Vice President and Associate Publisher; Mary Bednarek, Acquisitions and Product Development Director; Kristin A. Cocks, Editorial Director

Dummies Trade Press: Kathleen A. Welton, Vice President and Publisher; Kevin Thornton, Acquisitions Manager

IDG Books Production for Dummies Press: Beth Jenkins Roberts, Production Director; Cindy L. Phipps, Manager of Project Coordination, Production Proofreading, and Indexing; Kathie S. Schutte, Supervisor of Page Layout; Shelley Lea, Supervisor of Graphics and Design; Debbie J. Gates, Production Systems Specialist; Robert Springer, Supervisor of Proofreading; Debbie Stailey, Special Projects Coordinator; Tony Augsburger, Supervisor of Reprints and Bluelines; Leslie Popplewell, Media Archive Coordinator

Dummies Packaging and Book Design: Patti Crane, Packaging Specialist; Kavish + Kavish, Cover Design

◆

The publisher would like to give special thanks to Patrick J. McGovern, without whom this book would not have been possible.

◆

Contents at a Glance

Introduction 1

Part I: Getting Started (Before Your First At-Bat) 7

Chapter 1: What Is Baseball? 9
Chapter 2: Suiting Up: Equipment 17
Chapter 3: The Rules of the Game 27

Part II: Taking Your Swings — How To Play the Game ... 35

Chapter 4: Training: How to Get into Baseball Shape 37
Chapter 5: Swinging the Lumber: HittingLike a Major Leaguer 59
Chapter 6: Winning the Arms Race: Pitching like a Major Leaguer 99
Chapter 7: The Third Dimension: Defense 115
Chapter 8: The Science of Baserunning 175
Chapter 9: Joe's Baseball Playbook 199

Part III: From the Little Leagues to the Major Leagues: Organized Baseball 225

Chapter 10: T-Ball to College Baseball and Everything in Between 227
Chapter 11: The Minors and Other Leagues 231
Chapter 12: There Are Tricks to This Game: Coaching 241
Chapter 13: Major League Baseball 247
Chapter 14: Measuring Performance (How to Calculate Baseball's Statistics) 251
Chapter 15: Going All the Way: The League Championship Series and the World Series 259

Part IV: We Don't Care If We Ever Get Back — A Spectator's Guide 265

Chapter 16: Following the Bouncing Baseball 267
Chapter 17: Keeping Up with the Show: Baseball Online, on the Air, and on the Newsstand 287
Chapter 18: Fantasy Baseball 295

Part V: The Part of Tens 303

Chapter 19: Joe Morgan's Top Ten Players, All-Time and Current 305
Chapter 20: Joe Morgan's Top Ten Pitchers, All-Time and Current 317
Chapter 21: Joe Morgan's Top Ten Fielders, All-Time and Current 327
Chapter 22: Joe Morgan's Top Ten Future Stars 335
Chapter 23: Ten Baseball Records that Are Least Likely to Be Broken 339
Chapter 24: Ten Events that Transformed the Game 343

Part VI: Appendixes 349

Appendix A: Baseball Speak: A Glossary 351
Appendix B: Major League Records 365
Appendix C: Baseball Organizations 379

Index 389

Book Registration Information ...... Back of Book

Table of Contents

Introduction **1**
  About This Book 1
  Why You Need This Book 1
  How To Use This Book 2
  How This Book Is Organized 2
    Part I: Getting Started (Before Your First At-Bat) 3
    Part II: Taking Your Swings — How to Play the Game 3
    Part III: From the Little Leagues to the Major Leagues: Organized
      Baseball 3
    Part IV: We Don't Care If We Ever Get Back — A Spectator's Guide ... 4
    Part V: The Part of Tens 4
    Part VI: Appendixes 4
  Icons Used In This Book 4

Part I: Getting Started (Before Your First At-Bat) **7**
  Chapter 1: What Is Baseball? **9**
    The Roots of the Game 9
    The Objective of the Game 9
      When nine isn't really nine 10
      Extra innings 11
    Making Your Way around the Playing Field 11
    The Action of Play 13
    Coming Home (Eventually) 13
    Who Is in Charge 14
    The Umpires and Official Scorer 14
    The Strike Zone 16

  Chapter 2: Suiting Up: Equipment **17**
    Choosing Your Weapons: Bats, Balls, and Gloves 17
    Getting Good Wood (and Aluminum) 19
    If the Glove Fits 20
    Shodding Yourself Like a Pro 22
    Batting Helmets 23
    Batting Gloves 23
    Sweatbands 23
    Caps and Uniforms 23
    And if You'll Permit Us an Indelicacy 24

  Chapter 3: The Rules of the Game **27**
    Play Ball! 27
    The Batter 28
      Making an out 28
      A question of fair or foul 29
      Getting on base 30

Designated Hitter Rule 30
The Runner (Baserunning Etiquette) 30
Rules Governing the Pitcher 32
    The balk 32
    Warming up 32
    Visits to the mound 32
    On spitballs and other pitches that go bump in the night 33
Rules Governing Umpires 33

Part II: Taking Your Swings — How To Play the Game ... 35

Chapter 4: Training: How to Get into Baseball Shape 37

Warming Up 38
    Jogging knee lifts 38
    Skipping leg extensions 38
Let's Get Flexible: Stretching 38
    Torso twist 39
    Forward bend 39
    Forward leg bend 40
    Shoulder roll 41
    Triceps stretch 41
    Forearm and wrist stretch 42
    V-stretch 43
    Seated groin stretch 43
    Knee pulls 43
    Butterfly stretch 45
    Dip splits 45
Jumping for Joy — Pylometrics 46
    Good jumping form 47
    The pylometric drills 47
Taking Your Medicine — Using the Medicine Ball 48
    Basic rotation pass 48
    Basic chest pass 48
    Basic toss 49
    Hip toss 50
    Toe push 50
    Medicine ball jumps 50
    Lunges 51
High Intensity Leg Work — Sprinting 51
    Hurdling sprints 51
    Sprinting for home 51
Playing Heavy Metal — Working with Free Weights 52
    Bench press 53
    Dumbbell bench press 54
    Close grip bench press 54
    One arm dumbbell row 54
    Squats 54
    Lunges 54
    Hammer curls 55
    Upright row 55

Curl to press 55
Shrugs 55
Lateral raise 56
Lying triceps extension 56
It Ain't Over 'til It's Over 57

Chapter 5: Swinging the Lumber: Hitting like a Major Leaguer 59
What You Need to Hit 60
Picking Your Lumber 61
Get A Grip — Holding the Bat 62
Where does that label go? 63
Your body and your bat 64
On chicken flaps and other eccentricities 64
Stepping Up to the Plate 66
The benefits of being up front 67
Stuck in the middle 68
Tales from the deep 68
Getting Close 68
Your Stance 69
What's Your Body Doing? 70
Going into your crouch 71
Can you dig it? 72
Why a Stride? 72
Look before you stride 72
The length of your stride 73
Troubleshooting your stride 73
Slightly Up or Slightly Down: Two Approaches 74
Making Contact 75
Some Fine-Tuning 76
A Word About Follow-Through 77
Dealing with the Strike Zone 78
That First Pitch 79
Going to All Fields 79
Hitting to center field (straight-away) or to the opposite field 80
Pulling the ball 80
Analyzing the Pitcher 82
The Dying Art: Bunting 82
Your bunting stance 83
The sacrifice 85
Bunting for a hit 86
The squeeze play 86
Faking the bunt 87
The Hit-and-Run 88
The Run-and-Hit 88
Walking Aggressively 89
Getting the Most Out of Batting Practice 89
Working with Your Batting Practice Pitcher 90
Other Practice Tips 90
Hit from a batting tee 91
Swing in front of a full-length mirror 91

Play pepper 91
Work with grips and rollers 92
Develop your hand-eye coordination 92
Troubleshooting Your Batting 92
Hitting off your heels 92
Chopping 92
Extreme uppercutting 93
Hitching 93
Locking the front hip 93
Lunging 93
Bobbing your head 94
Stepping in the bucket 94
Fear of Getting Hit 94
Post Script: Some Pinch-Hitting Advice From Rusty Staub 95

**Chapter 6: Winning the Arms Race: Pitching
like a Major Leaguer** **99**
It All Starts with Your Stance 100
Your Wind-up, Thrust, and Release 100
The Follow-Through 104
Pitching from the Stretch 105
Heat and Other Weapons: Your Pitching Arsenal 106
The four-seam fastball 106
The two-seam fastball 107
The slider 108
The split-fingered fastball 108
The curveball 109
The three-fingered change-up 110
The circle change-up 110
The palmball 111
The screwball 112
The knuckleball 112
Before You Take the Mound 113

Chapter 7: The Third Dimension: Defense **115**
The Good Hands People 116
Picking a Position 116
Catcher 116
First base 118
Second base 118
Shortstop 119
Third base 120
Left field 120
Center field 121
Right field 121
Pitcher 121
Loading the Cannon: Getting Your Arm Ready for the Field 122
The grip 122
Delivering the throw 123
How hard is too hard? 125

A Word about Errors 125
　　Don't short-leg 126
　　Avoid those hidden errors 126
Six Tips for Fielding Grounders 126
Positioning Yourself for a Strong Defense 127
Fielding Line Drives 128
Fielding Fly Balls 128
Playing the Field: Position by Position 129
From Behind the Plate: Catcher 130
　　Setting up 131
　　Signs: The secret language of catchers 132
　　When you're ready to catch 133
　　Receiving the pitch 135
　　Tracking errant pitches 135
　　To catch a thief 136
　　Derailing the double steal 137
　　Blocking the plate 138
　　Getting help 139
　　Pick-offs and pitchouts 139
　　Fielding pop-ups 140
　　Thwarting the bunt 140
　　Let the force be with you 141
You Can't Hide at First Base 141
　　Footwork and balance are keys 142
　　Target practice 142
　　When a throw is bad 143
　　Holding on 143
　　Covering bunts 144
　　Cut-off plays 144
　　When the pitcher must cover first 145
　　Doing the 3-6-3 (first-to-short-to-first double play) 145
Second (Base) to None 146
　　Setting up 146
　　Whose ball is it, anyway? 148
　　Blocking the ball 148
　　Getting it to first 149
　　Preventing grand larceny — defending against the steal 149
　　Picking them off 150
　　Run-downs 101 150
　　Tagging the big league way 151
　　Covering first 151
　　Relays and cut-offs at second 152
　　Turning two 152
　　The care and feeding of your shortstop 154
　　Dealing with the runner 154
　　A last word on second 155
Cookin' at the Hot Corner 155
　　The basic stance 155
　　That word again — anticipation 155

Checking the real estate 156
Fast hands for slow rollers 156
Playing mind games 157
A basic rule to get two 157
Some last words from third 158
Ranging Wide: Playing Shortstop 158
Setting up 158
Backhanded compliments 160
The wisdom of an open-glove policy 160
Doubling up 161
A last word on playing shortstop 162
That Extra Infielder: The Pitcher 162
Your follow-through: The key to getting into fielding position 162
Be aggressive 163
Keeping those runners close 163
When the runner strays too far: Pick-offs 164
Where Fly Balls Go to Die: Playing the Outfield 166
Setting up 167
Taking your basic stance 168
Taking off from jump street 169
Making the catch 170
Don't fall into the gap 170
Coming in on a ball 171
And going out on a ball 171
You have to catch grounders, too 172

Chapter 8: The Science of Baserunning **175**
That First Step out of the Box 176
Taking Your Lead 177
Leading off first 177
Leading off second 179
Leading off third 180
That Sense of Where You Are 182
Rounding the Bag 182
Tagging Up 182
Working with Your Coaches 183
Putting the Run in the Hit-and-Run 184
Sliding 184
The straight-leg slide 185
The bent-leg slide 185
The head-first slide 186
The hook slide 188
Breaking Up Is Hard to Do: Preventing the Double Play 190
Collision: When the Catcher Blocks Home Plate 191
Profile of a Thief: Stealing 192
What every base thief should know: How to read the pitcher 193
Lead — and runs will follow 194
Stealing third 194
Stealing home 195
Delayed, double, and fake steals 196

Chapter 9: Joe's Baseball Playbook 199

Part III: From the Little Leagues to the Major Leagues: Organized Baseball 225

Chapter 10: T-Ball to College Baseball and Everything in Between 227

A Good Place to Start: T-Ball 227
If You're Looking for a League 228
From Big 10 to Ivy League: Collegiate Baseball 230

Chapter 11: The Minors and Other Leagues 231

The American Minor Leagues 231
Minor league franchises — where are they? 232
The lower minors 233
Experience not always necessary 233
Baseball in Japan 235
Baseball's New Asian Frontiers 237
Baseball in the Tropics 237
The Cuban Juggernaut 239
Adding to Your Baseball Library 239

Chapter 12: There Are Tricks to This Game: Coaching 241

Know Your Players 242
Avoid having a happy bench 243
But don't let them get too unhappy 243
Know the Elements of a Winning Team 243
Use Those First Five Innings 244
Criticize in Private 245
Work with Your Coaches 245
Keep It All in Perspective 245

Chapter 13: Major League Baseball 247

Major League Baseball Today 247
The Major League Franchises 248

Chapter 14: Measuring Performance (How to Calculate Baseball's Statistics) 251

Offensive Measurements 251
Batting average 252
On-base percentage 253
Slugging average 253
Base-on-balls percentage 253
Home run ratio 254
Stolen base percentage 254
Strikeout ratio 254
Pitching Measurements 254
Winning percentage 254
Earned run average (ERA) 255
Opponents' batting average 255

Defensive Measurements: Fielding Average 256
Team Measurement: Won-Lost Percentage 256

Chapter 15: Going All the Way: The League Championship Series and the World Series 259

The League Championship Series 259
Expansion brings change 260
Adding more playoffs to the League Championship Series 260
The World Series 261
The first "world series" 261
The end of the American Association 262
National League expansion 262
The Temple Cup 262
And yet another cup 262
The World Series takes off 263

**Part IV: We Don't Care If We Ever Get Back —
A Spectator's Guide 265**

Chapter 16: Following the Bouncing Baseball 267

Picking the Best Seat (It Depends on What You Want to See) 268
Looking for a Souvenir? 269
The Other 98 Percent of the Time: When You Can't Get to the Park 270
Real Fans Keep Score 270
The scorekeeper's codes 272
Tracking the runner 273
The Stadiums 275
The National League stadiums 275
The American League stadiums 281
Stadium Statistics 285

Chapter 17: Keeping Up with the Show: Baseball Online, on the Air, and on the Newsstand 287

Baseball in Cyberspace 287
MLB@Bat 287
The Negro Baseball Leagues 288
The Baseball Server 288
The National Baseball Hall of Fame and Museum 288
Total Baseball Online 288
Ballparks by Munsey & Suppes 289
The Sports Network 289
Major league team sites 289
Baseball on the Tube 290
ESPN 291
Fox Broadcasting 291
NBC 291
The Sports Network 292
The Classic Sports Network 292
Caribbean League telecasts 292
Baseball in Print 292

Chapter 18: Fantasy Baseball **295**

What the Heck Is Fantasy Baseball? 295
How Do I Play? 296
    Starting a league 296
    Drafting a team 297
    Filling out your roster 298
    Managing your team after the draft 298
    Taking care of administrative tasks 299
    Figuring your point total and winning 299
Some Tips for Fantasy Baseball Success 300

Part V: The Part of Tens *303*

**Chapter 19: Joe Morgan's Top Ten Players,
All-Time and Current** **305**

The Ten Best Players of All Time 305
    Willie Mays (New York-San Francisco Giants, New York Mets) 306
    Babe Ruth (Boston Red Sox, New York Yankees,
        Boston Braves) 306
    Hank Aaron (Milwaukee-Atlanta Braves, Milwaukee Brewers) 306
    Ty Cobb (Detroit Tigers, Philadelphia A's) 307
    Mickey Mantle (New York Yankees) 308
    Frank Robinson (Cincinnati Reds, Baltimore Orioles, California
        Angels, Los Angeles Dodgers, Cleveland Indians) 309
    Joe DiMaggio (New York Yankees) 310
    Roberto Clemente (Pittsburgh Pirates) 310
    Jackie Robinson (Brooklyn Dodgers) 310
    Ted Williams (Boston Red Sox) 311
The Ten Best Current Players 312
    Ken Griffey, Jr. (Seattle Mariners) 312
    Barry Bonds (San Francisco Giants) 312
    Frank Thomas (Chicago White Sox) 313
    Mike Piazza (Los Angeles Dodgers) 314
    Jeff Bagwell (Houston Astros) 314
    Tony Gwynn (San Diego Padres) 314
    Larry Walker (Colorado Rockies) 314
    Mark McGwire (St. Louis Cardinals) 315
    Mo Vaughn (Boston Red Sox) 315
    Juan Gonzalez (Texas Rangers) 315

**Chapter 20: Joe Morgan's Top Ten Pitchers,
All-Time and Current** **317**

The Ten Best Pitchers of All Time... 317
    Cy Young (Cleveland Spiders, St. Louis Red Stockings, Boston
        Americans, Cleveland Indians) 318
    Warren Spahn (Boston-Milwaukee Braves, San Francisco Giants,
        New York Mets) 318
    Walter Johnson (Washington Senators) 318
    Lefty Grove (Philadelphia A's and Boston Red Sox) 319
    Christy Mathewson (New York Giants).............................. 319

Steve Carlton (St. Louis Cardinals, Philadelphia Phillies,
San Francisco Giants, Chicago White Sox) 319
Tom Seaver (New York Mets, Chicago White Sox, Boston
Red Sox) 320
Sandy Koufax (Los Angeles Dodgers) 320
Bob Gibson (St. Louis Cardinals) 321
Juan Marichal (San Francisco Giants, Boston Red Sox) 322
The Ten Best Current Pitchers 322
Greg Maddux (Atlanta Braves) 322
Roger Clemens (Toronto Blue Jays) 323
Randy Johnson (Seattle Mariners) 323
Tom Glavine (Atlanta Braves) 323
John Smoltz (Atlanta Braves) 324
Pat Hentgen (Toronto Blue Jays) 324
Pedro Martinez (Boston Red Sox) 324
David Cone (New York Yankees) 324
Mike Mussina (Baltimore Orioles) 325
Alex Fernandez (Florida Marlins) 325

**Chapter 21: Joe Morgan's Top Ten Fielders,
All-Time and Current 327**
The Ten Best Fielders of All Time 327
Willie Mays (New York-San Francisco Giants, New York Mets) 328
Ozzie Smith (San Diego Padres, St. Louis Cardinals) 328
Curt Flood (Cincinnati Reds, St. Louis Cardinals,
Washington Senators) 328
Bill Mazeroski (Pittsburgh Pirates) 329
Johnny Bench (Cincinnati Reds) 329
Roberto Clemente (Pittsburgh Pirates) 329
Brooks Robinson (Baltimore Orioles) 330
Keith Hernandez (St. Louis Cardinals, New York Mets) 330
Ken Griffey, Jr. (Seattle Mariners) 330
Luis Aparicio (Chicago White Sox, Baltimore Orioles,
Boston Red Sox) 331
The Ten Best Current Fielders 331
Ken Griffey, Jr. (Seattle Mariners) 331
Barry Bonds (San Francisco Giants) 331
Ivan Rodriguez (Texas Rangers) 332
Charles Johnson (Florida Marlins) 332
Roberto Alomar (Baltimore Orioles) 332
Omar Vizquel (Cleveland Indians) 332
Jim Edmonds (California Angels) 333
Rey Ordonez (New York Mets) 333
Ken Caminiti (San Diego Padres) 333
Barry Larkin (Cincinnati Reds) 333

Chapter 22: Joe Morgan's Top Ten Future Stars 335
Baseball's Future Stars 335
Vladimir Guerrero (Montreal Expos) 335
Nomar Garciaparra (Boston Red Sox) 336

Alex Rodriguez (Seattle Mariners) 336
Jose Cruz, Jr. (Toronto Blue Jays) 336
Derek Jeter (New York Yankees) 337
Andruw Jones (Atlanta Braves) 337
Scott Rolen (Philadelphia Phillies) 337
Edgardo Alfonzo (New York Mets) 337
Shawn Estes (San Francisco Giants) 338
Neifi Perez (Colorado Rockies) 338

**Chapter 23: Ten Baseball Records that Are Least Likely to
Be Broken** **339**

Records That May Stand Forever 339
Joe DiMaggio's 56-game hitting streak (1941) 340
Cy Young's 512 career wins (and his 313 career losses) ... 340
Babe Ruth's .690 career slugging percentage 340
Jack Chesbro's 41-win season (1905) 341
Johnny Vander Meer's two consecutive no-hitters
    (June 11, June 15, 1938) 341
Nolan Ryan's 5,714 career strikeouts 341
Rogers Hornsby's .424 batting average (1924) 341
Ed Walsh's 1.82 career earned run average (ERA) 342
Hank Aaron's 755 career home runs 342
Cal Ripken's consecutive games-played streak (2,478 and
    counting) 342

Chapter 24: Ten Events that Transformed the Game **343**

The Changing of the Game 343
Alexander Cartwright codifies baseball's rules (1845) 344
Baseball players form the first major league (1871) 344
The pitcher's mound is moved back 15 feet (1893) 344
Mr. Rickey builds a farm (1920) 345
The Black Sox scandal (1920) 345
The night the lights went on in Cincinnati (1935) 346
Jackie Robinson and Branch Rickey shatter the
    color line (1946) 346
The Brooklyn Dodgers and New York Giants go west (1957) 346
The Messersmith-McNally decision (1975) 347
The baseball strike of 1994 347

Part VI: Appendixes **349**

Appendix A: Baseball Speak: A Glossary **351**
Appendix B: Major League Records **365**
Appendix C: Baseball Organizations **379**

Index **389**

Book Registration Information .... *Back of Book*

Foreword

Joe Morgan ("The Little Man," as I like to call him) knows baseball. In fact, he was one of the most intelligent players to ever play the game. And I should know, I had the distinct pleasure to know and work with Joe for more than two decades. During my years as the manager of the Cincinnati Reds, Joe was an incredible ball player — not just for his Hall of Fame abilities but for his genuine love of the game. Joe was an unselfish player with a healthy respect for the rich history and tradition of baseball. His first priority was always the team; he never tried to selfishly pad his individual statistics. I love and respect Joe for his giving attitude, and he is universally respected by both his peers and baseball fans worldwide.

Now Joe gives back to the game through this grand slam of a book, *Baseball For Dummies* (I even helped out with a chapter or two). Joe explains the game with insight and down-to-earth information so that anyone can understand and appreciate the game. I'm so glad Joe had the opportunity to share his vast baseball knowledge. His gift for understanding baseball and people sets him apart from the "average Joe."

Today, Joe continues to give back to the game through his expert analysis and commentary and, of course, through *Baseball For Dummies*.

Joe was a very special player who turned out to be a total person.

— Sparky Anderson

Major-league manager (two teams) for more than 26 years and three-time World Series winning manager

Introduction

∙∙

Welcome to *Baseball For Dummies,* a book dedicated to the proposition that no one's education is complete unless it includes a thorough grounding in the principles of the greatest sport ever created. This book is much like a baseball game: orderly but spontaneous, filled with nuance and surprise, and packed to the brim with fun. We hope you enjoy reading it as much as we enjoyed writing it.

About This Book

We wrote this book to appeal to every level of fan from the novice who just recently purchased his first pack of baseball cards to the loyalist who has been sitting in the same seat at the ballpark since the Coolidge administration. Spectators will have an easier time watching and appreciating baseball's finer points after they finish our book. You will not only know what the players on the field are doing, but why they are doing it. If an extraterrestrial dropped out of the skies, we would hope it could read *Baseball For Dummies* today and attend its first baseball game tomorrow without experiencing any confusion.

If you're a player, there isn't any component of your game that can't be elevated by studying this volume. Pitching, hitting, fielding, and baserunning — we cover it all with the aid of some the game's legendary players. It doesn't matter if you are taking your first cuts in Little League or already sitting in a big league dugout, you can find something in this book to make you a better player. Whether you participate on the field or just watch, our mission is to increase your baseball pleasure by a factor of ten.

Why You Need This Book

Novices need *Baseball For Dummies* because no other book can offer them such a comprehensive introduction to the National Pastime. You are going to discover things about baseball that many die-hard fans still haven't learned. Do you know how the great outfielders are able to get a good jump on the ball? Where the first baseman should stand to receive a cut-off throw? How many stitches are in a baseball and who manufactures bats that meet major league standards? You can find the answers to these and many more questions within these pages. And if you already know a lot about the sport? You're about to learn a good deal more. This book is chock-full of inside tips and insights that you will rarely encounter anywhere below the professional ranks.

To be honest, we believe all human beings need this book because baseball is part of our genetic destiny. Archaeologists have unearthed evidence linking bat-and-ball games to our prehistoric ancestors. What compelled them to start smacking around a tiny sphere with a stick? No one knows for certain, but our guess is they did it because there was no television, no Oprah, no Seinfeld, no reruns of *Cheers*. What were the Cro-Magnons to do with all their leisure time? Cavemen would swing clubs to slay the odd raptor and throw stones to bring down an occasional pterodactyl. So it was a natural leap to utilize these talents for less-daunting sport. Ever since the prehistoric days, the urge to strike round objects with a stick or club has been encrypted in our DNA. You can't escape it. Try suppressing this drive, and there is no telling how much damage you can do to yourself. (*Ripley's Believe It or Not* has reported cases of spontaneous combustion in which people burst into flames for no apparent reason. We think they would still be alive today if they had only played a game of catch every few weeks.) So we offer this book to you as a kind of public service. Use it to find a safe release for your primordial urges.

How To Use This Book

You may use this book anyway you like. Read it from cover to cover or just pick a section and dive in. If you are a novice, you may want to read the glossary first (or at least refer to it often) so you can understand the language we use. Then read Chapters 1 and 2 for an understanding of baseball's rules. If you are a more advanced player or coach, you may want to start with Part II to improve various aspects of your game. This book is designed so that you never have to read any chapter or part in its entirety; you can often find many short paragraphs that can stand alone as mini-chapters. And Joe's Part of Tens should appeal to longtime fans or those of who you who are just learning the difference between a slider and a curve.

How This Book Is Organized

In each chapter, we start with the basics and build from there. For example, when Joe discusses hitting, we begin by advising you on what sort of bat you should use. Next we focus on your grip, and then gradually add all the other elements of a perfect swing until you're slashing line drives all over the field. Whenever we think a point needs further clarification, we cross-reference the appropriate chapter so you can immediately get any additional information you may need.

Part I: Getting Started (Before Your First At-Bat)

This is a baseball and this is a bat — yes, the book is that basic at the start. First, we give you a little history to tell you how baseball began. Then, we review the rules, so you won't commit any *faux pas* on or off the field such as running the bases in the wrong direction. Because you cannot take the field without the proper equipment, we also identify the tools of the trade, tell you where to acquire them, and show you how to take care of your bats, balls, and gloves so they can take care of you.

Part II: Taking Your Swings — How to Play the Game

In this part, we shape up your game so you look like a pro no matter what your level of play. First, we get you into baseball shape. When you finish your workout, you'll be able to chew horsehide (it's terrific with a nice Bordeaux) and spit split-fingered fastballs. Then, a group of major leaguers joins us to improve every facet of your game. We smooth the kinks out of your swing so you can maximize your bat speed to hit for power and average. Would you rather take a turn on the mound? We can add some zip to your fastball and show you how to throw a major league curve. Fielding? You discover the proper way to turn a double play and catch a foul pop. And you'll never again get your feet tangled while chasing a fly ball hit over your head (and if you think a lot of major league outfielders won't be reading that section, you haven't seen a game lately). For coaches and players, we include a playbook that reveals baseball's basic defensive alignments at a glance. No extra charge; we just threw it in the book as a bonus.

Part III: From the Little Leagues to the Major Leagues: Organized Baseball

In this part, we take you through every level of professional and amateur ball to impart some sense of where the game is played and how it is run. We also bring in future Hall of Fame skipper Sparky Anderson for some tips on managing. And we even show you some basic baseball math so that you won't be at a loss the next time your friends ask you to calculate their fielding percentage.

Part IV: We Don't Care If We Ever Get Back — A Spectator's Guide

If you'd rather watch than play, this is the part for you. In this part, you discover how to follow the game as a spectator, where to go for game coverage in the various media, and — best of all — how to keep score. You also get an analysis of all the major league parks with an eye toward how they affect player and team performances. Want a little more involvement without going onto the field? We devote a whole chapter to Fantasy Baseball.

Part V: The Part of Tens

It wouldn't be a ...*For Dummies* book without this part. Our lists of all-time players give you a taste of baseball history and you can use our lists of current players as mini-scouting reports. The rest is just interesting stuff we thought you should know.

Part VI: Appendixes

You can't understand the game if you don't understand its language. Our glossary in Appendix A broadens your baseball vocabulary and gives you a timeline of famous baseball players. Appendix B lists the major league baseball records that provide you with some context for player performances. And Appendix C is a contact list for the major baseball organizations around the world.

Icons Used In This Book

Baseball Speak: Talk like this and the folks in the bleachers will have no trouble understanding you.

Baseball Bookshelf : Some "must have" books to start or enhance your baseball library.

Joe Says: Tips from the Hall of Famer himself.

Heads Up: Information that can prevent you from making a bonehead play on or off the field.

Player Tip: Sage advice from one of the greats of the game.

Viewer Tip: Some insight that can enhance your baseball viewing whether you are in the stadium or in front of the TV.

Coach Tip: Advice that you can accept as coming from a coach or pass along to others you coach.

Warning: Beware! This situation can be dangerous.

Part I
Getting Started (Before Your First At-Bat)

The 5th Wave   By Rich Tennant

IN AN ATTEMPT TO CIVILIZE THE GAME OF BASEBALL, A VARIATION WAS INVENTED THAT ELIMINATED THE BAT AND BALL. INSTEAD, "PITCHERS" "THREW" DIFFICULT WORDS WHICH "BATTERS" HAD TO SPELL CORRECTLY IN ORDER TO ADVANCE TO 1st BASE.

Try throwing something from the botanical lexicon. "Lobularia" or "Heliotropium" should do it.

SPELLING BEE BALL HAD LITTLE INFLUENCE ON THE GAME WE KNOW TODAY.

In this part . . .

A father of one of the authors was a Marine drill instructor, who told him that the secret to succeeding in anything was to "have clear objectives." In this part, we start by describing baseball's objectives (to make sure you don't go wandering around the basepaths during a game). We also share some of the rules that give baseball its structure. We then tell you where to get the best ball, bats, and gloves — so you'll not only play like a pro, you'll also dress like one.

Chapter 1

What Is Baseball?

In This Chapter

▶ The origins and objective of the game

▶ Where the players play

▶ The layout of the field

▶ Moving around the bases

▶ The role of managers and umpires

▶ The strike zone

For those of you who still believe that Abner Doubleday invented baseball in Cooperstown, New York, we bring you a line from the gangster movie *Donnie Brasco:* "Fuhgedaboudit!" Abner didn't invent nuttin'. No one person actually conceived the sport. Baseball evolved from earlier bat and ball games including town ball, rounders, and one o'cat. Although there is no denying that the English game of cricket was also an influence, baseball is as singular an American art form as jazz. (Although during the early 1960s, the Soviet Union claimed baseball was a Russian creation. We should note, however, that they were also taking credit back then for the invention of the telephone, the electric light, whiteout, and — oh, you get the idea.)

The Roots of the Game

If anyone invented baseball it was Alexander Joy Cartwright. This gentleman bank teller founded the New York Knickerbockers, America's first organized baseball team, in 1842. Three years after that, Cartwright formulated the sport's first codified rules (which included three strikes per out and three outs per half-inning). These guidelines became the basis of modern baseball.

The Objective of the Game

The objective hasn't changed since Cartwright's day — it is for a team to win its game by outscoring its opponent.

In the major leagues, a game is divided into nine units of play called innings (and it's nine innings nearly everywhere else except some youth leagues where five to seven is the norm). An *inning* consists of a turn at bat and three outs for each team. Visiting teams bat in the first half (called "the top") of an inning; home teams bat in the second half (called "the bottom") of the inning.

While one club (the offensive team) is at-bat, the other plays in the field (the defensive team). Nine players compose the offensive team's lineup. The defensive team also consists of nine players: the pitcher, catcher, first baseman, second baseman, third baseman, shortstop, left fielder, center fielder, and right fielder. Check out Figure 1-1 of the playing field to see the basic positions for each of these defensive players. (Table 1-1 gives you the abbreviations for these players.)

Table 1-1	The Players
Abbreviation	*Player*
P	Pitcher
C	Catcher
1B	First baseman
2B	Second baseman
3B	Third baseman
SS	Shortstop
LF	Left fielder
CF	Center fielder
RF	Right fielder

When nine isn't really nine

Many baseball games are finished before the completion of nine full innings. For example, if the home team leads after the top of the ninth, it wins the game without taking a turn at bat in the bottom of that inning. The home team can also win the game in less than nine if it scores the winning run during the final frame. For example, the Colorado Rockies come to bat in the bottom of the ninth inning of a game against the San Francisco Giants. The Giants lead 8-7. With two men out, Colorado right fielder Larry Walker hits a two-run homer off Giants reliever Robb Nen. The Rockies win 9-8. The game is over even though the two teams combined for only $8^2/_3$ innings (remember, a team does not complete an inning until it makes the third out). This

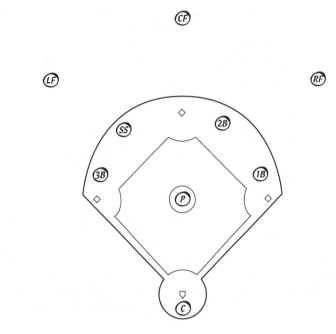

Figure 1-1:
The playing field with its players.

example illustrates a difference between baseball and the other major team sports. Either team can win a game that ends in regulation time in football (four quarters), basketball (four quarters), and hockey (three periods). In baseball, the home team can never win any game that lasts the full nine innings (except in the event of a forfeit).

Extra innings

Games that are tied after nine innings go into *extra innings*. The two opponents play until an inning is completed with the visiting team ahead or until the home team scores the winning run.

Making Your Way around the Playing Field

Baseball is played on a level field divided into the infield and outfield. The infield (also know as the *diamond*) must be a square 90 feet (27.45m) on each side. Home plate sits at one corner of the square, the three bases rest at the other corners. Moving counterclockwise from home, you see first base, second base, and then third base.

Baselines run from home plate to first base, as well as from home to third. Baselines also extend from first base to second and from second to third. The foul lines extend from the first base and third base lines and run straight to the outfield walls. The section of the outfield beyond first base is called right field, the outfield section behind second and short is center field, and the outfield section beyond third is left field.

Coaches pass on advice to players from the *coach's box,* the chalk rectangle in foul territory near first and third. When the players are not on the field, they sit in shelters in foul territory called *dugouts.* Between the dugout and home plate is the *on-deck circle,* where the next hitter awaits his turn at-bat. (See Figure 1-2.)

Major league rules require the distance from home plate to the nearest fence or wall in fair territory to be at least 250 feet (76m). Home plate must be a 17-inch (43cm) square with two of its corners removed to leave a 17-inch long edge, two 8^1/$_2$-inch (21.5cm) adjacent sides, and two 12-inch (30.5cm) long sides angled to a point. The result is a five-sided slab of white rubber with black borders. A regulation pitching rubber is a 24-x-6-inch (61 x 15.5cm) rectangular square made of white rubber, set in the middle of the diamond 60 feet, 6 inches (18.4m) from the rear of home plate. See Figure 1-3.

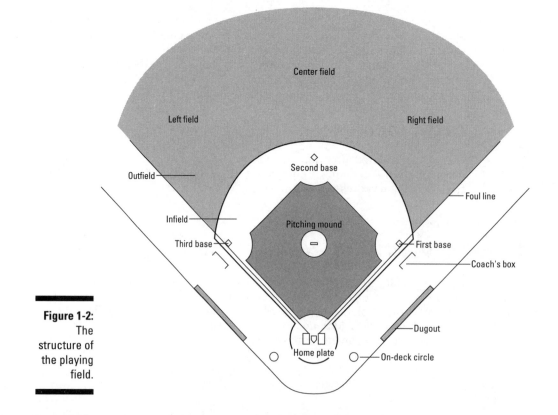

Figure 1-2: The structure of the playing field.

Figure 1-3:
Home plate
and the
pitching
rubber.

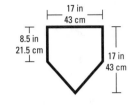

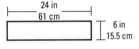

The Action of Play

The pitcher is the player who stands at the middle of the infield diamond on that hill called the *mound*. He throws the baseball, a white leather sphere, toward the catcher, a teammate who squats behind home plate. When the pitcher throws the ball to the batter at home plate, he is said to be *delivering a pitch*.

The opposing team's batter (or hitter) stands in one of two batter's boxes on either side of home plate. Each batter must come to the plate according to a specific order (the batting order or *lineup*) designated by the manager or head coach. As the ball reaches the home plate area, the batter tries to hit it with a clublike implement called a *bat*. Batters try to hit the ball into *fair territory* — that part of the playing field between and including the first and third base lines, from home base to the outfield fences — where it will either be fielded for an out or drop in safely for a base hit (we describe the various ways a batter makes out or reaches base safely in Chapter 3). A hit can take four forms:

- ✔ A *single* delivers the batter to first base.
- ✔ A *double* is hit far enough that the batter can reach second base.
- ✔ A *triple* gets the batter to third base.
- ✔ A *home run* means the batter can circle all three bases and touch home plate for a run.

  Home runs usually travel over the outfield fence in fair territory. If a batter hits a ball that stays on the field, but he is able to circle the bases and touch home before a play is made on him, it is called an *inside-the-park home run*.

Coming Home (Eventually)

Players score runs by getting on base and then moving around (and tagging) all three bases in order before crossing home plate. They must reach home before the offensive team tallies three outs in its half of the inning. When a club's hitters make three outs, its half-inning ends. Then it takes the field and the opposing team comes to bat. (Chapter 3 has all the details on how an out is made.)

Game called because of . . .

Umpires can *call* (end) games because of inclement weather, power outages, earthquakes (don't laugh, a tremor postponed the 1989 World Series between Oakland and San Francisco), a disciplinary action (a mob of fans runs on the field and refuses to vacate; no matter which team is ahead, the umpire forfeits the game in favor of the visiting club), or some other event that renders play impossible or dangerous. To be an *official game* (one that counts as a win or a loss in the league standings), the two teams must play at least five full innings. Exceptions to this rule occur whenever the bottom of the fifth concludes with the home team ahead or if the home team scores the winning run during that fifth frame.

You can advance on the bases at any time, but you do so at your peril. If you are off base when a member of the defensive team (a *fielder*) tags you with the ball, you are out. The exception to this occurs when the umpire calls "Time." At that moment, the ball is considered dead. You may step off base without being put out, but you may not advance.

Who Is in Charge

In professional baseball, *managers* are the team leaders (at some other levels, such as college baseball, this person may be referred to as the head coach). Managers plot strategy and decide which team members play which positions. They also determine a club's batting order. Managers have assistants, called *coaches,* who help them to train and discipline the team. Managers also use the first and third base coaches to pass along instructions to players through a series of signs.

The Umpires and Official Scorer

On-field officials known as *umpires* enforce the rules of play. In the major leagues, four umpires — one for each base and home plate — are assigned to each game. They decide whether a batted ball is fair or foul and whether a player is safe or out. The home plate umpire also calls balls and strikes during the pitcher-batter confrontation. Umpires have complete authority over the game. They can eject anyone from the field who violates the rules of conduct.

Baseball's Hall of Fame

To learn more about the history and evolution of this great game, there is only one place to visit: the National Baseball Hall of Fame and Museum in Cooperstown, New York. Its museum has over 6,500 artifacts, including examples of the earliest bats, balls (such as the 1954 World Series balls shown here), and gloves. Many of the exhibits are interactive. The Hall's library and archives boast the world's most comprehensive collection of printed baseball matter, including box scores from the late 1800s.

The Hall of Fame gallery is this institution's Valhalla, the place where baseball's immortals are commemorated in bronze. Members of the Baseball Writers Association of America elect honorees from a list of players with ten years or more of major league service. All candidates must have been retired from baseball for at least five years before they can be considered for induction. The Hall of Fame Veterans Committee votes for managers, pioneers of the sport, baseball executives, umpires, players from the Negro Leagues, and players who missed election their first time through the Baseball Writers Association of America voting process. A candidate must collect 75 percent of all ballots cast by either the writers or the Veterans Committee to earn a plaque in the gallery.

National Baseball Hall of Fame Library, Cooperstown, N.Y.

All professional games also have *official scorers*. These people are hired by the league to record on a scorecard all the events that take place on the field during a game (see Chapter 16 for scoring information). They cannot overrule an umpire nor can they affect the outcome of a game. They do, however, often rule on whether a batted ball should be labeled a hit or an error for the official record. (In high school, college, and so on, the home team provides a scorer who usually consults with the visiting team score-keeper on a close call.)

The Strike Zone

BASEBALL SPEAK

Pitchers must throw the ball through a *strike zone*, an imaginary box that, according to the rules, is the width of home plate and extends from the bottom of the kneecap to the uniform letters across a player's chest. (See Figure 1-4.) Any pitch that passes through the strike zone without being struck by the batter is a strike — provided that the umpire calls it a strike, that is. If a pitch is hit foul (no matter where the batter makes contact with the ball, in or out of the strike zone), it is also a strike.

Pitches outside the zone that a batter does not swing at are called *balls*. During his at-bat, if a batter tallies three strikes before the pitcher throws four balls (pitches outside of the strike zone), he is declared out.

If the pitcher throws four balls before registering three strikes, the batter is awarded first base. If a batter has two strikes on him, he can foul balls off indefinitely without any of them counting as third strikes. (The foul tip is an exception to this; check Appendix A for an explanation of the foul tip rule.)

Figure 1-4:
The strike zone.

Chapter 2
Suiting Up: Equipment

. . . .

In This Chapter

▶ Finding the best equipment

▶ Choosing a bat

▶ Choosing a glove

▶ Choosing your shoes

▶ Wearing a helmet

▶ Selecting the rest of your outfit

. . . .

*W*hen Pittsburgh Pirates shortstop Dick Groat was hitting his way to a batting title and MVP award in 1960, his manager Danny Murtaugh claimed, "Groat could hit .300 using a piece of barbed wire as a bat." Perhaps Groat could, but no one expects you to attempt that feat. When you take the field, you should be accompanied by the best equipment available. You don't need to spend vast sums to purchase top-quality accessories provided you know what to look for and where to find out. Hence, as the late sportscaster Howard Cosell would say, this chapter tells it like it is.

Choosing Your Weapons: Bats, Balls, and Gloves

Unless you are under ten years old, buy equipment that meets all the major league specifications. To be considered major league, a baseball must

✔ Have a circumference between 9 and $9^{1}/_{4}$ inches (22.9cm and 23.5cm).

✔ Weigh between 5 and $5^{1}/_{4}$ ounces (141.8g and 148.8g).

✔ Have an outer covering constructed from two pieces of white horsehide or cowhide stitched together with red thread.

✔ Have a cork or rubber core wrapped in yarn.

You don't have to go to your local sporting goods store armed with a tape measure, a scale, and scalpel (for filleting the ball to check its innards) to make sure you're buying a baseball that conforms to major league standards. Rawlings (800-729-5464) is the only company licensed by both major leagues to manufacture their official baseballs. So if you buy one of their balls, you know you're getting the genuine article. Rawlings' major league baseballs carry the designation "Official Baseball of the American (or National) League" and are signed by a league president (Gene Budig for the American League, Len Coleman for the National). You can buy first-rate baseballs manufactured by other companies, but you have no way of knowing if these products are of major league quality. (Figure 2-1 shows a typical baseball.)

Figure 2-1:
A standard
baseball.

WARNING!

Reducing injuries with innovative baseballs

Many baseball-playing youngsters live in fear of being struck by a batted or thrown ball. Likewise, many parents fret while watching their child face live pitching for the first time. To ease such fears, Worth, Inc. (931-455-0691) manufactures Reduced Injury Factor (RIF) baseballs, a softer ball that reduces the peak force of impact, lessening the chance of serious injury. Although slightly spongier, a RIF ball has the exact size and weight of a regulation baseball giving children a safer, yet realistic training tool.

Worth manufactures three types of RIF baseballs with varying injury protection:

✔ Level 1, the softest of the three, is recommended for players age 5–7 or as a training ball for all ages.

✔ Level 5 is a medium-firm ball recommended for players age 8–10.

✔ Level 10, the firmest RIF baseball, is recommended for players age 11 and up.

You can find RIF baseballs at many sporting goods stores; contact Worth, Inc. for the location nearest you.

A ball whose insides are poorly wrapped rapidly becomes misshapen with use. If your baseball is poorly stitched or constructed from inferior leather, it will fall apart. Avoid balls made with synthetic leather covering wrapped around a core of hard plastic. These balls make good toys or first balls for toddlers, but if you're a young adult or older, you'll tear the cover off of it in one good afternoon of batting practice. The toy balls are also so light, you risk throwing out your arm if you use one for a serious game of catch. Keep your baseballs in a warm, dry place.

Getting Good Wood (and Aluminum)

Choose a bat (see Figure 2-2) that you can swing comfortably with control and speed (we go into this factor in greater depth in Chapter 5). Major league bats must be a single, round piece of solid wood, no more than $2^3/_4$ inches (7cm) in diameter at its thickest and no more than 42 inches (1.06m) long. Bats made of white ash have greater durability than bats constructed from less dense woods. When you choose a bat, look for one with a wide grain, the mark of an aged wood. These bats are more resistant to breaking, denting, chipping, or flaking than bats made from less mature wood. Hillerich & Bradsby's Louisville Slugger (800-282-2287) is a popular bat among major league hitters. It is also the official bat manufacturer for major league baseball. (In Chapter 5 you can find out how to pick out the bat that's right for you.)

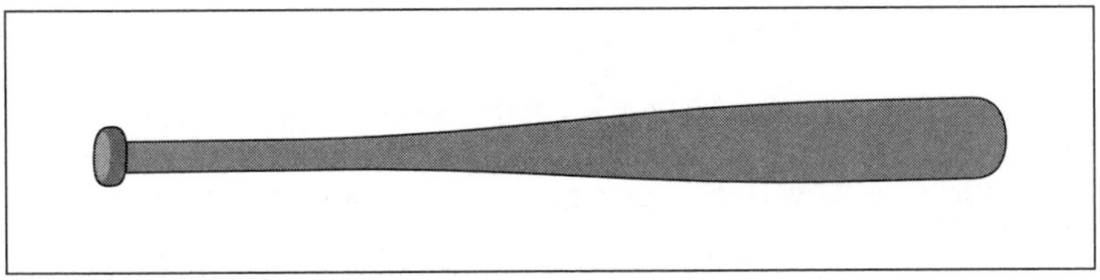

Figure 2-2:
A typical
baseball
bat.

Aluminum bats are currently popular in many levels of nonprofessional baseball. The choice of aluminum over wood is largely an economic one. Most nonpro leagues find the cost of regularly replacing broken wooden bats budget busting. Hitters love these bats because they are hollow and light, yet they have more hitting mass than the heavier wooden bats. This quality enables the hitter to generate greater bat speed and power. Balls that are routine outs when struck by a wooden bat are out of the park when launched by aluminum. Pitchers dislike these bats for obvious reasons.

Caring for your wood bat

To keep your wood bat in the swing of things, be sure to perform the following maintenance:

- Clean your bat with alcohol every day, especially if you cover its handle with pine tar. Alcohol cleansing prevents pine tar and dirt buildup.

- Keep it away from dampness. Absorbed moisture adds weight to your bat (which is why Ted Williams never, ever placed his bats on wet ground). If your bat gets wet, dry it off immediately and rub it with linseed oil.

- "Bone" your bat to maintain its hard surface. Rub it hard along the grain with a smooth piece of bone or another bat.

- Store your bats vertically, barrel down in a dry place.

If your league insists that you use an aluminum bat, buy one that rings or lightly vibrates when you strike its barrel on something hard. Bats that don't ring have no hitting life left in them. Ceramic and graphite bats are the new kids on the block. They have the durability of the aluminum bats, but are closer in weight/mass ratio to wooden bats so they don't give hitters an unfair advantage over pitchers. Their price, however, can be prohibitive. Top-of-the-line models can cost as much as $220.

If the Glove Fits . . .

Major league baseball rules regulate the size of gloves at each position. Most leagues for young adults and up adhere to these directives. (In Chapter 7 you can find out how to choose a glove for the position that you want to play.)

Catcher's mitts can be no more than 38 inches (96.52cm) in circumference nor more than 15$\frac{1}{2}$ inches (39.37cm) from bottom to top. The first baseman's mitt must be no longer than 12 inches (30.48cm) from top to bottom and no more than 8 inches (20.32cm) wide across the palm. The web of your mitt — which can either be a lacing, a lacing through leather tunnels, or an extension of the palm with lacing — cannot exceed 5 inches (12.7cm) from top to base. Other fielders' gloves must not measure more than 12 inches (30.48cm) long from the tip to any one of your four fingers or 7$\frac{3}{4}$ inches (19.7cm) wide. All major league gloves and mitts are made of leather.

Children can get by with using vinyl gloves and plastic balls. However, once you are playing serious baseball, leather is the only way to go. Pick a glove that conforms to the major league standards and fits your hand comfortably.

Gloves with open webbings allow you to watch the ball until you catch it, which is always a good policy. You don't have that advantage with closed-web gloves, which are also more difficult to break in (though if you're a pitcher, you need the closed webbing to better hide your pitches). Major league baseball licenses Wilson Team Sports (773-714-6400) to manufacture fielding gloves. (See Figure 2-3.)

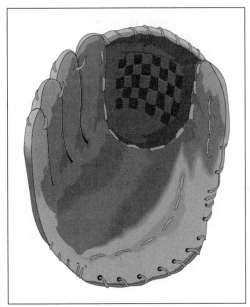

Figure 2-3:
A typical (left-handed) fielder's glove.

Besides their gloves, catchers have to wear the traditional tools of ignorance to survive behind the plate (as shown in Figure 2-4):

- ✔ Chest protector
- ✔ Mask
- ✔ Shin guards
- ✔ Protective helmet
- ✔ Throat guard

If these items are of sub-par quality, you are jeopardizing your health every time you drop into your crouch. All-Star Sporting Goods (508-425-6266) produces catcher's gear that meets major league standards.

Caring for your leather glove

The best way to break in a leather glove is to play catch with it frequently. You can also make it more pliable by rubbing it with linseed oil, saddle soap, or — here's a Helpful Hint from Heloise — shaving cream (though, you may want to avoid the gel-type creams, which tend to dry out quickly). If your glove gets wet, let it dry naturally. Placing it on a radiator or some other heat producer cracks the leather. When your glove is idle, place a ball in its pocket, and then tie the glove with a leather strap or wrap a rubber band around it. This practice maintains its catching shape.

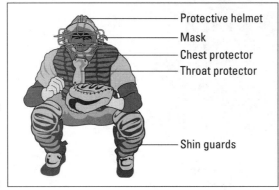

- Protective helmet
- Mask
- Chest protector
- Throat protector
- Shin guards

Figure 2-4:
The catcher's equipment.

Shodding Yourself Like a Pro

Most nonprofessional players give little thought to their shoes; they just put on whatever they can. In fact, standard baseball shoes are no longer obligatory for many pro players. I've seen Frank Thomas hit in tennis shoes. I'm a traditionalist in this area. I believe you should buy a light shoe with metal spikes so that you can get maximum traction in the batter's box and on the basepaths (slipping in the batter's box, on the bases, or in the field could cost your team a ball game). If you don't want to wear spikes, at least get shoes with rubber cleats so you can grip the playing surface as you run.

Your shoes should fit properly and offer your feet adequate support, otherwise you risk damaging your lower leg's connective tissue. Choose a sturdy shoe with support that runs its entire length. Because your shoes stretch with use, choose a pair that fit snugly when you first wear them.

Batting Helmets

Both major leagues require hitters to wear batting helmets with at least one ear flap (protecting the side facing the pitcher). Anytime you go to bat against live pitching without wearing a batting helmet, you should have your head examined. And if you're unlucky, that is exactly what you will have to do. Even a low-grade fastball can permanently damage or even kill you if it collides with your unprotected cranium. A solid batting helmet with double ear flaps is the best insurance policy a hitter can buy. American Baseball Caps, Inc. (610-565-0945) is the official manufacturer of batting helmets for major league baseball.

Light plastic batting helmets, such as the freebies that major league teams give away on Helmet Day at the stadium, are too flimsy to protect your head from an errant fastball. Do not wear them to the plate.

Batting Gloves

Batting gloves protect a hitter's most important tools — his hands — from painful blisters, cuts, and scrapes. Runners can wear them on the basepaths to protect their hands while sliding; fielders can don them under their fielding gloves to reduce the sting of hard-hit balls. Franklin Sports, Inc. carries batting gloves designed to withstand the rigors of a major league season. For hitting, choose gloves that do not detract from your "feel" for the bat.

Sweatbands

When the temperature is scorching and perspiration soaks your body, sweatbands will keep your hands dry at the plate. Two companies hold the major league licenses in this category: Wilson Team Sports (773-714-6800) and Easton Sports (415-347-3900). (Make sure you clean those sweatbands regularly or the aroma they exude will clear out entire stadiums.)

Caps and Uniforms

Want to dress your head like a major leaguer? New Era Cap Company is the official manufacturer of major league caps. Most major retail sporting goods chains, which include Foot Locker, Modells, Lids, Sports Authority, and Sears, carry baseball headwear. Your cap should fit snugly enough that the bill doesn't droop over your eyes to block your vision.

The way you wear your hat

We're not sure who wrote the major league rule book, but it surely wasn't Ralph Lauren or Alan Flusser. The rulemakers frown on any attempt at an on-field fashion statement that even hints at individuality. (As Jim Bouton, the irreverent pitcher for the New York Yankees and Seattle Pilots during the 1960s, once observed, "When baseball says it wants its players to show some flair, it means it wants us to wear our caps on a jaunty angle.") Baseball rules demand that teammates wear identical uniforms. Try to stand out by wearing different colored socks or donning a white fox cape and the umpires won't permit you on the field (especially if they are part of the anti-fur movement). Home team uniforms must be white; visiting teams are required to wear a darker color. (This requirement is meant to help fans, umpires, and, particularly, players to distinguish the teams from one another. If you have a baserunner trapped in a run-down play and you slap the ball on a player whose uniform is the same hue as yours, you just tagged out your third baseman.)

Russell Corporation (705-563-2773) holds the major league license to manufacture uniforms, batting practice jerseys, and baseball undershirts. However, Wilson and Rawlings also manufacture uniforms for several major league teams. Uniform fit is a matter of personal comfort; your pants and jersey should permit unrestricted movement at the plate and in the field.

And If You'll Permit Us an Indelicacy

Male ballplayers should never take the field without wearing a jock strap (athletic supporter) and protective cup. You don't really need to ask why, do you?

A reminder on equipment

As mentioned earlier in this chapter, be sure to play baseball with the best equipment that you can obtain. However, you don't always have to spend a lot of money in order to equip yourself well or just to have fun. The great Willie Mays used to play stickball, and he seems to have done pretty well for himself.

Who knows? In an attic or a garage somewhere, your family may have some good equipment just waiting to see daylight again. (And if you run across the old baseball spikes shown here, you've just found some shoes worn by Hall of Famer Ted Williams.)

National Baseball Hall of Fame Library Cooperstown, N.Y.

Chapter 3

The Rules of the Game

In This Chapter

▶ How a batter gets out — or on base

▶ The designated hitter rule

▶ The runner

▶ Special rules for the pitcher

▶ The umpire's decisions

Major league baseball has rules. Lots and lots and lots of rules. We considered presenting all of them to you, but then we glanced through an abridged version of the official rule book. It was over 200 pages long. We could jam them into this chapter only if we switched to the following font size:

A batter is out when a third strike is legally caught by the catcher.

And, of course, it would have to be single-spaced and the chapter would be three times as long. Not very practical, huh? You could just imagine the mountain of lawsuits our publisher would face from readers who suffered eyestrain while trying to discern the balk rule. So instead, we've opted to provide you with major league baseball's most important rules: The regulations you have to know if you want to understand what is happening out there on the field.

Play Ball!

Actually, the umpire doesn't have to be that verbose when ordering a game's commencement. He merely has to call "Play" after first ensuring that each member of the defensive team (the hometown team in this case, because the visiting club always bats first in an inning) is in position and that the hitter is in the batter's box. What happens if the defensive team doesn't take the field? The umpire calls "Play" and the fielders have five minutes to assume their positions. Otherwise the ump, unless he deems their absence unavoidable, can forfeit the game to the visiting team.

When an umpire calls "Play," the ball is considered "alive." No, it doesn't start tap dancing. The term merely means that players can use the ball to make outs or get on base. Whenever the ball is alive, runners may advance on the basepaths; the team in the field can also tag them out. If the umpire calls "Time," the ball is "dead." No action can take place on the field until the umpire once again calls "Play." The ball is also rendered dead whenever a fielder *falls* into the dugout or the stands while making a catch. If the fielder steps into the dugout and makes the catch without falling, the ball is alive. Runners may proceed at their own peril.

The Batter

Each team's manager must present the home plate umpire with their respective lineups before play commences. A hitter bats according to the order of that lineup throughout the entire game unless the manager removes him for a substitute.

After the pitcher comes to his set position or begins his wind-up, the hitter cannot leave the batter's box unless the umpire grants his request for "Time." (See Chapter 6 for details on pitchers.) Should the hitter leave without the ump's permission, the pitcher can deliver a pitch, which may be called a strike. If a batter refuses to get into the batter's box, the umpire can order the pitcher to pitch. In that situation, the rules require the ump to call every pitch a strike whether or not it passes through the strike zone.

Making an out

You are called out in the following situations:

- A fielder catches your fair or foul ball (unless it is a *foul tip* to the catcher with less than two strikes) before it touches the ground. (See Appendix A for the foul tip rule.)
- After hitting the ball, you or first base is tagged by another player holding the ball before you touch base.
- A third strike is caught by the catcher while you are at-bat.
- A ball that was initially hit or bunted fair hits your bat a second time while you are in fair territory.
- While running outside the foul lines, you obstruct a fielder's throw.
- You hit the ball with one or both feet outside the batter's box or step from one batter's box to another while the pitcher winds up.
- You obstruct the catcher from fielding or throwing.

✔ You use a bat that has been tampered with in defiance of league specifications.

✔ You bat out of turn in the lineup. (However, the umpire will call this only if the opposing team protests.)

✔ You hit a foul tip that is caught by the catcher for strike three.

A foul ball that is not caught counts as a strike against the hitter. However, the umpire cannot call a third strike on any *uncaught* foul. In that event, the hitter's at-bat continues.

A question of fair or foul

Right about now, you may be wondering which is fair territory and which is foul. Put simply, fair territory is that part of the playing field between and including the first and third base lines, from home base to the outfield fences. Foul territory is the section of the playing field outside the first and third base lines and behind home plate. (See Figure 3-1.)

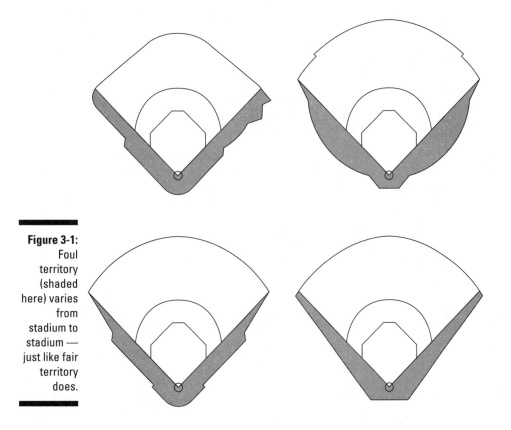

Figure 3-1:
Foul
territory
(shaded
here) varies
from
stadium to
stadium —
just like fair
territory
does.

Getting on base

Now that we've depressed all the hitters in the audience by revealing how you can fail, it's time for a little positive feedback. You can get on base in the following situations:

✔ You hit a fair ball that is not caught by a fielder before it touches the ground.

✔ You hit a fair ball that touches the ground and is caught by a fielder whose throw fails to beat you to a base.

✔ The umpire calls four pitches out of the strike zone during your at-bat.

✔ A pitch in the strike zone hits you without first touching your bat.

✔ The catcher obstructs your swing.

✔ You hit a fair ball beyond the playing field (a *home run*).

✔ You hit a fair, catchable ball, but the fielder makes an *error* (drops the ball, throws it away, and so on).

✔ A third strike skips past the catcher and you beat the throw to first.

✔ You hit a fair ball and a baserunner is tagged out or *forced out* at another base, but you are safe at first base. (See Appendix A for the definition of a force out.)

Designated Hitter Rule

As of the 1998 season, the designated hitter rule applies only to the American League. The *designated hitter* (DH) bats for the pitcher throughout the game without taking the field. Managers can let their pitchers hit, but if they do, it takes away the use of a DH for the entire game. If someone (a *pinch hitter*) bats for the DH or if someone runs for the DH, the substitute becomes the designated hitter. If a manager puts his DH in the field at some point in the game, the pitcher must bat in place of the substituted defensive player. After this move takes place, the DH role is terminated for that game.

The Runner (Baserunning Etiquette)

Generosity is a virtue, but, as a runner, you can never share a base with a teammate when the ball is alive. If you do, the defense can tag out the second runner. If you pass another runner on the basepaths, the umpire will call you out. When advancing from base to base, you must be sure to tag each bag in its proper order (especially on a home run). If you miss a base and the defense notices it, they can get you out on an appeal play (see Appendix A, the glossary, for an explanation of how an appeal play works).

Here are some other ways you can be *retired* (called out) on the basepaths (see Chapter 8 for more details):

- ✔ If a fielder tags you with a ball that is alive while you are off the bag (However, no one can tag you out if you overrun or overslide first, provided you return immediately to that bag without making a turn toward second.)

- ✔ If your teammate hits a ball that touches you in fair territory without it first touching or passing any fielder except the pitcher (The ball is dead; no other runners may advance or score on the play.)

- ✔ If, in the judgment of the umpire, you hinder a fielder from making a play

- ✔ If you run the bases in reverse order to confuse the defense (or if you are yourself confused!)

- ✔ When a batted ball forces you to advance to another base, and the fielder possessing the ball tags that base before you reach it (Say, for example, that you are on first and the batter hits a ground ball to an infielder. You have no choice but to try to advance.)

When you can't stray from the baseline

The baseline is a direct line running from home plate to first base, from first base to second base, from second base to third base, and finally from third base back home. Between first and second, and between second and third, you can't actually see the baseline because it is not marked — but it is still there for a reason. Normally, you need not worry about staying near the baseline when running the bases. In Chapter 8, you can read how you round first base to go directly to second, and how you lead off third base by moving into foul territory away from the baseline. In these and other situations, you are allowed to wander from the baseline because no opposing player is pursuing you with the ball. When someone is chasing after you with the ball trying to tag you out, however, you need to stay near the baseline: You are not permitted to go more than 3 feet (about a meter) to either side of the baseline to avoid being tagged. If you do, you are called out. Do you think that this baseline specification is unfair to runners? Just attend any Little League game and you'll soon see baserunning efforts that convince you of the wisdom of this ruling.

Rules Governing the Pitcher

Baseball mandates that the pitcher can throw from only two positions, the *wind-up* and the *set*. He can use either position at his discretion (see Chapter 6 for more information on pitching). With no runners on base, the pitcher must deliver the ball home within 20 seconds of receiving it from either the umpire or the catcher. If the pitcher fails to do so, the umpire may call a ball (but seldom does).

The balk

With runners on base, after the pitcher goes into his wind-up or makes any movement associated with delivering the ball to home, the pitcher must not interrupt his motion or the umpire can call a *balk* — which means that after a pitcher starts his delivery, he can't try to catch a runner off base with a pick-off throw. He cannot raise either foot from the ground *toward* home plate unless he is starting his delivery. The umpire also calls a balk if the pitcher drops the ball while trying to deliver a pitch. However, from the set position, the pitcher may deliver the ball home, throw to a base, or step back off the pitching rubber with his rear foot. (See Chapter 7 for more information on how to avoid a balk.)

Warming up

When the pitcher comes to the mound at the start of an inning, or when he enters a game in relief, the umpire can allow him no more than eight warm-up pitches. Play is suspended during these warm-ups. An exception to that rule occurs when a pitcher relieves an injured teammate. Then he can take as long as he needs to finish his warm-ups.

Visits to the mound

A manager or his coaches may visit the mound to consult with the pitcher only once every inning; if there is a second visit during the inning, the pitcher must leave the game. However, if the manager, coach, or trainer goes to the mound because the pitcher has apparently injured himself, the umpire does not count it as an official visit.

On spitballs and other pitches that go bump in the night

Any wet or rough spot on a baseball can make that ball move even more than usual — sometimes in unpredictable ways. At one time a pitcher could touch his lips with his pitching hand while he was on the pitcher's mound. Heck, he could shove his whole hand and the ball into his mouth if they would fit. However, since the major league spitball ban of 1920, a pitcher cannot touch his mouth as long as he is on the mound. He may not apply any foreign substance (such as mud or petroleum jelly) or spit to his hand, ball, or glove. The regulations also forbid pitchers from defacing the ball in any way. (Some pitchers try to make their breaking balls drop or curve more sharply by nicking them with nails or scratching them with sandpaper. Some pitchers would bring a Black & Decker power saw out to the mound if they could figure out a way to hide it from the umpires.)

If the ump catches you throwing a doctored pitch, he can automatically call the pitch a ball even if it passes through the heart of the strike zone. The rules then require him to warn you of the consequences if a second infraction occurs during that game. What happens if you throw another illegal pitch? The ump will boot you from the field and the league will lighten your wallet with a large fine. Immediate ejection is also the penalty if the umpire finds you in possession of a foreign substance on the mound, even if you don't apply it to a pitch (so leave those tubes of Sassoon hair mousse in your lockers).

Rules Governing Umpires

You can occasionally see two different umpires reach conflicting decisions on the same play. When that happens, the umpire-in-chief (the fellow standing behind the catcher at home plate) is the final arbiter. Any time anyone participating in the game — including the managers, coaches, and trainers — violates a rule, the umpire must report the infraction to the league's president within 12 hours. The president will then decide what penalties, if any, to impose. If a manager believes an umpire's decision violates the rules of baseball, he can protest the game to the league. He must declare his protest to the umpire immediately following the disputed decision and before the next play begins. Upon hearing the protest, the league president can order the game replayed if he believes the umpire was wrong and that his error adversely affected the protesting team's chances of winning the game.

Any player, manager, coach, or trainer, whose voiced disapproval of a decision is, in the umpire's opinion, excessively violent or profane, can be thrown out of the game by the umpire. Any voiced disapproval over a ball or strike call is grounds for automatic ejection (you can, however, dispute umpire's "judgment" calls: safe or out, fair or foul).

You have enough information in this chapter to follow any big league ball game. However, if you want to study the rules in greater depth while learning how they evolved, pick up a copy of David Nemec's *The Rules of Baseball* (Lyons & Burfurd).

Baseball and its rules

Baseball has been governed by very specific rules for more than a century — you could attend, for example, a game at Yankee Stadium (as shown here) in the late 1920s and probably not easily notice anything different from a modern game besides the designated-hitter rule. However, baseball rules have been much modified over the years as the game has grown and evolved. (Although you can find lots of differences between the way your local Little League team and the New York Yankees play the game, quite often the same basic rules apply. Always check with local amateur leagues to find out its specific regulations.) The current code of rules governing the major leagues and most any other professional baseball can be found online at the official major league web site (www.majorleaguebaseball.com).

In these rules, you can find the following information:

- Objectives of the game, the playing field, equipment
- Definition of terms
- Game preliminaries
- Starting and ending the game
- Putting the ball in play, dead ball, and live ball (in play)
- The batter
- The runner
- The pitcher
- The umpire
- The official scorer

National Baseball Hall of Fame Library Cooperstown, N.Y.

Part II

Taking Your Swings — How To Play the Game

The 5th Wave   By Rich Tennant

"The pitcher's having a little trouble with his inside curve and I'm trying to help him out."

In this part . . .

Baseball may not appear to be as physically demanding as basketball, hockey, football, or soccer, but don't kid yourself — you need to be in top condition to play a full season. In this part, we start out training camp by getting your muscles stretched and pumped (and stretched again). Then we've invited nine major league superstars to give you advice on your hitting, pitching, throwing, running, and fielding.

Our guest coaches have a combined 47 All-Star Game appearances, 30 Gold Gloves, 8 Most Valuable Player Awards, and 2 Cy Young Awards. In this part, our guest coaches reveal some secrets of their success and help you strengthen any weaknesses in your own game. Read this part even if you intend only to be a spectator; Part II gives you a deeper appreciation of what takes place on the field during a game. You'll quickly realize that something is always happening during a ball game, even when it looks like nothing is going on.

Chapter 4

Training: How to Get into Baseball Shape

In This Chapter

▶ Warming up

▶ Stretching

▶ Jumping and bounding

▶ Using the medicine ball

▶ Sprinting

▶ Working with free weights

*B*aseball players have to be in peak condition to survive the rigors of a long season. This game requires intense concentration and quick reactions; you can't allow yourself to be hindered by fatigue. A comprehensive training program can enhance your endurance, balance, coordination, speed as well as quickness (these are two different issues), flexibility, agility, and strength. The exercises described in this chapter are safe. However, you should have a complete physical before attempting all but the least stressful of them.

Trainers who transform 90-pound weaklings into Arnold Schwarzenegger will be of little value to you if they don't understand the demands of your sport. Ideally, you should work with people who possess a baseball background, either as trainers, coaches, or players. Stay away from drill sergeant types who demand one more rep even when the veins in your neck are flexed to bursting.

We've asked Gene Olivieri, who has trained pro athletes and helped get Richard Gere into buff shape for *An Officer and a Gentleman,* to oversee this chapter.

Warming Up

Your program should start lightly and then gradually increase in intensity. Never start a workout cold. If you do, you risk an injury that could jeopardize your health and career. A good warm-up does exactly that: It raises your body temperature several degrees while rushing blood deep into the muscles and connective tissues you are about to challenge. A warm-up reduces the chance of ligament strains, muscle tears, and general soreness. You don't have to run a marathon to open up your capillaries; a continual 15-minute regimen should do the trick. Jumping jacks, bicycling, rowing on a machine, or bouncing on a trampoline will warm your muscle groups. Skipping rope is especially good because it also improves coordination.

A jogging circuit can provide an ideal aerobic warm-up and it requires no equipment except running shoes. Begin with a light 20-yard (18.3m) jog, going back and forth six times. Rest for a minute, and then repeat the exercise — only this time swing your arms in circles on both sides. Rest for a minute, and then repeat the exercise while raising your arms over your head. Now that your heart is pumping a tad faster, use the exercises in the following sections to further raise the your muscles' temperature.

Jogging knee lifts

Start jogging again, but this time lift your knees toward your shoulders. Work your arms up and down in *opposite* step with your legs as you move. Repeat this three times over 20 yards (18.3m).

Skipping leg extensions

Extend both your arms in front of you to shoulder height. Skip forward slowly while extending your right leg toward your right hand. As you bring the right leg back down, extend the left leg in the same manner. (See Figure 4-1.) Do this for 15 yards (13.7m). Do four repetitions.

Hamstring pulls are nagging injuries that too often sideline players whose legs are heavily muscled. Focus on your hamstrings during both of these exercises to ensure you are getting a full stretch.

Let's Get Flexible: Stretching

Baseball is a game of sudden stops and starts, of instant acceleration. Tight muscles tear easily under such demands. Long, limber muscles increase your range of motion while decreasing the injury risks that accompany abrupt, jarring movements. Do these after your warm-ups.

Figure 4-1:
Skipping leg
extensions.

It is important to take long, slow breaths while you stretch. If you hold your breath or breathe too quickly during these exercises, you won't get the full benefits (you might also hyperventilate!). Breathe into the stretch and visualize exhaling any muscle tension. Hold each stretch for at least 10 seconds and as long as 30 seconds. Perform three sets per stretch, increasing your range of motion with each succeeding set. Do not bounce.

Torso twist

Stand with your feet shoulder width apart, your knees slightly bent, and your head erect. Using only your waist and thighs to provide torque, slowly twist your trunk and torso to the left, and then to the right. Your head should follow the torso. Rotate until you can see directly behind you. Let your arms flail out so that they gently slap against your upper chest with each rotation. Keep your elbows, wrists, and shoulders loose, your arm muscles relaxed. (See Figure 4-2.) Do 30 repetitions. This exercise limbers the muscles supporting the spinal column.

Forward bend

Stand with your feet shoulder width apart, your knees straight and locked. Loosely fold your arms across your chest. Bend forward gently. Slowly drop as low as you can with your folded arms hanging down. Gradually bring them to a point a foot above your ankles. (See Figure 4-3.) *Do not force anything.*

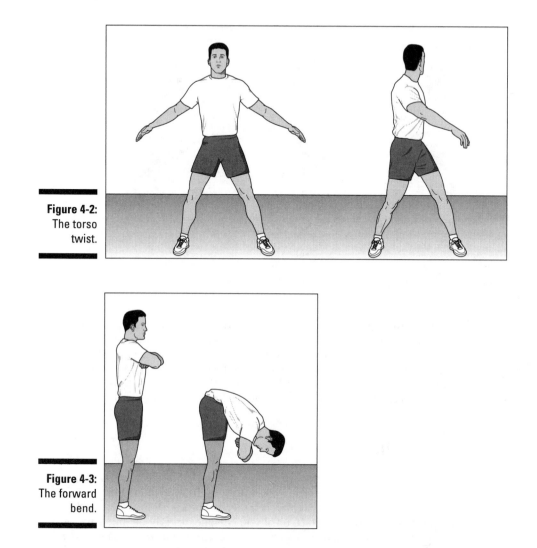

Figure 4-2:
The torso
twist.

Figure 4-3:
The forward
bend.

After you've reached your lowest point, take a deep breath and start rocking gently up and down. Your head and neck should be loose and dangling. Rock up and down 12 times, shift to the left for 12 more repetitions, and then do a final 12 on the right. This exercise stretches your vertebrae.

Forward leg bend

Stand in front of some form of waist-level support such as a wall or a dance bar. Facing the support, raise up your right leg and place your heel on it. Starting at your thigh, slowly pull your hands up the upraised leg until you can wrap your fingers around your toes.

Place your forehead on your knee (or as close to it as you can get) while gently pulling the toes back toward your head. Take ten deep breaths, and then switch legs. (See Figure 4-4.) Do two repetitions. This exercise stretches the tendons in back of your legs.

Figure 4-4:
The forward
leg bend.

Shoulder roll

Stand with your feet shoulder width apart and your knees slightly bent. Your arms should hang loosely at your sides. Roll your shoulders in a wide arc up toward your ears, circle toward the back, and then lower them. (See Figure 4-5.) Do 12 repetitions. Reverse the direction for a dozen more. Then simultaneously roll one shoulder forward and the other backward. Reverse those directions for the last 12 reps. This exercise stretches your shoulder muscles, tendons, and joints.

Triceps stretch

Stand with your feet shoulder width apart and your knees slightly bent. Bending your elbow, bring your right hand behind your back and place the palm on the middle of your neck. Raise your left hand and place it on your right elbow. Gently pull the elbow to the left. Hold for 20 seconds, and then do the opposite side. (See Figure 4-6.) Do two reps for each side. This exercise stretches your rear deltoids as well as your triceps. It will limber your throwing arm.

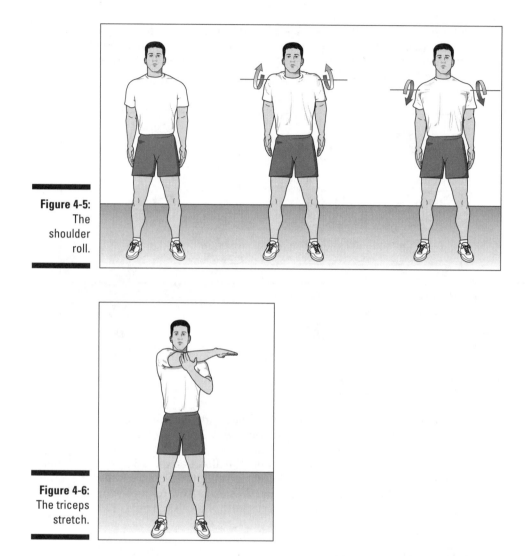

Figure 4-5:
The
shoulder
roll.

Figure 4-6:
The triceps
stretch.

Forearm and wrist stretch

Stand with your feet shoulder width apart and your knees slightly bent. Extend your right arm in front of your torso with your palm parallel to the ground. Lift your right hand until its fingers point to the ceiling at a 90-degree angle.

Take the top of your right fingers in your left hand and gently pull the hand toward you. (See Figure 4-7.) Hold the stretch for 15 seconds. Then point your right fingers to the ground and gently pull them toward you with your left. Hold for 15 seconds, and then repeat for the opposite side. Do one rep for each side. This exercise stretches the muscles of your lower arm.

Figure 4-7:
The triceps
forearm and
wrist
stretch.

V-stretch

Sit on a flat surface with your legs straight and spread as far as they can go without straining in a V-shape. Place your left hand on your right knee to keep your leg straightened. Lowering your chest to your right thigh, slowly reach out with your right hand and grab the toes of your right foot. (See Figure 4-8.) Hold the stretch, and then do the opposite side. Do two reps for each side. This exercise stretches the glutes, lower back, and hamstrings.

Seated groin stretch

Sit with your heels drawn together and as close to the groin as possible. Gently push your knees to the floor with your elbows while keeping your back straight. Then hold your ankles and pull your upper body forward while maintaining your posture.

Knee pulls

Lie on your back with your knees up at a 90-degree angle. Place both hands around your right knee and gently pull it toward your chest. Hold for 15 seconds, and then do the left knee. (See Figure 4-9.) Do four reps for each side. This exercise stretches your lower back.

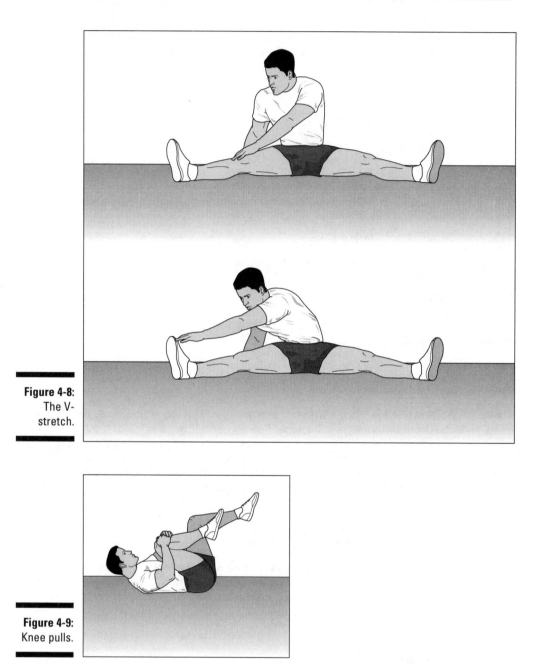

Figure 4-8:
The V-stretch.

Figure 4-9:
Knee pulls.

Butterfly stretch

Sit on a flat surface with your legs in front of you in a V. Grab your ankles and pull them toward your groin. Let your knees raise off the ground. Then slowly lower your knees to their original position. (See Figure 4-10.) Hold the stretch for 20 seconds. Do two reps. This exercise stretches the inner thigh and groin.

Dip splits

Stand upright with your feet together. Step forward with your left foot, as far as you can without straining. Balancing yourself on your left leg, slowly slide your right foot back while dipping your knee down (you may want to brace yourself against a support the first few times you try this).

Figure 4-10:
The butterfly stretch.

Your left thigh should be parallel to the ground. Your right knee should be suspended just above the ground. (See Figure 4-11.) If you don't use a support, extend your arms out to both sides for additional balance. While maintaining this position, gently rock up and down. Do six reps, and then repeat with the other leg. Do three sets for each side. This exercise stretches the hamstrings as well as the large muscles and tendons at the front of the thighs. It will also strengthen your ankles.

Figure 4-11:
Dip splits.

Jumping for Joy — Pylometrics

Pylometrics are a series of jumping and bounding drills to develop explosive leg muscles that react quickly and forcefully, exactly what you need to play a game filled with sudden, unexpected movements. To execute these drills, you need a padded, heavy-duty box with a solid base to support your weight. You can construct your own or better still, buy one at an athletic equipment store.

Before taking to the air, warm up for ten minutes with a light jog. Jumping (or rather landing out of your jump) can jar your ankles, knees, and hips, so your shoes should be shock absorbent and provide your ankles with support. Gel-soled footwear is a good choice. If you have problems with your lower joints, don't attempt these drills without consulting your physician.

Good jumping form

Your upper torso should be relaxed but upright. As you prepare to leap, swing your arms up from your sides to create momentum. When you land, bend your knees to absorb shock. Start with a 12-inch-high pylometric box and gradually progress to the 24-inch version. Position the box on a surface with give to it, such as grass (the best choice). Avoid doing pylometrics on a hard floor or concrete. Rest for several minutes between sets. Whenever possible, do these drills with an instructor or a partner who can monitor and correct your form.

The pylometric drills

The following sections describe the types of drills you can do for your pylometric workout.

The box jump

Stand approximately 12 inches (30.5cm) from the front of the box (you can adjust the distance as you discover your jumping abilities). Bend your knees and jump onto the box. (Don't forget to swing those arms up!) Jump backward immediately. As soon as your feet touch the ground, jump back on the box. Start with 5 reps, and work up to 12. Start with one set, work up to three. This exercise works the calf and quadriceps.

The jump and run

Stand on the box. Jump to the ground, landing with your knees bent and feet shoulder-width apart. Immediately break into a 15-yard (13.7m) dash. Jog back and repeat. Start with four reps, and work up to ten. This exercise improves your start-and-go reactions while working your glutes, quadriceps, hamstrings, and calves.

Box jumps at alternating heights

As you progress in strength and agility, you can use higher boxes. Attempt this exercise only after becoming comfortable with the 24-inch model. You need five pylometric boxes of varying heights for this drill. Their heights should increase from 12 to 24 inches (30.5 to 61cm).

Position each box (in ascending height order) 24 inches apart (61cm) from each other in a straight line. Take your usual stance in front of the smallest box. Jump onto it, jump immediately forward onto the ground, and then jump onto the next box. Complete the circuit without pausing. Rest for 30 seconds and begin again. Do four sets, and work up to six. This exercise works a wide range of leg muscles while building endurance.

Side-to-side jumps

You don't need a box for this exercise. On grass, mark off two points 2¹/₂ feet (76.2cm) apart. Stand by one marker with your feet together and jump sideways to the other marker. Do 6 reps, and work up to 12. This exercise develops hip strength, which enhances your torque at the plate (see Chapter 5 to see how important torque is for hitting).

Taking Your Medicine — Using the Medicine Ball

COACH TIP

Medicine balls may seem like relics from the 1890s, but they are making a comeback with baseball's strength trainers. Used properly, the balls can work a wide range of muscles; they target your abdominals, glutes, hip muscles, upper leg and back muscles, while also working the upper torso. These muscles provide balance as well as explosive rotational power (just what you need whether you're pitching or hitting). Medicine balls come in a variety of weights — generally 2 to 16 pounds (7.3kg); if you've never used one before, start with nothing heavier than a 6-pound ball. Work slowly and concentrate on form. Rest one minute between sets (you can slice that to 30 seconds as you build wind and endurance). Do these exercises two or three times a week.

Basic rotation pass

Standing back-to-back with a partner, pass the ball back and forth in rapid rotation. You hand off the ball to your right and immediately accept the return on your left. (See Figure 4-12.) Do this for 30 seconds for one set. Gradually work up to three sets and then start again with a heavier ball. This exercise builds your obliques and abdominals.

Basic chest pass

You and your partner should stand approximately 10 feet (3.04m) apart (if you don't have a partner, you can throw the ball against a wall). Hold the ball at chest level. Using your wrists and fingertips, pass it to your partner as if your were passing a basketball. (See Figure 4-13.) Pass it rapidly back and forth for six repetitions. Work up to 12. Do two to three sets.

Figure 4-12:
The basic
rotation
pass.

Figure 4-13:
The basic
chest pass.

Basic toss

With your partner standing at your feet, lie on a comfortable, flat surface with your knees bent at a 90-degree angle. Raise your shoulders by slightly contracting your abdominals. From this position, toss the ball to your partner. Catch his or her immediate return, lie back, raise and contract again and repeat your toss. Start with 15 reps and work up to 25. Do one set. This exercise builds the chests, wrists, and fingers.

Hip toss

Stand laterally 10 feet (3.04m) from your partner (you can also use a wall). Hold the ball with both hands at your hip. While keeping your lower body stationary, twist your torso and arms toward your partner while firing the ball. Try to use the same motion you employ while swinging a bat.

Do a complete set, and then switch to work the opposite side. Start with 8 reps, and work up to 12. Do two to three sets. This exercise works your obliques, hip, and lower back. It's another good drill for building torque.

Toe push

Lie on your back with the medicine ball on your chest. Bring your legs up on a 90-degree angle. Push the ball as close to the top of your toes as you can (your shoulders should lift from the ground). Hold this position for a moment, and then return to your starting position. (See Figure 4-14.) Start with 15 reps, and work up to 25. This exercise works the lower back, abdomen, chest, and shoulders.

Figure 4-14: The toe push.

Medicine ball jumps

Squat as close to the ground as your balance will allow while holding the medicine ball in front of you at your knees. Jump up as high as you can while swinging the medicine ball upward. Land with your knees bent to absorb any shock. Return to your squat and repeat the exercise. Start with 6 reps, and work up to 12. Do one set, and work up to three. This exercise works your quadriceps, hip flexors, and hamstrings. It gives you explosive drive for leaping.

Lunges

Do this drill slowly. Hold the ball above your head while standing with your feet at shoulder-length width. Lunge forward with your right leg until your chest is behind your knee. As you lunge, bring the ball forward until it is just above or parallel to your right ankle. Return to standing and repeat the drill using your left leg. Start with 6 reps, and work up to 12. Do two to three sets. This exercise works your leg's entire muscle group while limbering your hamstrings and lower back.

You can also build upper body strength by cradling the ball in your arms and jogging short distances. Start at a weight and distance that are comfortable, and then gradually increase both.

High Intensity Leg Work — Sprinting

Jogging makes for a great warm-up and, when done over a long distance, builds wind and endurance. However, in baseball, running is done in short, sudden bursts, so sprints should be a regular part of your workout routine. The best place to sprint is a baseball field. When you lack access to one, go to any field and set up your own "diamond" with markers 90 feet (27.45m) apart.

Make sure you warm up with a light jog and stretch (especially those hamstrings!) before attempting any sprints.

Hurdling sprints

After warming up, do this drill prior to sprinting. It teaches you the arm swing, stride, and leg lift that compose proper sprinting mechanics. Place 12 1-foot-high (30.5cm) hurdles approximately 20 inches (50.8cm) apart in a straight line (you should be able to take two sprinting strides between each hurdle). Start by running the circuit slowly while pulling your legs up high (or you'll trip) and swing your arms up at your side with each stride. After you are comfortable, sprint back and forth across the hurdle line. (See Figure 4-15.) Start with two complete circuits per set, and work up to four circuits. Start with two sets, and work up to four.

Sprinting for home

When you are ready, stand at home plate as if you were at-bat (you can use a real bat or an imaginary one), swing, and then sprint to first as if you were trying to beat out a close play. Jog back to first, swing again, but this time sprint to second. Retrace your steps with another jog, swing, and sprint at top speed to third. Catch your breath, and then sprint for home as if a teammate had just hit a sacrifice fly and you were challenging Dodgers outfielder Raul Mondesi, one of baseball's deadliest arms. Finish the rotation by hitting an "inside-the-park" homer and circling all the bases (and if you want to fantasize that the pitch was delivered by Greg Maddux with the score tied in the bottom of the ninth of a World Series seventh game, it's all right with us). Do one complete circuit, and work up to two.

You can add variations to your sprinting drill. Stand at first and pretend to be stealing second or sprint to third on a ball hit into the gap. Start at second and try to score on a single to left-center. By replicating these situations, you're gaining speed while practicing your game.

Figure 4-15:
Hurdling
sprints.

Playing Heavy Metal — Working with Free Weights

Baseball's approach to conditioning has changed radically over the last 20 years. Until the late 1970s, trainers frowned upon players lifting weights; it was believed that weight training made you bulky and limited your range of motion. However, in 1979, Brian Downing, a catcher with the California Angels, used a rigorous weightlifting regimen to transform himself into the Incredible Hulk (yes, that is what they called him). In his new body, Brian added 70 points to his batting average and over 100 points to his slugging average. Those numbers caught everyone's attention. It wasn't long before clubs were opening weight training rooms and actively encouraging their players to press the metal. Today, most players train with weights. It's one of the reasons — genetics is the other — they are bigger and stronger than ever before.

However, before you even look at a dumbbell, a word or four of caution. Start your weightlifting program with a certified trainer. A professional will teach proper form and devise a schedule that alternates body parts while allowing your muscles to heal (they do tear during lifting). Proper form and a balanced schedule reduce injury risk and help you get better, faster results. Use a spotter — someone who will assist you if you slip or need help completing a rep — whenever you lift a heavy weight (especially when you are benching). Generally speaking, you should be able lift a weight for at least eight reps. If you can't do eight, go lighter. After you can do 12 reps easily, go to the next higher weight and start at 8 reps again.

You'll be able to lift more if you work large muscles groups such as the chest before working smaller muscles like the biceps. To discover more about choosing trainers, proper form, weight-training equipment, vitamins, and nutrition, you may want to read *Fitness For Dummies* and *Weight Training For Dummies* by Susan Schlosberg and Liz Neporent (from IDG Books Worldwide, Inc.).

Whatever weight-training program you follow, combine it with a regular stretching regimen. You don't want to sacrifice flexibility in pursuit of bulk. And remember, you don't have to pump iron to excel in baseball. Texas Rangers slugger Juan Gonzalez returned to the ranks of elite sluggers and won the 1996 MVP award after he *curtailed* his weight-training program. During the two prior seasons, his megamuscles had hampered his swing. Hall of Famers Mickey Mantle, Ralph Kiner, and Jimmy Foxx hit the ball as far as anyone playing today and they didn't touch free weights. However, weightlifting drills can strengthen your baseball muscles, provided you know which exercises to use. Performance specialist Jeff Sassone and the folks at the International Performance Institute (at the Bollettieri Sports Academy), a world-class sports facility devoted to improving all aspects of athletic performance, in Bradenton, Florida (941-755-1000), have offered us some weight training exercises for any player who wants to pound some metal. These are the people who helped train 1997 Rookie of the Year shortstop Nomar Garciaparra, so listen closely to what they have to say.

Bench press

The bench press works your chest muscles. Lie with your back flat on a bench with your feet on the ground to either side. Grasp the barbell with and overhand grip at points that leave you a few inches wider than shoulder width. Tighten your abdominals and tuck your chin into your chest. The bar should be directly over your eyes. Lower the bar slowly to the middle of your chest, and then press it back up over your eyes.

Dumbbell bench press

This exercise also works the chest while emphasizing muscle balance. Lie flat on the bench with your feet on the floor. Grab the dumbbells in an overhand grip. Press them up directly over your shoulders with your palms facing forward. Lower them with control until your elbows are slightly below your shoulders. Push the weight back up while keeping your shoulder blades flat on the bench.

Close grip bench press

Lie flat on the bench with your feet on the floor. Grip the barbell with both hands, about 6 inches (15.24cm) apart. Lower the bar with control until it touches the chest. Then press back up to the starting position.

One arm dumbbell row

Grab a dumbbell with your palm facing in. Keep your abdominals tight. Bend at the hips until your upper torso is parallel or nearly parallel to the floor. Keep your back slightly arched, and your knees slightly bent. Place your free hand on the bench for support. Allow the arm with the dumbbell to hang straight down from your shoulder. Pull the dumbbell up to your waist. At the top of this motion, your elbow should be tight to your side (keep it tight throughout) and pointing straight in back of you.

Squats

Place the barbell across your shoulders so that the weight feels evenly distributed. You feet should be parallel to one another and spread slightly wider than shoulder width. Place your hands shoulder width apart on the bar. Keep your head up and your shoulders back. Maintain a straight back with a slight arch at its base. Slowly bend your knees until your thighs are parallel to the floor. Rise back up. Do three sets. This is a power-hitter's exercise; it works all the large muscles, including the hips and glutes, that help you to drive a ball for distance.

Lunges

Set up as you did for the squat. However, instead of bending with both knees, step forward with your right leg. Slowly bend your right knee and lower your body while bending your left leg behind you. Keep your chest behind your right knee. Push back to your starting position and work the other leg. As an alternative to using the bar, you can also do this while holding a dumbbell in each hand at your side.

You must use a spotter for this exercise and wear a weight belt to protect your back. You may also want to lightly wrap your knees for additional support. And don't let your front knee pass your foot.

Hammer curls

Grab a dumbbell in each hand. Hold them to you down along your sides with your palms facing each other. Raise the dumbbells simultaneously to the shoulders while keeping the palms facing each other and your thumbs up. Lower the weights with control and repeat.

Upright row

Grab a barbell with your hands about 6 inches (15.24cm) apart in an overhand grip. Start with the bar resting on your thighs. With your elbows to the outside, pull the bar up to the chin. Keep your elbows above your wrist and straight. Lower the bar to your starting point with control and repeat.

Curl to press

While standing, hold a dumbbell in each hand with your palms facing forward. Raise the dumbbells to your shoulders while keeping your elbows at your sides. With your palms facing outward, press the dumbbells overhead by extending your arms. Return the dumbbells to the starting position by lowering the weight with control.

Shrugs

Hold your dumbbells in an overhand grip at your sides. Lift and rotate your shoulders back without moving your arms. Lower your shoulders and repeat the lift. (See Figure 4-16.) Do four sets. This exercise works your shoulders. Strong shoulders are the key to upper-body strength.

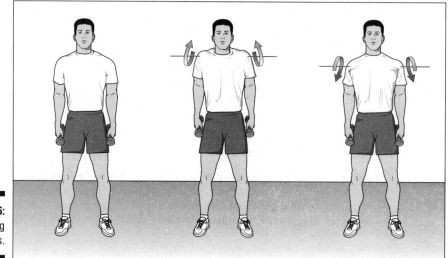

Figure 4-16:
Doing
shrugs.

Lateral raise

While standing, hold your dumbbells in an overhand grip at your sides.
Laterally raise the weights to shoulder height with your palms facing down.
Your arms should be parallel to the ground and your elbows should be
slightly bent. Slowly return the weights to their original position and repeat.
Do three sets. This exercise works the deltoids and strengthens the area
around the rotator cuff. You use the deltoids to swing your arms; the rotator
cuff keeps your arm in its socket. These are good muscles to take care of if
you're planning to hit or throw a baseball.

Lying triceps extension

Lie on a bench while grasping your barbell in an overhand grip that is
slightly less than shoulder width apart. Without locking your elbows,
straighten your arms until you raise the weight directly above midchest.
Hold your elbows stationary as you bend your arms to *gently* lower the
weight to your forehead. Raise the weight back above your chest and repeat.
(See Figure 4-17.) Do three sets. This exercise builds up your triceps, those
muscles that allow you to straighten your elbow. Strong triceps provide
added insurance against elbow injuries and discomfort.

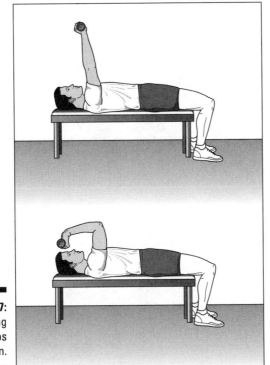

Figure 4-17:
Lying
triceps
extension.

When you are doing lying tricep extensions (a.k.a. brainbusters), one slip can cause serious injury. Start the exercise with a light weight (you may even use only the bar without any weights on it) and use a spotter.

It Ain't Over 'til It's Over

Just as you had to warm up before working out, you have to cool down afterward. Do some light jogging or stretching. Then lie on the floor with your legs straight up and resting against a wall. Taking 10 or 15 minutes to gently "come down" from your workout will limit your soreness while increasing your flexibility.

Chapter 5

Swinging the Lumber: Hitting like a Major Leaguer

In This chapter

▶ Getting ready to hit

▶ Taking your stance and stride

▶ Making contact with the ball

▶ Hitting the ball where you want

▶ Bunting and moving runners

▶ Practicing and troubleshooting your swing

▶ Taking some advice from Rusty Staub

I could talk about hitting for five minutes or five hours without repeating myself. Advice on the subject can be as complex as an in-depth explanation of hip rotation or as simple as saying, "See the ball, hit the ball." Ted Williams has said, "Hitting big league pitching is the most difficult thing to do in sports." Coming from the greatest hitter of the past 50 years, that statement may seem like bragging. However, most athletes who have taken their cuts on a diamond would agree with Mr. Williams. Just ask Michael Jordan how hard it is to get good wood on the ball. The greatest basketball player of our time — perhaps of all time — struggled to hit .220 during his season in the minor leagues. Bo Jackson was a football superstar. As a major league baseball player, he was a fine outfielder with great speed, a prodigious arm, and awe-inspiring power — but Bo's lifetime batting average was only a modest .250. Jim Thorpe, undoubtedly the finest athlete in Olympic history, also hit little more than .250 during his six-year stint in the major leagues (which means that both players were barely more than "average" hitters).

What makes hitting so difficult? Geometry for one thing. As coaches have reminded hitters since baseball's earliest days, "The game is played with a round ball and a round bat and you have to hit it square." Geography and physics complicate that challenge. Only 60 feet 6 inches (18.4m) separates the pitching mound from the batter's box. The average major league pitcher throws his fastball 87 mph. This means it takes the average fastball less than $2/3$ of a second to travel from the pitcher's hand to your hitting zone. How quick is that? In the time it takes to think of the phrase "$2/3$ of a second," strike one is already by you.

So, unless the hurler is soft-tossing a *knuckleball,* a hitter has barely an instant to read the pitch. Is it a *fastball,* a *slider, change-up,* or *curve?* If it is a fastball, is it a *four-seamer,* a *two-seamer* — or the dreaded split-fingered version? (Read all about these pitches in Chapter 6.) Will it be inside or out, up or down? Can you pull this pitch down the line or should you hit it to the opposite field? As you make these assessments, you must move your bat into the hitting zone. Of course, once you make contact, you have eight fielders in front of you (and one behind you), and all of them are committed to transforming the ball you just hit into an out. No wonder the best hitters succeed only three times out of ten.

What You Need to Hit

If you are willing to put in the hours, you can overcome all these obstacles to make yourself a good hitter. How good depends on what you have to work with. To succeed, hitters need

- ✔ **Excellent Vision:** As the baseball adage declares, "You can't hit what you can't see." You need strong vision and depth perception to judge a ball's distance, speed, and spin. (By the way, this doesn't mean you have to have 20/20 vision in both eyes. Many major league hitters have excelled while wearing corrective lenses. Michael Tucker, an outfielder for the 1997 Atlanta Braves, is not quite the nearsighted Mr. Magoo without his contacts, but he's close. He hit .283 in 1997 while playing excellent defense. Frank Howard wore glasses as an outfielder/first baseman with the Washington Senators during the 1960s and '70s. He led the American League in home runs twice.)

- ✔ **Quick Reflexes:** After you've recognized (or *read*) the pitch, your hand-eye coordination must be sharp enough to get your bat on the ball. The better your reflexes, the longer you can wait on a pitch.

- ✔ **Focus:** When you're up at the plate, fans, players, and coaches are yelling at you (and it's often not encouragement), planes may be flying overhead, the wind might be swirling objects across your field of vision, the pitcher can have a funky motion, and you may be tempted to think about the error you made last inning. You must block out all of those distractions and concentrate on the task at hand.

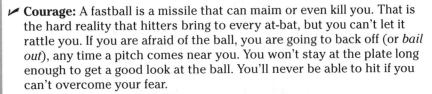

- ✔ **Upper Body Strength:** To swing a wooden bat (which often weighs two pounds or more) with controlled velocity, you must build up your arms, shoulders, chest, and wrists. You also need strong hands. If you have a weak grip, a pitcher will knock the bat out of your hands.

- ✔ **Courage:** A fastball is a missile that can maim or even kill you. That is the hard reality that hitters bring to every at-bat, but you can't let it rattle you. If you are afraid of the ball, you are going to back off (or *bail out*), any time a pitch comes near you. You won't stay at the plate long enough to get a good look at the ball. You'll never be able to hit if you can't overcome your fear.

- ✔ **Sound Strike Zone Judgment:** Hitters who come to the plate swinging at every pitch they see handicap themselves. Learn to recognize the strike zone while developing the patience not to swing at pitches outside of it.

- ✔ **Adaptability:** You've opened the season crushing inside fastballs. Now the pitchers around the league have gotten the message. (And, trust me, they will. Federal Express doesn't operate as quickly as the pitchers' grapevine.) So you're suddenly seeing a steady diet of outside breaking stuff. Adjust to the change — or your batting average will plummet.

- ✔ **Hitting Hunger:** Some batters get two hits in their first two at-bats and think, at least unconsciously, that they are done for the day. Great hitters are never content. As Stan Musial, the former St. Louis Cardinals outfielder and batting champion, has repeatedly said, "When I got two hits in a game, I came up wanting a third. If I got a third, I had to get a fourth. I never knew when I might go 0 for 4, so I was always *hungry* for more base hits."

That last item is something you either have or you don't, but you can develop the other attributes. We'll be working on most of them throughout this chapter.

Picking Your Lumber

Before we write another word explaining how to hit, take a look at what you'll be hitting with. The bat you choose should feel comfortable. Big league bats generally weigh between 32 and 36 ounces (907g to 1kg). If you can snap a 36- to 38-ounce bat through the strike zone with control and velocity, go for it. When a pitched ball collides with a heavyweight bat, it travels farther.

However, don't choose a large, heavy bat thinking it will magically transform you into a power hitter. Big bats don't necessarily produce big hits. If you can't control your bat, your swing will be awkward and long. You may have to start it early in the pitcher's delivery — and once you get it going it will be hard to stop. Pitchers, taking advantage of that swing, can continually fool you with breaking stuff. Pretty soon, you won't be hitting for power, you won't be hitting for singles, you won't be hitting *period.* You may as well use that big bat for kindling.

Bats come in various shapes. Find one that suits you. For instance, a bat with a medium handle and large barrel offers you more hitting surface. However, you won't be able to snap it through the hitting zone as quickly as a bat with a very thin handle and a large barrel. Throughout most of my career, I swung an average-sized bat — it weighed 32 ounces and measured $34^1/_2$ inches (87.6cm) long — yet I still managed to lead the National League in slugging in 1976. It had a thin handle and a small barrel. Bat speed was the key to my power. With my light bat, I could wait longer on the ball, which allowed me more time to recognize the pitch. I could whip through the strike zone with a quick, compact swing. The large barrel added momentum and gave me all the hitting surface I wanted.

Some big-league hitters change bats depending on the pitcher. I would occasionally go to a heavier bat against soft-throwing left-handers. I knew I didn't have to be quite as quick against them, and the bat's additional mass helped me drive the ball. Other than those instances, however, I stayed with my regular bat. It gave me the bat speed, control, and balance I needed to cope with most situations.

If you're a younger player, you may want to think "light." When you are unsure of the proper bat weight, choose a bat that is comfortable.

Get A Grip — Holding the Bat

The first thing you should consider when gripping a bat is *to glove or not to glove.* Almost all big leaguers wear batting gloves (some because it gives them a better hold on the bat, others because they have large endorsement contracts with glove companies). I *didn't* wear a glove when I hit (though I did wear a golf glove when I was on base to protect my hands while sliding) because I liked the feel of the wood against my fingers. Whether you wear batting gloves is a matter of personal preference. If gloves improve your grip, wear them. (Some players prefer, of course, substances such as resin or pine tar to improve their grip.)

When you hold your bat, your hands should touch so they can work as a unit. Begin by placing your bat handle at the base of the fingers of both hands. Grip the bat with your fingers rather than in your palm. Holding it with your palm deprives you of wrist action, flexibility, and bat speed. Align the middle knuckles of your top hand between the middle and lower knuckles of your bottom hand.

Choking up on the bat gave me better control. I would slide my hands an inch or two above the knob of the bat. Many people believe that choke hitters can't generate power, but Ted Williams choked up and he has over 500 career home runs on his résumé. You *will* sacrifice some power with an extreme choke (five or more inches above the knob). (See Figure 5-1 for an illustration of both grips.)

If you're strong enough, you can slide your hands down to the knob without surrendering any control; this grip will also give you a tad more plate coverage. Some sluggers bury their little fingers beneath the bat knob: They believe it helps their wrists and hands to work in better sync. You have to be extremely powerful to do this, though. Most readers should stick with one of the more conventional grips.

HEADS UP

When you are at-bat, hold the bat firmly but don't squeeze it; the tension slows down your wrists and hands. Your grip automatically tightens as you swing. Hold the bat more firmly with your bottom hand than with your top one. Your bottom hand pulls your bat through the hitting zone.

Where does that label go?

As kids, we were told that our bats would break if we hit a ball on the bat label. That's an old wives' tale, but you should keep the label turned away from the pitcher anyway. The grain side of the bat gives you a harder hitting surface.

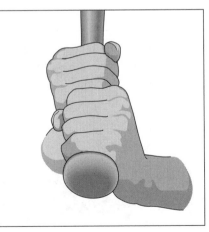
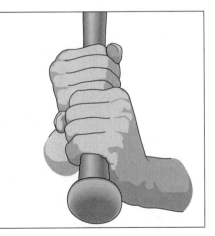

Figure 5-1:
The basic
bat grip and
choking up.

Your body and your bat

Now that you have your bat in your hands, how close should you hold it to your body? Again, let comfort dictate your choice, but it should be no less than 5 inches and no more than 7 inches from your torso (about 13 to 18cm). Holding your hands near your body also keeps you on the inside of the ball. Hold the bat out farther than that, and your swing will have too large an arc; you lose leverage and find it difficult to coordinate your hip and arm into your swing. Bring the bat in closer, and you restrict your movement; this will cost you bat speed. There will be a large loop to your swing, and it requires a long push to get your bat into the hitting zone. By the time you do, that fastball is already past you (see Figure 5-2).

Hold your hands somewhere between the letters on your uniform front and your shoulders. Your elbows should be away from your body (as shown in Figure 5-3).

On chicken flaps and other eccentricities

Whenever I brought by arms too close to my body, I tended to upper-cut the ball. The result? Too many fly ball outs. It was a tough habit to break. The late Nellie Fox, a Hall of Fame second baseman and a player/coach when I played with the Houston Astros, suggested I flap my elbow whenever I was at the plate as a reminder to keep it away from my torso. I was only supposed to do this for a few days, but the "chicken flap" became part of my hitting routine. It kept my elbow out and also got me cocked to hit.

Figure 5-2:
Holding your hands too near or too far from your body changes your swing.

Figure 5-3:
A proper
way to hold
your bat.

Will flapping your elbow make you a better hitter? If you had the same problem I did, it may. However, rather than emulate my or some other player's quirk, you must develop your own method for getting comfortable at the plate. My Cincinnati Reds teammate Tony Perez — one of the best clutch hitters I ever saw — used to continually regrip his bat. First, the fingers of one hand would open and close on the handle, and then the fingers of the other would do the same. It was as if he were playing a flute as he waited for the pitch. This method was nothing more than a rhythmic device that relaxed Tony while preparing him to hit.

Some players step out of the box after every pitch to windmill their bats. Next time you watch a game, pay attention to the hitters as they enter the batter's box. You'll probably detect a different idiosyncrasy with each player.

The point of all this is you can do anything you want with the bat *before you start your swing.* However, as you attack the ball, your stride must carry you into your hitting zone. Stan Musial had a peek-a-boo crouch at the plate that made him look like a man peering around a corner (see Figure 5-4). Carl Yastrzemski, the great Boston Red Sox outfielder and batting champion, stood nearly upright at home — he only slightly flexed his knee and hip — while holding his bat high above his left ear (Yaz was a left-handed hitter). He looked as if he were ringing a church bell. Musial and Yastrzemski had dissimilar stances. Yet, their strides and hip rotations would leave them in the same positions as they made contact with the ball.

So however you choose to carry your bat to the plate — on your shoulders, close to your body, parallel to the ground, whatever — is fine, as long as it allows you to quickly reach your ideal hitting position. Whether your quirk does something, you can't know until you get into the batter's box to take some swings.

Figure 5-4:
Musial demonstrates his unique hitting style.

National Baseball Hall of Fame Library Cooperstown, N.Y.

Stepping Up to the Plate

When you come up to hit, the first thing you must decide is where to stand in the batter's box. This is a matter of personal preference. Edgar Martinez, the great hitter for the Seattle Mariners, stands so far back in the box he's nearly out of it (this gives him more time to look over each pitch). Other batters stand in the rear of the box but far from the plate, up in the box and near the plate, or up in the box and far from the plate.

Any number of combinations is possible. I have short arms, so I stood close the plate. This position gave me a better opportunity to reach strikes on the outside corner (and if your stance doesn't allow you access to those outside pitches, find another one). Because I had a very quick bat, I felt comfortable standing far up in the batter's box. To discover what will serve you best, hit from various positions in the box against live pitching.

The benefits of being up front

When you stand at the front of the box (see Figure 5-5), your stride brings you in front of home plate. Anything you hit in front of the plate has a better chance of staying fair. Standing in front will help you against sinkerball and breaking ball pitchers; you'll be able to hit the ball before it drops below your swing.

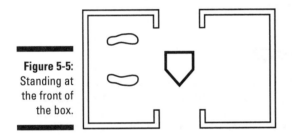

Figure 5-5:
Standing at
the front of
the box.

Stand deep in the box against a good sinkerballer, and you're giving him an advantage; his ball will have more time to sink. Standing at the front of the box also allows you to hit the curveball before it fully breaks. Even knuckleballs are easier to hit from this location; they have less time to dance. (I used to move as far up in the batter's box as I could against certain breaking ball pitchers; it took their best weapons away from them.) However, fastballs will provide your up-front stance with its ultimate test. They will be on top of you that much quicker. If you can't handle them, you'll have to step back.

To develop bat speed and strength, I would swing a lead bat only with my front (right) arm. This exercise strengthens your front side which pulls the bat through the hitting zone. I would do this 50 times a day during the off-season and 10 times before a game. You should also take 25 full swings with a bat that's heavier than the one you normally use in a game.

Stuck in the middle

Some batters take their swing from the middle of the box (see Figure 5-6). Hitting from the middle gives you a little more time to catch up with the fastball — but curveballs, sinkers, and knucklers also have more time to break. However, if you have only medium bat speed (something a coach can tell you), this is the place for you (until you develop a faster bat).

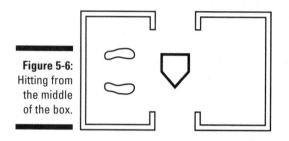

Figure 5-6: Hitting from the middle of the box.

Tales from the deep

Obviously, standing deep in the box allows you the maximum time to cope with the fastball. But you have to be a great breaking ball hitter to consistently succeed in this location; you're giving the curve, sinker, and knuckler their best opportunity to work their magic. Because you'll be hitting balls on the plate and the angle of your bat is toward foul territory, their trajectory will carry more of them into foul territory. If you stand deep in the box and far from the plate, you'll find it difficult to hit outside pitches (see Figure 5-7).

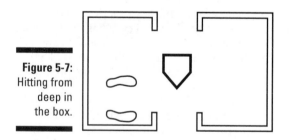

Figure 5-7: Hitting from deep in the box.

Getting Close

The toughest pitch to hit is the ball out and away from you. After getting in the batter's box, swing your bat to make sure you have full plate coverage. Stand close enough to home to reach pitches 4 inches (10cm) off the outside corner. When you're close to the plate, the outside part of it becomes your middle. You are taking away a strength from the pitcher. Sure, the pitcher can throw even farther outside, but if you're a disciplined batter you can take those pitches for balls. In the ninth inning of the 1975 World Series final game I drove in the winning run when Red Sox left-hander Jim Burton threw me a slider that broke down and away. It would have been a perfect pitch *if I had been standing farther off the plate.* Because I was close to the dish I was able to reach over and hit it into left center field.

Your Stance

Hitters can choose from three basic stances (all shown in Figure 5-8 for a right-handed hitter):

- ✔ **The Open Stance:** Your back foot is closer to the plate than your front foot.

- ✔ **The Even** or **Square Stance:** Both feet are equidistant from the plate.

- ✔ **The Closed Stance:** Your front foot is closer to the plate than your back foot.

I always preferred the closed stance. Only hitters who cannot rotate their hips out of the way properly need a somewhat open stance. (Your coach can tell you if you have the right hip action.) The open stance frees their upper torsos and automatically opens their hips, allowing them to drive their body and hands through the hitting zone while generating bat speed. It also lets you to turn your head so it faces the pitcher, which allows you to use both eyes simultaneously.

Everybody rotates away from the ball in order to hit. Open-stance hitters are already a half-step away from the plate. They must, therefore, remind themselves not to *pull off* the pitch (move away from the plate a split second too soon) or they won't be able to hit the ball with any authority. For that reason, most major leaguers choose the closed stance or square stance.

Novice hitters should start with an even stance. It will help you to keep your weight distributed evenly on the balls of both feet (and now you know how the stance got its name). As you gradually develop balance, reduce your stance an inch at a time until you find the closed stance that generates the most power.

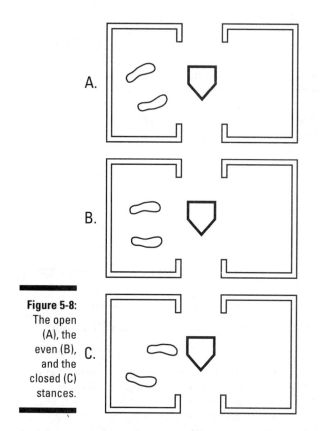

A.

B.

C.

Figure 5-8:
The open
(A), the
even (B),
and the
closed (C)
stances.

What's Your Body Doing?

Your shoulders will be slightly closed in a closed stance and more squared in the even or open versions. No matter which stance you choose, point your face toward the pitcher's mound so that you can see the pitcher with both eyes.

Young hitters often make the mistake of looking out of only one eye. Sometimes they slightly cock their heads to the side so that one eye is closer to the pitcher than the other. This stance alters your depth perception. You need both eyes on a parallel plane if you are going to read the ball's spin and speed as quickly as possible. Tucking your chin behind your shoulder will also limit your vision. Keep your head square and still throughout your stride and swing. You will hear broadcasters discuss how a hitter kept his head down throughout his swing. That's always good policy. Keeping your head down keeps your eyes on the ball. Move your head and your body follows. Your swing will suffer.

When taking your stance, bend your knees slightly to allow greater freedom of movement. An erect stance restricts your lower body's maneuverability. How far you spread your legs apart is a matter of personal preference. I always felt more balanced with my feet spread slightly more than shoulder width (see Figure 5-9).

Figure 5-9:
A balanced
batting
stance.

Going into your crouch

Some players, like the outfielder Rickey Henderson, go into an extreme wide crouch to shorten their strike zone. Rickey is probably going into the Hall of Fame after he retires, so you can be productive hitting that way. My former Cincinnati teammate Pete Rose hit out of a deep crouch with his bat on his shoulder. I don't think young players should copy that stance, but Pete used it to get more base hits than anyone in major league history. It all comes down to comfort. I recommend a slight crouch with some flex in the knee and your upper body only slight tilted toward the plate.

Bending too much from the top will hinder your swing; as you straighten up during your stride, you will lose sight of the pitch. Stay in your crouch as you stride. If the pitcher takes a long time between pitches, step out of the batter's box to stretch so you don't become rigid.

Can you dig it?

You hear a lot about *digging in* at the plate. All it means is that the hitter is planting both feet firmly in the batter's box. Digging in gives you more traction and prevents you from slipping. Power hitters do it all the time because they want to rotate off a firm back foot as their hips open. This position helps them to explode into the hitting zone.

Why a Stride?

Try hitting without taking a stride. If you stand still and swing, you can't generate any power. Your stride releases your energy and takes you into the pitch. It helps you to pivot while bringing your hips, arms, and shoulders into action. You must hit from a strong front side; your stride ensures that you will be successful by allowing you to firmly plant your front foot.

Look before you stride

When I was first learning how to hit, someone gave me a poem that taught me a valuable lesson about strides. It went

See the ball before your stride,
Let it go if it's outside,
If it's a curve and should break down,
Jack up and hit it downtown.

This poem reminded me that I had to see the ball before starting my stride. If you move too soon, you'll be swinging at the pitcher's arm motion instead of the ball. You won't get too many hits doing that. Always remember that you have more time to see and hit the ball than you think.

Some hitters watch the ball from the moment the pitcher puts it into his glove to start his wind-up. Don't bother with that because different motions might deceive you. Pitchers can rear back as if they are going to throw the ball through a wall, and then deliver a soft change-up. Or they can give you an easy, rocking-chair motion while throwing something hard and nasty.

Start looking for the ball when the pitcher drops his hand behind him to begin his throw to the plate. A pitcher's motion is like a batter's stance. A lot of idiosyncratic bells and whistles may be at the start of it, but eventually the pitcher has to come to a conventional release point. Concentrate on that point — say, the corner of a right-handed pitcher's right shoulder — because the ball comes out of that slot. As soon as you pick up the ball leaving his hand, react. Stride toward the pitch.

To make sure that you don't move too soon, try this exercise. Take batting practice and instruct the pitcher to occasionally complete his delivery *without throwing the ball.* If you find yourself moving into this phantom pitch, you need to discipline yourself at the plate.

The length of your stride

Pitches loose speed from the moment they leave a pitcher's hand. When you stride toward the pitcher, you are helping the ball get to you quicker by shortening the distance it has to travel. So your stride should not be longer than your original batting stance. A long stride with a narrow stance also makes your head bob. The pitch will seem as if it is jumping in and out of view. If your stance is 8 inches (20cm) wide, make sure your stride is no wider than that.

When you overstride, your upper body becomes unbalanced. Remember, the only purpose of a stride is to get your lower body into hitting position. Because your eyes are focused on the ball (they better be!), don't move your head or upper torso toward the pitch; you don't want to throw off your field of vision. Instead, stride into the ball with your lower body. After you stride, your head should still be in the middle of your body rather than leaning forward or backward. A hitter should glide and pop; don't leap and sweep.

As you move toward the pitch, step away from your hands, or push your hands back, to let your body move forward (see Figure 5-10). If you take your hands with you as you stride, you lose bat speed and power. Keep your hands and shoulders in the same position they held in your stance. I started my stance with my hands at the end of my left armpit, just off of my shoulder. They would still be there after I took my stride.

Troubleshooting your stride

You know that your stride is too narrow and that you need to lengthen it when

- ✔ Your front side doesn't feel strong; or
- ✔ Your legs are collapsing in midstride.

You know if your stride is too wide when

- ✔ You can't generate any hip action; or
- ✔ The ball seems as if it's jumping.

Figure 5-10:
Beginning
your stride.

 Players who overstride can draw a line or lay a bat across the batter's box during practice to remind themselves not to stride beyond it. I always thought the best remedy for overstride was concentration. If you are focused, you can eliminate most mistakes from your game.

Slightly Up or Slightly Down: Two Approaches

Almost everyone agrees that the ideal swing starts about armpit high and levels out as your bat comes to the ball. How much it levels out is a point of divergence.

Some instructors tell you to hit slightly down or even chop at the ball (although Ted Williams has told me that hitters can't hit down on the ball; they can only hit the ball's top half). When I was playing, Matty Alou, a center fielder with the Pittsburgh Pirates, won a batting title (.342 in 1966) and posted a .307 lifetime batting average by slapping the ball on the ground. He was obviously a gifted hitter. Matty scored only 90 or more runs twice, a low total for someone who usually batted at the top of a great hitting lineup — but to be fair, Matty had a slender, almost frail physique. Power was never going to be his game, so his hitting style was probably best for him. After all, he did win a batting title.

The King of Swing, Mr. Ted Williams, took the opposite approach from Alou. Ted's swing ended with a slight, upward arc. It permitted him to hit for power without hurting his batting average (.344 lifetime). Ted still preaches the slight uppercut swing to every hitter he meets. He persuaded Tony Gwynn, the San Diego Padres outfielder and eight-time National League batting champion, to try it in 1997. Gwynn had his best all-around season at the age of 37; he won another batting title and drove in more than 100 runs for the first time in his career.

I'm in the Williams camp. Batters who hit the ball hard are going to put more runs on the board than those who can't. Runs, not hits or batting averages, win ball games. If you hit down on the ball, it will be difficult for you to drive it for doubles or home runs. Keep your swing level; and if you stay behind the ball, your swing will have a slight upward arc as your body rotates into the pitch.

Making Contact

Don't swing as soon as the pitcher releases the ball; wait until you recognize the pitch (its spin and speed) before attacking it. You have cocked your body with your stride and you took that step away from your hands. As you go after the pitch, uncoil everything. Pivot forward, opening your hips as you transfer your weight from front foot to back. Brace your front leg. Bend your rear leg while pivoting your back foot. You will know you have shifted your weight correctly if your rear toe ends up pointing directly downward (see Figure 5-11).

Figure 5-11: The anatomy of making contact.

During all this time, your hands and arms will direct the bat's movement. Keep your elbows close to your body so that the bat travels in a tight circle. (Your hands and arms do not stay close to your body; good extension creates more bat speed.) Your bottom hand should pull the bat into the hitting zone while your top hand pushes and guides it (as shown in Figure 5-12). The back surface of the bat should rest against your top hand's palm.

Figure 5-12:
Your hands as you make contact.

Your swing should bring your hands and arms in front of the plate with your bat trailing slightly behind for leverage — think of swinging an axe from the side. Make sure your wrists are firm as the bat moves into the hitting zone. Try to see the bat making contact with the ball (you probably won't be able to, but just the attempt ensures that you are watching the ball throughout your swing).

Remember that you want to hit the ball in front of the plate so it has a better chance of staying fair. As you finish your swing, the bat should make an almost complete circle around your upper body; most of your weight should be on your front foot.

Some Fine-Tuning

Depending on a pitch's location, you should make these small adjustments in your swing:

✔ **On pitches inside:** Rotate your hips out of the way quickly so that you can get the bat out in front faster. When you hit an inside pitch, the barrel of the bat should be covering the inside of the plate.

✔ **On pitches outside:** Do the opposite of what you do with inside pitches. Keep your hips closed and go to the ball with your upper body. Try to drive the ball to the opposite field (to left field if you're left-handed, to right field if you're a righty).

✔ **On low pitches:** You shouldn't have to bend to hit a low strike. Give your swing slightly more arc as you go down to get the pitch.

✔ **On high pitches:** Many coaches tell you to get on top of the ball, but if you take that advice to an extreme you can develop bad habits. Because your hands should be at the top in your stride just before you start swinging, simply stay level (or high) a little longer, and then hit through the ball.

✔ **When the pitcher has two strikes on you:** In this situation, you have to swing at anything near the plate. You can't count on the umpire calling a ball if the pitch is only an inch or so out of the strike zone. Shorten your stride and cut down on your swing by choking up another half-inch or so.

A Word About Follow-Through

Conventional baseball wisdom holds that the follow-through (shown in Figure 5-13), which occurs after the ball leaves your bat, is the last essential part of your swing. Some coaches tell you that if you don't have the proper follow-through, you can't hit the ball with power. It's true that concentrating on continuing your swing after the point of contact helps you to drive *through* the ball. But I think the people who emphasize the importance of follow-through have things backward. The reason you're not driving the ball with power is because you're not executing one or more of the other elements of your swing that produce a good follow-through. (Following-through ensures that you hit *through* the ball, not *to* the ball.)

By itself, a good follow-through doesn't help you hit. Why? Because the ball has left your bat! If you've done all the things we've talked about, your swing has already accomplished its purpose. A good follow-through results from properly executed mechanics: It is a finish, important only to the batter, not to the ball. A poorly balanced follow-through may tell you your swing is off, but the weak pop-up you just hit to the catcher already let you know that.

Figure 5-13:
The classic
follow-
through.

Dealing with the Strike Zone

The baseball rule book says the strike zone is a rectangle the width of home plate, extending from the top of the batter's knees to the letters across his uniform jersey. In practice, however, every player and umpire has his or her interpretation of the strike zone. (See Chapter 1 for a diagram of the strike zone.) Most umpires have a strike zone that starts at the bottom of the player's knee and finishes no higher than the top of his belt buckle. It is the rare ump who will call a strike on a pitch at the letters. Because the zone is supposed to have the same width as the plate, you wouldn't expect to see too much variance there. Yet, some umps call strikes on pitches 6 inches (15cm) off the plate (mostly outer edge, rarely inside), and some never call a strike on any ball that just nicks the plate's corners.

When you take batting practice, swing at pitches in your legally defined strike zone; you can adjust to an individual umpire's zone after you determine what it is. The best hitters take most of their swings at pitches in the strike zone. It's true that some players are so strong that they can hit a pitch that is 1 or 2 inches off the plate. However, the so-called good "bad-ball" hitters are rare. Discipline yourself to swing only at strikes.

To get a sense of your strike zone without swinging a bat, have a catch with someone. Stand 60 feet (18.3m) apart (nearly the distance between home plate and the pitcher's mound) and keep your throws between each other's chest and knees. Move your tosses up and down within this area. Because you are facing the thrower dead-on, you can immediately detect from the ball's trajectory whether it will be a strike or a ball.

After you have learned your strike zone, find out where your hot hitting spots are within it. In his book *The Science of Hitting* (a must-read for every ballplayer), Ted Williams broke down his strike zone in a diagram — which demonstrated that he batted .400 when he hit pitches down the heart of the plate, but only batted .220 when he hit pitches that were low and outside. This result reminded Ted that he shouldn't swing at those low, outside pitches unless he already had two strikes on him and the ball was over the plate. All athletes must develop that same kind of self-awareness. You can never be a good hitter or player unless you know your strengths and weaknesses. If you are not a good low ball hitter, lay off that pitch until you have two strikes.

That First Pitch

Should you swing or take the first pitch you see in an at-bat? It depends on the situation. I remember a minor league game I played in Durham, North Carolina. My team was facing some rookie pitcher and I opened the first inning by popping up on his first pitch. When I came back to the bench my manager, Billy Goodman, a former American League batting champion, asked me, "What does that pitcher have?" Well, I didn't know what the pitcher had other than a fastball and I couldn't even tell you how hard he threw that. I hadn't seen enough of his pitches. And that was Billy's point: The first time you face a pitcher you don't know, *take* as many pitches as you can. Find out how his curve ball breaks, which way his slider moves. Does he have a change-up? Does he throw every pitch from the same angle?

When you are facing pitchers you are familiar with, however, there are no hard rules about swinging or not swinging at the first pitch. Against them, I always went to the plate looking to hit the first good pitch I saw. If it came on the pitcher's first offering, I swung. However, I invariably took a lot of first pitches simply because so many of them were thrown out of the strike zone.

Going to All Fields

Novice hitters should learn how to hit the ball to all fields. If a pitch is away from you, hit it to the opposite field (**remember:** right field if you are right-handed, left field if you are a lefty). Smack the pitch down the heart of the plate up the middle of the diamond. If the ball is inside, jerk (or *pull*) it into left field if you're a right-hander or into right field if you're a lefty. As you get more experience, you'll discover whether you are predominantly a *spray hitter* (typically a player who may or may not hit with some power to all fields, for example Detroit Tiger second baseman Bip Roberts) or a *pull hitter* (generally a slugger such as Jim Thome of the Cleveland Indians). See Figure 5-14.

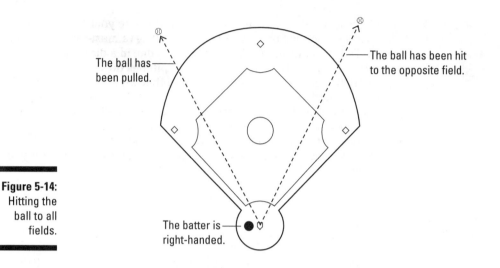

Figure 5-14:
Hitting the
ball to all
fields.

The ball has
been pulled.

The ball has been hit
to the opposite field.

The batter is
right-handed.

I started my big league career as a spray hitter but developed into a pull hitter as I got stronger. However, as a pull hitter, I could still slap a hit to the opposite field when the situation demanded it. A good spray hitter can pull the ball down the line when he needs an extra-base hit. The bottom line is you want to be as complete a hitter as possible.

Hitting to center field (straight-away) or to the opposite field

You have to hit the ball a little later in order to hit to center or to the opposite field. To do this, take an even stance at the plate. Aim everything through the middle — that strategy causes you to hit the ball later.

Pulling the ball

Hit the ball early enough so that the bat meets the ball in front of you. Right-handed hitters pull the ball to the left side; left-handers pull to the right. If you're using a closed stance, you're going to naturally pull a lot of balls (see the section "Your Stance," earlier in this chapter). The more closed your stance, the more you pull the ball. Crowd the plate as much as possible. This position expands the area from which you can pull. Make sure that your back foot is firmly planted; you want something stationary to drive from. Planting your back foot also gives your swing more arc. Don't upper-cut the ball; let your body, stride, and swing give it power. As you start your swing, shift your weight to your front foot. This shifting keeps your bat level in the hitting zone for a longer period of time. Want to hit for more power? Keep your weight back a little longer.

When the opposition gets shifty

Should you get a reputation as a pull hitter, opponents may try to stack their defenses against you. You could find yourself hitting against a *shift.* If you're a left-handed hitter, the shortstop moves toward the second base side of the infield, the center fielder leans toward right, and the left fielder comes closer to center. If you are right-handed, the fielders move the other way. The most extreme shift in baseball history was the *Boudreau Shift,* which the Cleveland Indians employed against pull hitter supreme Ted Williams. Whenever Williams came to bat, shortstop-manager Lou Boudreau would crowd the right side of the diamond with six fielders.

I hit against shifts during my career, though nothing as radical as the Boudreau version.

The best thing you can do when confronted by one is forget it's there. A shift's biggest impact is more psychological than anything else. If you look at it and think, "I'll never get a base hit against this, " you may as well drop your bat and return to the dugout. I always believed that if I hit a solid line drive it wouldn't be caught no matter how many fielders they stacked against me. Attack this stratagem with that same confidence. Of course, you can always destroy a shift by *dinking* (softly hitting) a single to the opposite field or bunting, but that is what the opposition wants you to do. They are trying to make you go away from your strength. Don't fall for it. Take your normal cuts at the plate (unless a single can drive in a run).

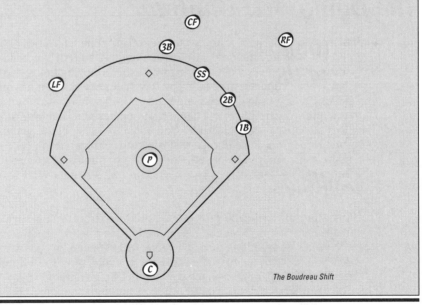

The Boudreau Shift

Analyzing the Pitcher

Most hitters don't keep written notes on pitchers; they keep "books" in their heads documenting how pitchers have come at them in the past. If a pitcher has been unsuccessful trying to get you out with inside fastballs, but has been burying you with outside breaking pitches, you can assume he's going to keep throwing those curves. However, you can't establish a pitching pattern off of any one game. Maybe the pitcher's fastball was sluggish the night he never tried to bust it by you inside. He may have had an unusually wicked curve working that evening. The next time you face him, if his *heater* is hopping, he may get you out with fastballs inside all night. You may not even see his curveball. So you have to discover what a pitcher has working for him on game day.

I would watch the opposing pitcher warm up in the bullpen to see what pitches he was throwing for strikes. Generally, if a pitcher can't control his slider or curve in the bullpen, he won't be able to control them in the game for at least an inning or two. Take those pitches for balls until he proves he can get them over the plate.

The Dying Art: Bunting

When you *bunt,* hold your bat in the hitting zone and let the ball make contact with it. The idea is to deaden the ball so that the baserunners can advance (or you can get to first) while the opposing fielders run in to make a play. There comes a time in every baseball season when anyone — even hulking sluggers like Cecil Fielder or Frank Thomas — should bunt. For example, you are playing a game that decides whether you or your opponent clinches a championship. You come to bat with the winning run on first and nobody out in the bottom of the ninth inning. I don't care how many home runs you hit all season, your job is to bunt that runner to second base. Bunts can win ball games — so everyone who swings a bat should know how to lay them down.

It is especially important for pitchers to learn how to bunt, even if they play in a league that invokes the designated hitter rule. Depending on how many substitutions are made during a game, pitchers can be called on to hit even in designated hitter leagues (for more on this rule, refer to Chapter 3). Or you may be playing an interleague game in the home park of a team whose rules don't provide for a designated hitter. In the fourth inning of the second game of the 1997 World Series between the Cleveland Indians and Florida Marlins, Cleveland pitcher Chad Ojea — who had never batted in the major leagues because of the designated hitter rule — bunted two teammates to second and third. It was a crucial play. A two-run single then broke open the game, which the Indians eventually won. Had Ojea failed to get the bunt down — or, worse, bunted into a double play — the outcome may have been different.

Your bunting stance

The most commonly used bunting stance is the *pivot*. Take your normal stance at the plate while waiting for the pitch. As the ball comes to the plate, pivot your upper body toward the pitch while keeping your feet in their stance position (see Figure 5-15). This method has several advantages:

✔ You can flow into a pivot quickly so you maintain an element of surprise.

✔ In the event of a fake bunt — where you "show" bunt to pull in the infielders and then swing away to drive the ball past them — the pivot allows you to easily resume a standard batting stance.

✔ With a pivot stance, getting out of the path of errant pitches is easier.

Figure 5-15:
An ideal bunting stance.

The *squared-stance* is your other bunting option — and perhaps best for players just starting out. Bring your rear and front feet parallel to home plate and each other while keeping them shoulder-width apart (see Figure 5-16). This stance gives you better plate coverage and a longer look at the ball than the pivot, but it also has its drawbacks. You become more vulnerable to being hit by a pitch, you risk stepping out of the batter's box (in which case the umpire may call you out), and, because you have to get set in this position early, you decrease your chances of surprising the opposition. I prefer the pivot, but you should adopt whichever position is most comfortable.

Figure 5-16:
The squared-stance bunt.

Whether you pivot or square around to bunt, make sure you drop into a slight crouch with your shoulder's squared toward the pitcher. Shift your weight forward as you stand on the balls of your feet. Hold the bat handle firmly with your bottom hand so you can control it, but don't squeeze the handle or you will hit the ball too hard. Slide your top hand up near the bat label. Pinch the barrel with your fingers and thumb, your thumb on top. This action forms the hand into a U that will absorb any impact when the ball strikes your bat. It also protects your fingers (see Figure 5-17).

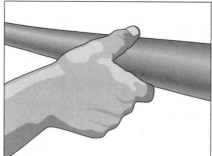

Figure 5-17:
Holding the bat for the bunt.

Many bunters hold their bat parallel to the ground while waiting for the pitch. I think it is better to hold the top of the bat barrel slightly higher than the handle. This strategy keeps you on top of the ball, which is where the bunter has to be. If you come up underneath the pitch, you will pop it up. If you hit the ball dead center, you'll produce a soft line drive that can be converted into a double play.

Hold the bat near the top of your strike zone so that any pitch over your bat will be a ball. This will keep you from offering at high pitches, which are hardest to bunt. Try to bunt a low pitch. Watch the ball make contact with the bat in front of you and the plate. Give with the ball, don't push it. You should experience the sensation of "catching" the ball with your bat and guiding it to its destination. Let your bottom hand direct the bat's angle.

The sacrifice

With the *sacrifice bunt,* the bunter advances the baserunners while giving up a chance for a base hit. With a runner on first, bunt toward the area between the mound and the first baseman. With a runner on second or runners on first and second, bunt toward the third baseman to bring him in off the bag. (See Figure 5-18).

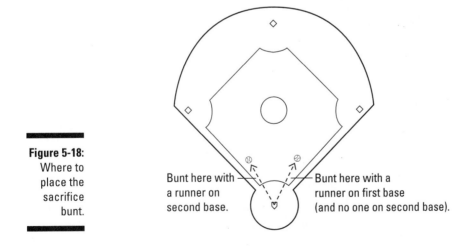

Figure 5-18:
Where to place the sacrifice bunt.

Bunt here with a runner on second base.

Bunt here with a runner on first base (and no one on second base).

Bunting for a hit

To successfully bunt for a hit, you must catch the opposition unaware. This is where the pivot gives you an advantage: It allows you to deceive the infielders longer than the squared-around stance. To bunt for a hit, you should be in motion as the bat makes contact with the ball. You should also grip the bat a little more firmly than you did for the sacrifice.

Drag bunts (so named because the bunter appears to drag the ball along the baseline as he runs toward first) are used by left-handed hitters (see Figure 5-19).

I beat out a drag bunt to get a hit in the seventh game of the 1975 World Series. To execute it, shift your weight into your right foot as you pivot and step toward first base. Hold the bat solidly with its head pointed toward third. Don't pull back the bat or the ball will go foul. You should be moving into your second stride as you make contact with the ball. With your running start, you should beat out the bunt, provided it stays fair (see Figure 5-20).

Right-handers or left-handers can execute *push* or *dump* bunts for base hits. If you bat right-handed, start with your weight on your right (the rear) foot. As you move to bunt the ball, quickly shift your weight forward into your left foot. Push the ball past the pitcher toward the hole between first and second. Run immediately after making contact. If you are a lefty hitter, reverse your weight shift and tap the ball down the third base line. Run immediately after making contact.

The squeeze play

The *squeeze play* is a sacrifice bunt with a runner on third base. If a manager calls for a squeeze play, it's usually during the later innings of a close game with less than two out. On a *safety squeeze,* the runner breaks for home only after you've dropped your bunt on the infield. If the bunt isn't good, the runner stays at third. As the bunter, your job is to push the ball away from the pitcher and toward the first or third baseman.

The *suicide squeeze* is a riskier play. It requires the runner to dash toward home plate as the ball leaves the pitcher's hand. *He is coming home no matter what kind of bunt you drop.* So you can't take the pitch even if it is out of the strike zone. You must bunt the ball somewhere.

Don't be too finicky about placement. With the runner bearing down on home, just bunt the ball to the ground in fair territory and you've driven in a run. Even if you bunt it foul with less than two strikes on you, the worst that can happen is the runner will be sent back to third. If you don't make contact with the ball, the catcher will have the runner dead at the plate (which is why it's called the *suicide* squeeze).

Figure 5-19:
Brett Butler
executes
the drag
bunt.

National Baseball Hall of Fame Library Cooperstown, N.Y.

Faking the bunt

You can fake a bunt when a teammate is trying to steal a base. A successful decoy may get the infielders moving in the wrong direction. When you pull back the bat, you force the catcher to stay back so it takes him longer to get to the ball. You can also fake a bunt, pivot back to your hitting stance, and take a short, easy swing (a swinging bunt) to slash or chop the ball past the infielders as they mistakenly charge toward home. Square around when you're attempting to help the base stealer; use the pivot stance if you are using the ruse to get a base hit.

Figure 5-20:
The drag
bunt.

The Hit-and-Run

As the batter on a hit-and-run play, your primary responsibilities are to protect the runner and to hit the ball on the ground. Swing and make contact with the pitch, no matter where it is thrown. If the pitch is out of the strike zone, lunge at it and try to get a piece of the ball. The runner will be taking off without a base-stealing lead; miss that pitch, and the opposing catcher will have little difficulty throwing him out. If you hit a line drive at a fielder with the runner moving, it is virtually an automatic double play.

Take your usual swing, but hit slightly down on the ball. You may hit the ball through an area vacated by an infielder who has moved to cover second base against the runner breaking from first. The play is usually initiated by the manager with one or no outs. However, a veteran hitter, suspecting the opposition is going to pitch him a certain way, can call the play with a sign to his baserunner.

The Run-and-Hit

The run-and-hit is generally called with a fast runner at first. It is similar to the hit-and-run, but the hitter's task is less specific. The runner breaks for second once the pitcher has committed to throwing the ball toward home. The runner should approach this like a straight steal. You are not obligated to swing at the pitch unless it is a strike (which is why the runner should be fast because, if you take the pitch, he has to steal second). You can also put the ball in play anywhere rather than having to hit through the right side of the infield. With his running start, the baserunner should be able to get to third on any ball hit out of the infield. An *extra-base hit* (anything more than a single) should score him from first.

Walking Aggressively

You can help your team by getting on base via a base on balls, but you shouldn't go to the plate looking to draw a walk; you will lose your aggressiveness. Instead, work the count against the pitcher by expanding and contracting the strike zone according to the count.

For example, I was a pull-hitter so I preferred to hit the ball inside. If the first pitch to me was a ball, I shaved 2 inches (5cm) off the outside portion of my strike zone. The next pitch could be a strike, but I wouldn't swing at it if it was on the outer edge of the plate. If it *was* a strike, I'd expand my zone by 2 inches (but I'd never let it become larger than the umpire's strike zone). However, if the ump called it ball two, I'd cut another 2 inches from the outside of my strike zone. On a three-ball and one-strike count, my strike zone would be about half its normal width: from the middle of the plate in. To get me out, the pitcher now had to throw two straight strikes rather than one. That 3-1 pitch was exactly where I wanted it, or I wasn't swinging. If the pitcher came inside where I was looking, I could drive that ball a long way. If he threw a strike on the outside corner, I still had another crack at him. Ball four would put me on first base. All the percentages were working in my favor. On a 3-2 count, I'd expand the strike zone out again and protect more of the plate. By altering my strike zone on each pitch, I increased my chances of drawing walks while remaining aggressive at the same time.

Getting the Most Out of Batting Practice

Batting practice is usually divided into rounds. On most of the teams I played for, we would take ten swings in the first round, seven in the second, five in the third, four in the fourth, three in the fifth, and one in the last. Use your first round of batting practice to get loose. Start by laying down two bunts, one as a sacrifice, the other for a base hit. Then work on your swing.

This first round is essentially a warm-up. You are getting comfortable with your timing, stance, and stride while working in your batting eye. Don't try to kill the ball. A lot of hitters are playing *long ball* (trying to hit a home run) when they take batting practice. They're not working on anything in particular, they're just trying to see who can hit the ball farthest. That's a waste of time, especially if you are not a home run hitter. Just make contact and aim to hit the ball through the middle. Starting with the second round, you should be simulating game conditions. Work on every aspect of your hitting. Try to pull the ball on one pitch and hit it up the middle on another. Poke one to the opposite field. Then let a swing rip without caring where the ball goes. Do this on every round.

If you want to play some long ball, do it on your last swing. After taking your last practice swing, trot around the bases to keep loose while practicing your left turns.

Working with Your Batting Practice Pitcher

During batting practice, have the pitcher throw you nothing but fastballs in the first round so that you can get your timing. Then have the pitcher work in some curves, sliders, and change-ups. If you take 30 swings, 8 of them should be against breaking balls. Facing a knuckleballer in tonight's game? If your pitcher can throw a knuckler, ask to see some of those too.

You may discover that pitches in a certain location are giving you trouble. Ask the batting practice pitcher to throw to that spot so you can work on them. Usually you'll know what the pitcher is going to throw. However, every so often you should take a round in which the pitcher can throw any pitch to any spot at any time without telling you in advance. This element of surprise helps hone your concentration and prepares you for actual game conditions.

Other Practice Tips

Besides facing live pitching during batting practice, you can do a number of things away from the ballpark to improve your hitting. Here are some of my favorites.

Hit from a batting tee

I used one throughout my career. Adjust the tee's height (see Figure 5-21) and set its position so that you are hitting the ball inside, outside, or down the middle of your strike zone. No matter which side you choose, always set the tee up in front of the plate.

Hitting off the tee forces you to concentrate on hitting a particular spot on the ball. It will help to keep you from *bailing out* (pulling away from the pitch) while quickening your bat.

Figure 5-21:
The batting tee is a great way to practice.

Swing in front of a full-length mirror

I'm not advocating narcissism here. Swinging in front of a mirror lets you check your entire stance and stride.

Play pepper

In *pepper,* the batter stands no more than 10 feet (3m) opposite several fielders who are lined up side by side. One fielder throws the ball; the batter taps it back. (Don't take a full swing or you may decapitate someone.)

The fielder who fields that ball quickly tosses it back toward the hitter, who taps it again. And so on. This game teaches you to keep your eye on the ball and make contact.

Work with grips and rollers

You need strong hands and wrists to hit. Use hand grips and wrist rolls to strengthen them. You can also squeeze a ball of putty to develop your grip.

Develop your hand-eye coordination

I used to punch a speed bag to develop my hand-eye coordination. Play catch with someone (yes, playing catch improves your fielding, but learning how to gauge the speed of the ball also helps you at the plate). Play paddle ball, tennis, racquetball, or any sport that demands quick reactions and excellent eye-hand coordination. Table tennis is an excellent choice because the ball moves so quickly toward you and you have to hit it out front — which is precisely what you have to do with a baseball.

Troubleshooting Your Batting

You can work on specific problems during batting practice. Here are some common hitting flaws that often lead to slumps and some suggestions for correcting them.

Hitting off your heels

If you have your weight back on your heels, your body and bat move away from the plate as you swing. Outside pitches and off-speed stuff will give you trouble. You won't be able to hit with any power. **Remedy:** Concentrate on keeping your weight on the balls of your feet while striding toward the pitcher.

Chopping

Slumping, novice hitters will often chop down at the ball just to make contact. Swinging in this manner decreases your hitting area. It is also impossible to drive the ball with this swing; you'll hit a lot of grounders (mostly for outs). **Remedy:** Make sure that you transfer your weight properly.

When you transfer your weight to your front foot, your bat remains level. Keep your weight on your back foot, drop your rear shoulder (you can't chop with your shoulder down), and take your usual swing.

Extreme uppercutting

When you *uppercut* the ball, you raise your front shoulder while dropping your rear shoulder and dipping your back knee. Batters who uppercut tend to strike out a lot. You can also forget about hitting high pitches with any authority. Raising your front shoulder moves your head out of its level plain, which prevents you from seeing the ball well. **Remedy:** Uppercutters keep their weight on their back foot too long; level your shoulder and make sure you transfer your weight from front to back. As I noted before, you should finish your swing with a slightly upward arc — but avoid any exaggerated uppercutting.

Hitching

If you have a *hitch,* you are dropping your hands just before you swing. A hitch is okay, as long as you can get your hands in good hitting position before the ball arrives. Frank Robinson had a hitch; he dropped his hands below his belt but he always got them back in time to hit. The last time I checked, his plaque was in the Hall of Fame. Unfortunately, too many hitters compensate for their hitches with rushed, upward swings. This hitch produces the same poor results as an extreme uppercut. **Remedy:** Keep your hands level and still.

Locking the front hip

Locking your front hip makes it impossible to transfer the weight from your rear foot to your front foot during your swing. You can't pivot properly. This fault significantly decreases your power. **Remedy:** Open your stance and concentrate on stepping toward the pitcher.

Lunging

Batters who *lunge* at the ball have stepped into the pitch too early. This misstep throws off your timing, power, and bat control. Hank Aaron would occasionally lunge with his upper body, but he could drive the ball because he always kept his hands back. **Remedy:** Be patient. Wait until you've read the pitch before swinging. Make sure your stride is no longer than your original stance. *Keep your hands back.*

Bobbing your head

If you bob or turn your head, you lose sight of the ball for a second. When you pick the ball up again (*if* you pick it up again), it is either almost past you or appears to be jumping at you. **Remedy:** Keep your head level and still throughout your stance, stride, and swing. If your stride is making your head bob, shorten it. Remember, your stride should be no longer than your stance.

Stepping in the bucket

Stepping in the bucket is another way of saying you are striding away from the pitch. The uneven weight distribution results in a loss of power. Because you're moving away from the plate, you can't hit the outside pitch. **Remedy:** Close your stance and concentrate on striding toward the pitcher.

Fear of Getting Hit

Some batters stride away from the pitch because they are afraid of being hit by the ball. To be successful, batters must be aggressive. If you can't overcome your fear, you won't be able to hit. I can't teach how not to be afraid, but perhaps I calm your concerns with a few facts:

- ✔ **It hurts only for a little while:** Many young players are afraid of getting hit by the ball because it's never happened to them before. They imagine the experience to be much more painful than it actually is. When batters do get hit, it's usually in a fleshy spot. Unless you've broken something (and as noted, that rarely happens), the pain subsides quickly.

- ✔ **Pitchers don't often hit batters:** It's rare that a hitter on any level — from Little League to the pros — is seriously injured by a pitched ball. I averaged around 600 plate appearances a season, stood way up front in the batter's box and close to the plate. Yet I rarely got hit by a pitch more than twice a year. Many of those were pitches that just grazed my uniform. I have been struck solidly by pitches, but I was never injured so badly that I had to leave a ball game or miss any playing time. Ground balls have hit me in the face during fielding practice (is that embarrassing!), but I've never been hit in the face by a pitch.

- ✔ **If your mechanics are sound, you can get out of the way:** Muhammad Ali, the great former heavyweight boxing champion, once said, "The punch that knocks you out is the one you don't see." Batters should remember that. If you keep your eyes (both of them!) on the ball, it's hard to get hit by a pitch, especially in the head. Your head is the easiest part of your body to move out of harm's way.

> ✔ **Batting helmets work:** Ron Cey, the former third baseman of the Los Angeles Dodgers, got hit in the head by a Goose Gossage fastball during the 1981 World Series. That's like taking a bazooka shell off the old noggin. However, Cey's batting helmet absorbed nearly the entire impact. He not only played the next game, he hit a home run. The moral: never step up to the plate without wearing your helmet.

Don't let the helmet give you a sense of false confidence. Getting hit in the head is dangerous and painful. It shouldn't happen to you, provided you stay alert at the plate.

Post Script: Some Pinch-Hitting Advice From Rusty Staub

When your manager asks you to come off the bench cold and go to the plate in a critical situation, he is handing you one of the most difficult assignments in baseball. Pinch-hitting is a specialized skill. I rarely pinch-hit more than ten times in any one season, so I've enlisted an expert to give us some advice on the subject. My good friend and former Houston Astros teammate Rusty Staub wasn't just a great pinch-hitter, he was a great hitter, period. He had a disciplined eye, superb bat speed, and excellent balance at the plate. During his career, Rusty amassed 2,716 base hits, 292 home runs, and 1,486 runs batted in while compiling a .279 lifetime batting average. He drove in 100 or more runs three times.

As a pinch-hitter for the New York Mets during his final three seasons, Rusty was the top of the line. He led the National League in pinch hits in 1983 and 1984. During the 1983 season, he tied a major league record with eight consecutive pinch hits; his 24 pinch hits that year also drove in 25 runs. That's delivering in the clutch. So when Mr. Staub talks about pinch hitting, he's like Smith-Barney on investing; we all have to listen.

"More than anything else, a pinch-hitter has to be emotionally strong. That season I tied the major league record for consecutive pinch hits, people forget that I was 0-for-April. I did walk a few times, but that didn't ease my frustration. It hurt because there were a couple of games we could have won if I had come through. And it's not as though you know you're coming back at the pitchers the following day like you do when you play regularly. A pinch-hitter might go four or five games before he gets another at-bat. So you can't let your failures eat at you.

"When you are primarily a pinch-hitter, you don't get too take as many batting practice swings as the regulars. Come to the park a little earlier and take extra b.p. (batting practice) as often as you can. Once the game starts, study that opposing starting pitcher intensely because you may be facing him in a later inning. What is working for him today? What is the catcher calling, and what does the pitcher seem to be shaking off? What sort of strike zone is the umpire giving

him? If the umpire is giving him the outside of the plate, you have to adjust, not the ump. Just look at what happened during the (the 1997 National League) playoffs between Atlanta and Florida. You had that game where Eric Gregg was calling strikes on pitches way outside all day. What do you do as a hitter? Complain throughout the game while you go 0-for-4? If you're smart, you move up on the plate and make the pitcher try to get you out inside.

"You should also talk to your teammates after they take their swings against a pitcher. Find out what kind of stuff he has. Then see if you can pick up some nuance that tells you what the pitcher is throwing.

"I picked up enough pitches in my career to know what was coming about 40 percent of the time. It wasn't difficult if you observed closely. For example, Rick Wise (a pitcher with the Philadelphia Phillies and other teams) used to hold the ball with his hand in the glove. Then he put the glove right in front of his chest. If he dropped the glove all the way during the wind-up, almost to touch his body, he was throwing a fastball. But when he gripped the curve-ball or his change-up, he would drop the glove only 6 inches. That was blatant. When Tony Cloninger pitched for the Braves, he wore a long sweatshirt, even if it was 110 degrees. When he was at the top of his stretch, that sweatshirt would recede from his wrist. If you saw a lot of wrist, Tony was throwing a fastball. If you saw a little bit of wrist, it would be the curve or slider. No wrist? He was throwing the change. At one time, when Nolan Ryan had to pitch out of a wind-up, he would look down at the ground before delivering the fastball; if he looked at the catcher, he was bringing the curve. With the stuff he had, that didn't always help, but at least you got a little better shot at him.

"Beside studying the pitcher, you should also examine the park conditions. Is the wind blowing in or out? Is it blowing in different directions in different parts of the park? Is there a sun field? If you hit the ball down the line, is it likely to stay fair or foul? Is the grass slowing down the ball? In Dodger Stadium, when I played, if you bunted the ball off the grass and it hit the mud, it stayed fair. In the old Astrodome, Joe and I knew that if you bunted the ball down the line, the turf moved the ball towards foul territory. Recognizing these idiosyncrasies helps you to bring as many plusses to the plate as you can. Every hitter should know these things, but it is especially important for pinch-hitters. You only have that one chance per game; you have to make the most of it."

Some thoughts on slumps

If you go into a slump, take extra batting practice and focus on the hitting fundamentals described in this chapter. Make sure your hands are properly positioned. Are they working together as a unit? Have a coach or teammate observe whether you're overstriding. Practice hitting the ball back through the middle of the diamond. Hitting the ball up the middle prevents you from uppercutting, pulling off the pitch, or hitting it too soon.

If practice doesn't seem to help, take a few days off. You may simply be fatigued. Remember that slumps are inevitable; there isn't a single Hall of Famer who didn't experience them. Babe Ruth was the greatest offensive force baseball has ever produced; he hit .118 in the 1922 World Series. Try to remain confident and optimistic. If you've hit before, you will hit again, so don't lose your aggressiveness. In 1976, I batted .000 in the National League Championship Series against the Philadelphia Phillies. I didn't get a hit or a run batted in (RBI). However, in the World Series that immediately followed, I hit .333 with one home run, three runs scored, and two RBIs in four games.

National Baseball Hall of Fame Library Cooperstown, N.Y.

Chapter 6

Winning the Arms Race: Pitching like a Major Leaguer

. . . .

In This Chapter

▶ Taking your stance

▶ Delivering the ball

▶ Following through

▶ Pitching from the stretch

▶ Discovering the different pitches

. . . .

*P*itching is the most valuable commodity in baseball. Teams don't reach the postseason without possessing solid starting rotations backed by deep bullpens. Any manager will tell you that strong pitching is the best insurance against long losing streaks. When your club surrenders only three or four runs every game, you can find a way to win even with the weakest offense. A gifted hitter can galvanize an entire lineup, but a dominant pitcher can do more to elevate a team than any position player. Even a last-place club can compete like a world champion if it has a top gun on the mound.

Find that opinion hard to believe? Open up a baseball encyclopedia and look up the 1972 Philadelphia Phillies. You'll see a team whose .358 won-lost percentage was the worst in the National League that season. Yet, when Steve Carlton pitched for the Phils, they played .730 ball. No team came within 110 points of that mark. If Philadelphia could have cloned Carlton, the club would have won its division by 22 games.

And Carlton is only one of a thousand examples we could have presented. Tom Seaver, Walter Johnson, Bob Gibson, Ferguson Jenkins, Gaylord Perry, Grover Alexander — the record books are filled with the names of men who transformed their clubs from victims to predators every time they strode to the center of the diamond. Each of these pitchers had powerful arms, sound mechanics, a genius for pitch selection, and an unquenchable competitive spirit. Now we can't give you Randy Johnson's arm, Mike Mussina's drive, or Greg Maddux's head. But, in this chapter, we show you the proper way to throw the various pitches you need to get hitters out. The rest you'll have to develop between the lines.

We've enlisted help from both sides of the mound for this section. Bob Gibson is our right-hander. During his 17-year career with the St. Louis Cardinals, Bob won 251 games, struck out 3,117 batters, posted five 20-win seasons, won two Cy Young Awards, and is one of the few pitchers to have a National League Most Valuable Player award on his résumé. He is a Hall of Famer.

Bob was a power pitcher, so for help with *off-speed* (nonfastball) stuff, we have Bill Lee. As a member of the Boston Red Sox and Montreal Expos, Bill was one of the leading left-handers of the 1970s. He wasn't overpowering; Bill got hitters out with movement and great control.

Note: For information on special rules for pitchers, see Chapter 3. And be sure to check out the defensive strategies for pitchers in Chapter 7, which also includes the pick-off move.

It All Starts with Your Stance

Stances are as individual as the pitchers who assume them. Find a stance on the mound that leaves you balanced and comfortable. Your weight should be evenly distributed and your hands relaxed. Keep your glove hand and ball hand together so you don't let the hitter see your grip on the ball (it may tip him off which pitch you intend to throw). As you take the sign from your catcher, your *pivot foot* (right foot for right-handers, left foot for left-handers) must touch the pitching rubber.

If you are left-handed, place your pivot foot on the left end of the rubber. If you are right-handed, do the reverse. Face the plate squarely.

Your Wind-up, Thrust, and Release

Your wind-up should get the full force of your body behind the pitch.

1. **Start releasing the momentum by taking a short step back behind the rubber with your striding foot (left foot for right-handers, right foot for lefties).**

   Avoid taking a large step or you will throw off your balance. You should be gripping the ball in the glove at some point between the top of your shoulder and high above your head. (See Figure 6-1.)

2. **Pivot as you lift your striding foot to bring it back over the rubber. Lift your striding knee to your chest.**

   This is your "leg kick," but if you actually do kick out, you'll disturb your balance. Keep your head steady and over your rear foot. (See Figure 6-2.)

Figure 6-1:
Starting the
wind-up.

Figure 6-2:
Beginning
your leg
kick.

3. **Bring your hands down (somewhere between your belt and chest) and break them while shifting your weight to your pivot leg.**

   That leg should be slightly bent. As you pivot back, your foot will turn until it is perpendicular to the rubber. Your hips and shoulders are closed to the batter.

   "Don't try to copy your wind-up from some other pitcher. Find out what is comfortable for you. If someone were to give you a ball and tell you to go into your wind-up, 99 percent of the time that basic motion is what will serve you best because it's what's most natural for you. We may have to alter your mechanics — the positioning of your arm or something like that — but not your natural motion. If you are a coach and you have a youngster who isn't comfortable winding up, don't make him do it. Let him pitch without a wind-up." — Bob Gibson

4. **Maintain the weight on your back foot until your leg kick is at its highest point. Then start shifting your weight forward toward home plate. (See Figure 6-3.)**

Figure 6-3:
Starting to
come
home.

5. **Bring your striding leg down and plant it with your foot pointed toward home.**

   As the striding foot hits the ground, your hips should open (but keep your front shoulder closed). Your throwing arm should be raised behind your head to its highest point with your wrist cocked back. Your striding leg should be slightly bent. Lower your body and thrust from the pitching rubber.

PLAYER TIP

"You have to get your hips into this. It's very much like playing golf or hitting. To play golf, you have to turn your hips away from the ball and then bring them back with your swing. To hit, you turn your hips away from the plate, and then come back. Same thing as a pitcher, you bring your hips to the side and then come back forward." — Bob Gibson

6. As you bring your throwing arm around, bring your glove hand forward just above your elbow with the palm up.

Keep your elbow high so you can trace a wide arc with your throwing arm. Do not, however, trace so wide an arc that it throws off your balance. To get the most movement on the ball, deliver your pitch with a three-quarters motion.

PLAYER TIP

"If you were to stand erect while facing home plate and pointed your arm out straight from your shoulder and then put your elbow and hand up at a 90-degree angle, you'd see and feel the proper angle (for delivering a pitch). You'll see pitchers who go higher or lower, but the 90-degree angle is the easiest on your arm. Most pitchers — and a lot of them don't even know they're doing this — will have their arm in this spot just as they begin their thrust." — Bob Gibson

7. Release the ball with your head over your striding leg and your arm fully extended.

Your elbow should be at or above shoulder level, your forearm parallel to the ground. Your pivot foot should come forward with its heel up as your hip (throwing-hand side) drives toward home plate. (See Figure 6-4.)

Figure 6-4:
Releasing
the ball.

"Don't try to muscle the pitch to get greater velocity. When you tighten the arm to throw, it's like a hitter trying to hit a home run and swinging too hard. His bat gets very slow. The same thing will happen with your arm. Keep your hand, wrist, and arm relaxed so you can pop the ball at the very last second. You get your velocity in front of the rubber, not behind the rubber. The ideal thing would be for you to use your arm like a whip, but not everyone is capable of doing that." — Bob Gibson

The Follow-Through

"Follow-through is very important for a pitcher. If you cut off your follow-through, you won't be able to pop the ball for velocity." — Bob Gibson

After you release the pitch, your pivot foot should continue to come forward until it is parallel or slightly in front of your striding foot. Bring the elbow of your glove hand back toward your hip (as if you were elbowing someone behind you). Your throwing arm should sweep across your body on a diagonal and end on the first-base side (if you are right-handed) or second-base side (if you are left-handed) of your knee. (See Figure 6-5.) Ideally, this follow-through should leave you in perfect fielding position: weight balanced evenly on the balls of your feet, knees bent, and your glove ready to field anything hit your way.

"If your follow-through ends with you in perfect fielding position, fine. But don't let it get in the way of your main objective, getting the ball to plate with location and something on it. If I had tried to come out in perfect fielding position all the time, I probably wouldn't have gotten anybody out because I would have had to cut my follow through off. I wasn't willing to do that. So I just made sure I recovered quickly enough after my follow-through to field the ball." — Bob Gibson

Authors' note: Mr. Gibson's follow-through often ended with him facing first base, but he recovered quickly enough to earn nine consecutive Gold Glove awards.

Figure 6-5:
Following-
through
with the
pitch.

Pitching from the Stretch

With runners on, you have to discard your full wind-up; it leaves your leg in the air so long that opponents will be able to steal bases easily. Instead, throw from the set or *stretch* position. Stand sideways with your rear foot against the front edge of the rubber and your front shoulder aligned with home. Your feet should be a little less than shoulder length apart with your front foot's heel even with the rear of your back foot's arch. (See Figure 6-6.)

Figure 6-6:
Getting into
the stretch
position.

Instead of winding up to deliver the ball, simply stretch your arms above your head and bring your ball and glove hands to a complete stop somewhere between your chest and belt. The rest of the delivery is similar to the one you use out of your wind-up except you need less kick and pivot and more push from the pitching rubber.

"Pitching from the stretch is no different from pitching with a wind-up. You're simply cutting off the wind-up, but at the point where you rotate your hips you should be in the same position as when you take your full wind-up." — Bob Gibson

Heat and Other Weapons: Your Pitching Arsenal

Ninety-two mph, 94 mph, 100 mph — the numbers reported by the speed-obsessed media may lead you to believe that a fastball's velocity is its most important attribute. It isn't. More critical to a pitcher's success is the fastball's movement and location. Pitchers should also be able to change speeds to throw off the batter's timing. If a fastball doesn't move much, a competent major league hitter can time it after a few viewings no matter how many speed records it shatters. Case in point: When Hideki Irabu, the Japanese League pitching star, made his American major league debut with the New York Yankees, his best fastball clocked in at 98 mph. Few pitchers can match his speed. However, during his first season with New York, Irabu's pitches were straight as a string. Once opponents got their swings grooved, they were hitting long shots off of him. Unless he learns how to make his ball move more or to pitch to spots, he's going to have a difficult time winning ball games.

"You can teach a pitcher to increase his movement on the ball. It's all a matter of how you hold and release the ball. If you release the ball with your fingers pointed straight up, there's a good chance the ball won't move. But if you just cock the ball to one side or the other, it will move if you work at it." — Bob Gibson

Atlanta's Greg Maddux, on the other hand, rarely throws harder than 88 mph. That's only a little above average for a major leaguer. However, Maddux is nearly unhittable because he can put the ball wherever he wants it and his pitches not only move, they move late. A batter may think that he has honed in on a Maddux pitch, only to find that the ball has darted in on his hands at the very last second. The right-hander rarely throws two consecutive pitches at the same speed. Like most great pitchers, Maddux throws a variety of pitches, including a slider, curve, and change-up. Every pitcher, no matter how hard he throws, should have at least three strong pitches — something hard, something that breaks (moves), and something off-speed — in his arsenal. With that in mind, take a look at your options in the following sections.

The four-seam fastball

The *four-seamer* is considered the basic fastball. Grip it with your top two fingers across the seams at their widest point. Nestle your thumb under the ball across the bottom seam. Curl your ring and little fingers along one side. Your middle and index fingers should be about $1/2$ inch apart. If they touch, the ball can slide, making it difficult to control. If you spread them too far, you can limit the wrist action you need to pitch. Hold the ball with your fingertips away from your palm. (See Figure 6-7.)

Figure 6-7:
The four-
seam
fastball.

Keeping your fingers in the center of the ball will limit its movement. However, if you bring your digits a bit closer together and move them off-center to the left, the ball will run or sink. Placing your fingers off-center to the right will cause the ball to break in on a left-handed batter and away from a righty.

The two-seam fastball

The *two-seam fastball* moves more than the four-seamer. To throw it, grip the ball along its two seams with your middle and index fingers. Position your thumb under the ball. Your ring and little fingers are off to the side of the ball, slightly behind your gripping fingers. Exert pressure with your middle finger and thumb. To throw a sinking fastball, move your top fingers so that they hook a seam. Throw the ball like a fastball and let your grip do the rest.

For a variation on this theme, you can grip the ball with your middle and index fingers across the two seams at their narrowest point (the portion of an official major league baseball that bears the league president's signature). Maintain pressure with your thumb and middle fingers. With this two-seam grip, the ball should move more to the side.

Some pitchers turn their hands down and in when they release the two-seamer. This action slows the ball's break, which can throw off a hitter's timing; however, if it doesn't, that pitch is an excellent candidate for a home run.

"As a right-handed pitcher, if I threw the two-seamer to a right-handed hitter, the ball would usually sink or curve into him. If I threw that same pitch to the left-hander, it would sink and move away from him. Most left-handed hitters are low ball hitters, which means that a two-seamer would be right in their wheelhouse. So I'm going to throw the four-seamer to him; that pitch will ride in on his hands." — Bob Gibson

The slider

A hybrid, the *slider* is part fastball, part breaking ball. It is listed with the other fastballs because it is more effective the harder it is thrown. The key to an effective slider is its late break. It should resemble a fastball until it approaches the hitter. Then it should veer sharply to the side.

Grip the slider with the index and middle fingers across the two widest seams. Keep your fingers slightly off-center, toward the outside of the ball. Your thumb is tucked under the ball, your ring and little fingers are off to its side. Exert pressure with your thumb and middle finger. (See Figure 6-8.)

Figure 6-8:
The slider.

When you throw the ball, *keep your wrist loose!* Throwing this pitch with a stiff wrist can strain and damage your elbow.

You also shouldn't twist your wrist as you release the slider. (A mistake commonly made by pitchers who think this will impart greater spin on the pitch. It does, but it also increases the chances of injury.) Instead, throw it like a fastball, but cut through the ball with your middle finger as you deliver the pitch. Keep your fingers on top of the ball until the moment of release.

"If you twist your wrist like you are throwing a curve, you won't get that extra bite on the pitch. That ball will have a big, slow break. Instead, turn the ball with your first two fingers and your thumb as if you were turning a doorknob."
— Bob Gibson

The split-fingered fastball

The *split-fingered fastball* is the child of the forkball, a pitch that was thrown with great effectiveness by such relief-pitching stars as Elroy Face and Lindy McDaniel during the 1960s. Pitchers held the forkball between the first two joints of their middle and index fingers. When thrown by a good fastball pitcher, it was more like a good change-up than a power pitch. You don't hold today's split-finger (or *splitter*) as high between your fingers as the forkball, which means you can throw it with greater velocity. Split your middle and index fingers and grip the ball along its seams. Do not jam it past the midway point of your fingers. (See Figure 6-9.)

Figure 6-9:
The split-fingered fastball.

PLAYER TIP

"Throw the pitch with a fastball motion and plenty of wrist. When properly delivered, the splitter should look like a fastball until it reaches the plate. Then the pitch should dive down as if the bottom had dropped out from under it."
— *Bill Lee*

The curveball

BASEBALL SPEAK

Good *curveballs* (also known as *deuces, hooks,* and *Uncle Charlies*) have put more hitters out of work than all the baseball strikes combined. If you have a hook that you can throw for strikes, batters can't *sit back on* (wait for) the fastball even when the count is in their favor. Hitters never look worse than when they swing at a curve after guessing a fastball.

To throw the curve, grip the ball with your middle and index fingers across the seams at their widest part. Hold it farther back in your hand than the fastball, but don't let it touch your palm or you won't get enough spin. Your object here is to get more of your finger surface in contact with the ball. Curl your ring and little fingers into your palm. Exert pressure with your middle finger and thumb; keep the index finger loose against the ball. (See Figure 6-10.)

Figure 6-10:
The
curveball.

"As you bring your arm forward in your motion, your wrist should be cocked and rotating inward. Your palm and ball should face you as your hand passes your head. While keeping your elbow high, turn your wrist and snap down as you release the ball over your index finger. The back of your hand should be facing the batter as the pitch leaves your fingers." — Bill Lee

Make sure you follow through with your motion, or your curve ball will *hang* (stay up in the strike zone where a hitter likes it). Pitchers who throw a lot of hanging curves often want to hang themselves because batters tend to smack those pitches a long, long way.

The three-fingered change-up

Change-ups make your fastballs more effective by making them seem faster by comparison. There are a variety of change-up grips; the *three-fingered change-up* one is the easiest to master. Hold the ball back against your palm with your index finger, middle finger, and ring finger spread across the seams at their widest point. Nestle the thumb and pinky against each other under the ball. (See Figure 6-11.)

"Exert equal pressure with all five fingers. Keep your wrist stiff. Bring it straight down as if you were lowering a window shade. Don't pick a corner with this pitch; throw it down the middle of the plate." — Bill Lee

The circle change-up

Hold the *circle change* like the three-finger change — only join the index finger and thumb in a circle on the side of the ball. (See Figure 6-12.)

Figure 6-11:
The three-fingered change-up.

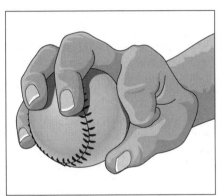

Figure 6-12:
The circle change-up.

The palmball

The *palmball* is an off-speed pitch, a change of pace designed to mess with the hitter's rhythm. Unlike all other pitches, the ball is held tight against the palm. Your middle and index finger rest across the top of the two widest seams. Your ring and little finger rest against one side, your thumb is slightly raised along the other. Exert pressure on the ball with your ring finger and thumb. (See Figure 6-13.) Throw this pitch with your usual fastball motion. As you release the pitch, straighten out your fingers and make sure your hand is behind the ball rather than on top of it. You want the ball to slip from between your thumb and fingers.

"Pitchers make the mistake of trying to underthrow their change-ups, reducing their arm's speed to slow the pitch. Throw the ball as if it were a fastball and let your grip and motion do the work." — Bill Lee

Figure 6-13:
The
palmball.

The screwball

Throw the *screwball* pitch only at your peril; it is murder on the arm. A
reverse curveball, the *scroogie* is held like a four-seam fastball (already
shown in Figure 6-7). The index finger and thumb provide all the pressure,
but you release the ball off your middle finger.

Come over the top with this pitch as if it were a fastball. However, just
before you release the ball, turn your wrist, forearm, and elbow inward in a
corkscrew motion. The rotation should be the opposite of your curveball.
When thrown by a left-hander (which most screwballers are), the ball breaks
down and away from right-handed hitters. However, it breaks down and in
on left-handed hitters, which is why they usually hit left-handed scroogie
artists so well (most left-handed hitters like the ball down and in).

The knuckleball

The *knuckleball* is the one pitch that is more effective the slower you throw
it. Knuckleballs are difficult to control because their movement is so erratic.
Often, the pitcher who throws one has no idea how it will move or where.
Knucklers dart, dance, jump, break, swerve, and rise. Sometimes it will
perform two or three of these motions in the same flight. Most batters hate
to hit against the knuckler; a good one can throw off their swings for weeks.

The trick to throwing the pitch is to eliminate as much of the ball rotation as
you can. Despite its name, the ball is rarely thrown off the knuckles. Instead, dig
the tips of your index, middle, and ring fingers (and make sure your nails are

always trimmed if you are going to throw this pitch) into just below the seams of the ball. Keep your thumb and little finger on the side. (See Figure 6-14.)

Figure 6-14:
The
knuckleball.

"Don't throw the ball; push it towards home plate with a stiff wrist out of your usual motion. Imagine you are tossing a pair of socks into the hamper. As you release the ball, extend your fingers straight out towards home plate." — *Bill Lee*

Before You Take the Mound

You will increase the effectiveness of all of your pitches if you throw them with the same motion. Have your coaches and teammates watch you on the mound to see if you are making any subtle gestures that reveal which pitch you are about to deliver. Never throw a half-hearted pitch. If you don't agree with the sign from your catcher, shake him off (shake your head "no"). Wait until he calls for something that inspires more enthusiasm or comes out to the mound to discuss the options.

Don't let a hitter beat on your second-best pitch. With the game on the line, go with your best stuff, even if it means matching your strength against the hitter's.

A word from Bob Gibson on throwing hard

"One of the lost arts in pitching is being able to throw the ball hard. Too many pitchers are throwing trick pitches at a very young age. Being able to throw the fastball with as much velocity as you can is more important. But the number one thing for any pitcher is control: being able to throw the ball where you want when you want to. Try using the same release point every time. If you don't know where your release point is, your ball is going to be everywhere. You also have to know yourself. For instance, if my ball was high, I knew there were two things I could be doing wrong. One was I had screwed up my release point, the other was I had taken too long a stride. When you understand that, you can make adjustments on the mound."

National Baseball Hall of Fame Library, Cooperstown, N.Y.

Chapter 7
The Third Dimension: Defense

- -

In This Chapter

▶ Discovering the requirements for each position

▶ Getting your arm ready

▶ Fielding and positioning

▶ Playing catcher (Johnny Bench)

▶ Handling first base (Willie McCovey)

▶ Making it at second base (Joe Morgan)

▶ Taking your position at third base (Ken Caminiti)

▶ Trying your hand at shortstop (Barry Larkin)

▶ Being a defensive pitcher (Bill Lee)

▶ Roaming the outfield (Ken Griffey, Sr. and Rusty Staub)

- -

*I*n 1997, each of the eight clubs in the major leagues that qualified for the playoffs had at least two Gold Glove recipients on its roster. (Gold Gloves are awarded yearly to the best defensive player at each position.) That shouldn't be surprising. Winning teams play good defense. We tend to think of power pitchers and sluggers as the dominant forces on a baseball diamond. But a great defensive player can be just as intimidating. When Seattle center fielder Ken Griffey, Jr. defies the earth's pull to make yet another leaping, rally-crippling snatch of what appeared to be a sure double, watch how many shoulders sag in the opposing dugout. Plays like that can slaughter hope before it gains full maturity; these defensive plays can deflate the victimized hitter and his club while elevating the team on the other side of the field.

Griffey, Florida Marlins catcher Charles Johnson, and New York Mets shortstop Rey Ordonez are among the premier fielders playing today. These Gold Glovers have sure hands, fast reactions, and strong, accurate arms. They get to balls that other fielders merely wave at. However, you wouldn't call any one of them a "natural" fielder — someone who was born to steal base hits — because there is no such thing. The only way to become a great defender is to work at it.

This chapter begins with some general fielding tips. Then the floor is turned over to an All-Star team of consultants for advice on how to play each of the nine positions (that's right, you pitchers, you're part of the defensive mix, too).

The Good Hands People

No matter which position you play, you need to have what ball players call *good hands*. However, *quick hands* and *soft hands* would be more accurate terms. If you have them, your hands adjust swiftly to bad hops, erratic bounces, or wild throws. Some people are born with quick hands, but most of us must develop them.

One way to develop quick hands is to play the game *short hop*. Stand 4 to 5 feet (1.2 to 1.5m) apart from a partner. Throw the ball to each other so that the ball bounces on a short hop, which forces the fielder receiving the throw to reach and adjust on every toss. Keep score to make the drill interesting. The first player to miss three short hops loses the round. Start again until you complete a five-round game. While practicing this drill, concentrate on using both hands for every catch. Training your hands to work in unison will make you a more coordinated fielder.

Picking a Position

Want to know which position is right for you? This section examines the particular qualities that each position requires so that you can see how you measure up.

Catcher

You must have a high threshold of pain to play catcher. Foul balls are going to ricochet off your fingers and feet, you'll take an occasional fastball or bat on the mask, and you can count on at least one home plate collision every week. Catchers must have strong legs — you spend half the game squatting while wearing heavy equipment. If you are going to play the position properly, you must possess a powerful, accurate arm, although you can compensate for an average throwing arm with a quick release.

HEADS UP

What's glove got to do with it?
(With apologies to Tina Turner)

Your glove (or mitt) is your most important fielding tool. It should fit snugly enough that it won't come off when you catch a ball in its tip. However, your glove should not be so tight that it restricts wrist flexibility or movement. How big should your glove be? That depends on what position you play.

✔ Catcher's mitts are always large, but yours shouldn't be so big that you cannot control it. Choose a mitt that you can open and close in a split second. (See Chapter 2 for some preliminary details on gloves and how to select them.)

✔ At first base, catching the ball is your primary concern. Digging the ball out of the mitt to get off your own throw is a secondary issue. Your first baseman's mitt should be as long as you can comfortably manage so that you can snag wide, errant tosses in the glove's webbing.

✔ Third basemen should also opt for large gloves. Balls are hit so quickly to third that you often only have time to block the ball or knock it down. You also have to field many balls hit wide to your left and right. A big glove helps you cover more territory.

✔ Second base is the position of quick throws; use the smallest glove possible here so that the ball won't stick deep in its pocket. Choosing a small glove to play second is also a matter of self-preservation — there will be times when you have 220 solid pounds of seething baserunner bearing down on you to break up the double play (as well as any part of your anatomy he can reach). In these cases, you don't want to spend a split second more time than necessary searching for the ball before unleashing your throw.

✔ Shortstops must get the ball out of their gloves quickly, too. But they must also be able to catch grounders cleanly when they range wide in the hole. A medium-sized glove is in order here.

✔ Outfielders are primarily interested in catching the ball. They have little need for a quick release. If you are playing the outfield, use the longest glove that the rules permit (see Chapter 2 for rules about gloves).

If you want an example of how a strong arm can completely neutralize base stealers, just watch Charles Johnson or Ivan Rodriguez intimidate a team from behind the plate. They both throw out a high percentage of potential base thieves, but what is more impressive is how few runners attempt to steal against them.

Besides having physical stamina, catchers must be mentally tough — catching is draining work; you are in on every pitch of the game. If your pitcher takes the mound without his best stuff, you're the one who has to improvise a strategy to retire batters with his secondary pitches. With every hitter, that computer between your ears is working in overdrive, trying to recollect or decipher the hitter's weaknesses and strengths.

Are you immersed in a batting slump? No matter how many 0-fors you've taken, you need to put your hitting woes out of your mind the moment you squat behind home plate. You must place your entire focus on aiding your pitcher in the battle against the hitter. Finally, you have to be a practical psychologist — if your pitcher is getting battered, you have to know whether he needs a pat on the back or a good swift kick in the rear.

Ideally, catchers should have a low center of gravity, like the 5-foot-8-inch Ivan Rodriguez. This body type gives the pitcher a better target and also offers the umpire a clearer perspective of each pitch. For example, seeing over a tall catcher like 6-foot-2-inch Charles Johnson can be difficult for an umpire; that size may occasionally cost his pitcher a low strike. (And that about sums up the only "weakness" — if you can call it that — in Charles's game. He is one of the best defensive catchers to ever pull on a pair of shin guards.)

First base

Left-handed throwers have an advantage playing first base. As a first baseman, all your throws to the infield go to your right; if you throw left-handed, the play is always in front of you. Right-handed throwers often have to whirl completely around before they can toss the ball to another base. First basemen don't need particularly strong arms; they rarely throw more than 60 feet. Your arm must be accurate, particularly on the 3-6-3 (first-to-short-to-first) double play when you are throwing into the runner.

First basemen should have enough range to cover their half of the hole between first and second. You need quick reactions and agility to cope with the opposition's bunting game. (Watch how San Francisco's J.T. Snow pounces on bunts with the nimbleness of a middle infielder.) First basemen catch more throws than any other fielders, with the exception of the catcher. Depending on how the ball is gripped prior to release, those throws can sink, rise, or dart to either side of you. You have to be prepared to gather in tosses from every angle. If catching the ball is a liability for you, move to another position.

Second base

Second base is a paradox. I've played enough of it to know that this can be the easiest infield position (as for catching the ball) — you don't have to cleanly catch a ground ball to record an out. Your proximity to first base allows you plenty of time to simply knock the ball down and make the short toss to the bag.

However, second base is also the most difficult position because you are a sitting duck on the double play. You often wait for a throw with your back to some runner who is eager to tear you in half with his slide. (Think football and hockey players are the only athletes who relish a little hard contact? George "Boomer" Scott — a hulking bruiser of a baserunner when he played with the Boston Red Sox and Milwaukee Brewers during the 1970s — often wore a necklace, which he gleefully claimed was constructed from retired second basemen's teeth. And George was one of the more genteel of baseball's crash artists.) Your attitude has to be, "The double play takes priority over my physical well-being. I'm going to turn the play first and *then* look for the runner."

Too many otherwise-skilled second basemen hurt their teams by letting their fear of injury prevent them from *turning two* (getting both outs on a double play). The key to not getting creamed is to catch your shortstop's ball cleanly so you have time to plant your left foot on the bag. When you throw toward first base, you gain the momentum to leap out of the way of the baserunner. Second basemen who bobble that toss from the shortstop freeze for a split second before they recover: This hesitation leaves them prone to collision.

In addition, a second baseman needs to be a take-charge type, an infield captain who can direct where a play should go (between pitches, the second baseman can indicate where the ball should be thrown if hit by the batter). Because you move around so much — for example, when you have to cover first base on a bunt — you must concentrate on positioning a little more than the other infielders. Chuck Knoblauch, a member of the 1997 American League Gold Glove team, is an excellent example of a second baseman who positions himself well on every hitter.

Because most of your throws are short, you don't need a powerful arm to play second base. However, your throws must be precise and quick (particularly when you are relaying an outfield throw to another base) and you must be able to throw under pressure (being exerted by that baserunner bearing down on you).

Shortstop

Shortstop is the most difficult infield position to play. Shortstops must be able to field grounders cleanly because they rarely have time to knock a ball down and throw out the runner. Because you have more territory to cover than any other infielder, you have to be far-ranging.

Tall, lean players, like Derek Jeter (6 feet 3 inches) and Edgar Renteria (6 feet 1 inch), are built ideally to play short; they can stretch out over more ground and reach out farther than smaller infielders. However, a relatively short player like 5-foot-9-inch Rey Ordonez can outplay almost anyone at this position because he is so quick. This position demands a powerful throwing arm to make the throw from the hole (near the third base side of the infield) or from deep behind second base.

Third base

Like the catcher, a third baseman must be willing to absorb a few body blows. You play close to home plate; if a right-handed hitter pulls the ball sharply, you often won't have time to get your glove into fielding position. That's when you have to throw your body in front of the ball, block it, get to your feet, and throw out the runner. That's why third basemen like Robin Ventura are studies in black and blue by midseason. You take a lot of punishment at third base.

Great third basemen usually have powerful arms; they need them to make long throws across the diamond. If you can throw with velocity, you can make up some of the time you lose blocking the ball and picking it up. However, Brooks Robinson, who is generally considered to be the best third baseman of all time, had an average arm at best. He compensated with a quick release and by positioning himself so that he seldom had to make the long throws required of most third basemen.

Third base is a reflex position; you must be able to react quickly to balls hit sharply to either side of you. Watch how Padres third baseman Ken Caminiti can go to the line to his right as well to the hole on his left. Ken's agility is one of the reasons he has several Gold Gloves sitting on his mantel (and a little later on, Ken tells you why he's so good at going to either side).

Left field

Left field is the easiest position to play. Of the three outfielders, the left fielder makes the shortest throws, so he can get by with a below-average arm. Fly balls hit to left don't curve as much as fly balls hit to right. When batters hit the ball to the opposite field, it tends to *slice*. Because so many more hitters bat right-handed than left-handed, the left fielder doesn't have to handle many sliced balls (those fly balls that seem to keep moving farther away from the pursuing outfielder no matter how hard he runs).

Left fielders must be able to *charge the ball* properly; their close proximity and direct angle to home offer them numerous opportunities to throw out runners at the plate. Charging the ball gives them the momentum to unleash strong throws. Barry Bonds is the player who defines this position today. He's fast, goes back well on balls hit over his head, expertly plays balls hit down the line, and has an above-adequate arm that rarely misses its target. Watch how he lines up his entire body behind a throw. He's a walking clinic on left-field play.

Center field

Center fielders should have accurate, strong arms; they are going to run down more balls than the other two outfielders and consequently have to make more throws. (If you charge the ball quickly and have a quick release, you can get by without having a strong arm.)

Speed and quickness are two more requisites for center field (a relatively slow player who positions himself well, on the other hand, can play either left or right field). However, you cannot play center unless you can run; there is just too much territory to cover. In addition to chasing after fly balls, you will be backing up your fellow outfielders on any fly balls or grounders hit their way.

Center fielders must be able to get a good jump on the ball; they need to be able to react and accelerate quickly. Players like Jim Edmonds of Anaheim and Arizona's Devon White move at the crack of the bat. Excellent lateral movement is another must. Edmonds and Griffey, Jr. are two examples of players who can go to either side to make a catch.

As a center fielder, you also have to understand your limitations. If you don't go back on the ball well, you cannot play too shallow. If you have trouble coming in, you cannot play too deep. A great center fielder like Ken Griffey, Jr. has no difficulty coming in or going out, so he plays deep to steal extra base hits from the opposition. Finally, the center fielder must be assertive — the entire outfield is your domain. If you call for a catch, the other outfielders must give way. On balls hit to the left or right fielders, you direct the play. (For more on where to go on a particular play, see Chapter 9.)

Right field

The first thing managers look for in a right fielder is a strong arm. Right fielders have to make longer throws than anyone else on the diamond. Someone like Seattle's Jay Buhner must make throws from deep in the right-field corner to third or home (and Buhner does that as well as anyone; he has a howitzer of an arm). Because hits to right tend to curve or fade away from the fielder, you must be proficient at reading the ball's angle.

Pitcher

For this chapter, we are looking at the pitcher solely as a defensive player. You are 60 feet 6 inches (18.4m) away from the hitter, so you must have quicker reactions than anyone else in the infield. For your own safety, you should be able to catch the ball cleanly, but this skill is not a requirement. If you can simply knock the ball down in front of you, you usually have plenty of time to throw out even the fastest runners. Young pitchers often ignore fielding fundamentals; they seem to think all they need to win ball games is a lively arm. However, most of baseball's elite pitchers — players such as Atlanta's Greg Maddux, Baltimore's Mike Mussina, and Toronto's Roger Clemens — are excellent fielders. They know how to execute, to do those little things that help them win close ball games. That's one of the reasons they are among their league's pitching leaders year after year.

Loading the Cannon: Getting Your Arm Ready for the Field

A poor throw can undermine the best glove work. In this section, we review the mechanics of throwing (before exploring any other aspect of fielding). To start, you need to warm up your arm. You and your throwing partner should stand 10 feet (3m) apart and gently lob the ball to each other. As your arm starts to feel loose and warm, gradually increase the velocity of your throws. If you are a young adult, toss the ball from four throwing angles:

- Over the top
- Three-quarters
- Sidearm
- Underhand

After you feel completely loose, stretch and strengthen your arm by gradually increasing the distance between you and your throwing partner.

Players under the age of 16 should throw only overhand or three-quarters; your arms aren't fully developed enough to withstand the strain of throwing sidearm or underhand.

The grip

When you grip the ball, your middle and index fingers should be approximately 1 inch (2.54cm) apart, *across* the seams. Place your thumb on the ball's underside directly below your middle finger. Press the ball with those two digits (thumb and middle finger). Because you want your throws to travel straight and true, always throw with your fingers across the seams (see Figure 7-1).

Figure 7-1:
How to grip
the ball
before
throwing.

Placing your fingers *with* the seams will cause the ball to sink or sail (a no-no unless you are a pitcher throwing to a hitter). Make sure that you hold the ball out in your fingers — if you hold the ball back in your palm as you throw, you won't generate enough velocity. Don't squeeze the ball. Hold it just firmly enough to maintain control. Practice grabbing the ball and finding your across-the-seams grip without peeking.

Delivering the throw

How you throw the ball depends on the position you play. Most outfielders throw the ball overhand for maximum power. The exception occurs on a *shoestring catch* (a ball caught, usually on the run, near your feet). If a runner is trying to advance on that play, the outfielder has to throw underhand or sidearm, or he won't get rid of the ball quickly enough.

Infielders rarely have time to straighten up and throw over the top; whenever you rear back to throw, you concede about 12 feet (3.6m) to the baserunner. So you should throw three-quarters, sidearm, or underhand — depending on the situation. On the double play, a second baseman or shortstop must throw from wherever he catches the ball. If you catch it high, throw overhand; catch it low, throw underhand.

To make an accurate, powerful throw

1. **Start the overhand throw by squaring yourself toward your target and swinging your throwing arm back to your side in an arc.**

   Tilt your upper torso back on your throwing side, while keeping your other shoulder (and your eyes) pointed toward your target. Your wrist should be cocked and ready to throw.

2. **Step and thrust forward as you swing your arm directly over its shoulder and toward your target.**

   Make sure you extend your arm fully. Keep your elbow higher than your throwing shoulder (see Figure 7-2).

3. **Plant your front (striding) foot while pushing off your rear (pivot) foot. To get maximum velocity on your throw, snap your wrist downward as you release the ball.**

   Your arm should continue to sweep in front of you and down to your side. As you follow through, your glove hand should come up behind you for balance. Allow your lower body to follow your upper body's momentum toward the target.

4. **Bring your pivot foot forward until it is parallel to your striding foot.**

   Use this same motion for the three-quarter throw from the outfield, but bring your elbow around on a 45-degree angle.

Infielders often throw sidearm. You don't have time for a lot of motion when you sidearm, so bring your throwing arm back in a short arc. Step toward your target and thrust forward as you swing your arm back in an arc that is parallel to the ground. You will often be unable to get your whole body behind this throw, so get as much shoulder and wrist into it as you can. Aim your throw for the middle of your target's torso.

Figure 7-2:
Making the
overhand
throw.

You usually must throw underhand when you are close to your target or have to quickly toss a ball you have caught below your knees and to the side. Using a bowling motion, flip the ball toward your target's chest. Because you cannot get anything behind this throw, give it a good wrist snap as you release the ball.

How hard is too hard?

You don't have to air everything out on every throw you make. I don't believe throwing consistently hard is likely to hurt or tire your arm. However, if you are trying to throw the ball through a wall on every play, you can strain your muscles over the course of a season. Rick Burleson, a first-rate shortstop for the Red Sox and Angels from the mid-'70s to early-'80s, had a cannon arm whose power he demonstrated on nearly every throw. By age 30, a torn rotator cuff (an arm injury more common to pitchers than fielders) finished his career as a starting shortstop.

A Word about Errors

The first thing you have to remember is that every player makes errors. Don't let it get you down, though. In 1976, for example, I made 13 errors (nearly one every two weeks) while still winning a Gold Glove at second base. In 1980, when I was with Houston, our left fielder Jose Cruz led the National League with 11 errors and he still managed to catch nearly 97 percent of the balls hit his way (Jose, by the way, was a fine outfielder, he just had one of those years).

On the upside, if you have good range and play aggressively, you're going to commit fumbles on balls that other fielders don't even reach. Most errors come on grounders that are hit directly at you (if you have any talent for catching a baseball at all, you will rarely muff a fly ball).

Fielders who fumble grounders tend to freeze for an instant instead of being aggressive. This lack of aggressiveness is what broadcasters mean when they say that the fielder *"let the ball play him."* Whenever a ground ball is hit toward you, charge it immediately so you can gauge its hop; fail to charge right away and you can misperceive the ball's bounce.

When you do commit an error, don't let it discourage you. Dwell on it and you'll probably boot another ball because you're not concentrating on the play at hand. As National League Gold Glove third baseman Ken Caminiti says, "If you know in your heart that you gave a ball your best effort, you just shrug the error off as part of the game. Keep your focus on the game and get ready for the next play. Don't spend any time thinking negatively.

Be aggressive. You should want that next ball hit to you because you *know* — not just *think* — you're going to make the play." That's the kind of confidence every fielder must have.

Don't short-leg

Fear of fumbles can sap you of aggressiveness. Some players, rather than charge a ball full-out, time their approaches so they and the ball arrive at a spot simultaneously. If they catch the ball, it looks like a dazzling play. If they miss it, the official scorer will usually score it a hit instead of an error. It's called *short-legging* the ball, and it is a capital crime. You aren't on the field to look pretty or compile a gaudy fielding percentage. You are there to help your team win. Short-leggers invariably cost their clubs victories. When you are on the diamond, give everything you do everything you've got.

Avoid those hidden errors

Mental errors don't appear in anyone's box score, but they are often more costly than physical mistakes. When you commit a *rock* (make a boneheaded play) like throwing to the wrong base, it's usually because you did not anticipate the situation.

When Tommy Henrich was excelling in left field for those great New York Yankee teams of the 1940s, he used to say, "Catching a baseball is fun; knowing what to do after you catch it is a business." If you want to field like a professional, you must take care of business. As each hitter steps up to the plate, review all your options.

For example, you're the second baseman with a man on first and one out. Right away you should not only be thinking double play, but how to execute it. If the ball is hit to the shortstop or third baseman, you have to cover second. Hit to the pitcher? You are backing up the shortstop's play at second base. And so on. Cover all the possibilities so that when the ball hits the bat, you are ready to execute. You don't have to waste a second wondering what to do — you can simply react.

Six Tips for Fielding Grounders

Fielding a ground ball is easy if you have sound fundamentals. To put yourself in position to make a play, you should do the following:

✔ **Charge the ball whenever you can.** If you hang back, the ball has more time to take a bad hop. Maintain a short, quick stride rather than one that is long and uncontrollable. You should be able to stop abruptly.

✔ **Stay down on the ball.** Keep your body, including your buttocks, low to the ground. Standing straight up makes it difficult to gauge the ball's hop. You want your eyes down low for a good look at the ball. Keep your eyes on the ball; watch it go into your glove. After you catch it, look where you are going to throw it.

✔ **Keep your weight balanced evenly on the balls of both feet when you take your fielding stance (unless you are anticipating a specific play).** Having your knees flexed rather than bent allows you freedom of movement.

✔ **Use both hands to field whenever possible.** Catch the ball with your glove near the ground facing up and your bare palm above it facing down. If a ball takes a bad hop, using two hands gives you a better chance to corral it. The ball may drop into your glove after hitting the palm of your hand, or it may drop in front of you. Then you can pick it up in time to throw out the runner. If you use only one hand and the grounder takes a bad hop, the ball will get by you. Using both hands also allows you to get your throws off quickly.

✔ **Let your hands "give" a bit when the ball makes contact with your glove.** Cradle the ball in your glove as if you were catching a raw egg.

✔ **Keep your arms extended so that you catch the ball in front of you.** Try to field the ball in the middle of your body so that if the ball hits you on the bad hop, it drops in front of you. If it hits off to your side, the ball can bounce away from you.

Practice your throws so that you can take the ball out of your glove without looking at it. You should know whether you get more velocity on the ball by gripping it across or with the seams. You must be able to get your preferred grip on the ball while looking at your target, *not the ball.*

There will be times when you shouldn't even attempt a throw. For example, suppose that Kenny Lofton is speeding toward first on a slow hit grounder. If you realize that you have no chance to make an accurate throw, hold the ball. Yes, you just put a runner on first, but that decision is better than letting Mr. Lofton take second or third (and he will) if you throw the ball wildly.

Positioning Yourself for a Strong Defense

No matter where you play on the field, knowledge and anticipation are the keys to positioning. Prior to the game, your pitcher should have told you and your teammates how he plans to throw to the opposing batters. You need to combine that information with all the data you have on those hitters. For example, when I was with the Reds, Jack Billingham might try to catch Billy Williams, a terrifying left-handed hitter with the Chicago Cubs, off-balance with a slow curve. I knew Billy would probably pull that pitch toward right field. If Jack threw his fastball away, Mr. Williams would probably shoot it to the opposite field. However, if Reggie Jackson — a slugger who hit over 500 home runs in the American League — were the hitter, Jack might throw a fastball away. Most left-handed hitters would hit that pitch to the opposite field in left. But Reggie was strong enough to pull the fastball away into right field — with authority. I had to know all these tendencies so I could position myself accordingly.

After your data file on the opposing players is complete, you can reposition yourself for each hitter that comes to the plate; you may even change your position from pitch to pitch. Say that your catcher calls for the fastball inside, you are going to lean to the left or right depending on the hitter's tendencies. Because smart hitters adapt to situations, you must do the same. For example, with the first baseman holding a runner on first, a left-handed hitting genius like Tony Gwynn can shoot balls through that big hole on the right side of the infield. If you were playing second in that circumstance, you would lean more toward first to get a better jump on balls hit toward the hole. If no one was on base, you would play closer to second. However, if the pitcher was going inside on Tony, you would cheat toward first.

Fielding Line Drives

Catching a line drive is a reaction play — you either catch it or you don't. However, if you can't catch a line drive cleanly, you must knock it down so you have some opportunity to pick it up and throw. Whenever you have to leap for a line drive, look the ball into your glove (watch the ball until it enters your glove).

Fielding Fly Balls

Later in this chapter, some fine major league outfielders give you tips on the proper way to catch a fly ball. For the moment, I want to talk about pop flies, those weakly hit fly balls that don't make it out of the infield. On pop flies, you should run to wherever you expect the ball to drop. Catch the ball in front of you on your forehand side. Don't play the ball so that you have to run to catch it at the last moment. If you have to go back on a pop fly, run sideways rather than backpedaling (though you can backpedal if it is only a few steps). You don't want to risk tangling your feet. Get stationary so the ball comes straight down into your glove. Position yourself so that if you fail to catch the ball, it will hit you in the chest (rather than the head or shoulders). Keep your arms extended but loose: That way, if you bobble the ball, you have a second chance to catch it before it hits the ground.

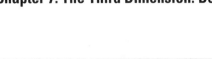

Infield flies

A word about infield flies: Umpires may invoke the *infield fly rule* only when all three of the following conditions are met:

✔ There are less than two outs.

✔ Baserunners must occupy first and second base; or first, second, and third.

✔ The batter hits a fair fly ball to the infield, which the umpire believes can be caught by an infielder making "an ordinary effort."

By yelling "infield fly!" (usually while waving his arms), the umpire automatically rules the hitter out, even if the ball is not caught. The runners may advance only at their peril.

Why have such a rule? When a pop fly is hit to the infield, the runners assume the ball will be caught, so they stay anchored at the bases. If there were no infield fly rule and the fielder deliberately dropped the ball, the runners would be forced to advance (to make room on the bases for the hitter). Because they could not begin running until the ball came down, the runners' late starts could make them easy victims of a double or even a triple play. Baseball's rulemakers saw this as "stealing outs through deception," so they enacted the infield fly rule in 1895.

Whenever you see infielders or outfielders collide on a pop fly, you know that someone wasn't paying attention. I always told our outfielders to yell so I could get out of the way if they were going to catch a pop-up. If you both yell for the catch, you won't hear each other. When I was with the Astros, our left fielder, Jesus Alou, and our shortstop, Hector Torres, were both yelling as they went after a pop fly. They collided and Hector nearly choked to death on his tongue. Make sure that you have your signals straight before each game so you can avoid that kind of catastrophe.

With a fast runner on first base, I've seen infielders deliberately drop pop flies so they could get the force-out at second. The idea is to erase a base-stealing threat or replace a speedy runner with a slower one. I don't believe that is ever good policy. Baseballs can take funny hops; if a pop fly hits the ground and bounces away from you, you may not get anybody out.

Playing the Field: Position by Position

I played second base my entire career (well, almost my entire career. I did play 16 games in left field while I was with the Astros and three games at third base for the San Francisco Giants). So I've enlisted some of the best fielders of the last 30 years to help us grasp the nuances of the other positions. You can find examples of their expertise sprinkled throughout the rest of this chapter.

JOE SAYS

A thought about mound conferences

Managers, coaches, catchers, or infielders sometimes initiate *mound conferences* when a pitcher is in a jam (the opposition is smacking his best stuff all over the lot). Mound conferences are sometimes used to stall for extra time while a reliever warms up (which usually means that the opposition is smacking the starter's best stuff all over the lot). The pitcher and his teammates discuss his mechanics (if anyone detects a flaw in his delivery), his emotional well-being (they want to calm and encourage him), the situation (as if he doesn't know that already), or even the weather (sometimes you just want to take his mind off his troubles).

Participate in these meetings only when you have something specific to accomplish. I would go to the mound when I thought our pitcher was throwing a certain pitch too often or to give him a breather in a tight spot. If he had just thrown a long series of bad pitches, I might tell him to approach the next pitch as if it were the first one of the ball game, just to get him out of the rut. If you don't have anything constructive to add to these conferences, stay put — small talk slaughters genuine communication. The player who keeps running to the mound when he has nothing to say risks not being heard when he finally does have something to contribute.

From Behind the Plate: Catcher

BASEBALL SPEAK

Good catchers are field generals. Because they call the pitches from behind the plate, they dictate a team's defensive strategy. The better *receivers* (catchers) can also set a tone for an entire ball club. For example, when Johnny Bench joined the Reds in 1968, he brought an intimidating presence to the field that immediately transformed Cincinnati into a cockier, more aggressive team. Yankee receiver Joe Girardi is an intense individual who raises his pitchers' concentration level the moment he squats behind the plate. Florida's Charles Johnson is the epitome of cool; he could even compose the emotive volcano that is Kevin Brown when that talented but temperamental right-hander got into one of his rare jams.

A catcher must be able to recognize the strengths and limitations of his pitchers and the opposing hitters. His arm must be powerful enough to provide base thieves with some incentive not to run. Receivers are often thought of as slow, blocky types. Most of them aren't swift, but they need to be quick enough to scurry from behind the plate on bunts.

All of a game's action flows from the catcher's *signs* (see the upcoming section "Signs: The secret language of catchers"). Because everything starts with his position, this is an appropriate place to begin our defensive tour. Throughout this section, you get tips from the player who redefined the position — Johnny Bench. Johnny came to the major leagues with the Cincinnati Reds in 1968 and promptly won the first of his ten consecutive Gold Gloves — a record for major league catchers.

I could go on for pages about this Hall of Famer's accomplishments — among them two Most Valuable Player Awards and 12 All-Star Game starts. However, no roll of honors or litany of dry statistics could summarize the Bench career better than the words of his former Reds manager, Sparky Anderson, who stated, "Johnny Bench is the standard against which all other catchers must be compared. As the total package, no one who has ever played the position can touch him."

Setting up

Catchers are the only players in baseball who set up defensively in foul territory. How deeply you position yourself behind the plate will depend on the hitter: You should get as close to home as you can without getting struck by the bat. Hitters who stand back deep in the box will keep you back. If a hitter moves up in the box, you should also move forward. The closer you come to home plate, the better positioned you'll be to handle bunts, foul tips, wild pitches, and would-be base thieves.

Though each player may bring a different wrinkle to their job, all catchers assume two basic stances behind home plate: The first is a set-up that puts you in position to deliver signs to your pitcher. Drop into a squat; keep your knees parallel with your weight evenly distributed on the balls of your feet. (See Figure 7-3.) Or put one foot slightly behind the other to help maintain balance. Spread your knees so that they provide a strong but comfortable base. Drop your rump until it is below your knees but slightly above your heels. Your upper body should be straight but never stiff.

Figure 7-3: A basic catching stance.

"You don't have to follow any 'Spalding Guide' model when you get behind the plate. People have different physical makeups, so they are going to squat differently. If you try to assume a position that doesn't fit your body, it will not work. Do whatever feels comfortable and balanced so that you can move either way on a pitch or block a ball in the dirt. Don't restrict yourself by holding your elbows too far in so that you are blocked from reaching across." — Johnny Bench

Signs: The secret language of catchers

To flash signs, extend your right hand between your thighs. Point your right knee at the pitcher; this position shields your signals from the opposition's first base coach. You can prevent the third base coach from stealing your signs by holding your glove in front of your left knee. Most catchers give signs by extending one or more fingers. To avoid confusion, keep your signals basic: one finger for the fastball, two for the curve, three for a change-up, four for any other pitch your pitcher throws, such as a slider or screwball. Spread your fingers as wide as you can when you give signs. You want to make sure your pitchers can see each digit clearly. (See Figure 7-4.)

"Depending on the shadows and your pitcher's vision, you might want to tape your fingers to give him a better look at what you're flashing. Sometimes you have to improvise. When I was with the Reds, one of our pitchers, Wayne Simpson, had a corneal abrasion on the day he was scheduled to pitch. He couldn't wear his contacts on the mound. I could have painted my fingers in neon and he wouldn't have seen them. So I set the glove on the side of my knee for a fastball, on top of my knee for a breaking ball. Wayne pitched a two-hit shutout." — Johnny Bench

Figure 7-4:
Giving
signs.

You can also transmit signs through the *pump system*. Using this method, you indicate which pitch you want by the number of times you flash the sign (pump one fist for a fastball, two for a curve, and so on). Call for pitch location by holding your palms up (for high pitches) or down (for low). Pointing away from or toward a batter will tell your pitchers whether the next pitch should be inside or out.

"You might go to the pump if you have an indication that the other team has stolen your signs, or with a runner on second. Whatever method you use, always make sure you and your pitcher are on the same page. The worst nightmare is to be giving signs during a game and suddenly realize that you have no communication whatsoever with the pitcher." — Johnny Bench

After a runner gets to second, where he has almost as good a view of the catcher's signs as the pitcher, things get more complicated. You must alter your signs so the runner cannot decipher them. One way to confuse him is to give several different signs in sequence after first deciding with your pitcher which of these is the genuine article. Or you can prearrange with your pitcher to combine two signs to get the appropriate signal. For example, you can flash one finger (fastball) as your first sign, three fingers (change-up) as a second, and two fingers (curve) as a third. If you and your pitcher have agreed to combine sign one (one finger) and sign three (two fingers) when a runner is on second, the addition produces the three-fingered signal for the change-up. (It is important that your infielders are also privy to your signs in all their various guises so they can set up properly on each pitch.)

"You can use physical signs to indicate an addition. For example, I might go to my mask to add one, or touch my chest protector to add two. Hitters will try to peek at your signs to gain an edge. If you catch them doing it, you can set it up with your pitcher to throw an inside pitch after you call for something outside. And I mean way inside — like around the hitter's neck. That will give him some incentive to stop peeking. If you think he's checking out your location behind the plate, to see if you're setting up inside or out, set up inside — but call for something away. Or stay centered and don't move in or out until your pitcher starts to unwind with his pitch." — Johnny Bench

When you give signs, make sure that neither your fingers nor hands extend below your thighs (where an alert opponent can observe them). Keep your elbow as still as possible; if the opposition detects you wiggling your elbow when you call for a breaking pitch, they can feast on your pitcher's fastballs.

When you're ready to catch

After you've given your sign, you can hop from your set-up position into your receiving (or *ready*) stance. Bring your rump up to just below knee level while keeping your thighs parallel to the ground. Stay low to give your pitcher a good target. This alteration shouldn't raise you as much as it makes you more compact. Shift your weight forward onto the balls of your feet until your heels are lightly touching the ground. Your feet should be shoulder width, with your right foot a few inches behind your left. Turn your knees and feet slightly out. (See Figure 7-5.)

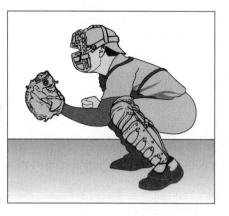

Figure 7-5:
Getting
ready to
receive the
pitch.

In front of your knee, bend the forearm of your catching hand at a 45-degree angle from your body. Don't lock your elbows or place them inside your knees — if you do, catching pitches far out of the strike zone will be nearly impossible. When nobody is on base, protect your bare hand by tucking it behind you. With runners on, keep your bare hand in a relaxed fist behind the webbing of your glove. Grab the pitch with your throwing hand as soon as it is delivered.

Your pitcher should be able to look directly into your mitt after you set up a target. Centering your glove to your body (while remembering to keep it outside your knees!) gives the pitcher a clearer view. If you call an inside pitch, you have to shift your target inside; do the reverse for outside pitches. Don't shift your body until the last possible moment or you'll tip off the opposition. Always keep your target within the strike zone. After you set up your target, maintain the target until the ball has left the pitcher's hand.

PLAYER TIP

"You have to know what your pitcher wants to use as a target. For instance, Tom Seaver might throw to my shinguards — right shinguard, left shinguard — depending on which side the batter swung from and whether we wanted to go in or out. Or he would pitch to one of my shoulders. Other guys looked to my glove. When you set a target with your glove, do not hold it straight up so your wrist is cocked into a L-shape. Angle the glove so you can stay flexible enough to rotate to the left or right." — Johnny Bench

Receiving the pitch

Catch the ball in the strike zone. If you receive it on the edge of the zone, the pitch's force can move your glove enough to transform a strike into a ball. Don't stab at the pitch; let it come to you. If you must, sway with the pitches on the borders of (or just outside) the strike zone. However, avoid any extreme movements: Any radical body shift might persuade the ump that the pitch is a ball even if it is in the strike zone.

When a pitch is legitimately outside the strike zone, don't try to steal a call by pulling them back into the zone with your glove. Umpires resent this trick; they can punish you by refusing to call borderline pitches in your favor for the rest of the game. You can, however, *frame* a pitch by subtly rolling your wrists to rotate the glove up or down. To do this, keep your arm and torso stationary. Rotate the glove down on high pitches, up on low pitches.

"On an outside pitch to a right-handed hitter, keep the largest portion of your glove over the plate while catching the ball in your web. Do just the opposite against a left-hander. Always try to catch the ball in the web." — Johnny Bench

Tracking errant pitches

With runners on base, your pitcher must know he can throw a low pitch without having to worry that you'll let it skip by you. He'll have that confidence after you demonstrate your ability to dig those babies out of the dirt. To do that, you must forget about catching when runners are on base. Instead, concentrate on blocking the ball while anticipating that every pitch will be a bad one.

If the ball in the dirt comes directly to you, drop to your knees and face the ball squarely. Get your hands low and centered. Drop your chin onto your chest to protect your throat. With your shoulders hunched, push forward to smother the ball. Should the pitch look as if it will veer to your right, step toward the ball with your right foot while dropping to your knee with your other leg. Move your glove and bare hand to the space between your foot and knee. Keep both hands between your legs but close to your body. (See Figure 7-6.)

On high pitches, raise your glove slightly higher than the ball. Angle your glove downward so that if you miss the catch, the ball drops in front of you. If you keep your glove too low or angled upward, the ball can glance off it and skip in back of you. The runners will like that; it means extra bases for sure.

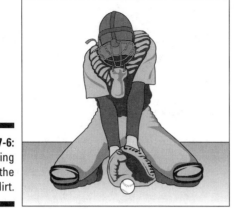

Figure 7-6:
Blocking
balls in the
dirt.

To catch a thief

Though it's not fair, catchers usually establish their defensive reputations with their throwing arms (though a receiver's game-calling ability provides a better measure of his value to a team). Most teams prize those catchers who can curtail the opposition's running game. Like the other fielders, you must practice gripping the ball and removing it from the glove without looking. Your speed with this maneuver improves with repetition.

"You have to be quick. The good base stealers get down to second in about 3.1 seconds. It takes the average pitcher about 1.5 seconds to get the ball to home plate (from the start of his wind-up). That leaves you 1.5 seconds to throw the ball 127 feet, 3 inches to a target 6 inches above the bag on the first base side so the infielder has $^1/_{10}$ of a second to make the tag. And then you have to hope the umpire is in position to make the call." — Johnny Bench

As a catcher, throws must be straight and true. A proper grip ensures that they are. Grab the ball across the seams where they are widest apart. If your grip is off on your first try, rotate the ball as you cock your arm to throw.

Your grip, cock, and release should constitute one continuous motion. As you grip the ball, bring your glove hand back to your right shoulder while closing your left one. With the ball in hand, bring your right arm slightly above and past your ear. As your right arm comes forward to throw, aim your left shoulder at the target. Keep your glove arm parallel to the ground. Throw overhand; side-arm deliveries tend to tail away from their targets. As you release the ball, snap your wrist downward.

"You can't practice enough the transfer of the ball from glove to hand. You have to keep doing it until reaching in and grabbing that ball across the seams becomes second nature. Practice this even when you are having a simple

catch. When you're behind the plate, you make the transfer with your shoulder closed, step straight with your toes pointed towards your target so that your arm follows your body line." — Johnny Bench

To catch today's speediest runners, you have to get the ball off to your fielders quickly. Therefore, you must try to throw while still coming out of your crouch. Major league catchers generally choose from among three throwing styles:

- ✔ **The step and throw:** Recommended for catchers with average arms, it allows you to put more of your body behind each throw. Just before you catch the ball, step forward about 6 inches (15.2cm) with your right foot while pointing it toward second base. Once you possess the ball, turn your hips as you draw back your arm, stride forward with your left foot, and throw.

- ✔ **The jump pivot:** The moment the ball hits your glove, jump to your feet and plant your left foot below the spot where you just gave your target while making a 90-degree turn to plant your right foot. Take a short stride toward second and throw.

- ✔ **The rock and throw:** This throw requires a powerful throwing arm because it entails little body movement. As you receive the ball, rock back on your right foot. Rise from your crouch with your arm cocked. Shift your weight forward to your left foot and throw.

"When people talk about throwing out baserunners, they are almost thinking about arms, but they should be thinking about feet. A catcher has to have quick feet so he can 'get under himself' and move fluidly from a receiving position to a throwing position. Your feet will get your shoulders turned and in position to throw." — Johnny Bench

Derailing the double steal

With baserunners on first and third, the catcher must be alert for the *double-steal*. On this play, the runner on first breaks for second hoping to draw a throw while the runner on third scores. Before stepping toward second to throw (if that is your choice), check the runner at third. If he has just broken for the plate, throw to third or hold the ball and get him in a rundown. You are virtually conceding second base to the runner on first, so failing to get the man at third leaves you with two runners in scoring position. If the runner on third breaks for home as your throw heads for second, be prepared for your second baseman or shortstop to cut off your throw and return the ball to you at the plate.

Blocking the plate

Throughout the season, the catcher is involved in numerous collisions at home. How well he blocks the plate determines if he gets the out while staying off the disabled list. As the runner steams toward home, spread your legs a little wider than shoulder width and anchor your left foot about 18 inches (45.7cm) in front of the plate. (See Figure 7-7.)

Figure 7-7: Blocking the runner from scoring.

"When you block the plate, remember it is better to be a live coward than a dead hero. I always let the runner see at least half the plate, so he had the option of going around me. If he can't see the plate, he has no alternative but to try to go through you or over you. If you persuade him to slide, you have him on the ground, where you can control what he is trying to do. As you block the plate, keep your toes pointed up the third base line and aimed directly at the runner. Should you angle the leg, the impact of the collision could permanently damage your knee." — *Johnny Bench*

After you have the ball and the runner has committed to sliding away from you, move your left leg, until you block the plate entirely. Grip the ball in your bare hand while turning the back of your glove toward the runner to protect your inner wrist. As the runner slides in, drive down on top of him with your shin guards to prevent him from reaching the plate. With the ball held firmly in the glove, you can tag him with the back of your mitt. If other runners are on base, see if any other plays are developing as soon as you make the tag at home.

These instructions assume that you are handling an accurate throw. If the throw is slightly off to either side, you can pull it in by shifting your right foot without leaving your position. However, if the throw is far off-line, abandon the tagging position and do what you must to get a glove on the ball. If the runner decides to come in standing up, roll away from him as you apply the tag. Avoid head-on collisions. ***Note:*** A catcher cannot block the plate unless he is receiving a throw or is already in possession of the ball — otherwise, it's obstruction.

Getting help

Catchers should have no difficulty seeing runners break from first when a right-handed hitter is at the plate. However, a left-handed hitter may block his view. Your first baseman has to let you know when the runner is taking off (and you should anticipate the steal on every pitch).

Neither lefties nor righties can obstruct your view when a runner tries to heist third. However, with a righty at the plate, the angle of the pitch determines the launching point of your throw. On outside pitches, step forward with your right foot and then step toward third with your left so you can throw in front of the hitter. If the pitch arrives inside, throw from behind the hitter. Step to the side with your left foot, shift your weight to your right, step toward third with your left, and throw.

Pick-offs and pitchouts

Pitchers aren't the only players who can pick a runner off base. The catcher can also initiate a pick-off play whenever a runner strays too far from a bag. If the count is favorable (1 ball or less), you can begin the pick-off play with a *pitchout.* After first signaling your pitcher, step into the opposite batter's box just as he starts to the plate; jump in earlier and you risk committing a balk. Ideally, the pitchout should come to you at your letters, but be prepared for a throw that is either too low or too high. As soon as you get the ball, throw to the fielder covering the targeted base.

When the count is not in your favor, call for a strike on the outside corner to set up the pickoff. As your pitcher delivers the ball, step back into throwing position with your right foot. Close your body by bringing both hands to the top of the letters. Pivot off your right foot, step with your left in the direction of your target with your left foot and throw. ***Important:*** You want the umpire to call a strike, so don't pop up too soon or you may obstruct his view of the pitch.

Fielding pop-ups

The best way to field pop-ups is to do it by the numbers:

1. **As the ball goes up, turn your back to the field and scan the sky for the ball.**

2. **Move toward the ball with your catcher's mask in your bare hand (if you throw it too early, you risk tripping over it).**

3. **After the ball reaches its apex and you sense where it will descend, toss your mask away and move in for the catch.**

4. **Catch the ball over your head with both hands.**

   The fingers of your glove should be slanted upward. Don't stab. Allow the ball to come to you.

After judging where a pop is going to come down, it's usually wise to back up one more step so that the ball doesn't wind up behind you — fouls usually drift back a little more than one expects.

The pop-up behind home plate will drift toward the stands as it goes up and come back toward the field when it descends. Right-handed hitters usually pop up inside pitches to the right and outside pitches to the left. Left-handed batters do the reverse.

"The pop-up behind home plate reacts like a banana. The ball will drift towards the stands as it goes up and curve back towards the field when it descends. So when the ball is popped up in back of you, turn around quickly, stop, and slowly move towards the ball while remembering it will come back to you a few feet." — Johnny Bench

Thwarting the bunt

The catcher is in the best position to field and throw balls bunted directly in front of the plate. When the ball is bunted in your territory, stay low as you pounce in front of the plate, scoop the ball up with both hands, and then make your throw. (See Figure 7-8.) Your attention should be on the bunt, so call for the ball loudly to avoid a collision with any incoming fielders. When the bunt is beyond your reach, become a traffic cop. Call out which fielder should handle the ball and tell him where to throw it.

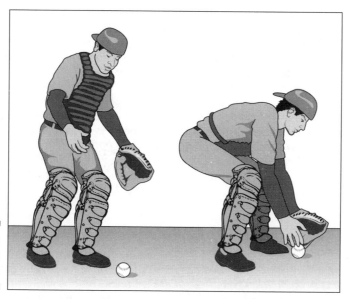

Figure 7-8:
Scooping
up a bunt.

Let the force be with you

When the bases are *loaded* (a runner on every base) and a ground ball is hit, anticipate that the infielder will throw home for the *force out.* You do not have to tag the runner to get the out. You simply must touch home plate while possessing the ball. When a force at home is in order, toss your mask away. Plant your right foot in the middle of home plate so you can move in either direction on a bad throw. Put your left foot in front of the plate. Be prepared to stretch like a first baseman to snare a short throw. With less than two outs, forget about the baserunner as soon as you catch the ball. He's out! (Remember, your foot was on the plate.) Immediately pivot to your right, face first, and throw to complete the double play.

You Can't Hide at First Base

Willie McCovey is our guide at first base. This Hall of Famer played first base for 22 seasons, most of them with the San Francisco Giants and San Diego Padres. Willie won the Rookie of the Year Award in 1959 and was named MVP in 1969. His work at first base earned him the name "Stretch" — an homage to his ability to keep one foot on the bag while reaching wild throws.

"We have to dispel the myth that first base is an old man's position, and that you can put just anybody at the bag and expect them to play it well. The first baseman handles the ball more than anyone on the field except the pitcher or catcher. So you must have good hands. You have to have a little quarterback in you to lead the pitcher with your throws when he goes for the putout at first. A first baseman has to save wild throws from his infielders. Quick reactions are a must. If you charge in on a bunt, and the ball goes to the third base side, you must immediately retract to get back to cover first. First basemen have so many responsibilities. You cannot hide a player who is weak defensively at this position. One way to develop the quick reflexes and good hands you need to play the position is to stand about 20 feet from a wall, throw a rubber ball against it, and field the hot smash that ricochets back at you. Gradually come closer to the wall so you can practice fielding short hops." — Willie McCovey

Footwork and balance are keys

"You have to be graceful; a first baseman should have loose muscles so he can move easily. Rudolf Nureyev, the ballet star, once came to me after a game and said I moved like a ballet dancer in the field. That was the greatest compliment I ever received for my fielding. If you are awkward, take a ballet class or study tai chi or some other discipline to improve your balance. If you weight train, make sure you stretch those muscles to stay loose." — Willie McCovey

Target practice

First basemen should generally play as deep as they can in the field. However, they must be able to get to the bag and set a target in time for the other fielders to make their throws. Taking those throws while putting your foot on first for the out has to become second nature. Your foot should hit the front inside corner of the bag. (See Figure 7-9.)

"If you're looking for the ball and the base simultaneously, or you have to spend time searching the bag with your foot, you'll miss making the out. Practice until your foot goes right to the bag without your looking. Avoid placing your foot on top of the bag where the runner can injure you by stepping on it." — Willie McCovey

You should have your target at first set when the infielder looks up to throw. Keep your weight evenly balanced on the balls of your feet so you can immediately shift to your left or right. "A good first baseman," says Willie, "will anticipate a bad throw on every play. That way he can easily adjust." Make sure your body is facing the fielder. Don't stretch for a ball until it is in the air and you are sure of its direction.

Figure 7-9:
Taking the throw at first.

When a throw is bad

Low throws are usually the toughest to handle. Try to take the low throw before it bounces. If you can't do that, get to it as soon as it hops so it won't bounce away from you. On high throws, you can stay on the bag while stretching for the ball, make a leaping grab off the bag, or move back into foul territory.

"Anytime you get a bad throw, your first objective is to catch the ball. Don't worry about keeping your feet on the bag or getting the baserunner out. If you catch the ball but it's too late to get the runner, you have a man on first. However, if the ball gets past you because you were stuck on the bag, the runners can advance an extra base." — Willie McCovey

On plays where the pitcher or second baseman are too close to you to make a hard overhand throw, they will probably try to feed you an underhanded toss. Help them by setting a big target with your glove.

"You would be surprised by the number of pitchers who cannot properly throw to first base after making a play. On those soft toss plays, you have to antici-pate that the pitcher will throw it over your head." — Willie McCovey

Holding on

When you *hold a runner on,* you shorten his lead to first to deny him a head start to second. Place the back of your right foot against the front inside corner of first while keeping your left foot along the base line. Your feet should be no more than shoulder length apart. Give your pitcher a good waist-high target with your glove.

As the ball is delivered to the plate, cross over with your left foot and bounce as quickly as you can toward second base. Get in a position to cover as much fair territory as possible. As the pitch approaches the plate, you should be in your crouch, facing the batter.

When runners are on first or second, or the man on first is slow, the first baseman can *play behind the runner* rather than hold him on. To play behind the runner, position yourself just inside the runner's left shoulder.

Make sure that the pitcher knows when you play behind a runner and second base is not occupied. Pitchers need to be reminded not to make a pick-off throw. Never assume that the pitcher knows instinctively that you've chosen to play behind a slow runner.

Covering bunts

Play bunts aggressively or you won't play them at all. Charge the plate as your pitcher delivers the ball home. Countless baseball instructional guides advise first basemen to listen for their catchers to tell them where their throws are going (first, second, or third). This advice is fine if you are not playing in a packed stadium where the roar of the crowd makes it impossible to hear yourself think. Under those conditions, you must be able to immediately recognize where the play is developing and throw accordingly.

*"Usually everyone in the stadium knows when a bunt is in order. However, there are some players and managers who will try to surprise you with a bunt. (**Note:** This usually occurs when the batter is trying to bunt for a base hit rather than a sacrifice.) If you study hitters closely, you can pick up some signs that telegraph a bunt is coming. For instance, some batters will look down towards you for an extra moment or two before bunting the ball your way. Other guys might choke up on the bat a little bit more. Watch what each hitter does when he bunts, and remember any quirks you can detect."* — Willie McCovey

Cut-off plays

If runners are in scoring position, the first baseman is responsible for cutting off the throw on balls hit to right or center. The third baseman will take most cutoffs from left, but if he can't get into position, you have to cover for him. Give your outfielder a good target by holding your hand and glove chest high (all infielders should do this). Where should you stand to receive the cutoff? Some coaches advise that you take it at a midpoint between second base and the pitcher's mound. Others want you to cut the ball off from behind the mound.

"There is an advantage to cutting the ball off between second base and the pitcher's mound. If you are behind the mound, on the home plate side of the diamond, you risk having the ball hit the mound or pitching rubber and bouncing away from you." — Willie McCovey

As you accept the relay from the outfield, wave your arms so the outfielder doesn't waste time trying to find you. Listen for a teammate (usually your catcher) to tell you where your throw is going (or if you should let the ball go through). The instructions should be this simple:

- ✔ "Cut, Cut!"— Cut off the ball and hold it.
- ✔ "Cut and Relay!" — Cut off the ball and throw to a specific base.

If the fielder thinks you should let the ball go through, he shouldn't yell anything. When you are setting up for a relay, line up your body in the same direction as your target. For example, if you are throwing to third, your body should be facing left center.

"Catch the ball on your glove side so you don't have to turn all the way around to throw. Practice catching the ball, taking it out of your mitt, and delivering the throw all in one graceful motion. Too many first basemen break this down into two parts. That extra motion is often the difference between a runner being safe or out." — Willie McCovey

When the pitcher must cover first

If you play deep, the pitcher is going to cover on many of those grounders hit to the right side. He's going to first in case you can't get there in time to make the tag on your own. If you can get to the ball and field it near first base, make the tag yourself. Make sure you wave off the pitcher so he is out of harm's way.

When fielding the ball takes you too far from first to make an unassisted putout, you must get the ball to your pitcher. If the distance is short enough, lead the pitcher to first with a firm underhanded toss that hits him chest-high. Balls fielded on their way to the second base hole may require you to throw overhand. Again, you should lead the pitcher to the bag with a chest-high toss.

Doing the 3-6-3 (first-to-short-to-first double play)

Many first basemen will tell you this play is the most difficult play they make. To initiate this double play if you are left-handed (as most first basemen should be), pivot clockwise — to your glove-hand side — to unleash a throw. If you are right-handed and the ball is hit directly at you, turn clockwise to throw. However, if the ball is hit to your left, you will probably have to pivot counter-clockwise before throwing.

Your first throw is the key to making this double play. Nine out of ten times, you will field the ball in the same line as the runner going to second. You must be able to throw the ball to your shortstop without hitting that runner. Then you have to get back to bag for the return throw. Because this play is always going to be close, you will need to stretch before catching the ball on the return. (Sometimes this play goes 3-4-3, first-to-second-to-first. If he must throw to the second baseman, the first baseman's responsibilities remain the same.)

*"Make sure you get that lead runner. Too many first basemen are so concerned with getting back to the bag to get that second out, they end up throwing the ball away and fail to get anyone. If you don't have a clear shot, take an extra sidestep to create a throwing lane to the shortstop. Try to get the throw to your shortstop in a spot to his liking. (**Note:** Many favor receiving the ball chest high.) But if you can't do that, make the best throw you can and depend on the shortstop's athleticism to complete the play."* — Willie McCovey

Second (Base) to None

Joe couldn't find a second baseman for this team, so he is doing the honors himself. His collaborator, editor, and publishers couldn't be more pleased. From 1973 to 1977, Mr. Morgan's play at second won him five consecutive National League Gold Glove awards. He was tutored in the field by two of the greatest second basemen in baseball history — Nellie Fox and the Grand Master of the Keystone, Bill Mazeroski.

Setting up

A second baseman's stance in the field should distribute his weight evenly on the balls of both feet. This position allows you to move easily to one side or another. As the pitcher goes into his wind-up, look directly at the batter. Not at his body. Instead, imagine he is swinging through a rectangular box that is as wide as home plate and extends from his shoulders to the tops of his toes. Watch that box. The ball will come to you from some spot within it. Make sure you are on the balls of your feet and ready to move when you see bat and ball collide. (See Figure 7-10.)

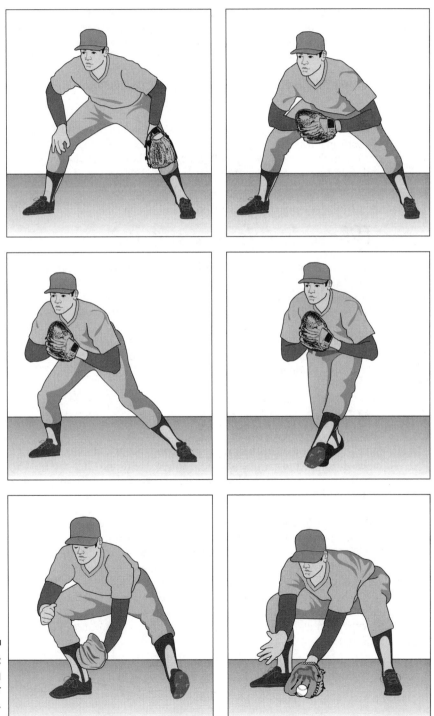

Figure 7-10:
Getting
ready for
the play.

"Be relaxed but alert at all times in the field. If you stay in one position too long, your body will tense; this will slow your reactions when the ball is hit. To alleviate tension, move your hands while you are in your stance. I often rested my hands on my knees as the pitcher wound up. An infielder has to do that to ensure that he is bending forward far enough. But as soon as the pitcher released the ball, I would raise my hands about 5 inches to give myself greater freedom of movement." — *Joe Morgan*

Your skills and the situation will determine how deeply you play your position. However, if you are fielding on artificial turf, the ball will shoot to you much quicker than it will on grass. Play two to five steps deeper. You should also remember that you cannot slide to a ball hit to either side of you on the turf. You have to field the ball and continue moving.

Whose ball is it, anyway?

On balls stroked up the middle of the diamond, who has first call, the shortstop or the second baseman? That's the shortstop's ball. Because he is moving toward first base on the play, he can make a stronger, more accurate throw than the second baseman (who is moving away from first).

"Just because it's the shortstop's play doesn't mean you don't have any responsibility. Get behind your shortstop and be ready to catch the ball in case it gets by him." — *Joe Morgan*

Blocking the ball

Nellie Fox was a three-time Gold Glove winner who led American League second basemen in putouts nine times. He taught me the best way to stop a ball you cannot catch cleanly from entering the outfield: Get down on one knee and block it with your body.

If this posture is not comfortable, find another way to get down on the ball. With a runner on second, do everything possible — dive in front of it if you have to — to prevent the ball from rolling into the outfield. Your methods can lack grace provided they get the job done.

"Because the second baseman rarely makes a long throw, he doesn't always have to catch a ball cleanly. Always remember that if you simply knock a ball down, you will usually have plenty of time to toss out the runner. "— *Joe Morgan*

Getting it to first

When you have to throw the ball to someone like our friend Mr. McCovey at first base, aim for an area from his belt buckle to his chest. This strategy allows you some margin of error if your throw is too high or low. Your throws should be on the money as often as possible. If you have to take a throw from a teammate, give him a chest-high target.

In most situations, you can wait until the first baseman reaches his bag before throwing to him. However, if the runner is some flash like a Lance Johnson or Eric Young, you may not have time to see if the first baseman is in place. Your job in that instance is to throw the ball across the bag; it's the first sacker's responsibility to somehow get to it.

"Make sure any player you are throwing to gets a good look at the ball. Take it out of your glove as quickly as possible so he can see it in your hand. This will help him to better gauge your throw's velocity and trajectory. When you bring back your arm to throw, make sure your glove doesn't block your target's view of the ball." — Joe Morgan

Preventing grand larceny — defending against the steal

One of the oldest maxims in baseball dictates who covers second — the shortstop or second baseman — on an attempted steal. The shortstop covers if the batter is left-handed. When the batter is right-handed, the second baseman has to make the play. However, like all good rules, this one does have its exception. If the batter is a good hit-and-run man or opposite field hitter like Arizona's Jay Bell, the second baseman and shortstop can switch assignments. Jay is a right-handed batter who excels at hitting behind the runner. Any second baseman who covers the bag on every steal attempt is inviting Jay to slap the ball through the vacated hole and into right field. So you have to play the major league version of cat-and-mouse with him. Your shortstop may cover for a pitch or even two. Then you may cover for the next couple of pitches. Keep switching so he doesn't know whether to pull the ball or go the other way.

"You and your shortstop must communicate to each other who will cover on the attempted steal. Before the game, decide between yourselves who will make the call. Keep the signals simple. Shield the front of your face with your glove. When you want your shortstop to cover second, open your mouth and purse your lips as if you were saying, 'You!' If you are going to take the catcher's throw, keep your mouth closed with your lips tightened to indicate, 'Me!'"
— Joe Morgan

Picking them off

On a *pick-off play,* the pitcher tries to catch a runner off base with an unexpected throw. You're not merely jockeying for an out with this play; you are also attempting to reduce the runner's lead. Just the threat of a pickoff can appreciably change the game. With the runner anchored at the base, your outfielders will have a better opportunity to throw him out on a base hit; you will have more time to execute plays in the infield.

"If the second baseman is covering the bag on the pick-off play, the shortstop must get behind him to back up any errant throws. If the shortstop is covering, the second baseman must reciprocate." — Joe Morgan

Pick-off plays come in two basic varieties:

- ✔ In the **time play,** the pitcher signals to the infielder covering second by glancing at him before looking toward the catcher. As the pitcher faces home, he and the infielder start counting, "One second, two seconds, three seconds." On three, the pitcher spins and throws; the infielder breaks for the bag. If everything is in sync, the infielder and the throw should arrive at second base simultaneously.

- ✔ **Daylight pick-off plays** don't require a count. The pitcher whirls and throws to second as soon as he sees a large enough space or "daylight" between the infielder and the runner.

"I dislike daylight plays because they can so easily backfire. Suppose you're trying to fake a runner back to the bag. The pitcher might mistakenly think you're breaking for second. If he attempts a pick-off, you have to scramble back to make the play. Often, you can't. The ball flies untouched into center field, the runner races to second or even home. Stick to the time play; there's less opportunity for error." — Joe Morgan

Run-downs 101

Run-downs occur (among other times) when a pick-off traps a runner between two bases. While tossing the ball to each other, you and your teammates chase the runner back and forth until he can be tagged. Making as few throws as possible is the key to an effective run-down. The more throws you make, the greater the chance one of you will toss the ball away.

After the run-down begins, you should try to force the runner back to the base he just left. The fielder with the ball should hold it high and away from his glove so the other fielders can see it. Whoever is waiting to receive the throw must give the player with the ball a target. For example, say a right-handed throwing teammate is chasing the runner back to you at second. You should stand to the left of the incoming runner. This position affords the thrower a clear view of your glove. If the thrower is left-handed, take a step to the other side. By using your glove as a target, your teammate is less likely to hit the runner with the throw.

During run-downs, fielders must stay out of the baseline while they are awaiting the ball. If you stand in line with the runner, his body may prevent you from seeing your teammate's throw. If the runner crashes into you on the base line when you don't have the ball, the umpire can award him the bag on fielders' interference.

"Never fake a throw during a run-down; you might fake out your teammates as well as the runner. Always hold the ball high so your teammate can see it. Cock your arm back only when you intend to release the ball. When you're not involved in a run-down, choose an unoccupied base to back up. Stay out of the action unless the ball gets by someone and comes in your direction." — Joe Morgan

Tagging the big league way

When a runner slides into a base you're defending, tag him on his foot, toe, or whatever other part of his anatomy is closest to the bag. Try to tag his hand if he attempts a head-first slide. Tag a runner who arrives at the base standing up anywhere you can reach him.

Don't attempt a tag with the pocket of your glove facing the runner or he may kick the ball away from you. (And yes, that's a legal play. New York Giants second basemen Eddie Stanky pulled it on New York Yankees short-stop Phil Rizzuto during the 1951 World Series. The ball went trickling into center field. Instead of being called out, Stanky was safe. The Giants went on to score five runs that inning.) Instead, hold the ball firmly as you swipe the runner with the back of your glove.

Covering first

Both your pitcher and first baseman usually try to field any slow-hit balls between first and the pitcher's mound. With first base unattended, the second baseman must cover. You must become a first baseman. Go to the inside of the bag with your rear foot. Lean into the diamond to give the thrower a proper chest-high target with your glove. Maintain your balance so you can spring to either side on a bad throw.

Relays and cut-offs at second

You are playing second base. With a man on first, the batter smacks the ball down the right field line. Cinch double. What do you do? Don't stand at second waiting for a throw. Instead, turn to face the right fielder from a point midway between first and second base. If the runner on first tries to score, your job is to relay the right fielder's throw to the catcher at home plate. If the runner is heading toward third when you get the ball, try to nip him at that base. (Check out Joe's Baseball Playbook in Chapter 9 to study your assignments on all of baseball's basic plays.)

Anytime the batter drives a ball into the gap (between the outfielders), there's going to be a relay. Make sure the outfielder makes the longest throw; between the two of you, he should have the stronger arm. Go out just far enough for the outfielder to reach you with a throw. After you get the ball, your job is to deliver a short, accurate throw to the appropriate base.

On balls hit to the left or left center field gaps, the shortstop accepts the relay. The second baseman must back up any balls that get by him. You must also let the shortstop know where to throw the ball. If he has to turn and look, he surrenders about 12 feet (3.6m) to the runner. While the outfielder's throw is in flight, observe the runners so you can tell the shortstop which base offers the best opportunity for a play. Identify the bag by yelling to the shortstop, "Home plate! Home plate!"

Turning two

Ask any infielder: The double play (DP) is the greatest play in baseball (other than the triple play, but they are so rare, you can't even think about them). When you turn a double play in a crucial situation, you immediately become the most popular guy on your club. Teammates will shower you with high fives, pitchers want to buy you dinner, and managers will name their firstborn after you. Nothing short of a win is more pleasing to a fielder than getting two outs with one ball.

Carly Simon knew the secret to executing the double play: Anticipation (great, now we're going to have *that* song humming in our heads for the rest of the month!). Whenever the opportunity for the double play presents itself — runners on first, first and second, or first, second, and third with less than two out — the second baseman must automatically think about turning two. Move a couple of steps closer to second and in toward the plate. You sacrifice a little range with this positioning, but it enables you to get to the bag quickly.

Charge for the base as soon as the ball is hit to the left side of the diamond. When you get within three steps of second base — and with practice, you instinctively know when you are — shorten your stride. Take choppier, quicker steps to ensure that you don't overrun the bag. You must maintain body control as you reach second, or you'll have trouble adjusting to a poor throw.

If you are a novice at second, look for the bag when you first run toward it. Once you know where it is, put your focus on the fielder. Give him the best chest high-target you can. However, stay alert in case the ball veers off on an angle. As the fielder cocks to throw, your attention should go the ball.

"The double play transpires so quickly, you must eventually learn to locate the bag without looking. When I first came up to the major leagues, I would work on starting the double play with our first baseman and shortstop for an hour and a half a day. Before practice. We did this until I was able to get the bag without even glancing at it." — *Joe Morgan*

To complete the double play, you must catch the ball, force out the runner from first by tagging second base, pivot, and relay the ball to your first baseman. It sounds like several parts, but they are all parts of the same motion held together by your pivot. (See Figure 7-11.) You have different ways to pivot on the double play.

✔ Many second basemen straddle the bag. As they catch the ball, second base is between their feet. They touch the bag with their left foot while throwing to first.

✔ Second basemen with unusually strong arms will sometimes use the push-off method. They catch the ball behind the bag, tag the front of the base with their rear foot, and then push off it as if it were a pitching rubber for their throws to first.

Figure 7-11:
The pivot
for the
double play.

"I learned the quickest and, in my opinion, best way to pivot by studying Bill Mazeroski. As a Gold Glove second baseman with the Pittsburgh Pirates, Maz led National League second basemen in double plays a record eight consecutive seasons (1960 to 1967). He was, and remains, the unchallenged king of the DP. Like Maz, I would catch my shortstop's throw out in front of my body. While crossing second, I would step on the center of the bag with my left foot. Then I would pivot and throw from wherever I caught the ball. If I gloved the ball high, my throw would be overhand or three-quarters. Feed the ball to me at my waist, and I relayed it sidearmed. Any ball caught below my waist was delivered to first with an underhand toss. Your primary concern is to get rid of the ball as quickly and accurately as you can. Some players drag their foot across the bag when making the force-out at second. I think that practice upsets a fielder's rhythm on the double play. If you instead step on the center of the bag, your motion continues uninterrupted. This also helps build some momentum behind your throw to first." — *Joe Morgan*

The care and feeding of your shortstop

Some double plays require a role reversal: Your shortstop makes the pivot. You have to field the ball and then feed it to him for the relay to first. It is important to know where your double-play partner prefers to catch the ball.

Note: Many second basemen throw to the shortstop backhand in a double play — a backhand throw is less likely to sail high than an underhand toss. If you are close enough to the bag to do so, a backhand throw is preferred.

"For example, when I was with the Reds, our shortstop Davey Concepcion liked to take the throw on the outfield side of second. So I would give it to him chest-high (the easiest ball to handle and throw while on the move) on the bag's outside edge. I've also played with some shortstops who wanted my toss on the inside of the bag. However, no matter what your shortstop prefers, you shouldn't wait to make the ideal throw. If you're off balance, get the ball to your partner any way you can and let him make the adjustment. If your double-play partner hasn't reached the bag, feed the ball to him wherever he is. Never make him wait for the ball or you can disrupt his timing." — *Joe Morgan*

Dealing with the runner

As said earlier, the second baseman's job is to make the double play before looking for the incoming runner. If you are continually concerned about getting hit at second, you can't play the position. One way to defend yourself against a collision is to get the ball to first as soon as you can. Don't worry about hitting the runner. Your quick throw will compel him to slide that much sooner. The sooner he slides, the longer it takes him to reach you at the base.

A last word on second

None of the suggestions I've just passed on to you are absolutes. Eighty percent of the time, you execute a play at second in the manner I've described in this chapter. However, there will be situations — such as when a throw is off line or the runner arrives at second faster than you anticipated — that demand improvisation. When these situations occur, remember that your bottom line is to make the play anyway you can. Get the out!

Cookin' at the Hot Corner

Third base is called the *hot corner* because the third baseman is so close to home plate he tends to field a lot of hot smashes. The position demands a strong arm, hair-trigger reflexes, and a ton of heart. All three attributes come to mind when we think about our third base "coach," the 1996 National League Most Valuable Player Ken Caminiti of the San Diego Padres.

The basic stance

Plays develop so quickly at the hot corner that third basemen must be able to shift out of position in an instant. Many third basemen set up in the lowest crouch on the field so they can spring up to their left or right. Ken has won three consecutive Gold Gloves without the benefit of an exaggerated crouch.

"For my basic stance — we're talking about when I don't smell bunt or some other play — I put my left foot slightly behind my right foot and bounce back on it. Now my focus is on the hitter, but I watch the pitcher with my peripheral vision. As he brings his leg down and arm through in his wind-up, I bring my left foot parallel with my right while transferring my weight evenly to the balls of both feet. As the ball crosses the plate, I bend forward a bit but not in a full squat. This leaves me balanced and open to move freely to either side." — Ken Caminiti

That word again — anticipation

Ken doesn't rely solely on his reflexes and proper weight distribution to glove the bazooka shots aimed his way. Like all great third basemen, he combines a sixth sense with concrete data to anticipate where the batter is likely to hit the ball.

"Most of the time, I like to know what the pitcher is throwing to a batter, so I can prepare myself accordingly. So I will peek through the batter's legs to pick

up his signs to the pitcher. Or I might have the shortstop relay the sign. I prefer to take them directly from the catcher, so there is no chance of miscommunication. Let's say the catcher calls for something offspeed. If the batter begins to swing before that pitcher reaches the plate, you know he has to hit that ball down the line or into foul territory. You're going to lean towards the line. The trick is to focus not on contact but before the ball meets the bat." — Ken Caminiti

Checking the real estate

Before the first game of every away series, the third baseman (as well as the other fielders) should examine how a ballpark's topography may affect play. Never take anything for granted; groundskeepers or the elements may have altered a park since you last played there.

"I'll spend some time seeing just how far it is from my position to the stands; that tells me how far I can run without banging into a railing. I'm going to roll the ball down the line to see if it tends to stay fair or roll foul. That helps me decide if I'm going to pick up that bunt down the line or let it go." — Ken Caminiti

Fast hands for slow rollers

The grab and throw on bunts or slow rollers topped to third is among the most difficult of all infield plays. Ken fields those balls as well as anyone who has ever played the position.

"To make those plays, you have to first get a good jump on the ball. On the bunt, try to key off the hitter to see if he gives it away (before trying to lay it down). His back foot can tell you a lot. For instance, a lot of right-handed hitters will drop that back foot before attempting a drag bunt. Left-handed hitters can be more difficult to spot. Like Kenny Lofton — who's probably the best I've seen at this — waits to the last moment and then just drops the bat on the ball. Brett Butler (a center fielder with the Los Angeles Dodgers in 1997) did the same thing. I try to take the bunt away from guys like him by playing all the way in and daring him to hit it by me. On those slow rollers, you have to bust it as hard as you can the moment you see the play. But you also have to maintain your timing. Get to the ball with stutter steps so that your left foot is even with the ball when you drop down to scoop it. Depending on how quickly you get there and the runner's speed, you glove the ball, take a step towards the base you're throwing to, and let it rip. On some plays, though, you just have to bare-hand the ball and throw in one continuous motion. That's a do-or-die play; you don't think, just react." — Ken Caminiti

Figure 7-12 shows how to bare-hand the slow roller.

Figure 7-12:
Fielding and
throwing
the slow
roller in one
motion.

Playing mind games

Persuade a runner to hang close to third base, and you decrease his chances of scoring on a short fly ball or hard hit grounder. How do you get a runner to anchor near third? Ken uses numerous fakes and moves to keep the runner honest.

"I'll make a move towards third or fake one to get the runner back, to keep him thinking. If you suspect a squeeze play is on (when the batter tries to bunt the runner on third base home), you can stand right next to the runner so he can't get to big a lead. When the pitcher starts up, I'll dart back to the bag just to cross the runner up." — Ken Caminiti

A basic rule to get two

As already noted, middle infielders usually attempt to get the ball to each other in a particular spot — at the letters, to the inside of the bag — on the double play. Their proximity to each other allows them this luxury. As Ken points out, third basemen don't need to be quite as specific.

"Things happen so quickly at third, many times the shortstop or second baseman hasn't reached the bag by the time you're ready to throw. So I just try to throw the ball directly over the base and let the fielders get to it. If a fielder is already at the base, I try to deliver it to his glove side." — Ken Caminiti

Some last words from third

"You can't play this position scared. If you're just starting out, it may seem as if things happen too quickly at third, but your body will react in time if you let it. Take the field with the attitude you want every ball hit to you and that you are going to make the play. Third base calls for a lot of long throws, so you must be able to throw overhand. However, there will be some plays where you don't have time for anything but a sidearm throw; you've got to know how much time you have to make the play. Who the runner is, how the ball was hit, and the angle from which you are throwing all factor into that decision. You have to know all these things if you are going to do your job. The key to having good range and quick reactions at third is concentration. Lay back and you are going to miss some plays you could have made. You should be focused on every pitch of the game so that you can anticipate your next move. By the end of the game, the third baseman should feel drained." — Ken Caminiti

Ranging Wide: Playing Shortstop

All the infield fundamentals reviewed in this chapter — throwing, fielding grounders, positioning, and so on — can be applied to this position. Shortstops should also read our section on second base. The shortstop is nearly a mirror of the second baseman except he has more ground to cover and must make longer throws. A second baseman's longest throw to first is barely more than 90 feet. The average throw for a shortstop to the same base is 110 feet. Because of the greater distance, you must be able to catch grounders cleanly or you won't survive at this position. If you knock balls down as a second baseman sometimes will, you may not have time to throw out the runner. Because you are responsible for so much territory, you must study the hitters throughout your league so you can position yourself properly in every situation.

The shortstop on our All-Star team is Barry Larkin of the Cincinnati Reds. The National League's Most Valuable Player in 1995, Barry has won three Gold Gloves (1995–97) at short. He is one of this era's great double play artists as well as being one of the best-throwing shortstops ever.

Setting up

Because you must roam to either side at short, keep your weight balanced. Your feet should be a little more than shoulder width with your legs bent slightly in a semicrouch. You often have less time than any other infielder to make a play, so you must be continually thinking about how you will react if the ball is hit a certain way. It is hard to turn on the jet packs from a stationary position, so put your body in motion by taking two steps forward as the pitch approaches the plate. You have a direct view to home plate. Watching the catcher's signs lets you know what the pitcher is going to throw. If you feel the hitter is going to hit a certain pitch to your left or right, cheat a step in that direction.

"The most important thing is to field the ball cleanly, and — for the advanced player — catch it with your momentum carrying you towards wherever you are going to throw, second or first. You always hear that you should look at the ball into the glove, but you should also look at the ball as you remove it from the glove. A lot of times, guys catch the ball and immediately look for their target instead of at the ball — as if someone was going to move first base. Then they have to double-clutch or regrip the ball before throwing, and that can cost outs. When you throw, your weight should transfer to your planted rear foot as you cock to throw, then transfer it back to your front foot as you release the ball."
— Barry Larkin

Shortstops often must run full-out, so you must avoid tangling your legs. When you must dart to your right, pivot on your right leg and cross over with your left. On balls hit to your left, do the reverse.

"When you throw the ball to first, try to throw the ball through, not to, your first baseman's chest. If you just try to throw to him, and you're short, the ball will short-hop him. When you're in the hole and can't get on top of your throw, you might have to sidearm the ball to first base. You see a lot of inexperienced shortstops wasting a lot of motion trying to get something on that throw. If you are going toward first, get your wrist into the ball and snap off that throw. Your momentum will help put something on the ball. If I am moving toward third when I catch the ball, I contort my body to get off a throw. I try to keep my front (left) foot closed, so my toe is pointed toward the left field stands. Then I throw against my body and use torque to propel a snap throw. On a play like that, you don't have to throw the ball all the way to first. (Former Reds Gold Glove shortstop) Davey Concepcion taught me how to bounce the ball on one hop to the first baseman. Shortstops should work on that play in practice."
— Barry Larkin

If you dive for a ball — something shortstops do frequently — you must get to your feet immediately. However, don't rush the play.

"Too often, young shortstops who dive start trying to throw the ball before they really catch it. Catch the ball, hit the ground, pop up, and make the throw. When a guy tries to throw the ball before he catches it, he stands a good chance of dropping it. With practice, you'll learn to pop up quickly after a dive with the ball securely in your possession. This should leave you plenty of time to get off a good throw. Studying martial arts helped me with this. One of the first things I learned was how to roll with a fall so I wouldn't be rigid when I hit the ground. If you can learn how to roll with your dive, your momentum will help get you to your feet." — Barry Larkin

Backhanded compliments

After ranging far to your right, you may still be unable to get in front of the ball. You have to make a *backhand play* in those situations.

"This should always be a play of last resort. You should be trying to increase your range daily so that you don't have to backhand too many plays. During practice, have your infield instructor hit balls to your left and right at ever-increasing distances away from you. Keep working your way around the ball. Your goal is not to let him get to your backhand. If you're not rangy, play a little deeper to compensate. When you do have to backhand the ball as you go towards the hole, try to catch it just beyond your left foot. Stop your momentum, plant on your right foot, step to your left and throw. Another way is to open up your right foot, catch your ball in front of it, bring your left foot through, plant on your right foot, and throw." — Barry Larkin

Figure 7-13 shows you the position for a backhand play.

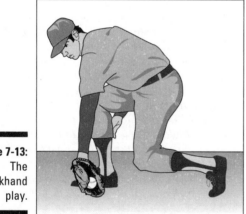

Figure 7-13: The backhand play.

The wisdom of an open-glove policy

This advice should be common sense: It is much easier to catch a ball with a glove that is fully open than with one that is half- or completely closed. All infielders should know this (although you would be surprised at how many major league infielders approach grounders with half-opened mitts), but it is especially important for the shortstop who has little time to bobble the ball.

As you reach the ball, slow down and bend with your legs rather than your back. Lower your glove on an angle to the ground and open the glove wide. The fingers should be touching the field and your palm should be lifted up slightly toward you. Keep the glove halfway open, or the ball can glance off its side. (See Figure 7-14.)

Figure 7-14:
The shortstop's glove has to be ready.

Doubling up

Like the second baseman, the shortstop can start double plays (his usual function) or act as the pivot man. If the ball is hit within three or four steps of second base, you usually don't need to involve your second baseman. Simply step on the bag with your left foot, push off, and throw off your right foot. Do this in one fluid motion.

- ✔ On balls hit near second, but not close enough to permit an unassisted play, give your second baseman a chest-high, underhanded toss. Throw sidearm to your second baseman on balls hit directly to you or just to your right.

- ✔ You must turn the pivot on the double play on balls hit to the right side of the infield. Get to the bag immediately.

- ✔ When the ball is hit so far to your right that you have to extend, take the time to plant your right foot and make a strong throw to second. You usually get only the lead runner on this play (which, by the way, should always be your priority), though the second baseman may be able to turn two if your throw is strong and accurate (and the runner heading toward first isn't very fast).

- ✔ On slowly hit grounders, forget about the double play. The shortstop must know the speed of each baserunner so he can decide whether to attempt the force at second or get the out at first.

"When I'm the pivot man on the double play, I prefer to receive the ball on the left field side of second. As I get to the bag, I slow my momentum so that I can adjust if the throw to me isn't where I expect it. On the pivot, if the ball is to my right, I step to it with my right foot and drag my left foot over the bag. If the throw is on my left, I step to it with my left foot and drag my right." — Barry Larkin

A last word on playing shortstop

"The great plays — the diving catches, the behind-the-back flips — are made because your fundamentals are sound. You've studied your positioning, you're aware of the situation and all the things that can happen. When you catch the ball, you look it into your glove and watch as you take it out. You do all the basics. Then when the ball is hit, your athletic ability and reactions take over. The great plays will come naturally because you will be in position to make them." — Barry Larkin

That Extra Infielder: The Pitcher

Retiring batters isn't the only responsibility pitchers have. When you are on the mound, you must cover a base or back up a fielder on nearly every play (refer to Chapter 9, the playbook, to learn your various assignments). You have to be quick enough to flag down hot smashes up the middle (or at least get out of their way so one of our infielders can catch them), and pounce on bunts. When runners stray far from the bag, you have to drive them back with a look or a pick-off move. On many infield plays, you are the traffic cop directing your teammates, so you must stay cool and alert.

For advice on how pitchers can field their position properly, we turn to one of Joe's opponents from the 1975 World Series, Bill Lee. The Red Sox left-hander was one of the smoothest fielders in the game, quick on bunts, fundamentally sound on grounders, and capable of the amazing play (the behind-the-back catch of line drives hit up the middle were a Lee specialty).

Your follow-through: The key to getting into fielding position

Pitching mechanics are covered in some depth in the Chapter 6. Ideally, when you emerge from your follow-through, you should be in a position to field anything hit toward you. Your body should be squared toward home plate, your feet should be parallel and shoulder width apart, and your weight should be evenly distributed over the balls of your feet. Few pitchers on any level come out of their follow through perfectly positioned to field. However, you should strive to come as close to the ideal we just described as you can.

"Never forget that your number one concern is getting the hitter out. If you can't come out of your follow-through in the ideal fielding position, you can compensate by keeping your eyes peeled on home plate and watching for the ball off the bat. Then let your reactions take over if the ball is hit towards you." — Bill Lee

Be aggressive

Try to field as many balls hit between you and first as you can. Anytime you can keep that first baseman near the bag, you are helping your team's defensive alignment.

- ✔ On bunt plays, charge balls that are hit directly toward you.
- ✔ On balls to the extreme side of you, field only those that look as if they will stop rolling before one of your infielders reaches it.

"As you go after the ball, don't focus on the runner. Instead, watch the ball into your glove. Don't rush your throw after fielding it. Get a good grip on the ball. Keep moving towards your target as you step and throw. If you have to spin and throw, keep a low center of gravity; it will make you quicker. If you are close to the base and the fielder isn't there, lead him to the bag with an underhand toss. However, if your fielder is on or near the bag and you aren't too close, hit the target he gives you with a strong overhand throw. Aim for his chest." — Bill Lee

On plays that require you to cover first base, go to a spot approximately 6 feet (1.8m) from first on the baseline. Run parallel to the base line as you cut toward first. As you reach the bag, shorten your strides so you can adjust to any bad throws.

"Touch the inside of the base on the home plate side with your right foot. This will prevent your momentum from carrying you into the runner (a must to avoid) or into foul territory." — Bill Lee

Keeping those runners close

Anytime you keep a baserunner anchored near a base, you not only reduce his chances to steal, you also make it more difficult to take an extra base or score on a long hit. Making numerous pick-off throws will chase a runner back to a base. Bill recommends three things you can do to hold a runner on without making a throw.

- ✔ Use the same motion to first as you do to home. Don't give the runner any extra movement to key off of. Be especially careful that you don't reveal your intentions with slight head or eye movements. Good baserunners are studying you constantly and pick up on the tiniest quirks.
- ✔ Disrupt the runner's timing by altering your rhythm as you move into your set position and go into your wind-up. Remember you're not changing movement here, just the timing of your movement. Don't fall into any consistent rhythms. Hold the ball during your set position for varying time periods.

✔ If you are left-handed, just watch the runner. If you don't move to throw, he can't go anywhere (well, technically he can, but the odds are you are going to throw him out).

"Always try to be quick to home plate. If the runner does take off, you will save your catcher a stride when he tries to throw the runner out. If you're slow to the plate, your catcher doesn't have a chance against the faster base stealers. He won't be able to get them unless he's Dirty Harry Callahan and he's toting his .44 Magnum." — Bill Lee

When the runner strays too far: Pick-offs

You can attempt to pick off a runner anytime your foot is off the pitching rubber (that's to say when you are in the set position or going into your stretch). If you are a right-hander trying to pick off a runner at first, push off your right foot while pivoting toward the bag with your left foot. Keep your upper torso open so you throw overhand rather than across your body. (See Figure 7-15.)

Figure 7-15:
The right-hander's pick-off move.

If you are a left-hander, you don't need to pivot because you are already facing first. All you have to do is snap off a sidearm throw while stepping toward first. When you raise your striding leg out of the set position, there will be a moment when it is pointed toward first. Unlike the right-hander, you now have the option of throwing to the bag or continuing your motion toward home plate. (See Figure 7-16.)

Pick-offs at second are more complicated. As Joe points out earlier (see "Picking them off"), you can employ a time play by signaling your second baseman or shortstop as you check the runner at second. On a 1-2-3 time play, the count begins when you turn back to face the hitter. On two, you should turn back toward second as the fielder breaks for the bag. On three, throw the ball at the knees and over the base. On the daylight play, the fielder sneaks up near the bag. You throw as soon as you see daylight between the fielder (usually the shortstop) and the runner.

"I know Joe prefers the time play, but, as a pitcher, I have to go the other way. I like the daylight play's spontaneity and the fact that you are reacting to your shortstop's movements. Time plays can go awry if you and your fielder aren't synchronized. That was always a problem for me. My middle infielders were usually on Greenwich time and I was on Somalian time." — Bill Lee

You shouldn't attempt many pick-offs at third because its a bad percentage play. Few runners steal home, and if you throw the ball away, you've just given the opposition a run. To pick the runner off, the right-hander and left-hander reverse the mechanics they use when throwing to first.

Figure 7-16:
The left-hander's pick-off move.

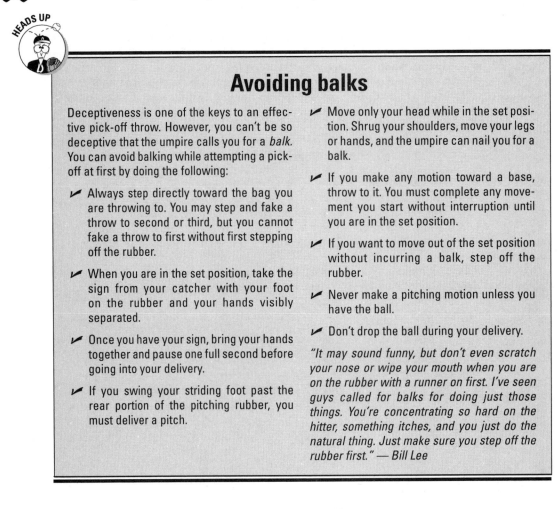

Avoiding balks

Deceptiveness is one of the keys to an effective pick-off throw. However, you can't be so deceptive that the umpire calls you for a *balk*. You can avoid balking while attempting a pick-off at first by doing the following:

✔ Always step directly toward the bag you are throwing to. You may step and fake a throw to second or third, but you cannot fake a throw to first without first stepping off the rubber.

✔ When you are in the set position, take the sign from your catcher with your foot on the rubber and your hands visibly separated.

✔ Once you have your sign, bring your hands together and pause one full second before going into your delivery.

✔ If you swing your striding foot past the rear portion of the pitching rubber, you must deliver a pitch.

✔ Move only your head while in the set position. Shrug your shoulders, move your legs or hands, and the umpire can nail you for a balk.

✔ If you make any motion toward a base, throw to it. You must complete any movement you start without interruption until you are in the set position.

✔ If you want to move out of the set position without incurring a balk, step off the rubber.

✔ Never make a pitching motion unless you have the ball.

✔ Don't drop the ball during your delivery.

"It may sound funny, but don't even scratch your nose or wipe your mouth when you are on the rubber with a runner on first. I've seen guys called for balks for doing just those things. You're concentrating so hard on the hitter, something itches, and you just do the natural thing. Just make sure you step off the rubber first." — Bill Lee

"Don't even think about this play with two outs. The runner cannot score on an out and no one wants to face his manager after making the inning-ending out on an attempted steal of home. Concentrate on the hitter; he's the one who can hurt you." — Bill Lee

Where Fly Balls Go to Die: Playing the Outfield

Oh boy, do outfielders have the life. They don't have to worry about kamikaze baserunners bearing down on them during the double play, hot line drives sizzling towards their craniums, or which base to cover on any given play. All they have to do is saunter after the occasional fly ball, throw it back toward the infield, and work on their suntans.

Yeah, right.

Playing the outfield is like playing any other position. It demands discipline, hard work, and knowledge. You must be able to gauge fly balls that come at you from diverse angles, understand the mechanics behind a good throw, and know what to do with the ball after you catch it. On balls hit into the gap, you must sprint full out, time your extension and catch, and then throw to the right base in one fluid move. Infielders can afford to take their time on many plays. Outfielders are so far from the action, they don't have a half-moment to spare on any ball that sets runners in motion. Infielders can bobble or even drop a ball and still record an out. If an outfielder drops a ball, the hitter is not only on first base, he probably takes an extra base. Outfielders don't collide with baserunners, but they can run into the occasional wall (and unlike human beings, those structures have no "give" to them). So you have to know what you are doing out there to avoid hurting yourself and your team.

Our outfield coach is Ken Griffey, Sr. The 1980 All-Star Most Valuable Player, Griffey patrolled all three outfield positions during a 19-year major league career spent largely with the Cincinnati Reds and New York Yankees. Sparky Anderson said, "Kenny is an example of how a person can make themselves into an outstanding fielder through hard work. He was a defensive weapon wherever he played and he charged the ball as well as any outfielder of his day." We're also going to bring in Rusty Staub, a smart outfielder whose powerful throwing arm was feared throughout baseball, for a word or two.

Setting up

Because they have more real estate to cover, outfielders have more positioning options than infielders. Where you play depends on the hitter, the pitcher, the situation, and the count. For example, Paul O'Neill, the right fielder of the New York Yankees, is a left-handed hitter with good power to all fields. He can hit the ball with authority anywhere. However, against a hard-throwing right-hander like Boston's Pedro Martinez, Paul is more likely to pull the ball when the count is in his favor. Conversely, if a hitter is *behind in the count* (he has more strikes on him than balls), he tends to protect the plate and hit the ball to the opposite field. So if Martinez has a 3-ball 1-strike count on him, his outfielders should shade closer toward right field.

However, if you were playing the outfield for Seattle and Randy Johnson were pitching, you may not move toward right if you don't believe O'Neill can pull Johnson's fastball. And even that is not an absolute. Suppose it's a close game in the late innings and Johnson has lost some of the hop from his fastball. You may think that O'Neill, who is looking to drive the ball for extra bases, may now indeed be able to pull on the tiring Johnson.

When setting up in the outfield, you must also consider your limitations and those of your teammates. Do you go back on balls well, but are less sure on balls that pull you in? Play shallow. Move to your left better than you're right? You have to compensate when a right-handed pull hitter is at the plate. Does your center fielder have a weak throwing arm? With the winning run on third and less than two out, you may have to take a ball that he would normally catch, so you can attempt the throw home. All of these factors — plus the field conditions for that day — determine where you play on each pitch.

Taking your basic stance

You should set up in the outfield with a square stance:

✔ Your feet are parallel, shoulder-width apart, and pointed toward home plate.

✔ Get into a semicrouch with your weight evenly distributed over the balls of both feet.

✔ Rest your hands on your knees but drop them as the ball approaches the plate.

This maneuver gives you momentum to chase the ball if it is hit beyond the infield. (See Figure 7-17.) If it looks as if the ball will be hit over your head, put the toes of whatever foot is on the ball side behind the heel of your other foot (this is called a *drop step*).

Figure 7-17:
The basic outfield stance.

"Get as loose as possible before the game starts. Give yourself 15 minutes to stretch, do calisthenics, and some light running. Don't bring any tension to the outfield; it will rob you of quickness." — Ken Griffey, Sr.

Taking off from jump street

What is the one thing you'll hear said about any great outfielder? He gets a good jump on the ball. Your eyes, ears, and head will determine how quickly you break for a fly ball. If you've done your homework, you should already know where the batter most often hits the ball. Concentrate on the pitcher-batter confrontation. You may not be able to tell what kind of pitch has been thrown, but you can at least observe its location. Notice if the batter is getting a late hack (swing) or is in front of the ball. Your knowledge of the hitter and pitcher should then give you some idea of where the ball is likely to land. Another indicator of how far a ball will travel is the sound made when the bat hits the ball.

"Here's a little game my teammates and I used to play during batting practice to sharpen our ears. We would stand with our backs to home plate and try to identify where a ball would be hit without peeking. All we had to guide us was the sound of the ball against the wood. Practice that day after day and, after a while, you can take off at the crack of the bat. It becomes instinctive." — Rusty Staub

"Depending on who was on the mound, I would key off of the pitcher's fastball and how the hitter was reacting to it. That would tell me if the hitter could pull the ball, or, if he was a little late, hit it the other way. Or just hit it back up the middle." — Ken Griffey, Sr.

Outfielders usually move laterally on fly balls. To achieve maximum acceleration, pivot and push off the foot nearest the ball as you rise out of your semicrouch. Cross over with your outside foot. If you must angle your run, stride first with the foot nearest the ball. Pivot on both feet whenever the batter hits the ball over your head.

"When you are going into the gap, don't keep your eyes on the ball. Train yourself to recognize where the ball will probably land and run to that area. After four or five steps, you can glance up to check the flight of the ball." — Ken Griffey, Sr.

You don't have to move much on balls hit right at you, but you do have to determine whether the ball will rise or sink. Don't take a step until you can read the ball's trajectory.

Making the catch

Pursue fly balls aggressively. If you drift over to time the catch of a ball, you aren't in position to throw. You may also be unable to adjust if you misjudge a ball's flight or a sudden gust carries it farther than you anticipated. Hustle on every play.

Using both hands, catch the ball out in front of your body and over your throwing shoulder. (See Figure 7-18.) If you are left-handed, your right foot should be forward; if you throw from the right side, your left foot is out in front. This position leaves you in the correct position to get off a good throw. Take a crow hop to close the shoulders and hips on your glove side, and then move through the ball as you throw overhand with a cross-seam grip.

You will instill sound habits if you catch every ball as if you have to throw it to a base. When you do have to unleash a throw, take a small hop to close the shoulders and hips on your glove side. Then move through the ball as you throw overhand with a cross-seam grip.

"You should be practicing taking the ball out of your glove in a cross-seam grip until you can do it blindfolded. Do it every time you grab a baseball. For maximum power, throw the ball over the top whenever you can and have your momentum pointed towards your target. The best way to build your arm strength for these throws is to play catch as often as possible. And I don't mean just randomly tossing the ball back and forth. Play catch with a purpose. Make a game of hitting a target every time you throw. If you deliver the ball up near your catching partner's face you get two points, at his chest one. Low point man buys the soft drinks. Try to hit a specific target even when you're just loosening up." — Rusty Staub

Don't fall into the gap

Any time a ball is hit into the *gap* or power alley, one outfielder should try to cut off the ball, while another should run at a deeper angle to back up the play. Usually the fielder closest to the ball goes for it. On plays where the ball is equidistant from both fielders, the center fielder has priority. However, to avoid mix-ups, especially on balls hit between two players, you and your fellow outfielders should call loudly for any ball you pursue.

Figure 7-18:
Catching
the fly ball.

Coming in on a ball

During practice, learn how to read the trajectory of balls far in front of you
so you can instantly decide if you should make the putout or catch it on a
bounce. If you have to play the bounce, slow down while keeping your body
and glove in front of the ball. That way, if you don't catch it cleanly, you can
knock it down.

*"Make sure you catch this ball belt-high or chest-high so that you keep your
eyes on the ball. It will be easier to handle." — Ken Griffey, Sr.*

And going out on a ball

Most major leaguers will tell you the most difficult fly ball to catch is the one
smacked over your head. Inexperienced outfielders often start back pedal-
ing on that ball, which is the worst thing they can do. If you back pedal, you
don't see the ball clearly because your head is bobbing up and down, you
can't generate any speed (which is why marathoners do not run backward),
and you can't jump if you need to. (See Figure 7-19.)

Figure 7-19:
Going back
on a fly ball.

"Outfielders tangle themselves on that play when they start off on the wrong foot. If a ball is hit over your right shoulder, drop step back with your right foot. Cross over with your left foot and stay angled sideways as you go back. If it is hit over your left shoulder, do the reverse." — Ken Griffey, Sr.

You have to catch grounders, too

With runners on, outfielders should charge ground balls as aggressively as infielders. They must catch the ball in a position that allows them to unleash a good throw. Field the ball on your glove side with your glove-side foot down. Close off your upper body with a crow hop, stride with your left foot, and throw over the top with a cross-seam grip.

"When there is no one on base, all you want to do is keep the ground ball in front of you. If it gets by, the runner is taking extra bases. Get in front of it, get down on one knee, and block the ball." (See Figure 7-20.) — Ken Griffey, Sr.

Okay, enough with all this theory. Now go grab a mitt, find a field, and start throwing some leather around with your friends. Nothing hones your fielding skills quicker than practice, practice, practice!

Figure 7-20:
Keeping the
ground ball
in front
of you.

In David Falkner's eloquently written *Nine Sides of the Diamond: Baseball's Great Glove Men On the Art of Defense* (Random House), some of the greatest fielders of all time — including Brooks Robinson, Willie Mays, and even Joe Morgan — reveal how they approach their craft. If you want to discover how players raise their defensive games to another level, this is the book to read.

Chapter 8
The Science of Baserunning

In This Chapter

▶ Running to first

▶ Leading off any base

▶ Running the basepaths

▶ Sliding

▶ Breaking up the double play

▶ Stealing

*B*aserunning has always been the most underrated aspect of baseball offense. Yet more games are won or lost on the basepaths than most fans realize. The teams that consistently win close games are the ones whose players can go from first to third on singles, break up double plays, score on short fly balls or ground-ball outs, and take the extra base whenever it is offered.

JOE SAYS

Anyone can be a good baserunner. You don't need speed; you simply need to be alert, aggressive, and smart. Pete Rose was one of the best baserunners I ever played with or against. From the stands, Pete appeared to be fast because he hustled all the time, but he had only average speed. In a game I played against him in the Houston Astrodome, Pete went from first to third on a sharp single to right. You didn't see that happen often on AstroTurf; singles bounced to the outfielders so quickly that baserunners usually advanced only one base. But Pete executed plays like that all the time because he was hustling from his very first step toward second. He also always knew where the ball was hit and the strength of the outfielder's arm.

Pete went from first to third as well as any player in the majors because of his head, not his legs. Take a page from his book: Always look to see where the outfielders are playing before each pitch.

That First Step out of the Box

You should be hustling toward first base the moment the ball leaves your bat. It doesn't matter which foot you lead with as long as you have good balance and your initial move propels you toward first. Always run in a straight line as close to the foul line as possible so that if a fielder's throw hits you, the umpire won't call you out for obstruction (see Figure 8-1). Don't overstride. Stay low for your first few steps to build acceleration and then explode into your normal running form.

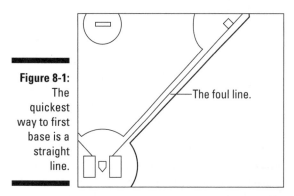

Figure 8-1:
The quickest way to first base is a straight line.

—The foul line.

If someone is going to make a throw to first base, don't just run to first base, run *through* it. Always touch the front of the bag as you cross over it. Continue running several steps down the right field line before making your right turn into foul territory. If you do this after touching first, you can't be tagged out for leaving the bag. However, turn left toward second base, and the fielder can tag you out before you get back to first. (See Figure 8-2.) As you run through first, glance over your right shoulder to see if you can advance to second on an error.

On grounders, don't bother to watch the ball as you dash toward first. Watching the ball slows you down. The only time you should watch the ball is if it is going toward one of the outfield gaps or over an outfielder's head. You can pick up most of those balls with a quick glance. If you can't, tilt your head slightly (and don't break stride) for a better view. Still can't pick it up? Then rely on your first base coach to tell you whether you should run through first or turn toward second.

Stay alert after singling to right field. If you make a wide turn at first, a charging right fielder may still get you out by throwing behind you to the first baseman.

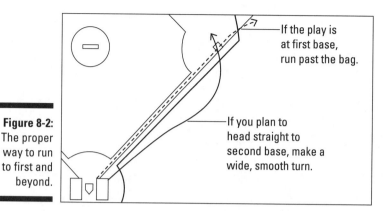

Figure 8-2:
The proper way to run to first and beyond.

If the play is at first base, run past the bag.

If you plan to head straight to second base, make a wide, smooth turn.

There will be times when you should slide into first base — for example, if a high throw draws the first baseman off the bag and he has to tag you for the out. If you slide while he's leaping for the ball, it will be nearly impossible for him to get the ball down in time to nail you. Some players slide into first on force outs, but I think this is bad policy. Sliding or jumping into first on your final step doesn't get you to the bag more quickly; it slows you down.

Taking Your Lead

Baseball is, as they say, a game of inches; you are often safe or out by the barest of margins. Any time you can use your lead to shorten the distance from one base to another, you gain an advantage for your team — you are inching that much closer to your ultimate objective: home plate.

Leading off first

After you're on first, keep your left foot against the bag while you check the alignment of the fielders and pick up any signs from the third base coach. Remind yourself of the number of outs. Don't move off first until you know the pitcher has the ball. While closely watching the pitcher receive his signs, take several shuffle steps from the bag (do not cross your left foot over your right; you can get tangled if you have to dive back to first on a pick-off). This position is your *primary lead*. (See Figure 8-3.)

Your goal is to gradually get as far from first base as you can without getting picked off. How far a lead you take depends on a number of factors: whether the pitcher is a righty or lefty, how good his move is, your size, and your reflexes. Tall players can take long leads — but so can short, quick players. Finding your ideal lead length is a matter of trial and error. However, most major league runners prefer to be a step or two and a dive away from first.

Figure 8-3:
Taking a
primary
lead.

When taking your lead, balance your weight evenly on the balls of both feet. Do not lean toward first or second. Drop into a slight crouch and flex your knees so that you can move quickly in either direction. This stance is known as a *two-way lead.* Your feet should be parallel to each other, shoulder width apart, and pointed toward the pitcher. (Maury Wills, who ran the bases well enough to steal 104 bases for the Dodgers in 1962, used to turn his right foot a little toward second base so he could pivot quicker.)

Let your arms hang loosely in front of you. Keep your eyes on the pitcher the moment you step from the bag. Watch for the pick-off play! Imagine a straight line leading from the outer edge of first base to the outer edge of second. Stand even with that line or a little bit in front of it. Leading off the bag from behind that line costs you extra steps (see Figure 8-4). It also makes it appear to the pitcher that there is a wider distance between you and first base than there actually is. You will be inviting additional pick-off throws.

As the pitcher throws toward home, you should assume your *secondary lead.* Take a crossover step and a hop toward second while watching the action at the plate. In a perfectly timed crossover, your right foot hits the ground a split second before the ball reaches home. When the ball passes the hitter or if the hitter hits the ball in the air directly at an infielder, stop on your right foot, turn, and get back to first. Should the ball get past the catcher or if the batter hits it, push off your right foot and run toward second. ***Remember:*** Don't leave the base until you know who has the ball. Baserunners must be constantly alert for pick-off plays and hidden ball tricks.

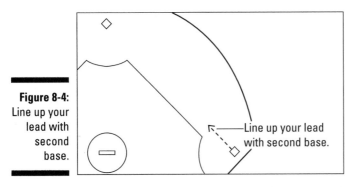

Figure 8-4:
Line up your
lead with
second
base.

Line up your lead
with second base.

On any catchable fly ball, you should be far enough from first that you can make it safely to second (or beyond, if the ball is dropped). If the batter hits a medium fly ball, run no farther than halfway to second base until you see how the play evolves. You can run farther toward second on a deep fly.

However, always remember that if the outfielder catches the ball before it touches the ground, you must get back to first. If the outfielder's throw reaches that bag before you do, you've just run into a double play. As you trot toward your dugout, you will notice a livid fellow with smoke coming out of his ears and the veins in his head threatening to explode. That is your manager. The doghouse you just slid into belongs to him.

Leading off second

You can take a longer lead off second than from first. No one is holding you close to the bag: The pitcher can't look directly at you, and he has to wheel and turn to pick you off.

If you are going to steal, set up in a straight line to third. Otherwise, stay a few feet behind the baseline. Take your primary lead. Advance as the pitcher delivers to the plate. You should be 15 to 18 feet (4.6 to 5.5m) from second as the ball reaches home.

With two outs, extend your primary lead off second to about 20 feet (6m) but set it about 3 to 5 feet (.9 to 1.5m) behind second base. This lead puts you in a better position to round third and head for home on a base hit. You don't have to worry about being doubled off, so you can take off at the crack of the bat. (See Figure 8-5.)

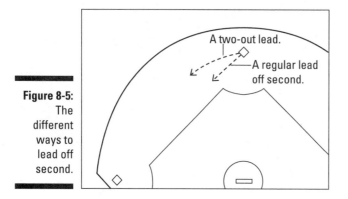

Figure 8-5:
The
different
ways to
lead off
second.

Leading off third

Managers have exiled baserunners to Devil's Island for getting picked off third base. Therefore, your primary lead off third should put you no farther from the bag than the opposing third baseman. Take this lead in foul territory so you won't be called out if you are struck by a batted ball. (See Figure 8-6.)

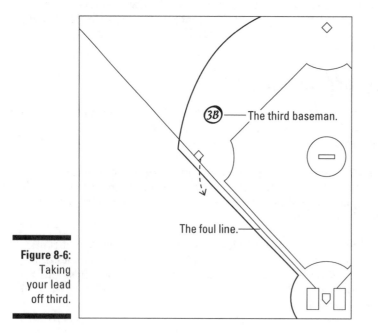

Figure 8-6:
Taking
your lead
off third.

The force out

Force out is a term that you need to be familiar with because it is a frequent occurrence in baseball — often misunderstood by the novice player and viewer alike (a trip to your local Little League game should convince you of that!). A force out (or *force play*) takes place when a batted ground ball forces a runner to advance to the next base, but that base is tagged with the ball before the runner reaches the base.

Under which circumstances does a batted ground ball force a baserunner to advance?

✔ A runner on first must *always* try to advance to second base.

✔ A runner on second base must try to advance to third base if another runner is on first base.

✔ A runner on third base must try to advance home if runners are on first and second base (in this case, the bases are *loaded,* and a force out is possible at any base, including home).

Of course, if you are the defensive player, it is easier to tag the base in a force play situation (or throw to another fielder who may step on

the base) rather than tag the runner — because tagging a runner may knock the ball out of your hand. You don't need to do both. And don't think that you must literally tag the base. Simply step on the base while holding the ball in either your bare or your gloved hand.

Under which circumstances does a baserunner not need to advance when the batter hits a ground ball? (If this information seems like overkill, don't forget your visit to the Little League game.)

✔ A runner on second base need not run if no one is on first base.

✔ A runner on third base need not run if either first base or second base is empty.

✔ Runners on both third base and second base need not run if first base is empty.

In the preceding situations, go to the next base only if you can make it safely — and remember that the defensive player must tag you with the ball instead of simply touching the base that you are running to. If you don't think that you can make it to the next base safely, simply stay put!

As the pitcher throws the ball home, take a two- or three-step walking lead toward home. You should land on your right foot, ready to break for home or return to third, just as the pitch approaches the plate. This movement leaves you in position to score easily on a wild pitch, passed ball, or ground out. It also allows you to pivot back toward third if the pitch is handled cleanly by the catcher.

That Sense of Where You Are

To be a great baserunner, you must take the extra base *before* the ball is hit. Prior to your game, watch the opposing fielders during practice to see the strength and accuracy of their arms. When you reach first base during the game, observe how deeply the outfielders are playing the hitter. Are they leaning in any particular direction? If the left fielder is playing deep, and your teammate hits a shallow fly in his direction, you can take off without holding up to see if the ball is caught.

If the outfield is *shaded* (leaning) toward left, and the hitter smacks the ball down the right field line, you can go for at least two bases.

You should also observe if any of the outfielders are left-handed throwers. If a left-handed center fielder has to go to his right in pursuit of a hit, he has to turn and make an off-balance throw to get you out at third. On a single to right center field, a right-handed center fielder cannot throw to third until he turns completely around. That gives you an extra moment to slide in safely.

Rounding the Bag

All right, you've just pounded a ball into the outfield and you are thinking double all the way. You're not running through first and up the right-field foul line on this play. Instead, head straight for first as you normally would. When you are about 15 feet (4.6m) from the bag, veer slightly toward foul territory, and then cut in toward the infield. As you pass first base on a nearly straight line toward second, touch the bag with your foot. It doesn't matter which one you use. However, you will have a shorter turn to make by touching the inside part of the bag with your left foot (see Figure 8-7). Make sure that you touch enough of first base for the umpire to witness the contact. Scamper to second base.

Tagging Up

After a fly ball is caught, baserunners must touch the base they occupy before advancing to the next bag. This action is known as *tagging up*. If you are halfway between first and second when a deep fly is hit, you must return to first to touch the bag. Take off for second only *after* the ball and fielder make contact. You can advance in this manner from any base.

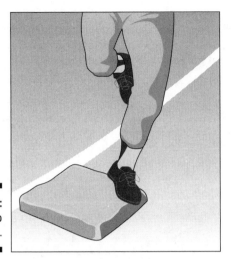

Figure 8-7:
How to
round first.

When you tag up from first, your right foot should be on the inside edge of the bag. This position leaves your right side open so it will be easier for you to follow the ball's flight. If you are tagging up from third, your left foot should be on the bag. Tagging from second? The situation determines which foot you should place on the bag. On a ball hit to left or left center, it's your right foot. When the ball is hit to right field or right center, switch to your left foot.

As you tag up, drop into a crouch. Extend your front foot 18 to 24 inches (46 to 61cm), depending on your leg length, from the base. Shift your weight forward. Watch the ball! The moment it touches the outfielder's glove, push into your stride toward the next base. You don't have to wait for the outfielder to catch it cleanly.

Note: When two outs have already been recorded, don't think that you must wait on a fly ball to be touched before you can run! (If the ball is caught, the inning is over, anyway.) With two outs, be prepared to run on any fly ball — and hope that the fielder misses or drops it.

Working with Your Coaches

You may feel as if you are alone on those basepaths; you're not. Think of the base coaches as part of your running team. Use them. When you get to first base, the coach there can be a fount of valuable intelligence. He will remind you how many outs there are (if he doesn't and you're not sure, ask him), reveal a quirk he has detected in the pitcher's motion (so you can get a better lead or steal a base), or tell you something about the outfielders (which one seems hobbled or isn't throwing particularly well that day). This is just the kind of information you need to make appropriate decisions on the basepaths.

The third base coach is your beacon. If you've lost sight of the ball or are unsure whether you should advance to the next base, watch his signs. No matter how much experience you have, heed the third base coach in most situations. He has a better view of the entire field than you. You may think you are running faster than you are, or you may not realize how quickly an outfielder has gotten to the ball. A good third base coach can gauge all of that for you.

Putting the Run in the Hit-and-Run

As the baserunner on the hit-and-run, don't depart from your normal lead or you may signal your intentions to the opposition. Timing is more important to the successful execution of this play than the size of your lead. You have to make sure the pitcher delivers the ball before you break from the base. (You can review how to execute the hit-and-run in Chapter 5.)

Sliding

"Slide, Kelly, Slide" — the popular saloon song from the 1890s — was written in honor of Boston Red Stocking superstar Mike "King" Kelly. While the lone umpire was looking elsewhere, Kelly would often help his team to an extra base by cutting across the infield from first and sliding into third without touching second. (Kelly wasn't the only guy to try this stunt back then, by the way.) You can't pull that play today (too many umps and TV cameras to catch you), but you can grab runs and wins for your team if you know how to slide properly. Often, the only difference between the umpire calling you safe or out on the bases is the quality of your slide.

 Practice sliding as diligently as you work on the other aspects of your game. You don't need to do this on a baseball diamond. My brothers and I used to practice in our backyard. Get into a pair of tennis shoes and sliding pads, wet some grass, put down a base, and practice all your slides. It's important to be able to slide on both sides. George Foster, one of my teammates on the Reds, could only slide one side no matter how a play developed. There were many times when he could have been safe but was tagged out simply because he couldn't elude the tag. As you practice, you will develop a feel for when you should start your slide.

The straight-leg slide

My favorite slide. The *straight-leg slide* gets you to the bag as quickly as possible while leaving you in position to bounce up and advance another base if a misplay occurs. Because your top leg is straight and aimed at the bag, you have less chance of catching your spikes in the dirt (a leading cause of ankle injuries).

Start this slide about 10 feet (3m) from the bag. Push off your rear foot and lift both legs up. Your body should glide forward feet first. Slide straight in (you can do this on either side) with the toe and foot of your top leg pointed in a straight line toward the middle of the bag. Your bottom leg is bent under you. (See Figure 8-8.)

Figure 8-8:
The
straight-leg
slide.

The bent-leg slide

The *bent-leg slide* is a variation of the straight-leg slide. To launch the slide, push off your rear foot and lift up both legs. Then tuck your rear leg under your slightly flexed top leg at a 90-degree angle (this pairing should resemble a figure 4). Maintain a semisitting position with your torso arched back and hands held high as you slide. Hold your chin close to your chest so you can see the base and the ball. Aim for the middle of the bag with your top leg. Touch the base with your heel (which prevents your cleats from catching on the bag).

The *pop-up slide* is the bent-leg with a wrinkle. You start this slide about 8 feet (2.4m) from the bag. Don't lean back. As your top leg hits the base, push up with your bottom foot. The momentum brings you to your feet, ready to advance if a misplay occurs.

Lou Brock, the all-time National League leader in stolen bases, used the pop-up slide to great effect (see Figure 8-9). It left him in position to take an extra base on a misplay. However, I don't like to see it used unless someone has already overthrown the ball when you start your slide. Too many runners have been called out when they were safe simply because their pop-up slides didn't afford the umpires a long-enough look to make the correct calls.

The head-first slide

This slide is nothing more than a dive into a swimming pool — without any water. You are hurtling yourself at great speed onto a hard surface that has no give. Pete Rose slid head-first for more than 20 years and he never even cracked a fingernail (see Figure 8-10). Don't let that fool you. The head-first can be dangerous. A descending fielder can spike your hands, the ball can hit you in the head, you can jam your fingers and hands against the base if you hold them too low. In the 1997 National League Championship Series, Florida Marlin shortstop Edgar Renteria knee-blocked a head-first sliding Kenny Lofton from reaching second base. If Kenny had slid straight in, Renteria couldn't have blocked him.

Figure 8-9:
Lou Brock is ready to pop up and run some more in a misplay.

National Baseball Hall of Fame Library Cooperstown, N.Y.

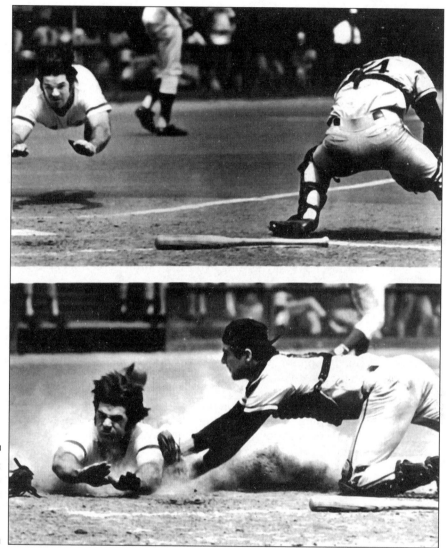

Figure 8-10:
Pete Rose
was known
for his head
first slides.

National Baseball Hall of Fame Library Cooperstown, N.Y.

If you are still not dissuaded from going in head first, at least minimize your
risk by executing the slide properly. Start the head-first slide by gradually
lowering your body until you are about 8 feet (2.4m) from the bag. Extend
your arms while you launch yourself off your rear leg. Keep your body
straight, but relaxed, so that your forearms, chest, and thighs hit the ground
simultaneously (this absorbs the shock). Stay alert and hold up your hands
and head up while sliding! See Figure 8-11. Should you attempt to execute a
literal head-first slide, you risk a sprained neck, concussion, or worse.

Figure 8-11:
The head-
first slide.

It's often hard to keep your hands up when attempting any type of slide. Wearing sliding gloves offers you some protection from injury.

The hook slide

The *hook slide* was supposedly the brainchild of Mike Kelly. It may have helped inspire that song they wrote about him, but it is basically a desperation play that you should use only when trying to evade a probable tag.

Let me set it up. You are on first. The batter hits the ball to right field. You cruise around second and burst toward third. The right fielder, however, has gotten a perfect bounce and has already fired the ball to the third baseman. As the ball beats you to the bag it pulls the third baseman toward his right. A hook slide to your right (the third baseman's left) is your only hope of avoiding an out.

Always execute the hook slide to the opposite side of wherever the tag will originate. If the throw comes in from the outfield side, slide to your left. Should it come from the infield side, slide to your right.

To hook slide to your left, push off on your right foot and drop to your left side. Your outer calf and thigh will absorb the slide's impact. Keep your right leg relatively straight with a slight knee flex (your right leg slides to the right of the bag). Scissor your left leg out toward the base. While sliding past the base, reach out with the toes of your left foot or either hand. Touch the bag at its nearest corner. See Figure 8-12.

If the fielder is about to tag your hand as you try to touch the base, you can pull your hand back. As the fielder's momentum carries him to one side, reach out to grab the bag with your other hand.

Figure 8-12:
The hook
slide.

To hook slide to your right (say, on a throw from the catcher), do everything I just described — only in reverse. Practice the hook slide from both sides. Don't use this slide on force plays; it slows you down when you need to get to the bag as quickly as possible.

Maury Wills was the greatest hook slider I ever saw. He could reach either corner of the base with the tip of his toe. This presented the fielder attempting a tag with the smallest target possible. With most runners, I only had to put the ball in the middle of the base to get them. They would slide right into it. I couldn't do that with Maury. You had to look for him, which is why he was so elusive.

You should also be aware of the risks involved with the hook. Your body's momentum can easily pull you too far past the base or make you miss it completely. Catching your spikes on the bag is another danger. Do this, and you can tear or break something. Keeping your knees slightly bent and both feet sideways offers you some protection. (See Figure 8-13.)

To avoid injury while sliding, try to hold both hands in the air. Many major league ballplayers hold a clump of dirt in each hand to remind them to hold their hands high on the basepaths. (Don't ask me how *that* custom started.) Wearing sliding gloves is a further precaution. And always remember the four cardinal rules of sliding:

- ✔ When in doubt, slide.
- ✔ Never be tentative (half-hearted slides are the most dangerous).
- ✔ It is always better to slide early rather than late.
- ✔ Never slide head first into home or when breaking up the double play (you don't want to expose your head and neck on contact plays).

National Baseball Hall of Fame Library Cooperstown, N.Y.

Figure 8-13:
Joe Morgan
himself
demonstrates
a hook slide
against the
master
hook slider
Maury
Wills.

Breaking Up Is Hard to Do: Preventing the Double Play

In the final game of the 1975 World Series, the Cincinnati Reds and I were losing 3-0 to the Boston Red Sox in the top of the sixth. Pete Rose led off that inning with a single against Red Sox left-hander Bill Lee. With one out, our catcher Johnny Bench hit a sure double play ball to Boston shortstop Rick Burelson. Burleson shoveled the ball to his second baseman Denny Doyle to start the double play. Doyle attempted to get a throw off to first, but Pete barreled into him just as the ball was leaving his hand. Though Pete was out, his hard (but perfectly legal) slide forced Doyle to throw wildly into the Boston dugout. Bench was safe; the inning, which should have been over, continued. The next batter, Tony Perez, hit a two-run homer that propelled us toward a 4-3 win and a world championship. Our comeback in that game started with Pete's slide.

Anytime you break up a double play, you are snatching an out from the box score; you are giving your team an extra opportunity to score and win. To execute this maneuver, you must know how to slide properly. You should also know the rules governing the play:

- ✔ You must be on the ground when you make contact with the fielder.
- ✔ You must be able to reach the bag with some part of your body during your slide.

As the runner trying to break up the double play, your assignment is to get to second base as quickly as you can while making a good, hard slide. You're not looking to hurt anyone, so forget about any rolling blocks. (I had one thrown at me in 1968. It crumpled my knee and put me on the disabled list for the entire season. Inflicting that sort of injury is not your objective.) The idea is to either knock the pivot man (either the second baseman or short-stop) off-balance or disturb his timing (by making him leap or hurry his throw).

You can start your takeout with your normal straight-leg slide. However, try to hook your top leg's foot under the pivotman's striding foot to knock it out from under him. Keep your weight on your bottom leg. When you take your usual slide, you are aiming for the base. Here, your objective is to reach the fielder. Slide on whatever side of the bag he pivots from.

Though you don't have to hit the pivotman to break up the double play, you should try to do exactly that. This potential collision forces him to jump out of the way. Minimize the chance of injury by sliding with your spikes held below the pivotman's knee. Should you make contact, it will be on his shins or lower, where there is nothing rigid to break. Avoid hitting any fielder from the knee up.

Collision: When the Catcher Blocks Home Plate

Catchers have this thing about opposing baserunners; they don't like to see them sliding across home plate. So the good catchers will do everything they can to stop you. Catchers are usually built like small condominiums. They wear heavy protective gear, and many of them enjoy a good crunch at the plate. Getting through them can be a daunting task, but you have to do it whenever you are carrying a run home. Take the easy route whenever it is available. If you can see the plate and know you can touch it, launch into your slide.

However, if the catcher has the plate completely blocked, you have to barrel through him. There is no elegant way to do this. Just get low so you have your center of gravity working with you and keep your head away from the point of contact.

The catcher can block the plate only if he possesses the ball. If he blocks it without having the ball, he is guilty of obstruction. The umpire will declare you safe at home after the collision.

Profile of a Thief: Stealing

All great base stealers have a love of larceny. They derive joy from picking the opposing team's pockets, especially in pressure situations. To excel as a base thief, you have to be cocky. When you get to first base, your body language and demeanor should announce, "I am stealing and there is nothing anyone can do to stop me!" You have to embrace the role of intimidator.

Base stealers make things happen. During that 1975 World Series, Boston pitcher Reggie Cleveland walked me to open the sixth inning of the fifth game. He threw over to first base seven times before throwing a strike to the batter Johnny Bench. Then he made four more throws to first. When he delivered another pitch, I took off for second but Johnny fouled off the ball. What did Cleveland do then? He made five more tosses to first. This didn't bother me a bit. Cleveland was concentrating more on me instead of the batter, which is precisely what I wanted. On Cleveland's next pitch, Bench singled and then Tony Perez came up to hit a three-run homer. The lesson here is that you don't need to steal a base to help your team; just the threat of a theft can be enough to rattle a pitcher into making a critical mistake. If the pitcher is playing cat-and-mouse with you, he can't possibly put his full focus on the hitter.

Stealing a lot of bases with your team far ahead or behind doesn't mark you as a great thief. It's easy to steal in those situations. The opposing pitcher is paying little attention to you. He's either cruising to a win or concentrating solely on getting your teammates out. Far more valuable are the runners who steal in the early innings to ignite their offenses or during the late portions of a close game.

A good base thief should be successful on at least 75 percent of his stolen base attempts. If your percentage is below that, you are probably hurting your team.

What every base thief should know: How to read the pitcher

Ninety percent of all stolen bases come off the pitcher rather than the catcher. If you waited until the pitch reached home plate before you stole, you would be thrown out 95 percent of the time. However, if you get a good jump as the pitcher delivers the ball, there is almost nothing a catcher can do to get you out, even if you aren't blessed with exceptional speed. In the fifth game of the 1997 World Series, Marlins first baseman Darren Daulton caught the Cleveland pitcher napping and stole second base. Darren has undergone nine knee operations, which have left him nearly immobile. Yet, he got such a good lead that he was able to steal second against Sandy Alomar, one of the best throwing catchers in the business. Had the Indians' pitcher been holding close at first, Darren never would have even attempted a steal.

Base stealers should study the opposing pitcher the moment he takes the mound. See if he has two distinct motions: one when he is going to throw home and another when he tosses the ball first to hold a runner on. Watch the pitcher throw to the plate from the stretch. Note what body parts he moves first and whether he does anything special when he throws to first base. See if he sets his feet up differently on his pick-off move. Try to detect any quirk that will reveal the pitcher's intentions.

Good pitchers are often the easiest to steal on. Erratic pitchers typically use different release points from pitch to pitch (which is why they are erratic). You never know when they are going to let go of the ball. The better pitchers have purer mechanics. They establish a rhythm and stick to it. Boston's Pedro Martinez will do the same thing to get to his release point on nearly every pitch. So you may be able to spot some clue in his motion. After you have a pitcher's pattern down, take off for second the moment he moves toward his release point. This might be a hand gesture or some slight motion with the leg. Even a pitcher's eyes can fall into a pattern. Many pitchers will take a quick glance toward first before throwing home; when they don't sneak a look toward you, they are throwing to your base.

You can also key off pitchers by observing their body language. Watch the pitcher's rear leg. If it moves off the rubber, the throw is coming toward you. To throw to the plate, every pitcher must close either his hip or his front shoulder. He also must bend his rear knee while rocking onto his back foot. After the pitcher does any of these things, the rules state he can no longer throw to your base. You should immediately break for the next bag. If the pitcher breaks his motion to throw toward any base, the umpire will (or should) call a balk. A balk allows you and any other baserunners to advance.

If you are on first base, left-handed pitchers are traditionally harder to steal on than right-handers because the lefty looks directly at the you when he assumes the set position. However, this also means *you* are looking directly at him so he is easier to read — if you know what to look for. Scrutinize his glove, the ball, and his motion. If a *southpaw* (a left-hander) tilts back his upper body, he is probably throwing to first; a turning of the shoulder to the right usually precedes a pitch to the plate. When he bends his rear leg, he is most likely preparing to push off toward home.

When a righty is on the mound, observe his right heel and shoulder. He cannot pitch unless his right foot touches the pitching rubber. Throwing to first requires him to pivot on that foot. If he lifts his right heel, get back to the bag. An open right shoulder also indicates a throw to first.

Lead — and runs will follow

Base thieves can choose between a stationary or walking lead. Lou Brock, the former Cardinal outfielder, used a *walking lead.* Lou was faster than most players, but he wasn't especially quick out of his first few steps (most taller players find it difficult to accelerate from a dead stop). He would walk two or three small steps to gain momentum before taking off toward second base. If it takes you a few steps to accelerate, this is the lead for you. A walking lead does, however, have one disadvantage: A good pitcher can stop you from moving by simply holding the ball. If you continue to stroll, the pitcher can pick you off.

For that reason, I preferred the stationary lead. The pitcher can still hold the ball, but I'm not moving anyway until he makes his first move to the plate. Whichever baserunning lead you choose, use the same one whether you are stealing a base or not. Set up the same way on every lead. You don't want to telegraph your intentions to the pitcher. He's watching you for clues as closely as you are watching him.

Stealing third

Stealing third is generally easier than stealing second. You can take a bigger lead at second than at first without drawing many throws. You can also take off from second before the pitcher releases the ball; when stealing from first, you have to wait for the pitcher to begin his motion. (The trick here is to time the pitcher's motion so you can leave just before he starts to the plate.)

Pitchers generally find it more difficult to pick runners off second than at first; the timing between the pitcher and his fielder must be precise. To catch you at second, either the second baseman or the shortstop has to cover or *cheat* (lean) toward the bag; this leaning opens up a hole for the batter. Alert coaches let you know when the fielders are sneaking in on you.

If a right-handed hitter is at-bat, the catcher must throw over or around him to get the ball to third. (Never steal third with a lefty at the plate unless you get such a good jump that even a perfect throw will not nail you.)

Despite the obvious advantages for the runner, stealing third is not a good gamble unless your success rate is 90 percent or better. Because you're already in scoring position at second, getting caught or picked off can devastate your offense. Stealing third when your team is more than two runs behind is foolish. (And making the first or last out at third, whether it be stealing or simply running the bases, is considered a big mistake.)

The only reason to steal third with less than two outs in a close ball game is so you can score on a fly ball or ground out. However, if you're a proficient base thief, it does makes sense to steal third with two outs; being on third rather than second in that situation offers you nine more opportunities to score. What are they? Memorize this list and dazzle your friends with your baseball erudition:

Nine Two-Out Events That Can Score You from Third (But Won't Score You from Second)

1. A balk

2. An infield hit

3. A wild pitch

4. A passed ball

5. A one-base infield error

6. A fielder's choice (where the hitter and any other baserunners are safe)

7. Baserunning interference

8. Catcher's interference

9. A steal of home

Stealing home

Speaking of stealing home (how's that for a segue?), this is rarely a good percentage play. It is best to attempt it during the late innings of a close, low-scoring ball game with two men out and a weak hitter at the plate. Obviously, this is the one base you steal entirely on the pitcher (the catcher makes no throw on this play). Your best victims are pitchers with unusually slow deliveries or long wind-ups. Having a right-handed batter at the plate when you attempt to steal home provides you with two advantages. The hitter obstructs the catcher's view of you at third. If he remains in the box until just before you arrive at home, he can prevent the catcher from getting in position for the tag.

Delayed, double, and fake steals

With the delayed steal, slide-step into your regular lead when the pitcher releases the ball and then count 1-2-3. This should slow your takeoff just long enough to persuade the catcher and infielders that you aren't stealing. Race for second after you count. (You may also first break out of your lead and return to first to camouflage your intentions.) Catchers have no way of knowing who will cover second base on a delayed steal until either the second baseman or shortstop moves toward the bag. If you've caught those two infielders napping and no one covers second, the catcher has to hold onto the ball or he will throw it into the outfield.

Double steals are possible whenever two bases are occupied. With runners on first and second, this play is nothing more than two straight steals occurring simultaneously. With only one out, the catcher will probably try to erase the lead runner heading to third. With two out, he may go after the slower of the two base stealers.

JOE SAYS

Stealing: Know when to say no

The 1975 World Series serves as a great setting for a base-stealing lesson. In the bottom of the ninth inning of the fourth game, I was batting with our center fielder Cesar Geronimo on second and Pete Rose on first. We were trailing, 5-4. Right-hander Luis Tiant was pitching for Boston. I was trying to concentrate on Tiant, always a difficult task because he had a thousand different herky-jerky moves and hesitations with which he distracted hitters.

Geronimo suddenly raced toward third just as Tiant went into his delivery. His unexpected movement pulled my attention away from the pitcher for a split second. By the time I looked back toward Tiant, the ball was nearly down the heart of the plate. A perfect pitch to drive for extra bases. However, that momentary lapse of concentration left me with little time to swing. My weak, late swing produced an inning-ending, rally-killing pop-up. That was the best pitch I had seen all night. I blew it.

However, Cesar should not have been running. He was already in scoring position, we were trailing by a run, and Tiant was tiring (he threw an arm-wringing 163 pitches in that game). Given those circumstances, a base runner has to give his team's number three hitter — usually an RBI man — a chance to drive him in. To be a great base stealer, you must be aggressive, but you also have to know when to throw on the brakes for the good of the team.

With runners on first and third, double steals become more complex. Imagine you are the runner on third. Your teammate on first should break full-out for second as the pitcher delivers the ball. You move down the line toward home. Halt as the catcher receives the pitch. Don't move until the catcher commits to throwing the runner out at second. Be alert in case he fakes a toss to the bag and instead throws to his pitcher, who will fire back the ball for a play at the plate. The throw's *trajectory* should tell you if it is going to second base or to the pitcher (the throw is going to be higher if it is going all the way to second base, so hesitate long enough to see this). Dash home as soon as the second-base-bound throw leaves the catcher's hand.

If you are the runner on first for this play, helping your teammate at third to score is your primary goal. You may break for second while the pitcher is in his set position. Should your movement distract the pitcher, he may balk (see Chapter 3 for details in the balk); both runners advance one base. Attract a throw to first, and you can force a run-down. While you jockey to elude the tag, the runner on third can score.

Fake steals open the infield for the batter at the plate. You can bluff the opposition by taking two and a half quick strides out of your primary lead before coming to a halt. Your movement should draw the infielders out of position (as one of them comes over to cover second).

Chapter 9
Joe's Baseball Playbook

- -

In This Chapter

▶ Situations with singles

▶ Situations with doubles or triples

▶ Where to go on bunts

▶ What to do on pop flies

- -

*W*e could do an entire book devoted to defensive situations and strategies. These 24 plays are the ones you encounter in almost every game. It doesn't matter whether you coach or play in Little League, high school, college, a professional league, or for your company's softball nine, these are the basic plays.

If you want to know more about the defensive role of each player on the field as well as some of the vocabulary used to describe these plays, be sure to check out Chapter 7. To read the diagrams that follow, here is all that you need to know:

Symbol	Meaning
ⓟ	Pitcher
ⓒ	Catcher
①ᴮ	First baseman
②ᴮ	Second baseman
ⓢˢ	Shortstop
③ᴮ	Third baseman
ⓡꜰ	Right fielder
ⓒꜰ	Center fielder
ⓛꜰ	Left fielder
⟶	Path of a player
------⟶	Path of the ball

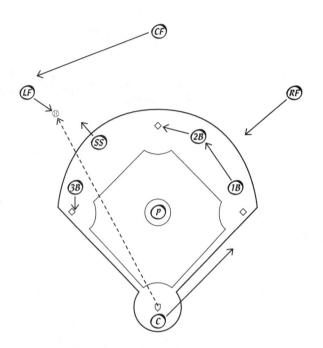

Single to left: bases empty

Catcher: Cover first base in case the runner takes a too-wide turn.

Pitcher: Back up any throw to second base.

First baseman: Check that the batter touches first base and then back up the incoming throw to second base.

Second baseman: Cover second base.

Shortstop: Pursue the ball; then line up between the left fielder and second base to take the cut-off throw.

Third baseman: Cover third base.

Left fielder: Field the ball and throw it to the cut-off man (the shortstop). If the shortstop is out of position, throw to second base.

Center fielder: Run to back up the left fielder.

Right fielder: Move toward the infield to cover a poor throw from the left fielder to the second baseman.

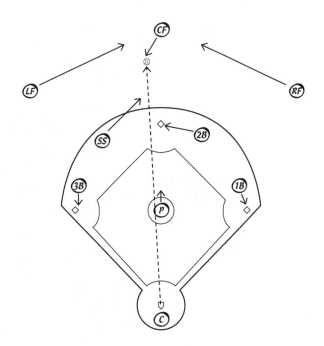

Single to center: bases empty

Catcher: Cover home plate.

Pitcher: Stay near the mound and back up any throw to second base.

First baseman: Make sure the batter touches first base, and then cover the base inside.

Second baseman: Go to second base to take the throw.

Shortstop: Go out to be the cut-off man for second base.

Third baseman: Cover third base.

Left fielder: Back up the center fielder.

Center fielder: Field the ball and throw it to second base.

Right fielder: Back up the center fielder.

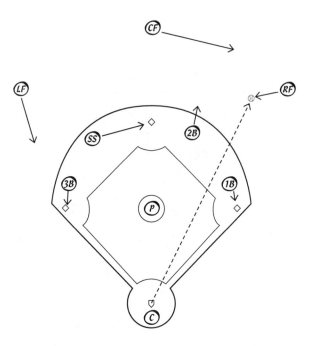

Single to right: bases empty

Catcher: Cover home plate.

Pitcher: Follow the flight of the ball and then decide where to back up (usually second base).

First baseman: Check that the batter touches first base; then cover the base inside.

Second baseman: Pursue the ball; then take the cut-off position between the right fielder and second base.

Shortstop: Cover second base.

Third baseman: Cover third.

Left fielder: Move toward the infield in case the right fielder makes a bad throw to second base.

Center fielder: Back up the right fielder.

Right fielder: Field the hit and make the cut-off throw to the second baseman. If the second baseman is out of position, throw it to second base.

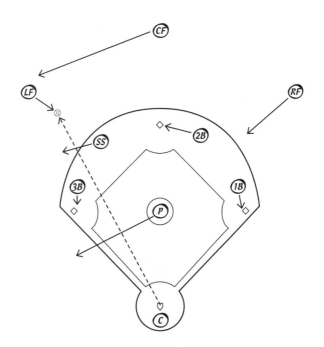

Single to left: runner on first, or runners on first and third

Catcher: Cover home plate.

Pitcher: Follow the flight of the ball and then decide where to back up (usually third base).

First baseman: Make sure the batter touches first base, and then cover the base inside.

Second baseman: Cover second base.

Shortstop: Line up between the left fielder and third base for the cut-off throw.

Third baseman: Back up the shortstop (but also cover third).

Left fielder: Field the ball and throw it to the cut-off man (the shortstop). If the shortstop is out of position, throw it to third base.

Center fielder: Back up the left fielder.

Right fielder: Move toward the infield to field any bad throws.

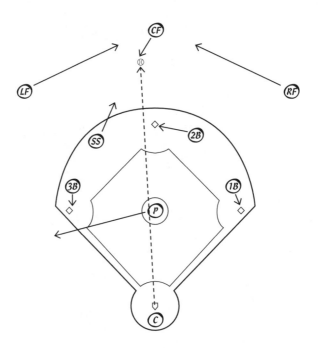

Single to center: runner on first, or runners on first and third

Catcher: Cover home plate.

Pitcher: Back up the throw to third base.

First baseman: Check that the batter touches first base; then cover the bag inside.

Second baseman: Cover second.

Shortstop: Line up for the cut-off throw between the center fielder and third base.

Third baseman: Cover third base.

Left fielder: Back up the center fielder.

Center fielder: Field the hit and throw it to the cut-off man (the shortstop). If the shortstop is out of position, throw it to third base.

Right fielder: Back up the center fielder.

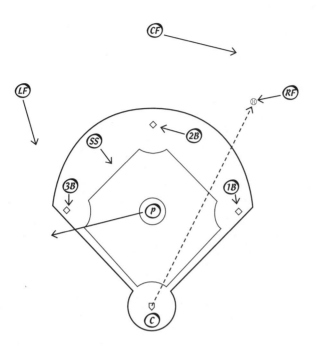

Single to right: runner on first or runners on first and third

Catcher: Cover home plate.

Pitcher: Back up third base.

First baseman: Make sure that the batter touches first base, and then cover the base inside.

Second baseman: Cover second base.

Shortstop: Line up for the cut-off throw between the right fielder and third base.

Third baseman: Cover third base.

Left fielder: Back up the throw to third base.

Center fielder: Back up the right fielder.

Right fielder: Field the hit and throw it to the cut-off man (the shortstop).

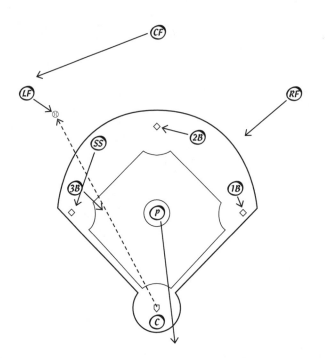

Single to left: runner on second, runners on first and second, or bases loaded

Catcher: Cover home plate.

Pitcher: Back up the throw at home plate.

First baseman: Cover first base.

Second baseman: Cover second base.

Shortstop: Cover third base.

Third baseman: Take the cut-off position for a throw to home plate.

Left fielder: Field the hit and throw it to the cut-off man (the third baseman).

Center fielder: Back up the left fielder.

Right fielder: Back up any throw to second.

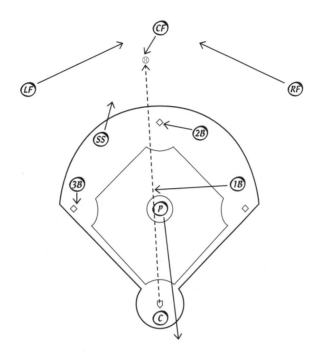

Single to center: runner on second, runners on first and second, or bases loaded

Catcher: Cover home plate.

Pitcher: Back up the catcher at home plate.

First baseman: Take the cut-off position near the mound for a throw to home plate.

Second baseman: Cover second base.

Shortstop: Take the cut-off position for a throw to third base.

Third baseman: Cover third base.

Left fielder: Back up the center fielder and then become a quarterback. Tell the center fielder where the throw is going.

Center fielder: Field the hit, listen for the left or right fielder's instructions, throw to one of the two cut-off men: the shortstop (if the play is at third base) or the first baseman (if the play is at the plate).

Right fielder: Back up the center fielder and then become a quarterback. Tell the center fielder where the throw is going.

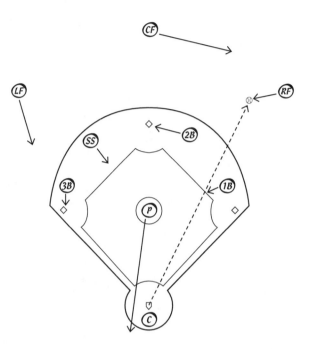

Single to right: runner on second, runners on first and second, or bases loaded

Catcher: Cover home plate.

Pitcher: Stand outside the base paths between third base and home plate, watch the play evolve, and back up the throw (usually at home plate).

First baseman: Take the cut-off position for the throw to home plate.

Second baseman: Cover second base.

Shortstop: Take the cut-off position for the throw to third base.

Third baseman: Cover third base.

Left fielder: Come toward third base in order to be able to help out at third or second base.

Center fielder: Back up the right fielder and tell him where to throw.

Right fielder: Field the ball, listen for the center fielder's instructions, throw to the appropriate cut-off man: the shortstop (on a play at third base) or the first baseman (on a play at home plate).

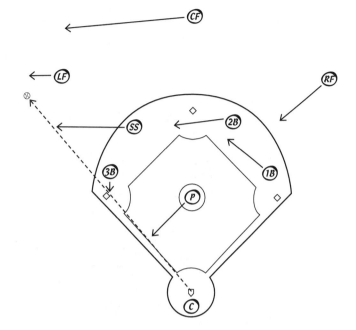

Double, possible triple down the left field line: bases empty

Catcher: Cover home plate.

Pitcher: Back up third base.

First baseman: Make sure the batter touches first base; then trail the runner to second base.

Second baseman: Go to the trail position behind the shortstop. Stay near second base.

Shortstop: Take the cut-off position down the left field line.

Third baseman: Cover third base.

Left fielder: Field the hit and make the cut-off throw to the shortstop.

Center fielder: Back up the left fielder.

Right fielder: Back up any throw to second base.

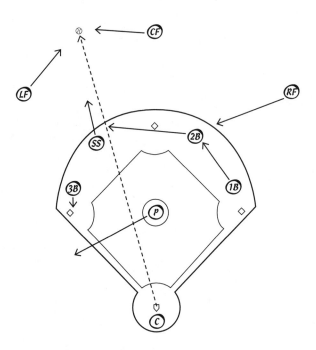

Double, possible triple to the left center field gap: bases empty

Catcher: Cover home plate.

Pitcher: Back up third base.

First baseman: Make sure the batter touches first base and then trail him to second.

Second baseman: Go to the trail position behind the shortstop.

Third baseman: Cover third base.

Shortstop: Line up with third base and the fielder for the cut-off throw.

Left fielder: Back up the center fielder.

Center fielder: Field the hit and then make the cut-off throw to the shortstop.

Right fielder: Back up any throw to second base.

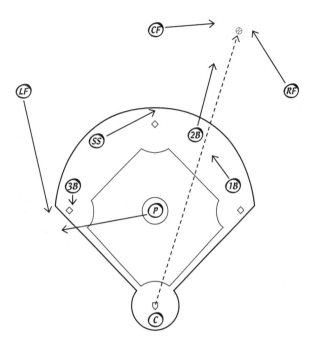

Double, possible triple to the right center field gap: bases empty

Catcher: Cover home plate.

Pitcher: Back up third base.

First baseman: Check that the batter touches first base, and then trail him to second base.

Second baseman: Line up with third base and the center fielder for the cut-off throw.

Shortstop: Get to the trail position behind the second baseman.

Third baseman: Cover third base.

Left fielder: Back up any throw to third base.

Center fielder: Field the hit and make the cut-off throw to the second baseman.

Right fielder: Back up the center fielder.

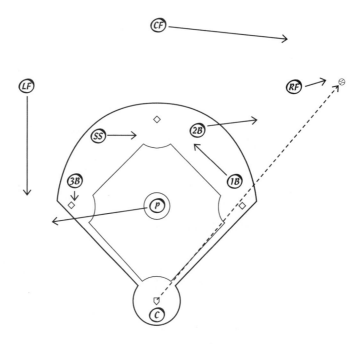

Double, possible triple down the right field line: bases empty

Catcher: Cover home plate.

Pitcher: Back up third base.

First baseman: Check that the batter touches first base, and then trail him to second base.

Second baseman: Line up with third base and the fielder for the cut-off throw.

Shortstop: Get to the trail position behind the second baseman.

Third baseman: Cover third base.

Left fielder: Back up any throw to third base.

Center fielder: Back up the right fielder.

Right fielder: Field the hit and then make the cut-off throw to the second baseman.

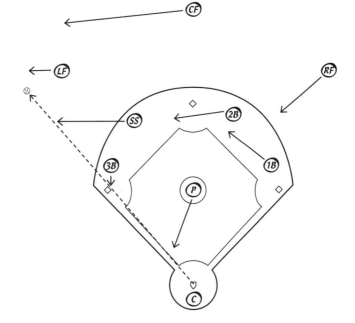

Double, possible triple down the left field line: runners on base

Catcher: Cover home plate.

Pitcher: Stand between home plate and third base (closer to home), watch the play evolve, and back up the throw.

First baseman: Check that the batter touches first base, and then trail the runner to second base.

Second baseman: Get to the trail position behind the shortstop. Let the shortstop know where to throw.

Shortstop: Line up between home plate and the fielder for the cut-off throw.

Third baseman: Cover third base.

Left fielder: Field the hit and make the cut-off throw to the shortstop.

Center fielder: Back up the left fielder.

Right fielder: Back up any throw to second base.

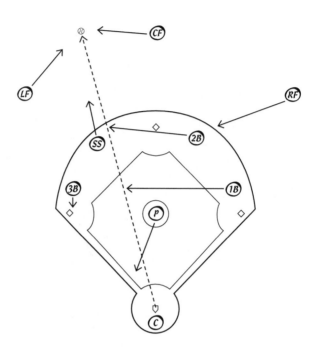

Double, possible triple to the left center field gap: runners on base

Catcher: Cover home plate.

Pitcher: Stand between home plate and third base (closer to home), watch the play evolve, and back up the throw.

First baseman: Take the cut-off position for a throw to the plate.

Second baseman: Get to the trail position behind the shortstop. Let the shortstop know where to throw.

Shortstop: Line up with home plate and the fielder for the cut-off throw.

Third baseman: Cover third base.

Left fielder: Back up the center fielder.

Center fielder: Field the hit and make the cut-off throw to the shortstop.

Right fielder: Back up any throw to second base.

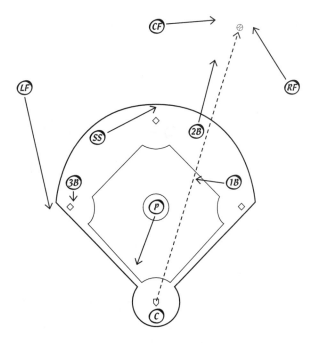

Double, possible triple to the right center field gap: runners on base

Catcher: Cover home plate.

Pitcher: Stand between home plate and third base (closer to home), watch the play evolve, and back up the throw.

First baseman: Take the cut-off position for a throw to the plate.

Second baseman: Line up with home plate and the fielder for the cut-off throw.

Shortstop: Get to the trail position behind the second baseman. Tell the second baseman where to make the throw.

Third baseman: Cover third base.

Left fielder: Back up any throw to third base.

Center fielder: Field the hit and make the cut-off throw to the second baseman.

Right fielder: Back up the center fielder.

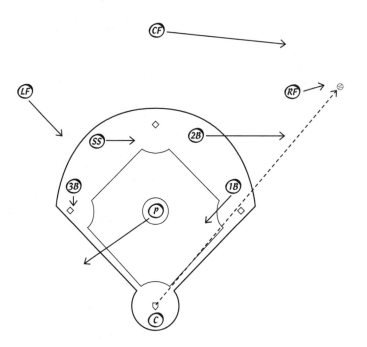

Double, possible triple down the right field line: runners on base

Catcher: Cover home plate.

Pitcher: Stand outside the base paths halfway between home plate and third base, watch the play evolve, and back up the throw.

First baseman: Take the cut-off position for a throw to the plate.

Second baseman: Line up with home plate and the fielder for the cut-off throw.

Shortstop: Get behind the second baseman. Tell the second baseman where to make the throw. Be the cut-off man for a play at third base.

Left fielder: Back up any throw to second base or third base.

Center fielder: Back up the right fielder.

Right fielder: Field the hit and make the cut-off throw to the second baseman.

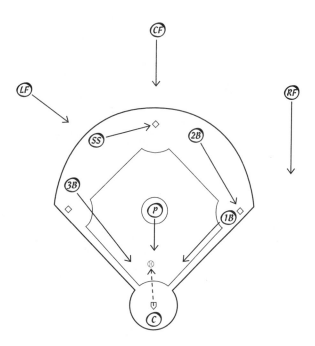

Sacrifice bunt: runner on first

Catcher: Tell the infielders where to throw.

Pitcher: Cover the middle of the infield. If you field the ball, listen to the catcher's instructions, and then throw to the appropriate base.

First baseman: After holding the runner on first base, charge and cover the right side of the infield. If you field the ball, listen for the catcher's instructions, and then throw to the appropriate base.

Second baseman: Cover first base.

Shortstop: Cover second base.

Third baseman: Charge toward home plate and cover the left side of the infield. (Be prepared to retreat quickly to third base to prevent the runner from advancing there.) If you field the ball, listen to the catcher's instructions, and then throw to the appropriate base.

Left fielder: Come toward the infield in order to back up poor throws.

Center fielder: Back up any throw to second base.

Right fielder: Back up any throw to first base.

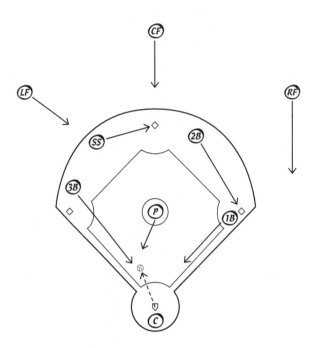

Sacrifice bunt: runners on first and second, the infield goes for the out at first

Catcher: Tell the infielders where the throw is going.

Pitcher: Cover the third base line. If you field the ball, listen to the catcher's instructions and then throw to the appropriate base.

First baseman: Cover the right side of the infield. If you field the ball, listen for the catcher's instructions, and then throw to the appropriate base.

Second baseman: Cover first base.

Shortstop: Cover second base.

Third baseman: Charge and cover the left side of the infield. If you field the ball, listen to the catcher's instructions, and then throw to the appropriate base.

Left fielder: Back up any throw to second base or third base.

Center fielder: Back up any throw to second base.

Right fielder: Back up any throw to first base.

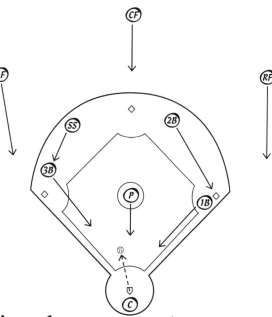

Wheel play: batter puts down a sacrifice bunt with runners on first and second, the defense goes for the force out at third

Catcher: Tell the infielders where the throw is going. (Catchers must remember that no one is covering second on this play.)

Pitcher: The shortstop should break for third base before you deliver the pitch. Cover the middle of the infield. If you field the ball, listen to the catcher's instructions, and then throw to the appropriate base.

First baseman: Cover the right side of the infield. If you field the ball, listen for the catcher's instructions, and then throw to the appropriate base.

Second baseman: Cover first base.

Shortstop: Get behind the lead runner's right shoulder and break for third base as the pitcher sets.

Third baseman: Charge and cover the left side of the infield. If you field the ball, listen to the catcher's instructions, and then throw to the appropriate base.

Left fielder: Back up any throw to third base.

Center fielder: Come toward the infield to cover second base.

Right fielder: Back up any throw to first base.

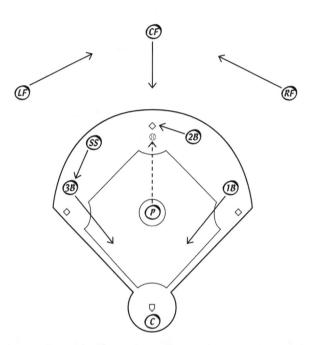

Wheel play fake: runners on first and second with a pick-off play going to second

Catcher: Cover home plate.

Pitcher: As the shortstop breaks for third base, make your pick-off throw to second base.

First baseman: Cover the right side of the infield as if the wheel play were on.

Second baseman: Fake a step toward first base, and then break for second base for the pick-off throw.

Shortstop: Position yourself behind the runner's right shoulder. Break for third base as if the wheel play were on.

Third baseman: Charge and cover the left side of the infield.

Left fielder: Back up the center fielder.

Center fielder: Back up the throw to second base.

Right fielder: Back up the center fielder.

For the wheel play fake to work, everyone must go about their initial assignments as if the play is actually on.

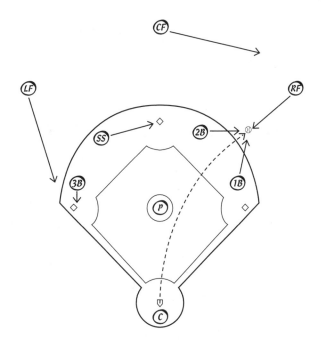

Pop fly to shallow right field

Catcher: If the bases are empty, back up a possible throw to first base; otherwise, cover home plate.

Pitcher: Call for a fielder if the ball is in the infield proper; if not, cover first.

First baseman: Call for a catch if you feel you can make the play; however, you must back off if the right fielder or the second baseman calls for the ball.

Second baseman: Call for a catch, but back off if the right fielder calls you off.

Shortstop: Cover second base.

Third baseman: Cover third base.

Left fielder: Back up any throw to third base.

Center fielder: Back up the right fielder.

Right fielder: Call for the catch if you feel you can make the play. All fielders must yield to you. (The right fielder is king on this play, but stay alert even if he calls you off. If he misses or bobbles the ball, you may be able to glove it for an out.)

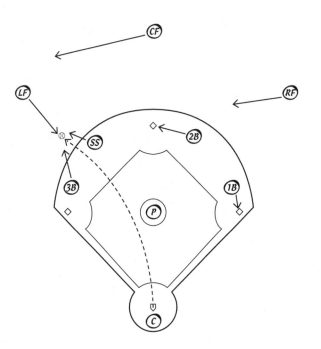

Pop fly to shallow left field

Catcher: If the bases are empty, back up a possible throw to third base; otherwise, cover home plate.

Pitcher: Call a fielder if the ball is close to the infield; if not, cover third base.

First baseman: Cover first base.

Second baseman: Cover second base.

Shortstop: Call for the ball if you think you can make the play. Give way if the left fielder calls for it.

Third baseman: Call for the catch if you think you can make the play. However, you must back off if the shortstop or left fielder calls you off.

Left fielder: Call for the ball if you think you can make the play. All other fielders must yield to you.

Center fielder: Back up the left fielder.

Right fielder: Back up any throw to second base.

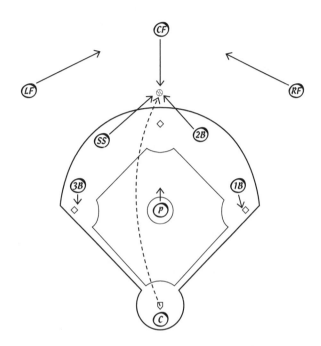

Pop fly to shallow center field

Catcher: Cover home plate.

Pitcher: Direct the infielders. If the shortstop and second baseman both go for the ball, cover second base if the first baseman is unable to do so.

First baseman: Cover first base unless the shortstop and second baseman both go for the ball. Then you must cover second.

Second baseman: Call for the ball if you think you can make the play. Back off if either the center fielder calls for it or if the shortstop calls for it before you do. Either you or the shortstop must retreat to cover second base.

Shortstop: Call for the ball if you think you can make the play. Give way if the center fielder calls for it or if the second baseman calls for it before you do. Either you or the second baseman must retreat to cover second base.

Third baseman: Cover third base.

Left fielder: Back up the center fielder.

Center fielder: Call for the ball if you think you can make the play. All other fielders must yield to you.

Right fielder: Back up the center fielder.

Part III
From the Little Leagues to the Major Leagues: Organized Baseball

The 5th Wave   By Rich Tennant

"Can I use it coach? My dad made it for me from an old telephone pole."

In this part . . .

Baseball is everywhere — you just have to know where to find it. In this part, we introduce you to all the various aspects of organized baseball. Weighing and comparing player performances is one of the great pleasures of baseball, so we also show you how to understand the measurements that do so — baseball statistics. Also in this part, Sparky Anderson joins us to show you how a major league manager's thought process works. Finally, we explain the League Championship Series and the World Series on the major league level.

Chapter 10

T-Ball to College Baseball and Everything in Between

* *

In This Chapter

▶ Getting started with T-Ball

▶ Discovering youth baseball leagues

▶ Playing baseball at the college level

* *

*W*hether you're 5 or 55, male or female, you don't have to regard baseball merely as a spectator sport. If you want to compete in an informal atmosphere, your local parks department can make a baseball diamond available for pick-up games. (You should always reserve field time in advance, especially if you have a number of leagues competing in your town.) Throughout the United States, thousands of baseball leagues and associations also offer nonprofessional players of all ages and genders an opportunity for organized competition.

The league you or your child joins does not have to be affiliated with **USA Baseball** (520-327-9700), but if it is you are assured that the organization conforms to a rigorous standard. USA Baseball is the national governing body of amateur baseball. Its members include the Little League, the Amateur Athletic Union, the National High School Coaches Association, PONY Baseball, the Police Athletic League, the YMCA, and the NCAA. USA Baseball is also responsible for picking (with the help of a national network of college coaches) and training the U.S. Olympic baseball team. Team USA players who have gone on to star in the majors include Mark McGwire, Will Clark, Robin Ventura, Nomar Garciaparra, and Charles Johnson. In the land of Blue Jays and Expos, **Baseball Canada** (316-267-3372) is the prominent amateur organization.

A Good Place to Start: T-Ball

T-Ball is baseball's version of miniature golf. The baseball is served on a batting tee, bases are never more than 60 feet apart, and everything else is scaled down, so that children (usually eight years old and under) can experience the joys of the National Pastime without risking physical harm. The **T-Ball USA Association** (212-254-7911) in New York City does not run any leagues or teams of its own, but it does assist many of leading amateur organizations with their T-Ball programs.

This nonprofit association also runs clinics to teach coaches and parents the rudiments of baseball. For more information about the program, pick up a copy of *The Official T-Ball USA Family Guide to T-Ball Baseball* (Masters Press).

If You're Looking for a League

Little League Baseball (717-326-1921) is played in all 50 states and 87 countries. With three million participants, one million volunteers, and 7,000 leagues, this is the world's largest organized youth sports program. Leagues are required to play a schedule of at least 12 games. Does Little League baseball provide a first step to the big leagues? It is estimated that 80 percent of all major league players played Little League baseball. Current major leaguers who have participated in the Little League World Series, held each year in Williamsport, Pennsylvania, include Gary Sheffield, Derek Bell, Be Dan Wilson, Charlie Hayes, and Wilson Alvarez.

The **Babe Ruth League** (609-695-1434) operates in 48 states (Hawaii and Alaska are the exceptions). Founded in 1951, it is currently composed of over 870,000 players on 43,800 teams in 6,200 leagues. Five- and six-year-olds in this league play T-Ball; seven- and eight-year-olds play with bases 60 feet (18.2m) apart and hit against a slow pitching machine or a coach. At 9 or 10 they are ready to face some live pitching. Babe Ruth League players will not, however, compete on fields with major-league dimensions until they are 13, when they enter a prep program. Age classifications top out at 18. This league stresses player participation over winning and is famous for teaching the proper way to play the game. And Joe Morgan will tell you that reputation is well-deserved. He participated in the Oakland chapter of the Babe Ruth League as a member of the Qwik Way Drive-In team.

Over 360,000 players on 24,000 teams in 11 states participate in **Dixie Baseball** (903-927-2255), the leading youth baseball program in the South. Five divisions compose the association's baseball programs. The Youth T-Ball division caters to children age eight and under. The oldest division, Dixie Majors Baseball, is for players age 15 to 18. Championship tournaments are held for the four oldest divisions during the first week of August.

Competition is probably fiercest in leagues sponsored by the **Amateur Athletic Union** (407-363-6170), which boasts 50 associations in all 50 states. Like professional clubs, many member teams will travel out of their locales to play games. Players participate in 12 divisions with age limits ranging from 9 to 20. Amateur Athletic Union championships are decided in tournaments featuring double-pool play. Teams are seeded before the first round. Winners go on to play in the National Championship Tournament; losers participate in a consolation bracket.

Other bona fide youth baseball organizations include

- **All American Amateur Baseball Association** in Zanesville, Ohio (614-453-8531)

- **American Legion Baseball** in Indianapolis, Indiana (317-630-1213)

- **Dizzy Dean Baseball** in Eupora, Missouri (601-258-7626)

- **Hap Dumont Baseball** in Wichita, Kansas (316-721-1779)

- **National Association of Police Athletic Leagues** in North Palm Beach, Florida (561-844-1823)

- **PONY Baseball** in Washington, Pennsylvania (412-225-1060)

- **Reviving Baseball In Inner Cities** (RBI) in New York, New York (212-339-7800)

- **U.S. Amateur Baseball Association** in Edmonds, Washington (206-776-7130)

- **Youth Baseball Athletic League** in Palo Alto, California (Fax: 415-843-1316)

Your child and the child within you can compete in the **National Amateur Baseball Federation,** which has 350,000 participants in 85 franchises across the country. Founded in 1914, this is the only all-volunteer amateur baseball organization in the United States. For younger players, classifications advance from Rookie (10 and under) to Senior level (18 and under). Players between the ages of 19 and 22 compete in the college classification. If you are over 22, you can recapture your youth at the Majors level, an unlimited classification. Many former college players and professionals who have reacquired their amateur status compete in this division. Member teams play anywhere from 30 to 100 games in local competition. The best of these teams participate in round-robin championship tournaments scheduled between mid-July and late August.

Two other organizations have unlimited classifications. The **American Amateur Baseball Congress** (616-781-2002) holds its August tournaments in seven divisions named for Hall of Famers: Roberto Clemente (eight and under), Willie Mays (10 and under), Pee Wee Reese (12 and under), Sandy Koufax (14 and under), Mickey Mantle (16 and under), Connie Mack (18 and under), and Stan Musial (unlimited). The **Continental Amateur Baseball Association** maintains competitive balance by spreading players out among 12 classifications (nine and under to unlimited). You can find out everything you need to know about this organization from its Web site (cababaseball.com).

From Big 10 to Ivy League: Collegiate Baseball

The first baseball game played between two colleges took place on July 1, 1859, when Amherst beat Pittsfield 73-32 (they thought they were playing football). Only 35 feet (10.6m) separated the pitcher from the batter, and the bases were a mere 60 feet (18.2m) apart. Few of the great college players of the late 1800s ever donned a major league uniform; most college men didn't consider baseball to be a respectable profession. However, the ascent of Christy Mathewson of Bucknell University, the elegant and erudite Hall of Fame pitcher for the New York Giants, considerably altered that attitude. Matty had been president of his class, a member of a literary society, and could simultaneously best ten opponents at chess. He demonstrated that one could play professional baseball without surrendering the title "gentleman." Largely due to his influence — as well as that of other turn-of-the century college stars who turned pro (such as Hall of Famers Eddie Collins and Harry Hooper), American campuses became incubators for major league talent.

Today, over two-thirds of all major league players have a college education. Collegiate baseball — which is intensely scrutinized by major league scouts — provides the perfect stage for any aspiring major leaguers to showcase their talents. The National Collegiate Athletic Association (NCAA), of course, is the Big Kahuna of the college game. Over 250 colleges — among them Mathewson's beloved Bucknell — compete in its 29 Division I conferences. Other NCAA college baseball squads play in either Division II or III. The NCAA Division I College World Series takes place during the first week of June. Both championship series for the other two divisions take place during the final week of May.

Chapter 11

The Minors and Other Leagues

In This Chapter

▶ A look at the American minor leagues

▶ Baseball in Japan and the rest of Asia

▶ Baseball in the tropics

▶ Beisbol Cuban style

▶ Required reading for minor league fans

Major league baseball isn't the only game in town (especially if you live in Helena, Montana, or Brisbane, Australia). Thousands of amateur and professional baseball leagues offer games to fans all over the globe. Japan, Mexico, Australia, Cuba, Venezuela, Italy, Korea, and China are just some of the countries that have embraced our National Pastime. And there is no way of knowing how many amateur leagues are flourishing through the world, but the number must easily reach five figures. Baseball Fever . . . it's catching and is spreading everywhere!

The American Minor Leagues

The minor leagues are where major league organizations send their young players to hone their talents before joining the big club. You will also find veteran ballplayers in the minors; they usually rehab their injuries in the minors before returning to the big leagues. Or their major league performances have slipped and they are trying to recapture the magic. Most minor league players have something to prove; the youngsters want to show their organizations that they are ready to advance, the declining veteran players are eager to convince some team that they can still compete in the major leagues.

Because nearly everyone on the field is highly motivated, you will see a hustling, often rollicking, brand of baseball in the minors. The level of skills on display varies from league to league, team to team, and player to player, but the level of thrills is consistently high from Triple-A ball down to the Rookie Leagues. Most minor leaguers have large dreams, but small salaries.

They play a game they love not for dollars, but with hope for glory. Their innocent, fervid aspirations will fail to touch your heart only if you don't possess one.

Minor league franchises — where are they?

In 1997, 19 minor leagues were operating under one umbrella organization: The National Association. The number of teams in these leagues may vary from year to year. Most minor league clubs are owned by major league organizations that absorb all of the operating costs. A few are independent entities, though even they have working agreements with clubs that underwrite much if not all of their overheads. At the end of the 1997 season, the National Association leagues and franchises were competing under the following alignments (1997 major league affiliation in parentheses):

Class AAA (Triple A)

- **The American Association:** Buffalo (Indians), Indianapolis (Reds), Iowa (Cubs), Louisville (Cardinals), Nashville (White Sox), New Orleans (Brewers), Oklahoma City (Rangers), and Omaha (Royals).

- **The International League:** Charlotte (Marlins), Columbus (Yankees), Norfolk (Mets), Ottawa (Expos), Pawtucket (Red Sox), Richmond (Braves), Rochester (Orioles), Scranton (Phillies), Syracuse (Blue Jays), and Toledo (Tigers).

- **Pacific Coast League:** Edmonton (Athletics), Salt Lake (Twins), Las Vegas (Padres), Calgary (Pirates), Vancouver (Angels), Tucson (Astros), Tacoma (Mariners), Phoenix (Giants), Albuquerque (Dodgers), and Colorado Springs (Rockies).

- **The Mexican League** is also a Triple A member of the National Association. All of its teams are independent entities with no major league affiliations. In 1997, the ML consisted of 16 franchises playing in three zones or divisions:

  - **Central Zone:** Mexico City (Reds), Mexico City (Tigers), Poza Rica, Aguascalientes, and Oaxaca.

  - **North Zone:** Monterrey, Monclova, Union Laguna, Nuevo Laredo, Saltillo, and Reynosa.

  - **South Zone:** Yucatan, Quintana Roo, Campeche, Tabasco, and Minatitian.

    The teams play a 122-game schedule that starts in March and ends in early August. The top two teams in each zone and the third-place clubs with the best records compete in a three-tiered playoff. The two finalists decide the Mexican League championship in a best-of-seven series.

The lower minors

We could present all the minor league teams and their affiliations, but then this would turn into a book of lists. So, instead, we present one last minor league list of the other National Association Leagues (see Table 11-1).

Table 11-1	National Association Leagues	
Class AA (Double A)	*Class A (Advanced)*	*Class A*
Eastern League	California League	Midwest League
Southern League	Carolina League	South Atlantic League
Texas League	Florida State League	
Short-Season Class A	*Rookie (Advanced)*	*Rookie*
New York-Penn League	Appalachian League	Arizona League
Northwest League	Pioneer League	Dominican Summer League
		Gulf Coast League

Ten independent minor leagues exist, most of whose clubs operate without any major league affiliation: the Atlantic League, the Big South League, the Frontier League, the Heartland League, the North Atlantic League, the Northeast League, the Northern League, the Prairie League, the Texas-Louisiana League, and the Western League.

If you want to know which teams are associated with any of the minor or independent leagues, refer to Appendix C for a league's address or phone number, or you can obtain the information from the most current copy of *Baseball America*'s Directory. To order the directory, call *Baseball America*'s toll-free number: 800-845-2726.

Experience not always necessary

Few players make it to the majors without first playing in the minor leagues. However, a fair number of those who made their professional debuts in the major leagues and were never sent down to the minors would eventually win baseball's highest honor — induction to the Baseball Hall of Fame in Cooperstown. Their ranks include

- Pitcher Walter Johnson (417 wins)
- Pitcher Catfish Hunter (224 wins)
- Pitcher Chief Bender (212 wins)
- Pitcher Ted Lyons (260 wins)

Minor league stars

Minor league audiences have witnessed some phenomenal performances over the years. In 1933, Joe Hauser, a first baseman with Minneapolis, hit 69 home runs to establish a professional baseball record that still stands. (Whose record did he break? His own. Hauser hit 63 home runs only three years earlier.) Tony Lazzeri, who would eventually star at second base for the New York Yankees, drove in 222 runs for San Francisco of the Pacific Coast League in 1925 (his team played 197 games that year). In 1922, pitcher Joe Boehler won 38 games for Tulsa of the Western League.

Some players' lifetime totals are equally staggering. Hector Espino, a slugging first baseman, hit a minor league career record 484 home runs, primarily for teams in the Mexican League. Bill Thomas won 383 games while pitching for various teams and leagues. Buzz Arlett won 108 games in his first six minor league seasons (1918–23) and twice won 25 games in a single season. However, after hurting his arm, he switched to the outfield and hit 432 career homers. In 1931, the 32-year-old Arlett earned a spot on the Philadelphia Phillies of the National League. In his only major league season, he hit .313 with 18 home runs and 72 runs batted in. Despite this fine showing, the Phillies released him after the season and no other major league picked him up. (Apparently, Arlett was considered a dreadful fielder, though many minor league historians claim he was an adequate glove man.)

The minors have also showcased their share of legendary teams. The best of these may be the 1937 Newark Bears, a New York Yankee affiliate that featured such future major league stars as second baseman Joe Gordon (an eventual American League MVP), outfielder Charlie "King Kong" Keller, first baseman George McQuinn, and pitcher Atley Donald. This group won the International League pennant by 25½ games with a 109-41 record.

✔ Pitcher Sandy Koufax (165 wins, 3 Cy Young Awards)

✔ Pitcher Bob Feller (266 wins)

✔ Pitcher Eddie Plank (326 wins)

✔ Pitcher Eppa Rixey (266 wins)

✔ Shortstop Ernie Banks (512 home runs)

   Banks, who played his entire career with the Chicago Cubs, spent half of it at first base. He won two consecutive MVP awards (1958-59) while playing shortstop.

✔ Shortstop Bobby Wallace (greatest fielding shortstop of his era)

   Wallace's glove work was so spectacular, he is one of the handful of men who played 25 years or more in the majors. In 1902, he was baseball's highest-paid player.

✔ Second baseman Frank Frisch (.316 lifetime batting average)

✔ First baseman George Sisler (.340 lifetime)

  ✔ Outfielder Mel Ott (511 homers)

  ✔ Outfielder Al Kaline (3.007 career hits)

Though he isn't eligible for induction until the year 2000, Dave Winfield (3,110 hits, 1,833 runs batted in) is a certain Hall of Famer who also by-passed the minor leagues.

Baseball in Japan

Historians credit Horace Wilson, an American professor based in Tokyo during the 1870s, with being the founder of Japanese baseball. Wilson's students called the game *yakyu* (field ball) or *beisu boru*. Amateur baseball flourished in Japan during the early part of the twentieth century. American teams regularly toured the country, and many top U.S. stars — including Frankie Frisch, Babe Ruth, and Casey Stengel — helped teach the nuances of the game to an enthusiastic Japanese audience. Ty Cobb, baseball's career hit king at the time, held baseball clinics in Japan in 1928.

Japan's first professional team, Nihon Undo Kyokai, was formed in 1920. Two more professional teams appeared in 1921, but all three disbanded by 1923 due to a lack of competition. Matsutaro Shoriki, a newspaper magnate, reintroduced professional baseball to his country when he formed the all-pro team Dai Nippon (the forerunner of the current Tokyo Giants) in 1934. Two years later, Shoriki and a group of businesspeople formed Japan's first professional league. In 1950, that league split into the Central and Pacific Leagues. Today, six teams operate in each of the two leagues (see Table 11-2):

Table 11-2	Japanese Baseball
Central League	*Pacific League*
Chunichi Dragons	Chiba Lotte Marines
Hanshin Tigers	Fukuoka Daiei Hawks
Hiroshima Toyo Carp	Kintetsu Buffaloes
Yakult Swallows	Nippon Ham Fighters
Yokahoma BayStars	Orix BlueWave
Yomiuri Giants	Seibu Lions

Both leagues include tie games in their standings. Japanese teams carry 28 players on their major league rosters, though only 25 are eligible to play in any one game. Each organization has a 70-man roster, including minor leaguers. Foreign (non-Japanese) players may hold four of these roster spots. Teams play a 130-game schedule (65 home/65 away) with no playoff format. Regular season games begin during the first week of April and end by the final week of September. The top teams in each league compete in the best-of-seven Japan Series — their version of our World Series — in mid-October.

The quality of Japanese baseball has improved dramatically during the last two decades, though it is not nearly on a par with the American game. Japanese outfielders and catchers lack the throwing strength of American major leaguers. Power hitters are also scarce in Japan. However, Japanese pitching is impressive. Whereas the league used to be dominated by control artists, fireballers such as Hideo Nomo (currently with the Los Angeles Dodgers) and Hideki Irabu (now of the New York Yankees) have emerged over the past few years. American scouts also have enormous regard for Japanese infield play, which generally equals, if not surpasses, U.S. major league standards.

The players

Like the United States, Japan has had its share of legendary baseball heroes, all of whom would have been stars no matter where they played. Their number includes

- Sadaharu Oh, who won 15 home run titles, nine MVP awards, 5 batting championships, and 13 runs-batted-in crowns while hitting — are you sitting? — 868 career home runs

- Tetsuharu Kawakami, Japan's "God of Batting," who hit .377 in 1951 and managed the Tokyo Giants to 11 pennants in 14 years, including nine straight Japan Series

- Katsuya Nomura, the "Johnny Bench of Japan," who hit 657 home runs from 1954 to 1980 while catching 2,918 games

- Left-hander Masaichi Kaneda, who posted 400 career wins and 4,490 strikeouts from 1950 to 1964 while playing with a club that finished in the upper half of the standings only once

- Yutaka Enatsu, who struck out 401 batters in 329 innings in 1968

- Kazuhisa Inao, who won 42 games as the Nishitetsu Lions ace in 1961

Americans who have starred in Japan include

- First baseman Randy Bass, a Central League Triple Crown winner (.350, 54 home runs, 134 runs batted in) in 1985

- Outfielder Leron Lee, who holds the Japanese record for highest career batting average (.320)

- Pitcher Joe Stanka, who won the 1964 MVP award when he went 26-7 for the Nankai Hawks

Baseball's New Asian Frontiers

Over the past 15 years, professional baseball has become wildly popular in two of Japan's neighboring countries. Taiwan is home to the Chinese Professional Baseball League. Founded in 1990, the league's six teams play a 100-game schedule. The Korean Baseball Organization has been operating since 1982. Its eight clubs compete in a 126-game season. Chan Ho Park, the ace of the Dodgers' pitching staff in 1997, is the first native-born Korean player to achieve stardom in the United States.

Baseball in the Tropics

In Mexico, Central America, and the Caribbean, baseball is nothing so sedate as a pastime; it's a passion. U.S. sailors and students introduced the game to Cuba around 1866.

The Cubans, in turn, brought baseball to Puerto Rico, the Dominican Republic, Panama, Mexico, Nicaragua, Venezuela, and Columbia.

As we noted earlier, the Mexican League is part of the American minor leagues, though none of its teams have major league affiliations. Most of the other teams south of the equator play in one of the leagues that comprise the Caribbean Baseball Confederation (CBC). These associations are referred to as *Winter Leagues* because their seasons begin in late October or November. There is no regular-season interleague play, but the league champions do compete against each other in the Caribbean World Series that is held in early February.

The following leagues comprise the CBC:

- **The Dominican League:** Founded in 1951. Its six teams play a 48-game schedule that begins in late October and usually ends just before the start of the New Year. Each organization has a 30-man roster. At the end of the season, the four teams with the best winning percentages meet in an 18-game round-robin tournament. The two survivors of that play a best-of-seven series to determine the league champion. Dominican League franchises include: Aguilas, Azucareros, Escogido, Estrellas, Licey, and the Northeast Tigers (located in San Fracisco de Macoris).

- **The Mexican-Pacific League:** Not to be confused with the Triple A Mexican League, the MFP was founded in 1958. Its eight teams play a 62-game schedule. The season opens around mid-October and ends in late December. Rosters are limited to 27 players. At the end of the season, the six clubs with the best winning percentages meet in a best-of-seven quarterfinals. The three winners of those series join the loser with the best regular season record in the best-of-seven semifinals. Two finalists emerge from those series to play a best-of-seven league championship. Mexican-Pacific League franchises include: Culiacan, Guasave, Hermosillo, Los Mochis, Mazatlan, Mexicali, Navojoa, and Obregon.

✔ **The Puerto Rican League:** Founded in 1938. The oldest of the Caribbean leagues features six teams and a 50-game schedule. Clubs begin regular season play in early November and finish in early January. Twenty-six players comprise each roster. At season's end, the league's top four teams meet in the best-of-seven semifinals. A best-of-nine final determines the league champion. Puerto Rican League teams include: Arecibo, Caguas Criollos, Mayaguez, Ponce, San Juan, and Santurce.

✔ **The Venezuelan League:** Founded in 1946. Eight teams in two divisions play a 60-game schedule that starts in late October and usually ends by New Year's Eve. Rosters are limited to 27 players. Each division's top two teams join a wild-card entry (whichever third-place club has the better regular-season record) in a 16-game round-robin series. The two teams that win that series meet in a best-of-seven playoff for the league championship. Venezuelan League teams include Caracas, La Guaira, Magallanes, and Oriente in the East Division; Aragua, Lara, Occidente, and Zulia compete in the West.

Three other leagues — two in this country, one on the other side of the world — also provide fans with baseball during the winter months. The Arizona Fall League, which begins its 50-game season in early October, is a terrific place to watch some of your favorite major league team's top prospects improve their games. Each of the league's six teams have multiple working agreements with various major league clubs. For more information, call the league office at 602-496-6700 or fax them at 602-496-6384.

Four teams play a 54-game schedule in the Hawaii Winter League. The season starts the first week of October and ends the first week of December. You can call the league office at 808-973-7247 or fax them at 808-973-7117.

The Australian Baseball League (ABL) opens in mid-October and closes during the first week of February. Eight teams play a 60-game schedule. The top four teams meet in a best-of-three semifinal. The survivors of that series play a best-of-three final to determine a league champion. Dave Nilsson, a left fielder-designated hitter with the Milwaukee Brewers, and Graeme Lloyd, a left-handed relief specialist who helped the New York Yankees win the 1996 world championship, are two current major leaguers who have played in the ABL. You can call the league office at 011-61-2-9437-4622.

The Cuban Juggernaut

Emilio Sabourin founded *Liga de Beisbol Profesional,* Cuba's first organized league, in 1878. Cuba eventually had a minor league entry, the Havana Sugar Kings, in the International League (AAA). Players from the island who went on to star in the American major leagues included Tony Oliva, Minnie Minoso, Camilo Pascual, Dolf Lucque, Zoilo Versalles, Luis Tiant, and Tony Perez.

However, shortly after Fidel Castro took power in 1959, the International League transferred the Havana franchise to Jersey City, New Jersey. Castro reacted by banning professional baseball throughout the country. He disbanded all pro teams and forbade Cuba's players from signing major league contracts. The flow of Cuban talent to the United States was stemmed at the source. Castro, a rabid baseball fan who had once been a middling pitching prospect, sought to fill the void by establishing the amateurs-only Cuban League. Its 16 franchises (representing 14 cities) start by playing a 65-game schedule. Eight of these teams go on to participate in a 63-game second season called the Selected Series. Four clubs from that competition continue playing during a February postseason that culminates with the *Series Nacional,* Cuba's version of the World Series.

Most observers agree that Cuba is the world's epicenter for amateur baseball. From 1987 to 1996, the island's national team posted an 80-1 record in international competition. It has not lost a Pan American Games baseball tournament since 1963.

Adding to Your Baseball Library

Your local library or bookstore is loaded with many fine books about minor league and international baseball. Here's a sampling:

- ✔ *Stolen Season* (Random House) by David Lamb. In this remarkable book, the author — a foreign correspondent — rediscovers America by traveling the minor league circuit.

- ✔ The Society of American Baseball Research's *Minor League Baseball Stars* and *Minor League Baseball Stars 2.* Both of these books offer complete surveys of minor league records. The two volumes include stats for 300 minor league stars as well as profiles of the most successful minor league managers. Both volumes are available through SABR. (You can find their contact information in Appendix C.)

✔ *The Story of Minor League Baseball: A History of the Game of Professional Baseball in the United States with Particular Reference to Its Growth and Development in the Smaller Cities and Towns of the Nation* edited by Robert Finch, Ben Morgan, and Henry Addington. Its title is the length of some books, but this volume delivers what it promises. Packed with records and stats, it is the most comprehensive book ever written on minor league baseball as it was played during the first half of the twentieth century.

✔ *Sadaharu Oh and the Zen Way of Baseball* (New York Times Books) by Mr. Oh and David Falkner. No book offers more insight into the life of a Japanese baseball player.

Chapter 12

There Are Tricks to This Game: Coaching

In This Chapter
- ▶ Knowing your players
- ▶ Knowing what it takes to win
- ▶ Getting the lead
- ▶ Criticizing the right way
- ▶ Using your coaches
- ▶ Keeping the game in perspective

*B*aseball managers (or *coaches* as they are often called outside the professional ranks) are responsible for all on-field decisions affecting their teams. The manager (usually with the help of an array of coaches) decides what is emphasized in training camp, which players make up his team's roster (though in professional baseball, contract considerations determine much of that), who bats where in the starting lineup, and who sits on the bench.

During games, managers decide which strategy should be employed from inning to inning (though many managers trust their veteran players to make those decisions for themselves). Managers call for, among other things, sacrifice bunts, hit and runs, stolen base attempts — and occasionally flash the *take sign* when they don't want a hitter to swing at a particular pitch. Managers can make their most dramatic impact on a game with their choice of substitutions. Picking the right pinch-hitter or relief pitcher often spells the difference between victory and defeat. It is said that a great major league manager can add six victories to a team's total during a 162-game season. That may not sound like much, but because every game you don't win is a loss, 5 additional wins represents a 10-game spread. (For example, a team with a mediocre manager may go 81-81 during a 162-game season. If a great manager milks five more wins out of that team, it finishes 86-76). That spread can mean the difference between having a disastrous season or a respectable one, between being a pennant contender or an also-ran.

It is difficult to calculate how many games incompetent managers cost their teams. If a manager's strategy is unsound or the line-up selections fail to maximize a club's offensive potential, you may be looking at another 10-game spread in the other direction. Although much depends on the makeup of the club, a well-schooled, veteran team can band together to overcome a poor *skipper* (manager). However, if the manager is also a divisive presence in the clubhouse, an entire season may be undermined.

Managerial responsibilities deepen and broaden below the pro and college levels. If you are coaching a high school or youth team, you must spend more time teaching fundamentals to your inexperienced charges. That task requires you to have patience. Besides being a manager, you at times have to assume the role of psychologist and parent figure. This advice is particularly true if your players are preteens. Many of your young players will be going nose-to-nose with loss, failure, and rejection for the first time in their lives. If you guide them with compassion, each defeat becomes an opportunity for growth and insight. If you ignore their pain, or worse, exacerbate it with ridicule or cold silence, you may scar them for life. Your responsibility is nothing less than that.

If you're a coach or manager, you can find hitting, pitching, training, and defensive tips that you can pass along to your players throughout Part II of this book. You can also find 24 defensive strategies in Joe's Baseball Playbook in Chapter 9. However, nothing written on any of those pages can illustrate how a manager thinks. To do that, we have brought in the most successful baseball manager of the last 30 years. In 26 seasons as manager of the Cincinnati Reds and Detroit Tigers, Sparky Anderson won 2,194 games (only two managers in baseball history have won more), 3 world championships, 5 league championships, and 7 division titles. He is the only skipper to guide teams to World Series championships in both leagues. So sit back and discover how a master manager approaches the game.

Note: Although Sparky Anderson's advice stems from his experience as a manager in the major leagues, what he says can be applied to coaching baseball at almost any level.

Know Your Players

"You should develop enough of a feel for your players that you can sense if something is off just by walking through the clubhouse. This means you have to be able to read a player's face and body language, his whole demeanor so that you can head off a problem before it threatens the team. This also means you have to talk to your players constantly to get some insight into how they think. Knowing your players also means understanding their strengths and limitations. If there is a left-handed junkballer on the mound, and you send up a pinch-hitter who has difficulty with slow stuff, whose fault is it when he makes out? That's your out because you asked him to do something he couldn't do."

Avoid having a happy bench

"You hear about those utility players who play very little but are content with their role on the club. I love those guys. As long as they are on someone else's club. I never wanted anyone on my roster who was happy about not playing. You want guys who want to be out on the field, so that when you give them a chance, they're going to bring some fire to the lineup."

But don't let them get too unhappy

"Keep your bench and your regular starters fresh by weaving players in and out of the lineup all season. In 1976, the Reds had a tremendous starting lineup, we won the division by ten games and were 7-0 in playoffs and World Series. Our eight regulars each had over 500 plate appearances, but we played them as a unit only 57 times during the season. We gave everyone a chance to contribute."

Know the Elements of a Winning Team

"Pitching, defense, speed, and power, in that order. Power is marvelous, but when you put up eight runs and the other team puts up nine, it can be draining. When you have great pitching you stop the other team from moving. You can create enough runs to win without using the long ball. On defense, if you give the other team only 27 outs, you have a chance. Give them 28 or 30 outs (by making errors or making mental mistakes), and you're handing their big sluggers extra at-bats to beat you.

The purpose of major-league spring training

"Number one, your team should leave camp in top physical condition. If a player is not in condition when the season starts, you're dead with him because he'll be out of shape all season. Number two, drill those fundamentals constantly. For example, in spring training games, anytime a runner was on first and a ground ball was hit through to center or right, I wanted him to go to third. I didn't care if we were down by ten runs. If they got thrown out, fine, it was part of the learning process. That's how they found out when they could take that extra base and when they couldn't. I never cared if we won a single game during spring training. My whole focus was on preparation for the regular season."

"When you have speed, you can drive the other team crazy. I'm not just talking about stolen bases here. I mean going from first to third, pulling the hit and run, faking steals, doing anything that injects movement into the game. When you do that, it is hard for the opposition to get set defensively. I always like playing against teams that could only slug; if you took away their long balls, you had them. But teams that are always on the go can beat you so many different ways."

Use Those First Five Innings

"Don't get the idea I don't like power. During innings one through five, I always wanted to destroy the other team, beat them up so badly that they went home crying to Mama that they didn't want anymore. So we'd play for the big inning and try to blow the opposition out of the park. One of the reasons you do that is that almost every club today has a big closer, a John Wetteland, a Jose Mesa, or a Mariano Rivera. You don't want to get into a war with those guys because nine times out of ten, you'll lose. If you bury the other team early, the closer never even gets up. However, come the sixth inning, if you don't have a lead, you have only 12 outs left to get something going. Now you have to grind it out, steal more, sacrifice runners over, do all the little things to create some runs. If your team can't do that, you're stuck."

Criticize in Private

"If you want players to be loyal, don't show them up. We had a game in Houston, where a player on second was thrown out on an attempted steal of third for the final out of the inning. Now, you should never make the last out of an inning at third, and when a player does it, everyone knows he pulled a rock. When the reporters asked me about it after the game, I said, 'I had a hunch and I sent him.' Well, of course I hadn't, but I was deflecting the blame away from him. Why humiliate him when he already feels bad? You can bet he and I are going to have a long discussion about the mistake, but we'll do that in private. Once a player knows you're going to protect him that way, he'll be receptive to anything you tell him; he'll give you the best effort he's got."

Work with Your Coaches

"Grant them full authority in their area of expertise. Trust that they will get everything done exactly as you discussed it. Don't be checking up on them in the field. Never second-guess anyone. If your third base coach sends in a runner and the player is thrown out by 20 feet, don't say a word. In 26 years, I never questioned any of my third base coaches' decisions. Once when a coach tried to apologize for a sending a runner who was thrown out, I said, 'Hey I'm glad you're out there and not me.' That should be your attitude. You also shouldn't think that just because you are the manager, you are superior to your coaches. Each of them will have an area of the game where they know much more than you ever will. Use that knowledge. Go to them for advice."

Keep It All in Perspective

"I never knew any manager who put together a great record without great players. They are what it is all about. Once you think you're the most important part of the team, it's time to look for another line of work. If you're coaching Little League, baseball is supposed to be fun for these kids, so don't overemphasize winning or losing. The best part of your game should be the hot dogs and soft drinks afterwards. And parents shouldn't take things too seriously, either. How can any parent get upset when their child goes 0 for 4 when I can take them to Children's Hospital and introduce them to kids who have only six months to live? Wipe your little ones' tears, give them a big hug, and let them know you'll love them even if they never get another hit."

Choosing a pinch-hitter

"I rarely picked pinch-hitters on a strict *platoon* basis (lefty hitters vs. right-handed pitchers, right-handed hitters vs. lefties). Instead, I looked at how you matched up against the pitcher's stuff. If there was a hard-throwing right-hander on the mound, and I had a lefty whose bat wasn't that quick and a right-hander who loved to hit the fastball, the right-hander is going up to the plate. I was more interested in what kind of pitches you could handle than what side of the batter's box you stood in. When I brought in relievers, I applied the same thinking, only in reverse. If I knew a hitter hated the breaking ball, I was bringing in a curveballer even if it meant bringing in a left-hander to face a righty. Now this means you not only have to know what your team can do, you have to know the opposition's personnel as well. I also always tried to save my best pinch-hitter for the late innings when he could come up with the game on the line."

Chapter 13

Major League Baseball

• •

In This Chapter

▶ Who runs the game?

▶ A look at the divisions

• •

*Y*ou can follow 30 major league teams — 16 in the National League and 14 in the American League — in 1998. Spring training starts in late February (when pitchers and catchers report) and continues through March. Each team plays 162 regular season games (81 games at home, 81 in opponents' parks) beginning around April 1. Interleague play (which started in 1997) between National League and American League clubs takes place during June, August, and September. The regular season ends during the final week of September, and postseason play starts in the first week of October with the two-round League Championship Series. These series produce a champion for each league (to find out how, see Chapter 15). They battle each other for the major league championship in the World Series in late October.

Major League Baseball Today

The Office of Major League Baseball is in New York City (see Appendix C for full contact information). As we went to print, the game still didn't have an official commissioner. Allan "Bud" Selig, the Milwaukee Brewers' owner, acts as chairman of baseball's executive council. The council enforces rules among the owners and proposes policy for both leagues. Paul Beeston, the former president of the Toronto Blue Jays, runs baseball's day-to-day business operations. Bob Gamgort heads Major League Baseball Properties, the highly profitable licensing and marketing arm for both leagues. And Randy Levine of the Major League Baseball Player Relations Committee represents the owners' interests in labor negotiations.

The American and National Leagues also maintain offices in New York City (and you can also find their addresses in Appendix C). Gene Budig is the A.L. president; Leonard Coleman is his N.L. counterpart. They implement policy, issue directives, approve contracts, and have jurisdiction over all league matters — including player fines, protests, and other disputes.

Donald Fehr doesn't own a club, swat home runs, or throw any high fastballs, yet he may very well be the most powerful man in baseball. Mr. Fehr is the executive director of the Major League Players Association, the baseball players' union. (The address for its offices is also in Appendix C.)

The Major League Franchises

In October 1997, Bud Selig announced that his Milwaukee Brewers of the American League Central Division would become the first major league baseball team to switch leagues in this century. The Brewers began play in the National League in 1998. Milwaukee's switch and the addition of the Arizona Diamondbacks expansion team currently give the National League 16 teams competing under the alignment shown in Table 13-1. (See Appendix C for contact information on all the major league clubs.)

Table 13-1	The National League	
NL East	*NL Central*	*NL West*
Atlanta Braves	Chicago Cubs	Arizona Diamondbacks
Florida Marlins	Cincinnati Reds	Colorado Rockies
New York Mets	Houston Astros	Los Angeles Dodgers
Philadelphia Phillies	Milwaukee Brewers	San Francisco Giants
Montreal Expos	Pittsburgh Pirates	San Diego Padres
	St. Louis Cardinals	

In the American League, the Detroit Tigers moved from the American League East to replace the Brewers in the Central division in 1998. The Tampa Bay Devil Rays, another expansion team, took Detroit's slot in the East (see Table 13-2).

Table 13-2	The American League	
AL East	**AL Central**	**AL West**
Baltimore Orioles	Chicago White Sox	Anaheim Angels
Boston Red Sox	Cleveland Indians	Oakland Athletics
New York Yankees	Detroit Tigers	Seattle Mariners
Tampa Bay Devil Rays	Kansas City Royals	Texas Rangers
Toronto Blue Jays	Minnesota Twins	

Each club carries 25 players on its regular-season roster (14 to 16 position players, 9 to 11 pitchers). Rosters expand from 25 up to 40 players on September 1. However, only those players who are on the roster before that time are eligible for postseason play.

A club captures first place in its division by compiling the best won-lost percentage. (You can discover how to calculate that percentage by consulting Chapter 14.)

Both leagues have a rich history that has been vividly captured in countless books. The best of these include

✔ Harold Seymour's *Baseball — The Early Years* and *Baseball — The Golden Years* (Oxford University Press). Critics have hailed Seymour as baseball's greatest historian. His first volume covers the game from the pre-Civil War years to 1903. Book two continues to 1970. Seymour presents baseball against a historical backdrop that provides the reader with a sociological context for changes within the sport.

✔ Lee Lowenfish and Tony Lupien's *The Imperfect Diamond: A History of Baseball's Labor Wars* (Decapo Press) was first published in 1980 and has been recently updated to include events up to 1996. This is the one book you must own if you want to make any sense of the constant turmoil between baseball's labor and management.

✔ *Total Baseball* (Viking Penguin) is the game's ultimate reference work. It is chock-full of statistics on every major league player who ever pulled on a pair of spikes. The 2,500-page volume also has league, team, and ballpark histories, all-time leader lists in every major category, and illuminating essays on such topics as Caribbean baseball, Jewish ballplayers, baseball journalism, and baseball movies. Each copy comes with a CD-ROM that provides a gateway to baseball on the World Wide Web. You can order a copy by calling 800-526-0275.

Society for American Baseball Research

Is Mike Piazza the best hitting catcher of all time? Did Babe Ruth really call his home run against the Cubs in the 1932 World Series? What team originally drafted Tom Seaver out of college and how did they lose him? You can find out the answers to these and many more questions by joining the Society for American Baseball Research (SABR). Founded in 1971, SABR is a nonprofit organization dedicated to the preservation of baseball history. Its two annual publications, *The National Pastime* and *The Research Journal,* are, by themselves, worth the $35 yearly membership dues ($20 for students or seniors, $45 for fans living in Canada or Mexico; $50 if you live overseas). However, members also have access to the SABR Lending Library, whose comprehensive inventory includes microfilm reproductions of *Sporting Life* (1883-1917) and *The Sporting News* (1886-1957). Besides the two aforementioned annual publications, SABR annually sends its members nine newsletters and a special magazine dedicated to a specific topic, such as the Negro Leagues, Minor League baseball stars, or nineteenth-century baseball stars. You can also participate on various research committees with top baseball historians. For membership information — and this is one organization every baseball fan should join — call SABR at 216-575-0500 (you can also find their address and fax information in Appendix C).

Chapter 14

Measuring Performance (How to Calculate Baseball's Statistics)

. . . .

In This Chapter

▶ Measuring offense

▶ Calculating pitching

▶ Judging fielding

▶ Evaluating your team

. . . .

*B*aseball fans are amazing. Math may have given them nightmares as students, but let their favorite player make a hit or an out, and they will have his slugging average computed before he takes a step from the batter's box. Statistics provide the game's followers with a context that allows them to compare players and eras. To hold your own in any conversation about the sport, you have to know what the numbers mean. So here's an introduction to baseball's primary stats.

Offensive Measurements

Mention the numbers 755, 4,256, or 61 to any avid baseball fan and they'll probably rattle off the famous baseball records that correspond to those numbers. (Just for the record, 755 = lifetime homers for Hank Aaron, 4,256 = lifetime hits for Pete Rose, and 61 = homers hit in 1961 by Roger Maris.) Even if you don't feel compelled to memorize baseball's legendary numerical feats, this section helps you make some sense out of the many ways that players and fans track and measure offensive ability.

70 = Mark McGwire
66 = Sammy Sosa

Batting average

The statistic used to measure what percentage of a player's at-bats results in a base hit. This statistic made its first appearance in 1874. To calculate it, divide the batter's total hits by his official times at bat:

Tony Gwynn, San Diego, 1997

$$\frac{220 \text{ hits}}{592 \text{ at - bats}} = .372 \text{ batting average}$$

(Yes, you might say Mr. Gwynn can hit a little.)

A hitter's at-bats do not include walks, sacrifice bunts, sacrifice flies, obstruction calls, catcher's interference, or being hit by a pitch. These events count as plate appearances and aren't used to calculate batting average. When the hitter is safe on an error, credit him with an at-bat, but not a hit.

To qualify for a major league batting championship (to lead the league in batting average over the course of a season), a player must have 3.1 plate appearances (not at-bats) for every game his team plays. In a regulation 162-game season, a hitter needs at least 502 plate appearances to qualify for his league's batting title. Today, the average major league hitter bats around .265. However, batting average doesn't tell you much about a hitter's ability. A player can have a high batting average, but if he doesn't draw walks or hit for power he may not be as productive as a low-average hitter who does.

For example, in 1969 catcher Manny Sanguillen of the Pirates batted .303 while Carl Yastrzemski, the Boston left fielder, hit only .254. Looking only at their batting averages, you might think Sanguillen out-produced Yaz. But consider these numbers:

Player	Homers	RBI	Runs	Walks	On-Base Pct.	Slugging Average
Sanguillen	5	57	62	12	.325	.407
Yastrzemski	40	111	96	101	.363	.507

As you can see, it was no contest: Yaz was far more productive than Sanguillen. Batting average alone couldn't adequately measure Yastrzemski's contribution to his team. To evaluate a hitter's full value, you must examine *every* aspect of his offense. (See the upcoming section "Slugging average" in order to see how this statistic is figured out.)

On-base percentage

Branch Rickey and Brooklyn Dodger statistician Allen Roth created this statistic during the 1950s. On-base percentage tells you what percentage of a hitter's at-bats results in his getting on base by any means other than an error, interference, or fielders' choice. To calculate this figure, add a batter's hits, walks, and hit-by-pitch (hbp) totals and divide by his at-bats plus walks plus hit-by-pitch plus sacrifice flies . . .

$$\frac{100 \text{ hits } + 100 \text{ walks } + 10 \text{ hpb} = 210}{530 \text{ at - bats} + 100 \text{ walks } + 10 \text{ hbp } + 10 \text{ sacrifice flies } = 620} = .3387 \text{ on - base average}$$

. . . which rounds out to .339. The average major league hitter is right around that number. Ideally, the first two hitters in your lineup, the players who jump-start your offense by getting on base any way they can, should have an on-base percentage of .375 or better.

Slugging average

You can derive a player's slugging average by calculating how many bases he averages with each at-bat. To do so, divide the total bases he accumulated with hits by his at-bats. A single equals *one* base, a double *two* bases, a triple *three* bases, and a home run *four* bases. For example, in 1997, Frank Thomas of the White Sox had 114 singles (114 bases), 35 doubles (70 bases), 0 triples, and 35 home runs (140 bases) for a total of 324 bases in 530 at bats:

$$\frac{324 \text{ total bases}}{530 \text{ at - bats}} = .661 \text{ slugging percentage}$$

The average major leaguer slugs around .420. A hitter with a .450 slugging has good power; the elite sluggers are at .490 or better. Now you can see why pitchers refer to Thomas as "The Big Hurt."

Base-on-balls percentage

This statistic tells you what percentage of a batter's plate appearances results in a walk. Divide the hitter's total walks by his plate appearances.

Home run ratio

This statistic measures how often a batter homers. To calculate it, divide the hitter's at-bats by his home runs. An average major league hitter will hit one home run approximately every 35 at-bats. (In 1997, Ken Griffey, Jr. averaged one homer for every 10.9 at bats!)

Stolen base percentage

You can judge a base stealer by the percentage of his stolen base attempts that are successful. Divide his stolen bases by his total attempts. In 1997, St. Louis Cardinals shortstop Royce Clayton stole 30 bases in 40 attempts for a .750 stolen base percentage. The average major league player is successful on 65 percent of his base-stealing attempts, but that is not a good rate. Expert base thieves succeed at least 75 percent of the time.

Strikeout ratio

The strikeout ratio discloses how often a hitter strikes out. Divide at-bats by strikeouts. An average major league hitter will strike out once every 5.5 bats or so. Some sluggers tend to chalk up a strikeout for every four at-bats or so. A great contact hitter like Tony Gwynn, however, may strike out only once every 14 at-bats or better.

Pitching Measurements

Not to be outdone by the hitters, pitchers also have a whole slew of stats to measure pitching performance. The stats covered in this section help you determine how effectively pitchers get out opposing hitters. Although dozens of pitching statistics exist, the critical indicator for any pitcher is wins. Flashy statistics are nice, but the name of the game for any pitcher is winning.

Winning percentage

This statistic tells you what percentage of a pitcher's decisions was victories. Divide the pitcher's wins by his total decisions (wins plus losses):

Jeff Fassero, Seattle Mariners, 1997

$$\frac{16 \text{ wins}}{16 \text{ wins } + \text{ 9 losses} = 25 \text{ decisions}} = .640 \text{ winning percentage}$$

Generally, the better pitchers post winning percentages of .540 or higher. However, if you pitch only .500 (which means you record as many wins as losses) for a club whose won-lost percentage is .400 or worse, your team-mates probably call you *ace*. Pitchers who consistently post winning percentages of .600 or better are among baseball's elite performers.

Earned run average (ERA)

This statistic measures how many earned runs (runs that score without benefit of an error) a pitcher surrenders every nine innings. To calculate, multiply the number of earned runs on a pitcher's record by 9 and then divide the result by his innings pitched:

Roger Clemens, Toronto Blue Jays, 1997

$$\frac{60 \text{ earned runs allowed} \times 9 = 540}{264 \text{ innings pitched}} = 2.05 \text{ earned run average}$$

Clemens's 2.05 ERA led the American League in 1997 and helped him win his fourth Cy Young Award.

Earned run averages have fluctuated widely over the years. When I played, an ERA under 3.50 was considered good. With all the offensive pyrotechnics in baseball today, a pitcher is doing well if he has an ERA of around 4.00. Because of the designated hitter rule, ERAs are usually .20 to .25 points higher in the American League than in the National League. (See Chapter 3 for information on the designated hitter rule.)

Opponents' batting average

This statistic reveals what percentage of batters faced by a pitcher hit safely. To calculate it, divide the number of hits a pitcher allows by the number of outs he records (innings pitched multiplied by 3) plus his hits allowed total. As you can see in the Mark Wohlers example, it's not as complicated as it sounds:

Mark Wohlers, Atlanta, 1997

In 1997, Wohlers recorded 208 outs in 69.1 innings pitched (69.1 × 3) . . .

$$\frac{57 \text{ hits allowed}}{208 \text{ outs} + 57 \text{ hits allowed}} = .2237$$

Getting a decision: the pitcher's dilemma

To earn a victory, a starting pitcher must pitch at least five innings (or four if the game goes less than seven innings) and his team must have the lead at the time he leaves the game. If that lead is never relinquished, he gets the win. If the game is tied when a pitcher who has pitched at least five innings is removed for a pinch hitter and his team goes ahead to stay during the inning in which he is batted for, credit him with the win. When the starter cannot get the win, the victory can go to any relief pitcher who is the pitcher of record at the time his team gains a lead it never loses. Credit a pitcher with a loss if he is charged with the run that beats his team.

If a reliever is the finishing pitcher for the winning team and does not qualify for the victory, credit the pitcher with a save in these situations:

✔ The pitcher gets the final three outs of a game that he entered with his team leading by three runs or less.

✔ The pitcher gets the final out (or more) when he inherits a situation in which the tying run is in the on-deck circle.

✔ The pitcher pitches the game's final three innings regardless of the score. (However, his pitching must be effective in the judgment of the official scorer.)

. . . which rounds out to an opponent's batting average of .224. The average pitcher is around .265. Outstanding pitchers, such as Randy Johnson and Pedro Martinez, consistently hold hitters below . 220.

Defensive Measurements: Fielding Average

Fielding average reveals what percentage of attempted plays is successfully completed by a fielder. To calculate it, add the fielder's putouts and assists, and then divide that total by his total chances (putouts, assists, and errors). Fielding average measures surehandedness rather than range. Players who don't reach a lot of balls have fewer chances to make errors.

Team Measurement: Won-Lost Percentage

This statistic is something of a misnomer because the number only tells you what percentage of games a team has won. You determine it by dividing a team's wins by the number of games played. Want to see a mind-boggling won-lost percentage? Check out the 1906 Chicago Cubs:

$$\frac{116 \text{ wins}}{152 \text{ games played}} = .763 \text{ won-lost percentage}$$

 Would you believe they lost the World Series that year? Every team wants to play at least .500 ball. Usually, a .550 winning percentage makes you a playoff contender. However, you can win a weak division with a relatively low won-lost percentage. The New York Mets won the NL East with a .509 won-lost percentage and then went to the World Series by beating the — oh, must I relive this memory? — Cincinnati Reds in the league championship series.

The lowdown on statistics

Statistics are often misleading. Everyone believes that a .300 hitter is a good player and that a pitcher with a low ERA is a good pitcher. That belief is not necessarily the case. To be a good player, you have to either drive in runs or score runs (depending on where you hit in the batting order), and the great players do both. A .300 hitter makes 7 outs every 10 at-bats, and if his 7 outs come with men on base and his 3 hits come with no one on base, these hits are not very productive. That is why run production is important. And there are a lot of pitchers who pitch just good enough to lose. Pitchers will tell you that it is just as tough to win a 5-4 game as it is a 1-0 game because they have to pitch out of more jams.

Run production is how you measure players. Wins and losses are how you measure pitchers. Batting averages and ERAs are personal stats.

Chapter 15

Going All the Way: The League Championship Series and the World Series

In This Chapter

▶ The arrival of the League Championship Series
▶ The difficult birth of the World Series

Getting to the World Series. That's the ultimate fantasy for every baseball player, manager, owner, or fan, or at least it ought to be.

I've participated in four World Series (including the Boston-Cincinnati classic in 1975, which many people have called the greatest World Series of all time) and seven National League Championship Series (NLCS). I knew the moment I stepped on the field to play the Eastern Division champion Pittsburgh Pirates for the 1972 National League pennant in my first NLCS, that the postseason is what baseball is all about. The stadiums are packed to bursting, and the spectators are continually on the edge of their seats or on their feet. Adrenaline is running high in both dugouts, and the media are everywhere. It feels as if the whole world is watching. Every pitch, every at-bat, every play assumes ten times as much significance than it held during the regular season.

If you can't get excited about postseason baseball, you better check for a pulse. To understand what all the hoopla is about, you can read up on the history of postseason play and examine the difficult road teams must tread to reach it.

The League Championship Series

Before 1969, all a team had to do to qualify for the World Series was to be the last team standing when your league's schedule came to a close. If you finished the season with the league's best won-lost record, you were its representative in the Series. If you were tied with another team after playing all your regular season games, a playoff determined the league champion. (In the National League, a best two-out-of-three game series broke the tie; the American League used a one-game, winner-take-all playoff.)

Expansion brings change

Major league baseball's 1969 expansion forever altered the postseason. Franchise owners voted to divide both the American League and National League — each of which had been single leagues of ten franchises — into two six-team divisions. Intradivisional opponents played each other 18 times during the season and met teams from its league's other division 12 times per year.

Both leagues also introduced a playoff format (since named the *League Championship Series,* or LCS), which required the teams that ended the season with the best records in their divisions to meet each other in a best three-out-of-five series. The winner of each playoff was declared league champion and went on to the World Series. If the season ended with two teams tied for a division lead, they met in a sudden-death, one-game playoff. Whichever club won that contest went on to the LCS. The survivors of those events represented their respective leagues in the World Series. Baseball tinkered with that format in 1985 when it expanded the playoffs to a best-of-seven game format.

Adding more playoffs to the League Championship Series

A more startling alteration came in 1994 when the two leagues adopted their present alignment (see Chapter 13 for more details) of three divisions each. The addition of a third division necessitated the creation of a second tier of playoffs — a three-of-five game series followed by a four-of-seven playoff to determine a league champion. It also required the inclusion of a *wild card* (an additional playoff qualifier) team in the postseason mix. To qualify for the wild card, a club must post the best record among its league's second-place finishers. If two teams tie for the division lead, but their records also qualify either for a wild-card berth, both teams make the playoffs. Which-ever of the two teams held the edge in their season series goes into the playoffs as the division champion. If there is a tie for the division lead, but neither team qualifies for the wild card (because some second-place team has a better record than either of them), the division championship is decided by a one-game playoff. Which teams oppose each other in the first round varies from year to year depending on the identity of the wild card.

As we went to press, baseball's general managers had proposed altering the system so that the club with the best record of its league's four playoff participants would meet the team with the worst record in the first round (for whatever silly reason, the wild-card team currently cannot meet its division leader in round one).

The World Series

People who watch very little baseball during the regular season often find themselves riveted to the television when the World Series is broadcast in late October. At its best, this best-of-seven confrontation between the champions of the American and National Leagues has a gradual, dramatic build that makes the Series the most compelling event in sports.

The first "world series"

Baseball's earliest "world series" in 1882 consisted of two informal post-season games between Cincinnati of the American Association and Chicago of the National League. The two teams split these contests, which received scant press coverage and were seen as little more than exhibitions. In fact, the National League chose not to see them at all. Up to that time, the National League had refused to consider the American Association as a legitimate major league. A standing edict forbade National League clubs from participating in contests against American Association teams. To defy that order without risking expulsion from the league, Chicago had to release all of its players from their contracts before they could face Cincinnati (those players re-signed with their club as soon as the games ended).

The National Agreement of 1883 brought peace between the two leagues. One year after the pact was signed, the National League champion Providence Grays met the American Association champion New York Metropolitans for a three-game set. It was billed as a battle for the baseball championship of the United States. However, after the Grays won, the media hailed them as world champions. Subsequently, the phrase "World Series" began slipping into the baseball lexicon, though the major leagues would not officially embrace the name until the early 1900s.

The end of the American Association

From 1885 to 1890, the American Association and National League pennant winners faced each other in series whose lengths varied from 6 games to 15. The National League won five of these six events. Friction between the two leagues forced the cancellation of the championship series in 1891. Shortly after that, the American Association folded.

National League expansion

In 1892, the National League expanded to 12 teams while dividing the season into two halves. Boston, the winner of the first half season, played Cleveland, owner of the second half's best record, for the league championship and "baseball's world title." The best-of-nine series was less than a sensation. Fan generally abhorred the split-season concept (it was abandoned after this one season), so they were unable to muster much enthusiasm for the confrontation it produced. A series packed with suspense may have won them over, but it was not to be. Boston shellacked Cleveland five games to none (there was one tie). Due to the disappointing response to the matchup, no championship series of any kind took place during the following season.

The Temple Cup

William C. Temple, a noted Pittsburgh sportsman, tried to revive postseason play by offering a prize cup to the winner of a best-of-seven series between the National League's top two finishers. For the next four years, baseball hailed the winners of the Temple Cup as world champions. Again, fans failed to embrace this concept and the Cup trophy went back to its original donor.

And yet another cup

In 1900, a Pittsburgh newspaper, the *Chronicle-Telegraph,* offered a silver loving cup to the winner of a best-of-five series between the National League's first-place finisher, the Brooklyn Superbas, and the second place Pittsburgh Pirates. Brooklyn won the set, three games to one, but the sparse attendance (the four games attracted fewer than 11,000 fans) convinced the National League owners to once again abandon postseason play.

The World Series takes off

Fortunately, baseball owners gave postseason play one last chance in 1903 after a new National Agreement recognized the recently formed American League as a major league. Barney Dreyfuss, owner of the National League champion Pittsburgh Pirates, challenged the American League champion Boston Pilgrims to a best-of-nine confrontation. Boston established the American League's credibility by winning the series, five games to three. More important, the series generated enthusiastic fan interest.

When the National League champion New York Giants declined to meet the once-again American League champion Pilgrims in 1904, the public outcry persuaded baseball's ruling body, the National Commission, to officially establish the World Series for the following season. The 1905 Series between the New York Giants and Philadelphia Phillies officially established the best-of-seven format, which is still followed today (the leagues experimented with best-of-nine format from 1919 to 1921, but deemed a nine-game series to be too long to hold the public's attention).

Except for 1994 when a players strike canceled the event, both leagues have participated in the World Series — or, to use its more elegant nomenclature, the *Fall Classic* — in every season since. The Series has endured to become an American cultural icon.

You can find all the essential records from both the playoffs and World Series in *The Complete Baseball Record Book,* published annually by *The Sporting News.* Donald Honig's *October Heroes* is an oral history of the World Series as told by such players as Tom Seaver, Gene Tenace, Johnny Podres, and Lloyd Waner.

The All-Star Game

Since 1933, the stars of the American and National Leagues have competed against each other in the All-Star Game, a midseason exhibition game (which means it is not counted as part of the regular season records) played in a different major league stadium each year. The AL and NL squads are led by the managers of the previous season's pennant winners. Fans participate in a nationwide poll to choose the starting lineups (with the exception of the pitchers) for both clubs.

The managers' own picks fill out the rest of their 28-player rosters. Each major league club must have at least one All-Star representative. The National League has a 40-27 lead in this "series," but much of that bulge was built from 1965 to 1985, when the NL teams — which were then much deeper in middle infield talent and power pitchers than their American League rivals — won 18 of 20 All-Star Games. Since then, however, the AL has won 8 out of 12.

Part IV

We Don't Care If We Ever Get Back — A Spectator's Guide

The 5th Wave   By Rich Tennant

"We track all the statistics from game to game – ERA, batting averages, TV ratings..."

In this part . . .

*I*ts time for our surgeon general's warning to baseball spectators: Once you're hooked on baseball, you won't be able to get enough of it.

In this part, we show you how to watch the game, where to sit, and how to keep score. As you become a diehard baseball fan, you'll undoubtedly want as much information as you can get on your favorite teams or players as soon as its available. So, this part covers where to get the most up-to-date baseball information. If you are on the Internet, we also tell you about a number of nifty Web sites to surf. Finally, we give you a brief introduction to the growing phenomenon known as "fantasy baseball."

Time to go to the park . . .

Chapter 16

Following the Bouncing Baseball

In This Chapter

▶ Viewing the action from the stands

▶ Waiting for a souvenir

▶ Watching the action on TV

▶ Keeping score

▶ National League stadiums

▶ American League stadiums

As a spectator, if you haven't experienced a baseball game live, well, you haven't experienced baseball. A ball field is more than mere backdrop; by juxtaposing speed against distance it provides a context for athletic miracles. Juan Gonzalez's latest 550-foot home run is merely a ball hit a long way when seen on television. But when viewed from a stadium seat, it becomes a thing majestic, almost unsettling in its celebration of raw, human power. Baseball is a sport of nuance, and nowhere but the ballpark can these subtleties be explored and appreciated. Is the shortstop cheating toward second to gain a step on the double play? Is the hitter choking up with a two-strike count? How will the left fielder shade this right-handed pull hitter? Sitting in the stands, you can get an immediate answer to all these questions by simply looking out at the field.

A visit to your local ballpark is also a healthful experience. You get to bond with fellow humans, soak up the sun's vitamin D (if you go during the day), fill your lungs with air made fragrant by freshly trimmed grass, and escape from life's anxieties. It is sort of like going to an outdoor consciousness-raising group only, it says here, vastly more entertaining.

Picking the Best Seat (It Depends on What You Want to See)

Given the emphasis stadium architects put on unobstructed sight lines, nearly every seat in a modern baseball park (any one built or refurbished in the last 30 years) is a good one. As you move around the stadium, you find that each section offers a different, often contrasting perspective of the game on the field (see Figure 16-1).

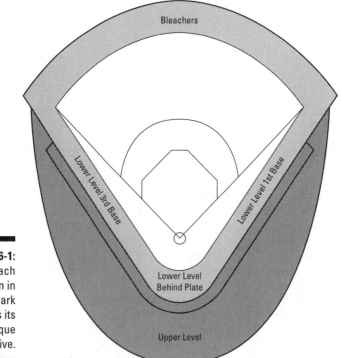

Figure 16-1:
Each section in a ballpark has its unique perspective.

Bleachers

Lower Level 3rd Base

Lower Level 1st Base

Lower Level Behind Plate

Upper Level

✔ For the best view of the pitcher-hitter confrontation, camp out behind home plate.

✔ Want to watch the double play unfold and the by-play between pitcher and runner? Head for the first base side — a seat here also grants you a bird's eye view of most of the game's putouts.

✔ From behind third, you can watch the relay and cut-off plays evolve as the runner races toward third or home against the right fielder's throw.

✔ Visit the upper deck and you can see the field as a giant chessboard with ever-changing defensive alignments.

✔ You get an appreciation of the various angles fly balls assume by sitting in the bleachers (if your park has them), which are located directly behind the outfield fence.

Looking for a Souvenir?

Almost everybody who goes to a ball game fantasizes about catching a foul ball or (even better) a home run. Foul-ball hunters have their best opportunities in the upper deck or lower boxes on the first or third base side of the park. If you want to add a home run ball to your trophy case, sit down the lines or in the bleachers — unless you are at Coors Field, where you can just wait out in the parking lot because of the way that the ball jumps out of there. (Figure 16-2 shows you some of the best places to sit if you want to get your hands on a baseball.) You are free to do whatever you want with any ball you catch, but you should know that in many ball parks, such as Chicago's Wrigley Field, hometown fans expect you to throw back onto the field any home runs hit by the visiting team.

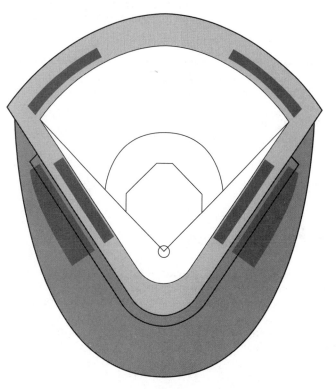

Figure 16-2:
Where to await a chance for a free souvenir.

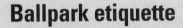

Ballpark etiquette

When you visit a stadium, have fun, get loose, but not too loose.

✔ Refrain from using foul language (children are usually nearby).

✔ Don't drink to excess (in fact, why drink at all?).

✔ Never, ever throw an object onto the field, run onto the diamond, or do anything that interferes with play.

The Other 98 Percent of the Time: When You Can't Get to the Park

If you're like most fans, you see the majority of your baseball on television, which is a terrific way to learn about the sport. When you watch games on the tube, you don't have to do any work. The camerapeople direct your attention to all the important action. If you miss a critical event — a fielding gem, a clutch hit, or dramatic strikeout — replays give you multiple chances to view it. Stop-action and slow-motion shots help you to dissect a play from a variety of angles.

All the major networks are using computer graphics to analyze pitch locations, *hit spreads* (those places on the field where a batter's hits are most likely to fall), defensive alignments, and batter-pitcher matchups. You don't have to look at a single scouting report. The announcers always have a wealth of data at their disposal, so you're going to get information you can't find anywhere else. And, best of all, if there is a rainout, you're already home.

Be sure to check out Chapter 17 for information on where and when you can catch a game on TV (and on the radio, too).

Real Fans Keep Score

Nothing focuses your full concentration on a baseball game like keeping score. You can purchase *scorecards* from stadium vendors (who sell cards for each game) or at almost any sporting goods store (where they are sold by the book). Or you can make your own. For every game you score, you need two cards — one for the home team, another for its opponents. Figure 16-3 shows what a typical, blank scorecard looks like.

	P	1	2	3	4	5	6	7	8	9	10	11	AB	R	H	RBI	E
TOTALS	R H																	

Figure 16-3:
A blank baseball scorecard.

The first thing that you should do is write the date, the weather, and whether the game is a day or night game (or the first game of a double-header, and so on) on the top of your scorecard, along with the teams competing. Lots of fans keep their scorecards (and ticket stubs) for a lifetime of memories.

Those numbers running across the top of the grid represent innings. Spaces on the left-hand side of the grid are reserved for the players' names, positions, and uniform numbers. You summarize a team's output of hits and runs for each half-inning in the spaces provided at the bottom of the scoring columns. When the game is over, record the player and team totals (at-bats, runs, hits, runs batted in, errors) in the grid's right-hand columns.

The scorekeeper's codes

The first time you encounter a completed scorecard, it may look as if some ancient sage had scribbled on it in hieroglyphics. Don't be intimidated. The scribbling becomes decipherable after you learn the basic symbols. Position players are represented by numbers (not to be confused with their uniform numbers), as shown in Table 16-1.

Table 16-1	The Numbers Assigned to Each Player
Player	*Number*
Pitcher	1
Catcher	2
First baseman	3
Second baseman	4
Third baseman	5
Shortstop	6
Left fielder	7
Center fielder	8
Right fielder	9

All scoring systems adhere to this numerical code. The symbols and abbreviations used to record the outcome of each at-bat, however, can vary from scorer to scorer. Novice scorers should stick to the basic forms shown in Table 16-2.

Table 16-2	Baseball Scoring Abbreviations
Event	*Abbreviation*
Single	1B
Double	2B
Triple	3B
Home run	HR
Base on balls	BB
Intentional base on balls	IBB
Balk	BLK
Caught stealing	CS
Double play	DP

Event	Abbreviation
Error	E
Fielder's choice	FC
Force out	FO
Flyout	F
Ground out	G
Hit by pitcher	HBP
Interference	I
Strikeout	K
Line drive	LD
Passed ball	PB
Stolen base	SB
Sacrifice hit	SH
Sacrifice fly	SF
Triple play	TP
Wild pitch	WP

Combine the position numbers and abbreviations to record the sequence of an out — which tells you who got the *assist* (a throw by a fielder that leads to an out), if any, and who made the putout. You can also pinpoint the location of a hit, or assign blame for an error. For example, if a game's lead-off hitter is retired on a fly ball to left field, mark F-7 in the first inning grid alongside the batter's name. If that ball drops just in front of the left fielder for a single, the proper notation is 1B-7. However, if the official scorer thinks that ball was catchable, enter an E-7. A double-play ball that is fielded first by the second baseman who throws it to the shortstop for the relay throw to the first baseman is scored 4-6-3 DP (second-to-short-to-first double play).

Tracking the runner

Most scorecards have tiny diamonds within the scoring blocks (if yours don't, you can draw them). Use these diamonds to record the progress of the baserunners. Treat the lower point of the diamond as home plate and work around the box counter-clockwise.

For example, if a batter singles to center field, darken the line of the diamond leading from home to first while recording the circumstances that put him on base in the lower right-hand corner:

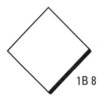

If the same player then advances one base on a wild pitch, darken the line from first to second and put the abbreviation WP in the upper right-hand corner:

When a short single to right moves this player up one more base, darken the line from second to third and note 1B 9 in the upper left-hand corner:

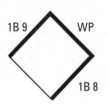

After a sacrifice fly to left field scores the runner, darken the line from third to home, fill in the diamond (to signify a run scored), and put a dot in the box of the batter who drove in the run. The result is a snapshot of a batter's entire one-inning history.

When the half-inning is over, draw a slash across the lower right-hand corner of the scoring block for any batter who makes the last out of a team's turn at-bat.

After you've mastered the rudiments of scoring, you can adopt such advanced techniques as color coding — which requires you to record walks in green, strikeouts in red, and hits in blue (you better own one of those multi-barreled pens for that one, or you'll need an extra seat at the ballpark just for office supplies).

Many books explain the various, complex scoring systems. But if you are looking for one that will entertain as well as inform you, purchase Paul Dickson's gracefully written *The Joy of Keeping Score* (Harcourt Brace).

The Stadiums

We think of the player who hits 40 home runs while playing half his games in Coors Field as a fearsome slugger. But would we hold him in such high regard if his club's home address were the Houston Astrodome and he struggled to hit 15 home runs a season? Conversely, the Colorado Rockies pitcher whose earned run average (ERA) is over 5.00 appears to be one step away from his release. However, let him pitch half his games in Oakland-Alameda County Coliseum, and he may find himself among the league's pitching leaders. Ballparks matter. They not only provide a pleasant setting to watch a game, they also profoundly affect run scoring and our assessment of a player's ability. In this chapter, I examine the impact each major league stadium has on performance and perception.

You can find great details about each of these stadiums on the Web at www.ballparks.com/baseball/index.html

The National League stadiums

William Hulbert founded the National League in 1876. Its original eight franchises were located in Chicago, New York, Philadelphia, Cincinnati, Louisville, Hartford, St. Louis, and Boston. National League stadiums tend to be a bit larger than their American League counterparts. With the notable exception of Coors Field, most of the stadiums seem to have been designed with pitching and defense in mind.

Turner Field: Atlanta Braves

A perfect example of how a stadium can affect our perception of a team. Through most of 1997, analysts struggled to explain Atlanta's loss of offensive vigor. Every Braves regular — with the exception of Jeff Blauser — was less productive than he had been in 1996. What was the cause of this hitting malaise? Age? Complacency? A shift in the setting of the Braves' sun sign? We'll answer the question by rephrasing a slogan from the 1992 presidential campaign: "It was the ballpark, stupid!"

Prior to 1997, the Braves played in Atlanta-Fulton County Stadium, a.k.a. "The Launching Pad." If parents did not want their children to become pitchers, this was the place they took them for discouragement. Atlanta's former stadium was the best hitter's park in baseball.

However, their new field appears to have been custom-designed for the Braves' Cy Young Award-winning pitching staff. It has a huge foul territory; a lot of foul balls that would give hitters a second chance by dropping into the stands in other parks are dropping into fielders' gloves for outs at the Turner. The ball doesn't carry well, especially for the left-handed power hitters who flourished in Atlanta-Fulton County. Atlanta first baseman Fred McGriff's home run production dropped dramatically in 1997.

On the road, the Braves were their usual, dangerous selves. It was the ballpark that had changed, not the team. One drawback to the new field: It's too early to tell for certain — perhaps improvements will be made during the off-season — but players are already calling this the worst infield in baseball.

Wrigley Field: Chicago Cubs

Since its opening, Wrigley has been considered a hitters' paradise, but the park is deceptive. When the wind is blowing in, this stadium favors pitchers, particularly those who throw ground balls. However, when the wind shifts outward, scoring goes up nearly 40 percent, and your chances of hitting a home run double. I hit my first major league home run in this park.

Cinergy Field: Cincinnati Reds

For me, it will always be Riverfront Stadium because that was its name when my teammates on the Big Red Machine and I called it home. This is not a park of extremes. Home run hitters get some help — though nothing like they receive in Camden Yards (Baltimore) or the Big A (Anaheim). It is difficult to hit a triple here. The turf is hard, but not to the point that it unduly hinders the infielders. When I was playing here, Cincinnati general manager Dick Wagner and I used to have a running debate about the hitting background. My teammates and I wanted something darker. However, some optometrist had told Dick that a gray background would make it easier for the hitters to pick up the ball. We couldn't convince him otherwise, but we still managed to score a few runs.

Coors Field: Colorado Rockies

Baseball's black hole for hurlers. Pitchers who visit Coors are often never seen or heard from again. This is the greatest hitters' park of all time. Since the field opened in 1995, Colorado and its opponents have scored nearly twice as many runs at Coors as they do on the road. Because of this, people are often surprised by the park's dimensions. They expect Coors to be a bandbox. Its playing field is actually slightly larger than average. Home runs launch themselves into orbit because of the thin, mile-high atmosphere. And it isn't just a home run park. Because the visibility at Coors is excellent, you can get a good read on a pitcher's offerings. The spacious playing field inflates extra-base hit totals and batting averages.

Complete games are a rarity at Coors. Few pitchers dare throwing anything near the heart of the plate, so you'll see an unusually high number of walks and deep pitch counts. Any Rockies pitcher who maintains an earned run average (ERA) under 4.50 should be congratulated. In 1997, Colorado's Pedro Astacio was 12-10 with a 4.14 ERA. He did not get any Cy Young Award votes — one has to wonder if any Rockies pitcher ever will — but someone should have given him the Purple Heart.

County Stadium: Milwaukee Brewers

County Stadium won't be with us much longer; Miller Park is scheduled to be the Brewers' new home by the year 2000. County Stadium demonstrates a bias for pitchers: Run scoring here is annually below the league average. However, it is a chamber of horrors for pitchers who lack pinpoint control. Apparently the mound is poorly maintained, so walk totals soar. (By the way, the Brewers were an American League team until they switched to the National League starting in 1998.)

Pro Player Stadium: Florida Marlins

It has two deep power alleys; so if you want to see baseball's most exciting hit, the triple, this is the park. Pitchers enjoy an advantage here because of the spacious outfield; the Marlins' ERA is nearly a full point lower at home than on the road. In 1997, Marlins ace Kevin Brown was an excellent pitcher no matter where he took the mound, but he was darn near unhittable on his home ground. Batters who spray hits to all fields also find success here, but hitters like that usually do well in any environment.

Pro Player is built for speed; a team needs an outfield composed of sprinters to track down those balls that shoot through the gaps.

The Astrodome: Houston Astros

The Astrodome is where pitchers go to lick their wounds after a series at Coors. It is the best pitchers' park in the major leagues. This was baseball's first fully enclosed stadium, the first to offer baseball played on a surface other than grass. Batted balls receive no help from wind currents; your best shots will often plummet before they get anywhere near the fence. When I was with Houston my teammate Jimmy Wynn, who was called the Toy Cannon, had as much power as anybody in the game. He hit more than 30 home runs in only two different seasons with us and he never hit as many as 40. So many of his dingers died at the Dome, I believe he would have won two or three home run titles had he played his home games anywhere else. Since that time, they have brought in the fences some 15 feet (4.6m). It is still a pitcher's park. To win in the Astrodome, your team has to be fundamentally sound. It must play tight defense — runs are at a premium so you can't give away any — and do all the little things on offense: steal bases, execute the hit-and-run, and bunt runners over. Of course, a club should be able to do those things in any park, but it's particularly important here.

Dodger Stadium: Los Angeles Dodgers

One of the reasons the Dodgers seem to have great pitching year-in, year-out is their ballpark (signing talented pitchers like Sandy Koufax, Orel Hersheiser, and Hideo Nomo is another reason). Hitters don't see the ball well here and the ball doesn't carry. Maybe it's the smog's fault. Dodgers batters usually hit 10 to 30 points higher on the road with much better power numbers. Dodgers first baseman Eric Karros is an exception; he hits better at Dodger Stadium than on the road. Mike Piazza also hits well here, but he's a tough out wherever he plays.

Olympic Stadium: Montreal Expos

Another pitcher's park with a fast artificial surface. They brought in the fences a few seasons back to make life easier for pull hitters, but there is still plenty of outfield in which to lose hits. Olympic Stadium features a hard, marble-smooth turf; batters can get a lot of base hits driving ground balls through the infield. Montreal shortstop Mark Grudzielanek has become a master at slashing the ball down either line for doubles.

This is not a good park for ground-ball pitchers; the infield is just too fast. Power pitchers who induce fly balls have an overwhelming advantage here.

Shea Stadium: New York Mets

It certainly isn't the Houston Astrodome, but Shea is a tough park for home run hitters. In the park's first 34 seasons, only seven different Mets have slugged 30 or more home runs; the Dodgers had three players with 30 or more dingers *last season*. As the ball leaves the pitcher's hand, it momentarily gets lost in the background and can be difficult to track. Pitchers are doubly tough at night. The field is relatively poorly lit and the air seems to thicken, making it hard to drive the ball. Strikeout pitchers — who don't give the hitter much time to see the ball anyway — can swagger as they take the mound at Shea. However, ground-ball pitchers who rely on brains rather than brawn don't usually fare as well, particularly during the day.

Hitters have an extra split second to recognize a soft-tosser's stuff, and the Shea infield is nearly as bad as the one in Anaheim. Ground balls are an adventure on this surface.

Veterans Stadium: Philadephia Phillies

They claim the field is composed of Astroturf, but put one cleat on it and you would swear the Phillies are playing on cement. You can't regularly play a slow third baseman or first baseman in this park; the ball will get by them too quickly. Outfielders also have to be fast and strong-armed or the opposing team will bury them with extra base hits. This has always been a good park for left-handed line-drive hitters. When the Phillies won their last N.L. championship in 1993, their lineup often contained six left-handed hitters and two switch-hitters. Only one of that bunch (catcher Darren Daulton) hit more than 20 home runs that season, but Philadelphia still managed to lead the league in runs scored and doubles. The park was no small factor.

Three Rivers Stadium: Pittsburgh Pirates

A neutral park if there ever was one. Pirates hitters generally hit as well here as they do on the road. If it offers a slight advantage to anyone, it is left-handed home-run hitters who hit towering fly balls; Three Rivers seems to work against batters with line-drive power. (This stadium — along with others such as Veterans, Busch, and Cinergy Field — is often given as an example of the "cookie cutter" stadiums built in the late '60s and '70s. See Figure 16-4.)

Busch Stadium: St. Louis

This used to be an atrocious park for home-run hitters. The Cardinals won National League pennants in 1985 and 1987 with only one batter (outfielder/first baseman Jack Clark) hitting as many as 20 home runs. They also captured a world championship in 1982 without a single 20-home-run man. Busch Stadium was carpeted in Astroturf in those days, and the Cardinals game was built around speed. Team management has moved in the fences a tad since then, so it's a bit easier to hit home runs. They've also torn up the turf and returned to natural grass. Despite these alterations, Busch is still a below-average power park; the ball gets no help in the still air.

Qualcomm Stadium: San Diego Padres

Here is all you need to know about Padres right fielder Tony Gwynn: He has won eight batting titles while playing in a park that decreases batting averages sometimes to an extreme. In 1997, Padres center fielder Steve Finley hit .216 at home while batting .303 on the road. It's as if he were two different players. Smog is a factor in the poor visibility, and the San Diego infield is slow. Would-be ground-ball base hits are gobbled up before they reach the lip of the outfield grass. Ground-ball pitchers are right at home here. Left-handed fly-ball/power pitchers, however, are at a disadvantage in San Diego. It is relatively easy to hit home runs in this park, particularly if you are right-handed.

Figure 16-4:
Three
Rivers
Stadium.

National Baseball Hall of Fame Library Cooperstown, N.Y.

3Com Park: San Francisco Giants

Whenever I think of Candlestick, I get an image of Juan Marichal throwing that high curve against the wind so it would drop straight down as it got to the plate. Tough pitch.

Fielders would love to torch this place. When it was Candlestick Park, the gust could roll in off the bay to chill you even on a midsummer night. The wind was so powerful it blew 5-foot 11-inch, 185-pound reliever Stu Miller off the mound during the 1961 All-Star Game. Runners were on base so the umpires charged Miller with a balk.

Now the park is somewhat enclosed and the wind doesn't blow straight in anymore. Instead, it swirls around, like a giant whirlpool. Third basemen will dance a fandango under a ball that is eventually caught by the shortstop. The minicyclone will even alter the path of a softly hit ground ball. The left field line at 3Com is only 7 feet closer than the one right, yet the park favors right-handed home-run hitters by a wide margin. Giants left fielder Barry Bonds would post better numbers in almost any park. Again, it's the wind. The currents pushing toward left field are usually stronger than those toward right. This is generally a good park for pitchers, provided their fielders don't mutiny. If you're a hitter, there is one type of pitcher you don't want to face here: a knuckleballer who can work the currents. He'll throw off your swing for two weeks.

Bank One Park: Arizona Diamondbacks

I've seen the model for this new park. Its dimensions suggest a neutral field with perhaps a slight bias toward the pitcher. However, we have no idea what effects the retractable dome and air conditioning will have on offense. The stadium is family friendly with a play area that features a swimming pool. Bank One's retractable dome is a state-of-the-art affair that will supposedly open and close much faster than the dome in Toronto.

The American League stadiums

Ban Johnson founded the American League in 1900 and declared it a major league in 1901. It was not officially recognized as a major league until 1903. The original eight franchises were located in Chicago, Boston, Detroit, Philadelphia, Baltimore, Washington, Cleveland, and Milwaukee.

Anaheim Stadium: The Anaheim Angels

The Big A. For years this was a pitcher's park. Then in 1979, the Angels erected three-tier seating behind the outfield walls. That construction enclosed the stadium, cutting off the wind. Now the ball flies out of here. Over the last four seasons, this has been the best home run hitter's park in the American League. It is especially friendly to left-handed power hitters. California center fielder Jim Edmonds is more of a home run threat here than on the road. However, the stadium depresses batting averages because visibility is poor. The infield is notoriously rocky.

You are more likely to see an infield error occur in this park than in any other American League stadium.

Oriole Park at Camden Yards: The Baltimore Orioles

Visit Camden Yards and step into a time warp. This park is a throwback to the great bandbox stadiums of the 1930s. Whoever the architect was, he had to be a hitter. The foul territory is tiny and the fences are cozy-close. You will see a lot of home runs and doubles in this park, but the small dimensions make triples a rarity.

Keep an eye on the right fielder. The ball can take any number of crazy hops off of that tall wall and scoreboard that stands behind him. Like Anaheim, this a park where left-handed power hitters flourish.

Fenway Park: The Boston Red Sox

Think Fenway and you think of the Green Monster in left field, Ted Williams, Jim Rice, Carl Yastrzemski, and all those 10-9 slugfests. Great hitters' park, right? Not anymore. Fenway represents the flip side of Anaheim Stadium. In 1989, Boston constructed 600 stadium club seats above the grandstand behind home plate. Broadcast booths and a press box were installed atop that. Fenway's home improvements altered the park's wind currents in favor of the pitcher. Scoring has decreased ever since. It's still a good place for enhancing your batting average (its small foul area contributes to that), but it actually suppresses home run totals. (See Figure 16-5.)

Comiskey Park: Chicago White Sox

A stadium that should warm the heart of any second baseman. Grounds-keeper Roger Bossard and his crew maintain the infield so meticulously that the ball rarely takes a bad hop. This is a pitcher's park. Batting and slugging averages tumble when hitters spend any time here; nearly all the White Sox hitters fare much better on the road than at home. It makes you appreciate what an extraordinary hitter Frank Thomas is.

This park is not as nice as the other newer parks because the upper deck angle is so steep you feel as if you are going to fall out of your seat.

Figure 16-5:
The Green Monster looms at Fenway.

National Baseball Hall of Fame Library Cooperstown, N.Y.

Jacobs Field: Cleveland Indians

If it's late or early in the season, bring an overcoat. The wind off the nearby lake can be frigid. Jacobs Field has a well-deserved reputation as a hitter's park; visiting batters love to take their cuts here. However, The Jake can be hospitable to pitchers during those cold spring and fall evenings. Balls do not carry well to left field under any conditions.

Tiger Stadium: Detroit Tigers

If you have a favorite left-handed slugger, this is the place to watch him play. The short porch in right field is an inviting target for the likes of Ken Griffey, Jr. and Tino Martinez. Other hitters don't fare as well. Many long fly balls — sure home runs or extra-base hits in other stadiums — are nothing but outs in this park's cavernous center field. Batters who hit the ball on the ground are usually thwarted by the unusually high infield grass. Ground-ball pitchers, of course, flourish here.

Kauffman Stadium: Kansas City Royals

Home run hitters know that this is the toughest long-ball park in the American League. Its dimensions are actually smaller than Anaheim's home-run haven (Royals management recently brought in the fences), but the ball just doesn't carry well. Line-drive hitters who can drive the ball into the gap for doubles and triples fare best in this environment. George Brett, who hit nearly everything on the line, almost hit .400 while playing here, and his teammate Hal McRae, a similar hitter, won the American League Runs Batted In (RBI) crown at the age of 37.

Hubert H. Humphrey Metrodome: Minnesota Twins

They called it the Homerdome when it first opened in 1982, but that was a misnomer. Only until very recently home runs were hit here at a rate below the league average. It is, however, a great park for doubles and triples. You won't see a lot of infield errors in the Metrodome; this is the fastest artificial turf in the game; the ball either scoots right to you for an out or zips past you for a hit. Visiting outfielders hate the place. If you are unused to doing it, tracking a fly ball against the backdrop of the Metrodome ceiling can be an imposing task. Balls seem to drop from out of nowhere and then they play hopscotch on the turf. This quirk contributes to Minnesota's enormous home field advantage. In 12 postseason games played in the Dome, the Twins are 11-1, including 8-0 in the World Series. It has fond memories for me because I got my 2,500th major league hit here.

Yankee Stadium: New York Yankees

The myth is that Yankee Stadium favors left-handed power hitters. Actually it is a boon for left-handed pull hitters. If you can jack the ball down the line, you'll get some extra short porch home runs. Left-handed Yankees sluggers who often hit the ball to the opposite field — Babe Ruth, Lou Gehrig, and

Reggie Jackson come to mind here — usually stroked more home runs on the road than at home. The park helps a hitter like Yankees first baseman Tino Martinez, though he is powerful enough to hit the ball out of anywhere. Yankees right fielder Paul O'Neill, who is just as big, strong, and left-handed as Martinez, hits the ball to all fields, so the park deprives him of home runs. With its expansive center field and generous foul territory, Yankee Stadium, despite the long-ball heroics that helped make it famous, is a pitcher's park.

Oakland Alameda County Coliseum: Oakland Athletics

The best pitcher's park in the American League. Visibility is poor at the Coliseum, so batters tend to strike out more often here than in other stadiums. Statistics demonstrate that the park gives a slight edge to right-handed power hitters. Now that Mark McGwire is no longer playing there, let's see if those numbers hold up in the coming seasons.

The Kingdome: Seattle Mariners

This is a neutral park whose short right-field porch establishes a slight bias for left-handed pull hitters. The turf here isn't particularly lively; you don't see as many strange bounces as you do on other artificial surfaces. Opposing teams never relish visiting the Kingdome. Seattle's hometown fans are the most raucous in baseball. They can electrify their team with their cheering while taking the opposition out of the game.

The Ballpark At Arlington: Texas Rangers

Strange park. Generally, hitters' stadiums promote power, but Arlington is brutal for home run sluggers. Juan Gonzalez would probably hit 50 or more home runs if he played his home games in another park. Yet, the field is conducive to scoring a lot of runs because so many triples and doubles are hit here. Players call the rock-hard infield the worst in baseball; grounders that would be outs in most stadiums rush past infielders for singles or down the line for doubles. Arlington's error rate is 25 percent above the league average, even though the Rangers have been a team of good fielders over recent seasons.

SkyDome: Toronto Blue Jays

Right-handed hitters who spray the ball around thrive here; left-handed sluggers don't. Otherwise, it's a fairly neutral park. SkyDome's artificial turf infield may be the truest in baseball; you get the feeling that customs officials turn away bad bounce base hits at the border.

Tropicana Field: Tampa Bay Devil Rays

This domed stadium hadn't opened as this book went to press, so I won't know what quirks it offers players. The dome is nonretractable, so the team will be playing on artificial grass. Judging by the park's dimensions, the fences down the lines will be so close that pull hitters from either side of the plate will pay to play here. However, it will be hard to score against pitchers who can induce fly balls to the rest of the cavernous outfield.

Tropicana Field looks as if it will have a lot of strange angles, so outfielders better be prepared for some tricky caroms.

Stadium Statistics

Table 16-3 gives you the details on all the major league stadiums. (Because of lack of room, all these dimensions are in feet. If you want to talk meters, just divide the feet by 3.28.)

Table 16-3			Major League Stadium Statistics				
Park	**LF Line**	**Left CF**	**Center**	**Right CF**	**RF Line**	**Surface**	**Capacity**
Anaheim	333	386	404	386	333	Grass	64,593
Camden Yards	333	410	400	373	318	Grass	48,876
Fenway	315	379	390	380	302	Grass	33,871
Comiskey	347	375	400	375	347	Grass	44,325
Jacobs Field	325	370	405	375	325	Grass	42,865
Tiger Stadium	340	365	440	375	325	Grass	52,416
Kauffman	330	375	400	375	330	Grass	40,625
Metrodome	343	385	408	367	327	Artificial	56,785
Yankee	318	399	408	385	314	Grass	57,545
Oakland	330	375	400	375	330	Grass	42,313
Kingdome	331	389	405	380	312	Artificial	59,166
Arlington	332	390	400	381	325	Grass	45,200
SkyDome	328	375	400	375	328	Artificial	50,516
Tropicana	315	375	410	401	322	Artificial	45,200
Turner	335	380	401	390	330	Grass	49,833
Wrigley	355	368	400	368	353	Grass	38,765

(continued)

Table 16-3 (continued)

Park	LF Line	Left CF	Center	Right CF	RF Line	Surface	Capacity
Cinergy	330	375	404	375	330	Artificial	52,952
Coors	347	390	415	375	350	Grass	50,200
County	315	392	402	392	315	Grass	53,192
Pro Player	335	380	410	380	345	Artificial	40,585
Astrodome	325	375	400	375	325	Artificial	54,370
Dodger	330	385	395	385	330	Grass	56,000
Olympic	325	375	404	375	325	Artificial	46,500
Shea	338	371	410	371	338	Grass	55,777
Veterans	330	371	408	371	330	Artificial	62,136
Three Rivers	335	375	400	375	335	Artificial	47,972
Busch	330	375	402	375	330	Grass	57,673
Qualcomm	327	370	405	370	327	Grass	46,510
3Com Park	335	365	400	365	328	Grass	63,000
Bank One	330	375	407	374	334	Grass	48,500

Chapter 17

Keeping Up with the Show: Baseball Online, on the Air, and on the Newsstand

- -

In This Chapter

▶ Surfing for baseball on the World Wide Web

▶ Finding baseball on TV

▶ Reading about baseball

- -

*T*he enormous amount of media coverage baseball receives reflects the sport's enduring popularity. And the coverage doesn't end with the regular major league baseball season. You can be lounging in front of the fire in the dead of winter and still enjoy plenty of baseball action — without even leaving the comforts of your living room.

Baseball in Cyberspace

Back in the "old" days, you had to travel to your nearest newsstand to get the latest scores and news. Now you can get scores, news, and a wealth of other information at the click of a mouse. Thousands of baseball Web sites abound on the Internet. This section highlights some of the more popular ones.

MLB@Bat

In 1995, baseball became the first major league sport to go on the Internet (and the Seattle Mariners were the first team to have its own Web site). You can access the big league site, MLB@Bat, at www.majorleaguebaseball.com.

Then get ready to dive into a treasure trove of baseball delights. During a recent tour of the Web site, we discovered a live conference call between all 30 major league managers, the latest results from the Arizona Fall League, trivia contests, the complete records for the 1997 season, and a bevy of highlight films. During the regular season, you can summon up the latest standings, league leaders, plays of the week, and live broadcasts of games you can't see anywhere else.

The Negro Baseball Leagues

James A. Riley, director of research for the Negro Leagues Baseball Museum, is the editor of this Web site at www.blackbaseball.com. The site is an archival resource that acquaints you with the rich history of the various Negro leagues, their players, managers, owners, and teams. This site also serves as a clearinghouse for Negro League books (sold through a discount bookstore) and memorabilia such as jackets, caps, and autographs.

The Baseball Server

Although it is chock-full of major league information, the Baseball Server at www.nando.net/sportsserver/baseball/mlb.html is also the site to visit if you want find out what is happening in the minor leagues, from AAA ball to the independents. The Baseball Server features standings, stats, records, players of the week, and new highlights.

The National Baseball Hall of Fame and Museum

The National Baseball Hall of Fame on the Web at www.baseballhalloffame.org cannot give you the same thrills as an actual visit to Cooperstown, but it's the next best thing. This site offers users an online tour of the Hall of Fame, its museum, and its library. The Fall Classic page presents the history of the World Series as told through audio and video clips.

Total Baseball Online

Who holds the record for home runs by a National League switch-hitter? How many games did Babe Ruth win as a pitcher? The best place to find out is this Web site (www.totalbaseball.com/), which is affiliated with *Total*

Baseball, the official encyclopedia of the major leagues. You can download all the material found in that volume, including its illuminating articles on various aspects of baseball history. (By the way, the answers to our trivia questions are: Howard Johnson, who hit most of those homers as a third baseman with the New York Mets, and 96 pitching wins for Babe Ruth.)

Ballparks by Munsey & Suppes

Are you a ballpark buff? Does just a glimpse of Wrigley Field's near mythic ivy-covered walls set you to swooning? Have we got a Web site for you! Ballparks by Munsey & Suppes (`www.ballparks.com/baseball/index.htm`) has all the information you could ever possibly want about major league ballparks present, past, and future — including seating plans, field dimensions, interior and exterior photos, turf type (which tells you, for example, that the Orioles play on Maryland Bluegrass in Baltimore's Camden Yards), and historical summaries.

The Sports Network

This Canadian network's Web site at `tsn.ca` is one of the most creative in all sports. Besides the usual stats, standings, and records, it has featured interactive games such as Diamondball, which allows the fans to perform as virtual managers. The Couch Master, fast becoming a Canadian Internet legend, runs a rollicking Chat Room. During the 1997 World Series, fans of this site had the opportunity to engage in lively chats with Blue Jays ace Roger Clemens and future Hall of Famer Dave Winfield.

Major league team sites

Many of major league baseball's 30 franchises now boast Web sites so you can keep up with your favorite team's latest doings with the click of a mouse (see Table 17-1).

Table 17-1	Major League Team Web Sites
Team	*Site*
Arizona Diamondbacks	www.azdiamondbacks.com
Atlanta Braves	www.atlantabraves.com
Baltimore Orioles	www.theorioles.com
Boston Red Sox	www.redsox.com

(continued)

Table 17-1 (continued)

Team	Site
Chicago Cubs	www.cubs.com
Chicago White Sox	www.chisox.com
Cincinnati Reds	www.cincinnatireds.com
Cleveland Indians	www.indians.com
Detroit Tigers	www.detroittigers.com
Florida Marlins	www.flamarlins.com
Houston Astros	www.astros.com
Kansas City Royals	www.kcroyals.com
Los Angeles Dodgers	www.dodgers.com
Milwaukee Brewers	www.milwaukeebrewers.com
Minnesota Twins	www.wcco.com/sports/twins
Montreal Expos	www.montrealexpos.com
New York Yankees	www.yankees.com
Oakland Athletics	www.oaklandathletics.com
Philadelphia Phillies	www.phillies.com
Pittsburgh Pirates	www.piratesball.com
San Diego Padres	www.padres.org
San Francisco Giants	www.sfgiants.com
Seattle Mariners	www.mariners.org
St. Louis Cardinals	www.stlcardinals.com
Tampa Bay Devil Rays	www.devilray.com
Texas Rangers	www.texasrangers.com
Toronto Blue Jays	www.bluejays.ca

As we went to press, three teams still lacked official Web sites: The Anaheim Angels, Colorado Rockies, and New York Mets.

Baseball on the Tube

Who said that baseball on television was boring? This is your chance to prove them wrong. This section is a guide to get you pointed in the right direction — toward baseball on the tube.

ESPN

This cable network, based in Bristol, Connecticut, begins its regular-season baseball coverage on Opening Day. ESPN broadcasts Sunday night games as well as two games each Wednesday for a total of 75+ regular-season exposures. It also carries divisional playoff games during the postseason. Fans can get the latest scores and game gossip on *Baseball Tonight,* which airs every evening throughout the baseball season.

ESPN also affords baseball wide coverage all year round on its flagship news program, *Sportscenter.* The show appears at regular intervals throughout each day. ESPN2, the little brother of ESPN, does not offer live coverage of baseball. However, the ESPN2 sports ticker, which runs during its broadcasts of other sports, offers you up-to-the-minute game scores, transactions, and additional bits of news. ESPN2 also covers some off-field baseball events such as the 1997 expansion draft and the Baseball Hall of Fame induction ceremonies. Both stations broadcast college baseball games. Consult your schedule to find out who plays and when.

ESPN Sports Radio — a network with 375 affiliates around the country — broadcasts all postseason games (including the World Series), the All-Star Game, and a selection of regular season contests. Its All-Star coverage includes two events that take place the day before the game: the popular Home Run Derby and the All-Star Game Gala.

Fox Broadcasting

Ruppert Murdoch's Fox Network brings you 18 regular-season Saturday games starting in late May. Fox/Liberty, the network's cable arm, divides 52 national exposures between its Fox Sports Network and FX. As explained in the next section, Fox alternates its postseason coverage with NBC.

NBC

The network that made television history with *Baseball's Game of the Week* does not broadcast regular-season games under the current TV contract (which runs until the year 2000). However, it does alternate coverage with Fox Network for the All-Star Game, the League Championship Series, and World Series. In 1998, NBC covers the All-Star Game and the American League Championship Series, while Fox covers the World Series and National League Championship Series. The two networks will switch assignments in 1999 and trade back once more in 2000. ESPN also covers some League Championship Series games as part of this postseason trio.

The Sports Network

The Sports Network (TSN) is an independent cable network in Canada. In 1997, a typical broadcast year, TSN featured 80 Toronto Blue Jays games, 25 Montreal Expos games, assorted games from the Fox Network, and full coverage of the postseason.

The Classic Sports Network

Yes, the snow is piled up to your rooftop, but you can still watch baseball. Tuning in to the Classic Sports Network is like stepping into a time machine. The cable station doesn't carry any live baseball telecasts, but it does bring you some of the greatest games ever played in their entirety. You'll see the Brooklyn Dodgers win their first and only world championship, Nolan Ryan pitch a no-hitter, the storied sixth game of the 1975 World Series between the Red Sox and Reds, and much more. Check your cable listings to see if your carrier provides the station.

Caribbean League telecasts

Many Spanish-speaking networks carry baseball from the Caribbean leagues during the winter months. You can watch players like Juan Gonzalez, Bernie Williams, and Ivan Rodriguez strut their stuff while you wrap Christmas presents. Consult your local TV listings for times and schedules.

Baseball in Print

If you don't want to play or watch baseball (or look for it on the Web), why not read about it? This section describes some great starting points for you.

- ✔ *USA Today* (1-800-USA-0001) provides fans with excellent national baseball coverage daily. Unlike many local papers, it rarely brings a hometown slant to a game or story. *USA Today Baseball Weekly* is the best source of week-to-week coverage, particularly during the off-season.

- ✔ *The Sporting News* (800-777-6785) is an excellent weekly magazine/newspaper that covers all the major league teams throughout the year as well as other sports.

- ✔ For comprehensive coverage of a particular baseball news story or event, read *Sports Illustrated* (800-992-0196).

✔ *Baseball America* (800-845-2726) has a fortnightly publishing schedule; therefore, many of its major league stories are old news by the time a copy reaches your hands. However, no publication can surpass its coverage of minor league and college baseball. If you are in a fantasy league and want to chart the progress of an up-and-coming prospect, a subscription to this magazine is a shrewd investment. (See Chapter 18 for more information on fantasy leagues.)

Other publications for your baseball reading pleasure include

✔ *Baseball Digest* (800-877-5893). A monthly compendium of baseball articles written by leading sportswriters from around the country.

✔ *Street & Smith's Baseball* (212-880-8698). The most respected of the pre-season baseball annuals.

✔ *Who's Who In Baseball.* The complete records, minor and major league, of nearly every current major league player. It is updated annually.

✔ *Beckett's Baseball Card Monthly* (972-991-6657). A guide to the fluctuating baseball card market — the Dow Jones often exhibits less volatility — by the leaders in the industry.

Chapter 18
Fantasy Baseball

In This Chapter

▶ The lowdown on Fantasy League baseball

▶ Playing the game

▶ Fantasy baseball tips

Millions of people play fantasy baseball every year. "What's the big deal" you ask? Fantasy leagues let you act as general manager for a team of major leaguers in a baseball universe of your own creation. You get to pit your executive skills against an entire league of virtual general managers who try to guide their teams to the pennant. After scouting and "signing" players, you spend the entire season modifying your club through trades, free agent drafts, and other transactions. If you win a championship, you get to take home a little prize money, bask in the applause of family and friends, and have a bottle of Yoo-Hoo poured over your head (one of Fantasy Baseball's more endearing rituals).

Daniel Okrent — whose contributions to baseball literature include the aptly named *Ultimate Baseball Book* (Houghton-Mifflin) — created the first fantasy league in 1980 while dining in the Manhattan bistro La Rotisserie Française with several other devotees of the National Pastime. The originators named the game Rotisserie Baseball after the restaurant (many players today often use the terms Rotisserie Baseball and Fantasy Baseball interchangeably).

What the Heck Is Fantasy Baseball?

Fantasy baseball is a game you play with 10 to 12 people; each team selects 23 major league players who compete against the other "owners'" teams of 23 players based on the real-life, regular-season statistics of the players. The week before the start of the major league season, you gather with the other owners in your league and hold an auction-style draft where each owner "purchases" players. After each of you fills his roster of players, the competition begins. Your team battles against the other teams based on the real-life statistics of the players drafted. You don't play individual games in fantasy baseball; instead, you try to accumulate the best totals possible in each statistical category.

What baseball statistics do you use? Most leagues use the eight categories (four hitting, four pitching) as shown in Table 18-1.

Table 18-1	Fantasy Baseball Scoring Categories
Offense	*Pitching*
Total runs batted in (RBI)	Team ERA (See Chapter 14 for information on calculating ERA)
Total home runs	Total wins
Team batting average	Total saves
Total stolen bases	Walks plus hits divided by innings pitched ratio (WHIP)

The goal is to select players who will amass the highest totals in the categories (except for ERA and WHIP, where the lowest total wins). Find out more about scoring in the section "Figuring your point total and winning."

How Do I Play?

Covering all the nuances of fantasy baseball in a single chapter is impossible, so you get only the general stuff here. Check out Glenn Waggoner's *Rotisserie League Baseball* (Little, Brown) to find out more and help establish the official rules for your league.

Starting a league

Starting a league is easy. Here's what you do:

1. Recruit 11 friends.

Twelve is the usual number of teams for a fantasy league, but you can play with fewer.

2. Select a date to hold your annual player draft.

Most leagues hold the draft the weekend before the major league season begins. If this date doesn't work for your busy schedule, try to hold the draft two weeks before the start of the season or the weekend after baseball's Opening Day.

3. Choose to play with either National League or American League players. (See Chapter 13 for more information on the two leagues.)

Limit your fantasy league to selecting players from only National League teams or American League teams. Nearly all fantasy leagues choose only one league.

4. Agree on an entry fee.

This dollar amount can be as high or low as you like. Pool the entry fees together to form the "pot," the cash paid out to the winners at the end of the season.

That's it. Start gathering information on your favorite players and get ready to draft!

Drafting a team

Fantasy leagues have a genuine salary cap; you can't spend more than $260 for your entire roster. You don't have to play for actual money, however. You may credit an imaginary $260 to each team. However, you must keep the $260 to 23 player ratio. See the section "Filling out your roster" for the position-by-position breakdown of the 23-player roster.

Although no team must spend all $260, spending less isn't wise. Always try to spend all your money on draft day to maximize your chances of getting all the players you want.

Assign a drafting order for calling up players to the auction block. For example, Team A may start the draft by saying, "Ken Griffey, Jr. for $1." The other owners begin calling out bids, always upping the bid in increments of at least $1. When the bidding slows, the owner who started the bidding, in this case Team A, gives fair warning ("Griffey going once, going twice . . .") and if no other owner ups the bid, the last bidder wins Griffey, Jr. Team B then calls up a player, and then Team C and so on until all teams have drafted 23 players. Setting up a draft order ensures fairness because all owners get equal opportunity to call up players for auction.

Designate two people as "official" secretaries to record all the players, dollar amounts paid for each player, and remaining dollar amounts for each team. Accurate records will help resolve any potential conflicts.

Filling out your roster

Your roster must consist of the following:

- ✔ Two catchers
- ✔ One first baseman (first and third basemen are also known as *corners*)
- ✔ One second baseman
- ✔ One shortstop
- ✔ One third baseman
- ✔ A back-up second baseman or shortstop
- ✔ A back-up first or third baseman
- ✔ Five outfielders
- ✔ Nine pitchers

If you are playing with "American League rules," you need a designated hitter (see Chapter 3 if you don't know what a designated hitter is!). If you play "National League rules," draft a utility player (an extra outfielder, infielder, or catcher).

A player qualifies at a certain position by playing at least 20 games at that position during the previous year. For example, if a player appeared in at least 20 games each at second base and shortstop last year, you may play him at either position. If a player played 125 games at catcher and 15 at first base, you may only draft him as a catcher. The "position qualifying" rule varies widely from league to league; refer to the book *Rotisserie League Baseball* for more information.

Nearly all leagues also draft a group of *reserves*. Use these players to fill in for injured or traded players. Because so many leagues treat the reserve list differently, refer to Glenn Waggoner's *Rotisserie League Baseball* to help you formulate a reserve list policy for your league.

Managing your team after the draft

After the draft, you can kick back, relax, and watch your team in action. Or, to really have some fun, you can start calling fellow owners to make trades. Trading players with other owners adds spice to any league and can help you improve your team in the process. For every player you trade to a team, you must get an equal number of players in return. After completing a trade, all teams involved (yes, you can negotiate multiteam deals) must have 23 players on their roster.

When a flesh-and-blood major league player is traded out of his league, released, put on the disabled list, or dispatched to the minors during the actual season, you can replace him in your lineup. For example, if Ken Griffey, Jr. breaks his leg in April and misses the entire season, you can replace him with a player from your reserves or acquire a new player.

Once again, thousands of rule variations exist for handling player movement during the season. Refer to the book *Rotisserie League Baseball* to help your league adopt a policy for picking up new players during the season.

Taking care of administrative tasks

As you may have guessed, running your own fantasy league involves some work. Here are some tips for minimizing the work and maximizing the fun:

- **Adopt a written set of rules:** Absolutely, positively do this or you'll face dozens of arguments throughout the season. Take an existing set of rules, such as the ones in Glenn Waggoner's *Rotisserie League Baseball*, and use them exactly the way they are or feel free to modify them.

  Don't be afraid to tweak the so-called "traditional" rules of fantasy baseball. Make up whatever rules you think will make the game as fun as possible.

- **Appoint a commissioner:** Choose someone, preferably the most ethical owner in your league, to wear the commissioner's hat to enforce rules and arbitrate all disputes.

- **Buy a good statistics software package or pay for a stats service:** A good software package allows you to download stats via computer and prepare detailed weekly reports and standings for each team. Appoint a statistician (preferably the computer guru in your league) to oversee the operation. If you don't have a computer or want to offload the work, subscribe to a statistics service which, for a fee, will calculate all your statistics and standings and mail the weekly results to each owner.

  Check the classifieds in *Baseball Weekly* or search the Internet under "Fantasy Baseball" to see what's available in both stats software and services. Stats services usually charge a yearly fee per player; you can purchase the software for a one-time fee. A service definitely costs more but is very, very convenient and involves almost no work on your part.

Figuring your point total and winning

Rank teams throughout the season from first to last in each of the scoring categories. In a typical 12-team league, you award 12 points for every first place finish, 11 for second, 10 for third, and so on down to 1 point for 12th place. For example, say your team has the rankings shown in Table 18-2 in a 12-team league.

Table 18-2	A Scoring Example	
Category	*Place*	*Points*
Total Home Runs	1st	12
Total RBI	3rd	10
Batting Average	6th	7
Stolen Bases	5th	8
Pitching Wins	2nd	11
Pitching Saves	10th	3
ERA	8th	5
WHIP ratio	12th	1
Total		57

You then compare your 57 total points to the other teams' point totals. At season's end, the club with the most points finishes first. If you play for cash, award the prize money as follows (or create your own prize money distribution):

✔ 50 percent of the total prize money pool for the pennant winner

✔ 20 percent for second place

✔ 15 percent for third

✔ 10 percent for fourth

✔ 5 percent for fifth

Some Tips for Fantasy Baseball Success

Use the following information to keep your team near the top of the standings and your sanity on an even keel:

✔ **Gather info, more info, and even more info.** Gather as much information on players as you possibly can. Information gathering is the key to drafting success.

Check out as many preseason publications as you can. *USA Today*'s *Baseball Weekly* puts out an excellent preseason fantasy baseball issue in mid-March that contains loads of info, including projected draft dollar values for each player.

- ✔ **Carefully monitor your money during the draft.** Remember, you have only $260 to spend on 23 players. Plan wisely.

- ✔ **Choose players who stay healthy.** Injuries can destroy even the strongest team. Try to avoid the injury-prone players.

- ✔ **Beware of Spring Training phenoms.** Just because a rookie has a great Spring Training (baseball's preseason) doesn't necessarily mean his success will carry over into the regular season. Don't overbid for a player based solely on his success in the preseason.

- ✔ **Watch out for the "World Series" factor.** If a player had a great World Series the year before, chances are owners will overbid for him in the next year's draft. World Series heroes usually remain fresh in everyone's mind on draft day. Don't get suckered in to overbidding for them.

- ✔ **Remember, there's always next year.** Is your team mired in last place? Don't worry — hope springs eternal — next year could be the year you win it all.

Economics 101: Supply and demand in fantasy baseball

Here's where you finally find a practical use for that high school or college Economics course you took years ago. Just as scarcity of oil in Saudi Arabia causes gasoline prices to rise in the U.S., supply and demand of players dictates the prices paid in fantasy baseball drafts. A short supply of certain types of players sends bids soaring through the roof. For example, each team in the majors typically includes a *closer* (a relief pitcher who finishes off games). Because closers accumulate most of the saves (one of the scoring categories in fantasy baseball), most drafts place a premium on the short supply of each league's outstanding closers (count on paying $25–$35 each). Similarly, demand rages for *four category players* — offensive players who excel in all four scoring categories: batting average, home runs, RBIs, and stolen bases. For example, in 1997 Larry Walker hit .366 with 49 homers, 130 RBIs, and 33 stolen bases — the type of season that fantasy owners drool over. Expect to pay around $35–$40 for scarce, four-category players like Walker.

Unique events during your draft may cause player values to fluctuate as well. For example, if three teams still need a first baseman and only one good first baseman remains available, you'll pay a pretty penny for him or, if you get outbid, get stuck with a lousy first baseman. Also, watch out for the favorite team factor: If most of your league's owners follow the Cubs, for example, expect a high demand and overbidding for Cubs players.

Part V
The Part of Tens

The 5th Wave   By Rich Tennant

In this part . . .

This part introduces you to Joe's pick of baseball's top players, pitchers, and fielders — past and present. One of our favorite chapters is our list of ten future stars. If you are as new to major league baseball as these rising stars are, you can grow up in the sport together! You can also read about ten events that shaped baseball into the game it is today as well as our ten nominees for records that are likely never to be broken.

Chapter 19

Joe Morgan's Top Ten Players, All-Time and Current

In This Chapter

▶ Willie Mays

▶ Babe Ruth

▶ Hank Aaron

▶ Ty Cobb

▶ Mickey Mantle

▶ Frank Robinson

▶ Joe DiMaggio

▶ Roberto Clemente

▶ Jackie Robinson

▶ Ted Williams

▶ Ken Griffey, Jr.

▶ Barry Bonds

▶ Frank Thomas

▶ Mike Piazza

▶ Jeff Bagwell

▶ Tony Gwynn

▶ Larry Walker

▶ Mark McGwire

▶ Mo Vaughn

▶ Juan Gonzalez

Some of these names are already household words — at least in a house inhabited by even the most rudimentary baseball fan. Other names may soon be household words. In any case, these players are the ones you'd want on your team.

The Ten Best Players of All Time

Just ask any group of baseball fans "Who are the best players of all time," and then stand back and watch the fireworks. They'll be debating for days; I argued with myself before finally whittling my list down to these ten megastars.

Willie Mays (New York-San Francisco Giants, New York Mets)

Willie could do anything on a baseball field and he did it all with show-stopping flair. When I think of Mays, I think of him in a hurry: streaking around the bases or running out from under his hat to make another rally-breaking catch. He won as many stolen base titles (four) as he did home run championships. My favorite part of his game was his baserunning; I never saw anyone better at taking an extra base. Willie had an instinct for where the ball was hit, where he was on the basepaths, and who was throwing from what angle. That's something you can't teach.

Babe Ruth (Boston Red Sox, New York Yankees, Boston Braves)

I didn't see Ruth play, so I can't rate him higher than Willie Mays. Comparing players from different eras is difficult, but Babe's record is impossible to ignore. Imagine if Randy Johnson, the best left-hander in baseball today, retired from the pitcher's mound and became Mark McGwire, the game's most prolific slugger. Ruth was a great pitcher first and an even better hitter second. He wasn't just an offensive force, either. Teammates remember him as an excellent outfielder with a powerful arm. Babe Ruth epitomized the America of the Roaring '20s, a country enthralled with its own size, power, and audacity. He will always be Mr. Baseball. (See Figure 19-1.)

Hank Aaron (Milwaukee-Atlanta Braves, Milwaukee Brewers)

Hank's 755 career home runs have overshadowed his other talents. He was an underrated outfielder who rarely made a mental mistake and was an excellent baserunner. Fans also tend to forget what an outstanding *base stealer* he was. A base stealer must be successful on 80 percent of his attempts to maximize his effectiveness. Aaron was right around that mark — and he usually stole his bags in crucial situations.

Figure 19-1:
Babe Ruth
was known
as the
Sultan of
Swat for his
home-run
hitting
ability.

National Baseball Hall of Fame Library Cooperstown, N.Y.

Ty Cobb (Detroit Tigers, Philadelphia A's)

Nobody liked Ty Cobb, but nobody could stop him. We are told that Cobb was arrogant, rude, bigoted, paranoid, and vindictive. And those were his close friends speaking; his enemies' opinions of him are unprintable. He often slid into bases with his spikes held high to slash opposing fielders. He once allegedly beat a man who had no hands. You might find Cobb's picture in the dictionary next to the word "sociopath," but he was a genius with a bat in his hands. He won 12 batting championships, including nine in a row. We don't think of Cobb as a power hitter, yet he led the American League in slugging eight times. He was the premier base stealer during a time when the stolen base was a primary offensive weapon. You can't win any game unless you score; Cobb put himself in position to score more runs — 2,245 of them — than anybody. His lifetime batting average: a career chart-topping .367. (See Figure 19-2.)

Figure 19-2:
Ty Cobb
was a
fearless
(and
fearsome)
competitor.

Mickey Mantle (New York Yankees)

The best switch-hitter ever. Mantle was the fastest man in baseball during his prime and he consistently hit the ball farther than anyone. Mickey always regretted that his lifetime batting average dipped below .300. However, he finished up with an on-base average and slugging percentage higher than either Aaron or Mays. He didn't run as often as Mays; the stolen base was rarely a part of the Yankee attack. But when Mickey wanted to steal a base, few catchers could stop him. From 1955 to 1961, he stole 100 bases while getting caught only 13 times. He was a converted shortstop who turned himself into a Gold Glove outfielder.

Frank Robinson (Cincinnati Reds, Baltimore Orioles, California Angels, Los Angeles Dodgers, Cleveland Indians)

One of the great field leaders, Frank Robinson was one of the toughest competitors I ever saw. He is still the only player to win Most Valuable Player awards in both leagues. Frank hit for power and average. He was a punishing baserunner who broke up the double play as well as anyone. In 1975, Frank became baseball's first black manager. He has always been a great leader. (See Figure 19-3.)

Figure 19-3:
Frank Robinson was as tough on the base-paths as he was in the batter's box.

National Baseball Hall of Fame Library Cooperstown, N.Y.

JOE SAYS

A case for Josh Gibson

I would have liked to have included Josh Gibson on this list. He was one of the great Negro League stars who didn't get an opportunity to cross the major league color line. Josh died of a brain hemorrhage at the age of 33 only months before Jackie Robinson made his major league debut. Gibson reportedly hit nearly 1,000 home runs in his 17-year career while batting .350. Satchel Paige told me Josh was the greatest hitter he ever saw — and Satch pitched against Williams, DiMaggio, and Mantle.

Joe DiMaggio (New York Yankees)

Joe DiMaggio, nicknamed the Yankee Clipper, possessed such formidable all-around skills that he won an MVP award in 1941, even though Ted Williams hit .406 that season. Ted didn't complain about the selection; he told me DiMaggio was the greatest player he ever saw. As a center fielder, DiMaggio had such a great, natural stride that he made the most difficult catches look easy. Sluggers usually run up big strikeout totals, so I was especially impressed with these two items from the DiMaggio dossier: 361 home runs with only 369 strikeouts.

Roberto Clemente (Pittsburgh Pirates)

Willie Mays and Robin Roberts both told me that Clemente was the best player they ever saw. He won four batting titles, an MVP, and a World Series MVP. A right-handed batter, Clemente hit the ball to the opposite field harder than most left-handed pull-hitters could. He didn't achieve the home run totals of Mays or Aaron, but he played most of his career in Forbes Field, a terrible park for homers. I remember the center field at Forbes being so deep that the grounds crew would store the batting cage out in its farthest reaches during games! Roberto was a great right fielder with a legendary arm. After he threw out 27 baserunners during the 1961 season, the league stopped running on him. His 13 consecutive Gold Gloves (1960-72) represents the record for outfielders.

Jackie Robinson (Brooklyn Dodgers)

Jackie Robinson's career numbers aren't as lofty as the others on this list. However, because of his color, the league didn't allow Jackie to play major league ball until he was 28 years old, so he missed some of his prime playing years. Despite the late start to his career, Robinson won the Rookie of the Year Award and National League MVP. He was the most intimidating base-runner of his time, and he reintroduced the stolen base as an offensive weapon. As the man who broke baseball's color line, he played magnificently under more pressure than any player before or since. We'll never know just how great he was because of the stress he lived with every day. (See Figure 19-4.)

Figure 19-4: Jackie Robinson broke baseball's longstanding color line in 1947.

National Baseball Hall of Fame Library Cooperstown, N.Y.

Ted Williams (Boston Red Sox)

Ted Williams was only an adequate fielder with a mediocre throwing arm. He was also an average runner. But once he got a bat in his hands, everyone forgot about his shortcomings. Known as the Splendid Splinter, Williams had the best combination of on-base percentage and slugging average of any hitter this side of Ruth. He won six American League batting championships and four home run titles. Ted also led the league in runs batted in (4 times), runs scored (6 times), slugging average (9 times), on-base percentage (12 times), and walks (8 times). He is, famously, the last of the .400 hitters (.406 in 1941). Ted won his first batting crown when he was 23 and his last at the age of 40.

The Ten Best Current Players

Looking over this list, you immediately recognize there is no talent drought in major league baseball. Most of these players are under 30 years old and possess multidimensional skills. I wouldn't be surprised if all of them reached the Hall of Fame. (The current team for each player is given in parentheses.)

Ken Griffey, Jr. (Seattle Mariners)

Ken Griffey is like a young Willie Mays. He has the same tools, though he doesn't steal bases as often as Willie did. He also plays the game with Mays-like flair. When you watch Jr. at the plate, notice the sound the ball makes when it jumps off of his bat. He hits the ball hard almost every time up and his home runs are usually long line drives to straight-away right field rather than arching fly balls. Another sign of greatness: Though a left-handed hitter, Jr. is deadly against left-handed pitchers; he hits them with even more power than he does right-handers. (See Figure 19-5.)

Barry Bonds (San Francisco Giants)

In 1996, Barry Bonds became the first National Leaguer to hit 40 home runs and steal 40 bases in the same season. That record sums up Barry's game: an equal blend of flash and crash that no one else in the National League can equal. How feared is Barry in major league dugouts? During the 1996 season, Reds manager Ray Knight ordered his pitcher to intentionally walk Bonds even though Bonds was leading off the ninth inning and the Reds had only a one-run lead. Conventional baseball wisdom says never intentionally walk the potential tying run, especially with none out in the ninth. That's Barry. He forces managers to rewrite their strategy books. Barry Bonds won three National League MVP awards and easily could have won four or five.

Figure 19-5:
Ken Griffey, Jr. is one of the brightest stars in baseball today.

National Baseball Hall of Fame Library Cooperstown, N.Y.

Frank Thomas (Chicago White Sox)

Defensively, Frank Thomas is an average first baseman, and a dead man walking probably beats him in a sprint. But the Big Hurt (Thomas's appropriate nickname) is here because of his big bat. Frank is the Ted Williams of this generation. Thomas hit over .300 with at least 25 homers, 100 runs batted in (RBIs), 100 runs, and 100 walks in seven consecutive seasons. No other player in major league history can boast of such a streak. I admire his work ethic. Frank is a "first to come, last to leave the ballpark" baseball soldier. Players with less talent should use him as a role model. Frank Thomas is a two-time Most Valuable Player.

Mike Piazza (Los Angeles Dodgers)

Mike Piazza is the foundation of the Dodgers' lineup; no current player is more indispensable to his team. When it comes to combining average and power, he is the best hitting catcher ever, and that includes Hall of Famers such as Johnny Bench, Yogi Berra, and Roy Campanella. He is especially deadly with runners in scoring position. Mike wasn't strong defensively when he first entered the major leagues. However, he has put in long hours working to improve his catching skills. Mike showed immense improvement in every defensive department in 1997.

Jeff Bagwell (Houston Astros)

Another former Most Valuable Player, Jeff Bagwell is a great runs batted in (RBI) man with power. Jeff has deceptive speed and will steal a base when his team needs one. He is also aggressive on the basepaths. If you're a second baseman, you don't relish hanging in on the double play when Bagwell is bearing down on you. Jeff plays Gold Glove defense at first. He has the reactions of a third baseman and is especially good at fielding bad throws.

Tony Gwynn (San Diego Padres)

We all know about the batting titles, but Tony Gwynn also has several Gold Gloves on his mantel. His throwing arm is average, but he makes up for it with accuracy. He's been slowed by several injuries over his career, but he's one of the smarter baserunners in the game. He knows when he can take an extra base and when he can steal a bag. (But don't forget that Tony is one of the all-time great hitters!)

Larry Walker (Colorado Rockies)

I rated him highly even before his 1997 breakout season. Walker has one of the best arms of any right fielder in baseball. Another deceptively fast runner, he's a threat to join Barry Bonds in the National League's 40-40 club (40 home runs and 40 stolen bases).

Mark McGwire (St. Louis Cardinals)

Here's how Larry Walker described a home run McGwire hit against the Rockies in 1997: "When the ball came down, it had moon dust all over it." Baseball has evolved into a home run hitting contest, and no one is better than McGwire at jacking the ball out of the park. And he's more than just a hitter. Mark is an excellent first baseman with surprising range, quick feet, and sure hands.

Mo Vaughn (Boston Red Sox)

Mo Vaughn is another big guy (6 feet 1 inch, 240 pounds) who looks like a one-dimensional slugger, but he isn't. Besides hitting for average and power, Mo is a disciplined, intelligent baserunner. He is faster than he appears. Mo will score from first on balls hit down the right field line because he studies the fielders and knows the nuances of the ballparks.

Juan Gonzalez (Texas Rangers)

Juan Gonzalez entered 1996 in the third year of a hefty, five-year contract. He had posted respectable numbers during the first two seasons of that pact, but he was not satisfied. Juan was no longer among the leaders in any major offensive departments. The two-time American League home run king felt he owed it to his team to rejoin the ranks of elite hitters. Juan missed a month of the 1996 season, yet he still hit 47 home runs and won the American League MVP award. He continued his improvement in 1997 by spending extra hours in the batting cage learning how to hit the inside pitch while *laying off* (not swinging at) breaking balls in the dirt.

Chapter 20

Joe Morgan's Top Ten Pitchers, All-Time and Current

In This Chapter

▶ Cy Young

▶ Warren Spahn

▶ Walter Johnson

▶ Lefty Grove

▶ Christy Mathewson

▶ Steve Carlton

▶ Tom Seaver

▶ Sandy Koufax

▶ Bob Gibson

▶ Juan Marichal

▶ Greg Maddux

▶ Roger Clemens

▶ Randy Johnson

▶ Tom Glavine

▶ John Smoltz

▶ Pat Hentgen

▶ Pedro Martinez

▶ David Cone

▶ Mike Mussina

▶ Alex Fernandez

*F*rom Cy Young to Greg Maddux, these are the pitchers you'd want on the mound for any important game — well, for *any* game, to be honest. Be sure to check out Chapter 6 for details on the pitching stuff mentioned here, and Chapter 14 describes how you can figure out some of the statistics associated with pitching.

The Ten Best Pitchers of All Time

How good were these ten? Nolan Ryan has 5,714 career strikeouts and he didn't survive the cut.

Cy Young (Cleveland Spiders, St. Louis Red Stockings, Boston Americans, Cleveland Indians)

Cy Young pitched at the turn of the century, so I don't know much about him. What I do know is enough: 511 career wins. All any pitcher has to do to match that total is win 20 games a year for 25 years. And he'd still end up 11 wins short. Young pitched more than 400 innings in five different seasons. I get a sore arm just writing that. Among his pitches, Cy reportedly threw a tobacco ball, which I guess was a spitball with something extra on it.

Warren Spahn (Boston-Milwaukee Braves, San Francisco Giants, New York Mets)

Warren Spahn didn't record his first major league victory until he was 25, a fairly late start. Yet he won more games (363) than any other left-hander. He was a crafty pitcher with power; Warren led the National League in strikeouts for five consecutive seasons. He lasted so long because he always made adjustments. When his fastball slipped, he added a screwball and change-up. When his curve flattened, he picked up a slider. Durability was his strength. At age 40, he led the league in wins (21) and earned run average (3.02). Two years later, Warren won 23 games and had a 2.60 earned run average. On July 2, 1963, he lost an epic 1-0, 16-inning duel to San Francisco's Juan Marichal. (He gave up a home run to Willie Mays.) Spahnie told me he mistreated his body in that game; he was never the same pitcher after that.

Walter Johnson (Washington Senators)

The pitcher everybody else is measured against. Nicknamed the Big Train, Johnson won 416 games for a Washington Senator team that finished in the second division in 10 of his 21 seasons. Most major league pitchers fail to notch 100 career wins; Johnson recorded 110 career *shutouts!* Do you know what that means? Those were 110 games his team could not lose. As hard as he threw — he was built like Nolan Ryan and apparently had the same kind of stuff — Johnson had excellent control. His lifetime earned run average of 2.17 looks like a typo. It isn't.

Lefty Grove (Philadelphia A's and Boston Red Sox)

Another pitcher who didn't win a major league game until he was 25. He was a dead-red fastball pitcher; old-timers claim his ball hardly moved at all, but it was so fast hitters couldn't catch up to it. Here's the most impressive thing about Grove: He won 20 or more games in seven consecutive seasons when his fastball was at its best. After his fastball cooled down, he developed a curve. His newly developed curveball was good enough to help him win 83 games and three ERA titles over a five-year span. Like Spahn, he adjusted.

Christy Mathewson (New York Giants)

His 372 wins are third on the all-time list. The most amazing aspect of his record is his control. In 1908, Matty pitched 391 innings and walked only 42 batters. He once won a nine-inning game using only 67 pitches. In the 1905 World Series, Mathewson pitched three shutouts in six days and allowed only one base on balls. His *out pitch* was the "fadeaway," a latter-day screwball that he consistently threw for strikes.

Steve Carlton (St. Louis Cardinals, Philadelphia Phillies, San Francisco Giants, Chicago White Sox)

One way to judge a pitcher is to see how much better his record is than his team's. In 1972, Carlton pitched for a Phillies club that won only 59 games. Twenty-seven of them belonged to the man nicknamed Lefty. He had a great fastball, a good curve, and the best slider ever thrown on this planet. Nearly all pitchers throw sliders with a twist of the elbow. Carlton, however, pulled across the ball. But Steve's fingers were so strong the result was a bat-breaking slider. Because the motion put no strain on his elbow, he maintained his power pitching into a relatively old age. (See Figure 20-1.)

Figure 20-1:
Steve
Carlton
brings it
home.

National Baseball Hall of Fame Library Cooperstown, N.Y.

Tom Seaver (New York Mets, Chicago White Sox, Boston Red Sox)

Tom Seaver had a great moving fastball that overpowered most hitters. He also loved center stage in New York. When he pitched at Shea Stadium, it was as if he were appearing on Broadway. I had a few home runs off him, fought him off now and then, but I usually didn't hit him hard. Tom also had a good slider and, around the middle of his career, he'd surprise you with an occasional change. But mostly he attacked you with hard stuff. He really didn't have much of a curveball; he didn't need one. (See Figure 20-2.)

Sandy Koufax (Los Angeles Dodgers)

Sandy's fastball and curveball were the two best pitches I've ever seen. You couldn't pick up any spin on his curve. It was nearly as fast as his fastball

National Baseball Hall of Fame Library Cooperstown, N.Y.

Figure 20-2:
Tom Seaver
knew how
to throw the
hard stuff.

and it didn't just drop; it exploded out of the hitting zone. His riding fastball had everything on it. He threw as hard as Nolan Ryan, but his control was better. I've faced a lot of great pitchers — Gibson, Seaver, and Carlton among them — on those rare days when they didn't have their best stuff. I never saw Sandy take the mound with anything less than his full arsenal.

Bob Gibson (St. Louis Cardinals)

During a game against the Pirates in 1967, Roberto Clemente hit a line drive off Gibson's leg. Gibby pitched to another batter before he realized the leg was broken. He was the toughest competitor I ever faced. Great slider, great fastball, and a tremendous will to win. Gibson's expression always said, "You can't hit me." You had to admire that attitude if you were his teammate, but if you were hitting against him it could get under your skin. Gibson was a gifted all-around athlete who won nine straight Gold Gloves and was a dangerous hitter with good power.

Satchel Paige

Satchel Paige was another great Negro League star who deserves mentioning. The color line came down just in time for the 42-year-old Satch to join the Cleveland Indians in 1948. In the midst of a grueling pennant race, Paige went 6-1 with a 2.47 earned run average. Though accurate records are scarce and not always substantiated, it has been estimated that Satch won over 600 games during a 30-year career with eight different Negro League and assorted barnstorming teams. Robin Roberts (a Hall of Fame pitcher who won 286 games in 19 major league seasons) told me Satchel Paige was the best pitcher he ever saw.

Juan Marichal (San Francisco Giants, Boston Red Sox)

Like Greg Maddux — only with better stuff. Juan was a magician on the mound. His bag of tricks included two different fastballs, a curve, a slider, a screwball, a palmball, a straight change, you name it. He threw them all for strikes from every conceivable angle. Juan pitched in and out, and up and down within the strike zone, and changed speeds. You could go an entire game without seeing the same pitch twice. At Candlestick Park, where he usually threw against the wind, Marichal would take something off his curve so that it would break more. When he pitched at the Astrodome, where wind was never a factor, he threw a harder curve. That's pitching.

The Ten Best Current Pitchers

Today's hitters are bigger and stronger than ever, and ballparks are becoming increasingly smaller. Fans expect every game to be a slugfest — except when these pitchers are on the mound. The following ten pitchers seemingly turn back the clock to the dead ball era of the 1900s, and teams become grateful for any runs that they score. (The current team for each player is given in parentheses.)

Greg Maddux (Atlanta Braves)

Four Cy Young Awards make this an easy choice. If a strike is a pitcher's best friend, Greg Maddux will never be lonely. He throws more strikes than any other pitcher in baseball. Maddux gets 75 percent of his first pitches over the plate for strikes. When he's behind in the count, he displays a jewel cutter's precision; he rebounds with a strike in over 80 percent of those situations. Maddux features the standard assortment of pitches — fastball, slider, and curve. He doesn't throw especially hard, but his ball moves so much it doesn't matter. His biggest asset? A preternatural instinct for knowing what pitch the hitter *isn't* looking for — five-time batting champion Wade Boggs claims Maddux has a crystal ball in his glove. His best weapons? Control and changing speeds.

Roger Clemens (Toronto Blue Jays)

In 1997, Roger Clemens tied his own major league, single-game record by striking out 20 batters. Power pitchers tend to mix in a lot of fly ball outs with their strikeouts. When you watch Clemens pitch, notice the high number of groundouts he records. His rising fastball accounts for most of his strikeouts, but his hard sinker and splitter induce batters to beat the ball into the ground when he needs a double play. Clemens knows how to finish games and finish off hitters; he is nearly invincible with a late-inning lead. His fourth Cy Young Award in 1997 makes him a lock for the Hall of Fame.

Randy Johnson (Seattle Mariners)

How do you spell unfair? Johnson is 6 feet 10 inches, throws about 1,000 mph, has a wicked, slashing slider, and is just wild enough to make hitters call their insurance agents between innings. Everybody has a hard time hitting him, but this southpaw (left-hander) is particularly damaging to the fragile psyches of left-handed hitters. When the Colorado Rockies played Seattle in 1997, Larry Walker — who was only hitting .400 at the time — benched himself rather than face Johnson. The two did have a memorable confrontation in the All-Star Game later that year — the left-handed Walker came to the plate batting right-handed for the first time in his major league career (and even took one pitch).

Tom Glavine (Atlanta Braves)

Tommy Glavine reminds me a bit of Warren Spahn. Both left-handers were known for spotting the ball, though they could also strike hitters out. Tommy doesn't throw Spahnie's screwball. Instead, he combines his 90-mph fastball with one of the best change-ups in the business. He has a good slider, which he will often run in on righties. Tommy is fearless; he never gives in to the hitter. Even when he's behind in the count, he'll still work the borders of the plate rather than just throw a strike near the middle.

John Smoltz (Atlanta Braves)

Pitch for pitch, John Smoltz might have the best pure stuff in baseball. His fastball hits the mid-90s, his *splitter* (split-fingered fastball) rates among the league's nastiest pitches, and his curveball is hard to pick up because it breaks late. However, his best weapon is a great slider. When John takes his full wind-up, he's virtually unhittable; he's more vulnerable pitching from the stretch. But to get him to pitch from the stretch, you have to get base-runners on against him when he's pitching from that full wind-up. That's the kind of paradox that transforms a lot of batters into Amway salesmen.

Pat Hentgen (Toronto Blue Jays)

Hentgen has two outstanding fastballs. He throws a hard cutter to get out left-handed hitters. He throws a rising, four-seam fastball to retire right-handed hitters. He also uses that four-seamer against sluggers — no matter what side of the plate they swing from — in key situations. His secret weapon is a *slurve,* a hard, twisting breaking ball that is a hybrid of the slider and curve. When he gets the slurve over on a two-strike count, many hitters are too surprised to swing at it.

Pedro Martinez (Boston Red Sox)

Pedro Martinez has a reputation for pitching inside. Way inside. He must lead both leagues in knockdown pitches. Because he throws in the mid-90s, he provides hitters with plenty of incentive to stay loose when they face him. Martinez offsets an explosive fastball with a sinking change-up that destroys a hitter's timing. He doesn't allow many baserunners. Mark McGwire says that Martinez — a 1997 Cy Young recipient — has the best stuff he has ever seen.

David Cone (New York Yankees)

David Cone throws two sliders: a conventional overhand version and his *laredo,* a sidearm pitch that backs right-handed hitters off the plate before he even releases it. Coney alters the movement on his 90+-mph fastball with a variety of grips. He will also change speeds with his curve. His big out pitch is a hard splitter. David has an ace's temperament. To get him out of a game you have to drag him from the mound. He's famous for throwing as many as 150 pitches in a single game. A tough competitor.

Mike Mussina (Baltimore Orioles)

Mike Mussina complements his cutter, four-seam fastball, and knuckle-curve with the best change-up in the league. Mussina is always among the American League leaders in wins. He had some of his worst numbers in 1996, but in some ways it may have been his most impressive year. Mike couldn't get the ball down that season; he surrendered 31 home runs and his earned run average (ERA) soared to nearly 5.00. Yet he still scuffled to 19 wins. That's what you want to see from a starting pitcher. Forget about ERAs and those other stats. Starters are paid to win; Mussina has proven he can do that even when he doesn't have his best stuff.

Alex Fernandez (Florida Marlins)

A warrior. Like David Cone, Alex Fernandez will throw as many pitches as it takes to win. Study his pitching motion: Smooth, compact, all silken violence, it's as near to perfect as a pitcher can get. Fernandez doesn't have any one big pitch. His fastball, curve, slider, and change-up are all way above average, though; Alex can get outs with any of them. He has a quick move to first that keeps baserunners anchored. Alex excels defensively because his mechanics usually leave him in good fielding position. Unfortunately, during the 1997 National League Championship Series, it was discovered that Fernandez had a rotator cuff injury. It remains to be seen how he will recover.

Chapter 21

Joe Morgan's Top Ten Fielders, All-Time and Current

In This Chapter

▶ Willie Mays

▶ Ozzie Smith

▶ Curt Flood

▶ Bill Mazeroski

▶ Johnny Bench

▶ Roberto Clemente

▶ Brooks Robinson

▶ Keith Hernandez

▶ Ken Griffey, Jr.

▶ Luis Aparicio

▶ Ken Griffey, Jr.

▶ Barry Bonds

▶ Ivan Rodriguez

▶ Charles Johnson

▶ Roberto Alomar

▶ Omar Vizquel

▶ Jim Edmonds

▶ Rey Ordonez

▶ Ken Caminiti

▶ Barry Larkin

You can't succeed in baseball without fielding. Getting leather on the ball (defense) is just as important as getting wood (offense) on it. Be sure to check out Chapter 7 for details on how to field at each position.

The Ten Best Fielders of All Time

Wide range, soft hands, and quick reflexes weren't enough to earn a player a spot on this list. All ten of these fielders made the grade because they also knew what to do with the ball *after* they caught it.

Willie Mays (New York-San Francisco Giants, New York Mets)

You can't teach a person to play defense the way Willie Mays did — he got to balls faster than anyone. His quick release was a bonus because he possessed one of the best arms to ever disappoint a baserunner. Willie was one of the few center fielders who came in on a ball as well as he went back on one. He could cut off a line drive over second before it had any chance to consider life as a single. Then, on the very next play, he would devour yards of real estate to yank yet another extra base hit out of the box score. Willie brought the same instincts to the field that he displayed on the bases. He always knew the pitcher, what he was throwing, who was hitting, how the ball left his bat, who was on base, what the score was, and the angles of the park. He won more Gold Gloves (12) than any other center fielder in baseball history.

Ozzie Smith (San Diego Padres, St. Louis Cardinals)

Gravity had no authority over Ozzie Smith. Ozzie brought an unprecedented array of acrobatic skills — he would do handsprings and backflips as he took the field — to his position. The ultimate turf (artificial grass) shortstop, Smith was one of the few infielders nimble enough to change direction in midstep when a ball took a bad hop. His speed and agility enabled him to reach the deepest portions of his position in time to cut off grounders that slashed through the turf. A few years before he retired, Ozzie tore his rotator cuff — a devastating injury for infielders because it drains the strength from their throwing arms. He compensated by developing a hop and jump that put his entire body behind each toss. On balls hit into the hole, Smith's slide toward third base allowed him to firmly plant his foot to make a throw while he was catching the ball. I'd never seen anyone do that before Ozzie; he was the Rolls Royce of shortstops.

Curt Flood (Cincinnati Reds, St. Louis Cardinals, Washington Senators)

Though he played a deep center field, Curt Flood was nearly Mays's equal at catching line drives hit just over the infield. Curt had a strong throwing arm when he first came to the majors; after he broke it in midcareer, the arm never regained its former strength. Throwing would remain the one weakness in his defensive game from that point on. Nevertheless, he won seven consecutive Gold Gloves (1963–69), led the league in total chances — a reliable indicator of an outfielder's range — three times, tied for the lead twice, and finished in the top two every season from 1962 to 1969. In 1966, Curt recorded 391 putouts without being charged with a single error.

Bill Mazeroski (Pittsburgh Pirates)

Mr. Second Base. I modeled myself after him. In the field, Maz epitomized athletic economy. He rarely took an extra step to elude an incoming runner. Mazeroski was so quick on the double play, Pirates fans called him "No Touch." He seemed to relay the ball from the shortstop to first base without pausing to touch it. Maz had plenty of practice on that play; his 1,706 double plays represent the all-time record for second basemen. Perhaps the best part of his stellar game was his positioning; Bill knew where to play every hitter, even those he had never seen before. He had that sixth sense that is common to all great fielders. Maz led the National League in assists nine times, double plays eight times, putouts five times, and chances per game ten times. He holds the National League record for his position with eight Gold Gloves.

Johnny Bench (Cincinnati Reds)

From the moment he came into the league, Johnny Bench was the best defensive catcher in the game. He had the quickest, strongest, and most accurate throwing arm of any catcher I have ever played with or against. Bench came straight over the top with his throws so they rarely sank or swerved. He was solid as a rock at home plate; enemy baserunners had to find a way around rather than through him. He had huge, powerful but dexterous hands; he would take the padding out of his catcher's mitt so he could handle the ball with an infielder's flexibility. Bench was the first catcher to pick pitches out of the dirt backhanded with one hand — it was a signature maneuver that allowed him to capture balls that would have skipped past other catchers. From 1968 to 1977, he was the National League's Gold Glove catcher.

Roberto Clemente (Pittsburgh Pirates)

In 1971, I was playing for the Houston Astros in a game against Roberto Clemente's Pirates. With two out in the eighth and Pittsburgh leading 1-0, I was on first with our left fielder Bob Watson at the plate. Clemente was playing medium deep in right center field when Bob hit a laser beam toward the right field corner. It looked as though the ball would strike just above the yellow home run line, which was *only* 10 feet above the ground. Most right fielders would have positioned themselves to play *off* the wall a ball hit that high, that far, and that fast. Clemente, who was 36 at the time, wasn't having any of that. He galloped at full stride into the corner, leaped, and caught the drive while crashing into the fence. The inning was over, the Pittsburgh lead preserved. It was a memorable catch, the kind of brazen, heartbreaking play Roberto Clemente made repeatedly throughout his career. He won the Gold Glove every year from 1961 through 1972.

Brooks Robinson (Baltimore Orioles)

No player at any position can match this third baseman's 16 consecutive Gold Gloves. Robinson introduced "The Dive" to hot corner play (the *hot corner* is the third base area). Before him, third basemen scurried or tumbled after balls hit far to either side of them. Brooks Robinson took to the air, and by diving, he got to balls no one else could reach. Robinson wasn't fast, but he was quick and heady. He positioned himself on every pitch. Brooks would shift left or right on each batter depending on the pitcher, the hitter, and the situation. When he fielded a ground ball, his glove was always down — so the ball couldn't skip under it — and open to the hitter. Text-book stuff. Infielders with the range of a Robinson often place among the league leaders in errors. However, Robby was so sure-handed that he led American League third basemen in fielding percentage a record ten times.

Keith Hernandez (St. Louis Cardinals, New York Mets)

The most intimidating first baseman ever to play the position; no one could match him at covering the hole between first and second and charging bunts. He was also a master strategist. Keith would sometimes move up on the grass, obviously set for the bunt, and then back up several steps as the pitcher released the ball. He distracted so many hitters with this move, he practically eliminated the bunt as an option for many opposing teams. Most first basemen go directly to the bag to receive an infielder's throw. Keith would instead often loop back to the foul line, and then step toward first on a straight line. This maneuver kept the evolving play in front of him — always a good policy.

Ken Griffey, Jr. (Seattle Mariners)

Ken Griffey, Jr., a Gold Glover from the moment he first stepped on a major league field, is the best of all young outfielders. Jr. ranges far to his left and right. He plays so deep he steals more extra-base hits from opposing hitters than any other center fielder. No one gets Jr.'s jump on the ball, and he is absolutely fearless. He will crash into walls, climb fences, and make body-jarring leaps to get to a ball. His arm is above average, and he rarely misses his target.

Luis Aparicio (Chicago White Sox, Baltimore Orioles, Boston Red Sox)

Luis Aparicio was one of the few ballplayers who gained admittance to the Hall of Fame for his glove work. With his wall-to-wall range, Aparicio routinely made plays on the right-field side of second base. He would get in front of balls other shortstops backhanded; he backhanded balls other shortstops couldn't reach. Before Aparicio's major league arrival, shortstops, like other fielders, were taught to field the ball with both hands — but Aparicio introduced a one-handed fielding style that left him in a better position to unleash a throw. He had an exceptionally strong throwing arm. Among shortstops, Aparicio holds the major league career records for games played, assists, and double plays. He led his league in fielding percentage eight times and earned nine Gold Glove Awards.

The Ten Best Current Fielders

Great fielders are exuberant; their pursuit of every batted ball is a dance of joy. When they take the field, none of these ten are merely playing a position; they are playing out their passions. (The current team of each player is indicated in parentheses.)

Ken Griffey, Jr. (Seattle Mariners)

Placing Jr. in the top spot was easy; he's the only current player who made our All-Time fielder's list. Griffey has won eight straight Gold Gloves. Jr. won his eighth Gold Glove in 1997 at the age of 28, putting him on pace to shatter Willie Mays's major league record of 12 Gold Gloves for center field play.

Barry Bonds (San Francisco Giants)

My all-time left fielder. Barry studied for his doctorate in outfield play under the tutelage of his father, Bobby, a three-time Gold Glover in his own right, and Professor Willie Mays (who also happens to be Barry's godfather). Even though he's left-handed, Barry is quick to the line; he has an accurate throwing arm and he's the most fundamentally sound outfielder in the game. Barry consistently hits his cut-off man. He goes back on fly balls hit over his head as though he carries a built-in honing device; this talent allows Barry to play shallow enough to swipe enemy singles without leaving him vulnerable to the extra-base hit.

Ivan Rodriguez (Texas Rangers)

Defensively, he's a Johnny Bench clone. Ivan Rodriguez has the best throwing arm of any catcher in the American League. He throws out better than 40 percent of would-be base stealers (30 percent is about average); many clubs don't even bother to run against him. Every year, he enhances some aspect of his game: pitch calling, plate blocking, digging the ball out of the dirt. He won six consecutive Gold Gloves by the age of 26.

Charles Johnson (Florida Marlins)

In 1997, Charles Johnson set a record for major league catchers for most games without an error. I don't know what kind of dishwashing detergent Charles uses, but he has *soft* hands; the ball nestles into his glove. His arm is even better than Ivan Rodriguez's; just as strong and a tad more accurate. He also has a quicker release. Though he's tall (6 feet 2 inches) for a catcher, Charles has no difficulty reaching down to block balls in the dirt; he makes that play as well as anyone. He has quickly earned a reputation as a first-rate handler of pitchers. Charles is entering only his fourth season of play, and the Marlin pitching staff is composed largely of veterans. Despite this disparity in experience, pitchers rarely shake him off (that's to say, they throw the pitch that he signals).

Roberto Alomar (Baltimore Orioles)

When healthy — Roberto Alomar was bothered by a groin injury in 1996 — he has so much range at second base, his outfielders often have to call him off fly balls. Alomar has stopped ground balls in right field and converted them into double plays (try it sometime). The most impressive thing about him isn't how well he goes to his left or right — and no one can match his lateral movement — but how *quickly* he gets into good position on either side. This quickness allows him to plant his right foot firmly, the key to getting off a strong throw from any angle.

Omar Vizquel (Cleveland Indians)

Omar Vizquel covers ground like a modern Luis Aparicio — he plays with a flair, but he doesn't allow it to intrude on his fundamentals. Vizquel pays attention to all the basics: He looks the ball into his glove, reacts instantly to short hops, and positions himself almost flawlessly. When he is fooled on a grounder, he has the speed to rectify his mistake. Vizquel is a cool head, prone to neither physical nor mental errors.

Jim Edmonds (California Angels)

The Human Highlight Film. *Sportscenter* features Jim Edmonds' perilous catches so often, ESPN must be paying him residuals. Edmonds has a "nose" for the ball and he's willing to sacrifice his body to get to it. He catches everything, rarely makes an error, and has a strong, precise throwing arm. If he has a shortcoming, it's that he occasionally runs down balls that are better handled by his left or right fielders. Edmonds will make the catch in those plays, but he won't be in a position to make the throw.

Rey Ordonez (New York Mets)

The new Ozzie Smith. If you look at a diagram of a baseball diamond, the shortstop's territory is usually that patch of real estate between second and third base. For Rey Ordonez, it is wherever he chooses to roam. He has breathtaking range. In 1996, his first full season, Rey made far too many errors (27); he had the lowest fielding percentage of any National League shortstop. However, many of those miscues came on balls no other short-stop could reach. In 1997, Rey reduced the errors by more than half without sacrificing any range. He fields with a crowd-pleasing flourish, and baseball highlight films have already introduced the nation to his signature play: a dash-and-slide to his right, followed by a backhanded stab of a grounder, and punctuated by a side-arm strike to first. When you see it, pay special attention to that throw. Rey's arm is so strong that he can get off a perfect toss without planting his feet.

Ken Caminiti (San Diego Padres)

Ken Caminiti is much faster than he appears, so he covers a lot of ground at third. He has the physical toughness that you need to play the position; Ken played most of 1996 through the pain of a partially torn rotator cuff and still won the National League MVP Award. He has the hot corner's quickest hands and best arm. Ken is especially adept at coming in on the ball well; he converts slow rollers that appear to be hits when they leave the bat into routine outs.

Barry Larkin (Cincinnati Reds)

When healthy, Larkin is the most consistent shortstop around. Barry has superb baseball intelligence; his on-field mental lapses are few. You could not pick a better shortstop to study if you want to learn the correct way to start a double play; second basemen seldom have to reach for a Larkin feed. Barry has a great arm, and he can get off an on-target throw from virtually any angle.

Chapter 22
Joe Morgan's Top Ten Future Stars

- -

In This Chapter

▶ Vladimir Guerrero

▶ Nomar Garciaparra

▶ Alex Rodriguez

▶ Jose Cruz, Jr.

▶ Derek Jeter

▶ Andruw Jones

▶ Scott Rolen

▶ Edgardo Alfonzo

▶ Shawn Estes

▶ Neifi Perez

- -

As baseball prepares to enter the next century, its future looks bright if this list of players is any indication of the quality of the game.

Baseball's Future Stars

If any of these players were publicly traded stocks, you would sell off your Microsoft to buy shares in him. In other words, watch out for these up-and-coming future stars.

Vladimir Guerrero (Montreal Expos)

Montreal manager Felipe Alou views Vladimir Guerrero, who came to the National League straight from Double-A ball, as the second coming of Roberto Clemente. This 22-year-old certainly has Clemente-like tools. During his last tour in the minors, the Eastern League named Vladimir its best defensive outfielder — not an award you would expect to be won by a right fielder. Major league scouts think he may already own the National League's best outfield arm. Offensively, Vladimir can hit for power and average, as well as steal a base. I like his feel for the strike zone; Vladimir is the type of player who can win batting championships and home run titles.

Nomar Garciaparra (Boston Red Sox)

All Nomar Garciaparra did in his rookie year was set a major league record for runs batted in (RBIs) by a lead-off hitter (98) and compile a 30-game hitting streak. Depending on the makeup of future Red Sox rosters, Nomar probably won't be a lead-off hitter for very long; he has too much power and RBI potential. His power and speed combination mark him as a potential 30 homer-30 stolen base man. And he can play shortstop with anybody in his league. Nomar's hands and feet are so quick, Red Sox manager Jimy Williams calls him the Viper. When I spoke to the shortstop during his rookie season, I was most impressed with his attitude. Nomar understands his role on the Red Sox is to produce runs and play solid defense. He doesn't carry his errors to the plate; he doesn't let a bad day with the bat hurt him in the field.

Alex Rodriguez (Seattle Mariners)

During his first full season (1996), Alex, who was barely 21, hit .358 to become the third youngest major league batting champion of all time. Ahead of him on that list? Hall of Famers Ty Cobb and Al Kaline. Alex was also the fifth youngest player to hit 30 or more homers and total more than 100 runs batted in. He led the American League in runs (141 in 146 games), doubles (54), and total bases (379). Alex continued to hit for power and average in 1997 while doubling his stolen base output. A-Rod, as Alex Rodriguez is nicknamed, is a steady, though unspectacular, shortstop. His range is only average; as he gets bigger, Alex may have to consider another position. No matter where he plays, he'll be a batting title contender for the next decade or more.

Jose Cruz, Jr. (Toronto Blue Jays)

His power propelled him from A-Ball to the major leagues in less than two years. Watch how the ball jumps off his bat; only Jr. (Griffey) hits harder line drives. Jose has the makings of a home run champion. He is still learning the strike zone and is prone to chasing bad breaking balls, but he is patient enough to work out his share of walks. He has good speed, so he can leg out infield hits. Jose is still not a competent outfielder, but he'll correct that flaw with experience.

Derek Jeter (New York Yankees)

As the Rookie of the Year in 1996, Derek Jeter performed as if he had never heard of the word "pressure." He played superior defense and did his best hitting in game-breaking situations. He displayed the composure of a veteran during crucial late-season games and all throughout the 1996 postseason as the Yankees went on to win the World Series. He is a line-drive hitter who uses the whole field. I don't see Jeter as a 30+-home run man like Garciaparra or Rodriguez, but he could hit 50 doubles. He does have to reduce his strikeouts. In the field, he displays excellent lateral movement, broad range in and out, and sure hands. His work on the double play is infield art. Given his quiet command, Jeter is destined to be the Yankees' captain.

Andruw Jones (Atlanta Braves)

Mark it down: Andruw will be one of the all-time great center fielders. He has unlimited potential. In 1996, the 19-year-old outfielder went from A-Ball to the World Series in six months. He can run, throw, and hit with power as well as play all three outfield positions. In 1996, he became the youngest player ever to homer in a World Series. To get the most out of his ability, however, he must develop a better sense of the strike zone. He will.

Scott Rolen (Philadelphia Phillies)

This third baseman has a short, compact swing and an excellent batting eye. In 1997, Scott Rolen flashed more home run power as the National League Rookie of the Year than he did in any level of the minor leagues. He is a throwback; he likes to get his uniform dirty and seems to play baseball for the sheer pleasure of the game. Scott compensates for his average speed with excellent baserunning instincts, and he's a panther with a strong, accurate arm at third. Scott can barehand a bunt and throw out the runner in one sleek motion.

Edgardo Alfonzo (New York Mets)

Edgardo Alfonzo looks to be a perennial Gold Glove candidate. He brings a shortstop's range to third and is rarely out of position on a hitter. What impressed me about his .315 batting average in 1997 was how it kept rising as the season wore down. That tells you that Edgardo was able to make continual adjustments to the National League's pitchers. The Mets enjoyed numerous thrilling, come-from-behind victories in 1997, and Edgardo seemed to be in the middle of every rally. He likes to hit with the game on the line.

Shawn Estes (San Francisco Giants)

Many fine young pitchers blossomed in 1997 — Brad Radke, Jason Dickson, and Livan Hernandez among them — but Shawn Estes is a left-hander, and that makes him special. Estes throws a terrific hard curveball, a 90+-mph fastball, and a change-up that hitters never seem to expect. Though 1997 was his first full season in the majors, he anchored San Francisco's pitching staff during a close pennant race; he was at his best pitching in games that followed a Giant loss.

Neifi Perez (Colorado Rockies)

Clearly, we are entering the Golden Age of Shortstops. Everything about Neifi Perez in the field says, "Hit the ball to me!" He's an aggressive short-stop whose daring play can elevate an entire team. Neifi's run-saving skills will be much appreciated by Colorado's beleaguered pitchers, who are forced to labor in baseball's most hitter-friendly park. He's fast enough to bunt .300, and he should get his share of doubles, triples, and stolen bases.

Chapter 23

Ten Baseball Records That Are Least Likely to Be Broken

. . . .

In This Chapter

▶ Joe DiMaggio's 56-game hitting streak

▶ Cy Young's 512 career wins

▶ Babe Ruth's .690 career slugging percentage

▶ Jack Chesbro's 41-win season

▶ Johnny Vander Meer's two consecutive no-hitters

▶ Nolan Ryan's 5,714 career strikeouts

▶ Rogers Hornsby's .424 batting average

▶ Ed Walsh's 1.82 career ERA

▶ Hank Aaron's 755 career home runs

▶ Cal Ripken's consecutive games-played streak

. . . .

Records are made to be broken — or so the saying goes. The records in this chapter are different, however. Read on to see why these records can be considered safe from any future update.

Records That May Stand Forever

We all thought Babe Ruth's record of 714 career home runs would last forever, and then Hank Aaron taught us that there are no guarantees of anything in baseball. That said, I believe these ten records will remain beyond any player's reach.

Joe DiMaggio's 56-game hitting streak (1941)

In 1978, I was Pete Rose's teammate when he made his assault on this mark. Pete was the perfect player to break the record. He was a .300 hitter who batted from both sides of the plate, made contact, and could bunt for singles. Pete had a good eye, yet he didn't walk so often that he would lose many at-bats. The Reds had a strong lineup that season and Pete batted lead-off, a situation that maximized his plate appearances in every game. Some players succumb to pressure when they get near a record; they can't cope with all the press attention. Roger Maris, for example, lost clumps of hair during his pursuit of Babe Ruth's single-season home run record. Pete thrived under pressure; he was so focused, he could have held press conferences in between pitches without being distracted. And yet Pete fell a dozen games short of DiMaggio.

No one will break DiMaggio's record because today's relief pitching is just too specialized and too good. When Joe played, relievers were usually pitchers who weren't good enough to make the starting rotation. Today, relievers might be the best pitchers on a team. When Rose's streak was finally stopped at 44 games, who struck him out to end it? Gene Garber, a relief pitcher for the Atlanta Braves.

Cy Young's 512 career wins (and his 313 career losses)

A pitcher would have to win 25 games a year for 20 years and he'd still be a dozen short. The 313 losses? A pitcher today will be long out of baseball before he suffers that many defeats.

Babe Ruth's .690 career slugging percentage

No hitter is within 50 points of Ruth. In the last half century, only eight batters in both leagues have slugged .690 or better in a *single season!* Of those eight, only Albert Belle has done it twice. Ken Griffey, Jr. and Mark McGwire slugged 56 and 58 home runs respectively in 1997; neither of them topped .690! What are the odds that any player can maintain that kind of slugging over an entire career? (Chapter 14 describes how to figure out a player's slugging percentage.)

Jack Chesbro's 41-win season (1905)

When Chesbro pitched, batters neither walked nor struck out very often. They came to bat looking for that first good pitch to hack. Home runs were a rarity, so pitchers could throw the ball down the middle of the plate without dread. Pitchers in 1905 would routinely hurl complete games while throwing 90 pitches or fewer (125 is approximately the present norm) — so they could pitch more often than starters do today. With today's trend of pitchers starting only every fifth game, certified workhorses like David Cone, Randy Johnson, and Greg Maddux rarely make 40 *starts* in a season. The last pitcher to win as many as 31 games was Denny McLain of the Detroit Tigers in 1968.

Johnny Vander Meer's two consecutive no-hitters (June 11, June 15, 1938)

Consider this: If a pitcher throws two consecutive no-hitters he doesn't break anything; he merely ties Vander Meer's record. It requires three consecutive no-hitters to set a new mark. How difficult is that to achieve? For as long as baseball records have been kept, *only three men have pitched three or more no-hitters in their entire careers!* Nolan Ryan, Bob Feller, and Sandy Koufax all did the trick. None of them came close to surpassing Vandy's achievement. No one ever will.

Nolan Ryan's 5,714 career strikeouts

All you have to do is strike out 200 batters a season for a little more than $28^1/_2$ seasons. Good luck.

Rogers Hornsby's .424 batting average (1924)

It's been 56 years since Ted Williams became the last man to bat over .400 and he was 18 points shy of Hornsby's mark. No one will break this record for the same reason that no one will ever again hit in 56 straight games: Modern relievers are just too tough on today's hitters. (Chapter 14 shows you how to figure out a player's batting average.)

Ed Walsh's 1.82 career earned run average (ERA)

Another mark that underscores how the game has changed since the turn of the century. Walsh compiled his record in an age of big ballparks, wide strike zones, deadened baseballs, and low-run games. The league ERA during Walsh's career (1904–1916) was about 2.70, which means if your ERA was over 3.00, you were probably scuffling to keep your job. In today's game — which has become a continual Home Run Derby — the ERAs of both leagues hover between 4.00 and 5.00. Pitchers with ERAs below 3.00 seem like an endangered species. With most of the new ballparks showing a bias toward the hitters — baseball owners have figured out that lots of offense attracts fans to games — ERAs will continue to soar. Big Ed's record will be with us as long as there are sunrises. (Refer to Chapter 14 for how to figure out this statistic.)

Hank Aaron's 755 career home runs

I doubt the modern player will put in the time it takes to break this record. With all the money players earn today, much of the incentive for longevity is lost. At 27, Jr. Griffey and his 294 home runs are well ahead of Hank's career pace. However, to catch Aaron, Jr. would have to average 46 home runs a year for the next decade. As great as Griffey is, I just think that is too much to ask of anyone.

Cal Ripken's consecutive games-played streak (2,478 and counting)

I think if Cal's record proves anything besides his obvious dedication to the game, it's that ballplayers need rest. The season is too long and grueling — mentally as well as physically — for anyone to compete in every game year in and year out. Ripken has a history of rough Septembers. His streak took on a life of its own so that he couldn't be benched even when he probably could have used a day off. Other managers are aware of this. I doubt they'll ever allow anyone else to start another streak like it.

Chapter 24

Ten Events that Transformed the Game

In This Chapter

▶ Establishing baseball's rules (1845)

▶ Forming the first major league (1871)

▶ Moving the pitcher's mound back (1893)

▶ Starting the farm system (1920)

▶ Betting on baseball: The Black Sox (1920)

▶ Turning on the lights for night baseball (1935)

▶ Shattering the color line (1946)

▶ Heading west with the Dodgers and Giants (1957)

▶ Removing the reserve clause (1975)

▶ Striking: The baseball strike of 1994

*B*aseball has a long history indeed, and any sport with such a history has undergone transformations. Baseball is no exception — but as difficult as some of these transformations were at the time they occurred, the game always seems to get better.

The Changing of the Game

The capability to change has made the game of baseball what it is today. If you were taking a test on important baseball events, these would be the ones to know.

Alexander Cartwright codifies baseball's rules (1845)

Thank you, Alexander Cartwright. Before you brought some order to baseball, fielders put out runners by hitting them with a thrown ball. How many bruises did you save me? Cartwright, a New York bank teller and member of the Knickerbockers baseball team, prescribed the dimensions for the modern diamond with bases 90 feet apart. He invented the three-strikes-you're-out rule, established the nine-man team in the field, and decreed that three outs would end the offensive team's half of an inning. These and other Cartwright rules became the basis for present-day baseball.

Baseball players form the first major league (1871)

It was called the National Association of Base Ball Players and, oh, was it a mess! There was no fixed schedule of games; teams played each other on a catch-as-catch-can basis. Franchises dropped in and out of the league without warning. Disputes over officiating were frequent and vociferous; the umpires were mostly untrained volunteers. Arguments and fights would delay games for as long as an hour. Players, regardless of their contracts, would jump from team to team during the season. Franchises engaged in continual battles over ticket pricing and the division of revenues. Most clubs lost money not because of poor attendance (most of the clubs had large followings) but due to mismanagement. The league folded in only four years. By now, I imagine you're wondering how such a misfit operation transformed baseball? In two ways. First, it proved that fans would pay money to watch a league of professionals cavort on the diamond. This encouraged the establishment of other professional leagues. Second, those organizations that followed the National Association learned from their predecessors' mistakes. They avoided the defects that led to the league's demise. So the association was a testing ground. It provided a vital first step in the development of the major league structure that remains intact, albeit with modifications, today.

The pitcher's mound is moved back 15 feet (1893)

Speaking for all hitters, someone should light an eternal flame at the gravesite of the man who thought of this. Could you imagine facing the likes of Nolan Ryan, Roger Clemens, or Randy Johnson if they were only 45 feet (13.7m) away? The thought of that is like something out of *Nightmare on Elm Street.* No one could get a hit under those conditions. History proves that offense drives baseball's turnstiles. If the rules committee hadn't fixed the pitching distance at 60 feet, 6 inches (18.4m) from home plate, baseball would be nothing more than two guys playing catch with each other with the hitter as a spectator. And he might be the only spectator because no one else would want to watch.

Mr. Rickey builds a farm (1920)

As the general manager of the financially challenged St. Louis Cardinals, Branch Rickey knew he could not outbid most of his major league competitors for players. So he decided to grow his own. Rickey created baseball's first farm system, a network of minor league teams designed to breed players for St. Louis's big league club. Some of these minor league franchises belonged to the Cardinals; others operated under working agreements with the team. By 1928, St. Louis controlled seven teams employing 208 players. As the system supplied a continual flow of talent, the Cardinals became a National League power; they would win five pennants from 1926 to 1934. Baseball took notice. It wasn't long before every major league franchise had a minor league network of its own.

The Black Sox scandal (1920)

Eight members of the American League champion Chicago White Sox accepted bribes to "throw" the 1919 World Series against the Cincinnati Reds. The scandal, unearthed during a grand jury hearing in 1920, couldn't have been more ill-timed. Baseball was in the midst of a postwar resurgence. Attendance had more than doubled in the previous two years. Reports that players and gamblers had fixed the Series threatened to decimate baseball's emerging fan base. To prevent that, team owners appointed Judge Kenesaw Mountain Landis — a jurist who positively seethed integrity — as its first commissioner. Landis promptly banned the eight White Sox conspirators. He clamped down on gambling throughout the sport (only the naive believe the Black Sox series was an isolated incident) and restored public confidence in the National Pastime.

Landis would rule over baseball until 1944, and his decisions during that time set precedents that still resonate today. Unfortunately, Judge Landis would not let integration occur while he was commissioner.

The night the lights went on in Cincinnati (1935)

When Reds general manager Larry MacPhail lit his club's diamond, it was not the first time baseball had been played under the lights. In 1883, a game between Pensinger's Paint Shop and Clay Henninger's Nine took place on an illuminated field in Chambersburg, Pennsylvania. Several minor leagues had been playing night games since 1930. However, when the lights came on in Cincinnati's Crosley Field, fans witnessed the first major league game played after sundown. The success of MacPhail's venture convinced other teams to follow his lead. Night baseball made the sport more accessible to that vast majority of fans who worked 9 to 5. The game may not have survived as a major force in sports if MacPhail (or somebody) hadn't brought it out of the darkness.

Jackie Robinson and Branch Rickey shatter the color line (1946)

Baseball drew its color line during the mid-1880s when all-white professional teams such as the powerful Chicago White Stockings refused to take the field against integrated clubs. By 1899, not a single African-American played in the major or minor leagues. When Brooklyn Dodgers general manager Branch Rickey signed Jackie Robinson, a 27-year-old shortstop with the Negro League's Kansas City Monarchs, to a contract in 1946, he effectively ended major league baseball's Jim Crow policy. Jackie's immediate success encouraged other clubs to scout and sign African-American talents. These men would revolutionize baseball. Players like Robinson, Sam Jethroe, Willie Mays, and Maury Wills revived the stolen base as an offensive weapon. They brought an edgier, more daring style of play to the field. Fans embraced it. Attendance soared throughout the major and minor leagues. Baseball's rising popularity coupled with the influx of previously untapped talent made expansion into new territories possible. Increased broadcasting and marketing revenues, higher player salaries, and further expansion followed. Rickey and Robinson started all of it by forcing the game to grow.

The Brooklyn Dodgers and New York Giants go west (1957)

I bet you can hear the teeth-gnashing in Flatbush over this entry. Though Brooklynites still lament the departure of their Beloved Bums — and please believe I do feel your pain, so no nasty letters — the departure of both teams had a positive impact on baseball. Prior to 1958, the National Pastime was hardly a national game. Major league baseball wasn't played west of St. Louis. When two of the National League's most prestigious franchises moved to California, the event opened up the entire country to baseball. The expansions into Canada and the soon-to-come moves into other international markets began with the transfer of these two franchises.

The Messersmith-McNally decision (1975)

The reserve clause virtually tied baseball players to their teams for life. A club could pay a player whatever it wanted or trade his contract — as well as his "reserve" — to any team it chose. In effect since the 1880s, the clause had survived numerous legal assaults, including a famous one by St. Louis Cardinals center fielder Curt Flood. Pitchers Dave McNally of the Montreal Expos and Andy Messersmith of the Los Angeles Dodgers didn't challenge the clause in court. They took their cases before an arbitrator and won. The victory ushered in baseball free agency; players with six years of major league service could sell their talents to the highest bidder. Freer player movement created more competitive balance and heightened fan interest, and sent baseball salaries soaring.

The baseball strike of 1994

The first impact of this event was negative. The always spiky relationship between the baseball owners and the players became more hostile, the World Series was canceled for the first time in 90 years, and fans abandoned the sport in droves. Out of all this carnage, however, came positive developments. Baseball has always been slow to change. Even prior to the strike, many wondered if the sport had lost its relevance. Now, exciting innovations such as the wild card, interleague play, and the push for international expansion are part of baseball's concerted attempt to rebuild its fan base while attracting new supporters. Teams and players are becoming increasingly fan friendly; the relationship between the players and owners appears to be more cordial. There is finally good reason to hope that they will work together for the game rather than against it. The strike of 1994 was a hellish time for the sport, but it may very well have ensured its prosperity in the coming millennium.

Part VI
Appendixes

IN PENITENTIARY BASEBALL, STEALING BASES IS NOT PERMITTED; HOWEVER, AN INMATE WILL OFTEN HAVE HIS ATTORNEY PLEA BARGAIN HIS WAY TO ANOTHER BASE.

In this part . . .

*A*round the horn . . . bang-bang play . . . high heat. . . . Baseball has a rich, colorful lexicon and you must understand it if you want to follow the action. We provide a list of key phrases, slang words, and terms in Appendix A. (And at the end of Appendix A, you can find a list of former players and the years when they played.) Appendix B is our baseball record book, where you'll find lists of standard-setting performances. Appendix C provides you with access to the world's major baseball organizations.

Appendix A
Baseball Speak: A Glossary

In this appendix, you discover the most common baseball terms (as well as a few uncommon terms here and there!) to help you in any baseball-lingo jam. In addition, at the end of this appendix you can find a chart to help you put into historical context some of the famous baseball names that you encounter in this book or in any baseball conversation.

Ace: The top card in a deck, the top gun on a pitching staff. Seattle's Randy Johnson, Toronto's Roger Clemens, and Montreal's Pedro Martinez are all considered aces. Teams can have more than one. In 1997, Atlanta's staff had a fistful of aces: Cy Young Award winners Greg Maddux, Tom Glavine, John Smoltz, and 20-game winner Danny Neagle.

Adjudged: Any judgment call made by the umpire, such as declaring a runner out at second base on a close play.

Alley: The section of outfield real estate between the center fielder and the left or right fielders. It is also called the *power alley* (where hits go to become doubles or triples) or the *gap*.

Appeal: When a player who has been fined or is subject to some other disciplinary action asks to plead his case to the league president or commissioner's office.

Appeal play: The defensive team's attempt to reverse a safe call by contending that a runner missed a base or left a base too early on a fly ball. An appeal must be called for immediately following a disputed play and before the pitcher throws a pitch toward home plate. Major league protocol requires the pitcher to step off the mound and throw to the base in question. The umpire at that base then rules if the runner was indeed safe or out.

Around the horn: A double play that goes from third base to second to first. The phrase comes from a time before the opening of the Panama Canal when ships had to sail around South America's Cape Horn to reach the Pacific from the Atlantic.

Assist: A throw from one fielder to another that puts out the batter or a baserunner.

At 'em ball: A ball that is hit directly at a fielder.

At-bat: Any time the batter gets a hit, makes an out, or reaches base on an error or fielder's choice. If the batter draws a walk, is hit by a pitch, completes a sacrifice, or reaches base on catcher's interference, he is credited with a plate appearance but not an at-bat.

Bag: A term often used in place of *base*.

Bad hop: A grounder that takes an unexpected bounce off the infield.

Bad-ball hitter: Someone who gets hits swinging at balls outside the strike zone.

Balk: A pitcher's motion that is deemed deceptive by the umpire. Runners who are on base when a balk is called get to advance one base.

Ball: A pitch out of the strike zone that the batter doesn't swing at and the umpire does not call as a strike.

Baltimore chop: A batted ball that bounces so high it cannot be fielded before the hitter reaches first base. It was popularized by John McGraw and the cagey Baltimore Orioles during the 1890s.

Bandbox: A small ballpark, one that favors hitters. The Baker Bowl, which was home to the Philadelphia Phillies until 1938, was a notorious bandbox. It was only $280^1/_2$ feet from home plate to the right field wall.

Bang-bang play: The baserunner and ball reach a base or home plate at nearly the same moment.

Banjo hitter: A batter who hits mostly singles.

Barrel: The thickest part of a bat.

Base: The 15-inch (38cm) square white marker found at three of a baseball infield's four corners (home plate is five-sided). They are placed 90 feet (27.45m) apart from each other.

Base on balls: What a pitcher surrenders whenever the umpire calls four of his pitches out of the strike zone (four balls) during a hitter's time at bat. The batter takes first base, the errant hurler's manager takes a Maalox — and, if the pitcher allows very many of these, he takes a trip to the showers. Also known as a *walk*.

Baseball: The white, red-stitched sphere that pitchers throw, fielders catch, and hitters whack during a baseball game. It is composed of a cork core under layers of rubber, yarn, and cowhide.

Baseball mud: Umpires rub this auburn mud into new baseballs to remove the sheen from the leather. Why? So that pitchers can get a better grip on the ball.

Basket catch: A catch made with your glove at belt level. Coaches frown on the practice, but Willie Mays won 12 consecutive Gold Gloves with his signature catch.

Bat: The sculpted, wooden implement (usually fashioned from pine or ash) that hitters use to assault a baseball.

Bat around: What a team does when its entire lineup bats during an inning, with the inning's lead-off hitter batting twice.

Bat speed: The time it takes a hitter to get his bat into the hitting zone.

Batboy or batgirl: The players' valet during the game. The batboy or batgirl picks up the hitter's bat and helmet when the hitter's turn at bat ends. He or she also brings new balls to the umpires between innings.

Batter: What a player becomes when he steps into the batter's box to take his swings.

Batter's box: The rectangle, marked by chalk, on both sides of home plate. The batter must stay within that box when hitting.

Battery: A team's pitcher-catcher combination for any given game.

Batting cage: A metal cage placed behind home plate during batting practice. It protects bystanders from being hit by foul balls.

Batting eye: A player's ability to judge the strike zone. Batters who average 100 or more walks per season (Frank Thomas, Barry Bonds, Rickey Henderson) have excellent batting eyes.

Batting glove: Batters usually wear this soft leather glove on their bottom hand (right for left-handed hitters, left for righties), though some batters wear them on both hands. Batting gloves prevent blisters and gives the hitter a better grip on the bat handle. Some fielders wear batting gloves underneath their fielding gloves to soften the impact of hard-hit balls.

Batting helmet: Hard plastic helmet that protects a hitter's cranium from errant pitches.

Batting order: The sequence in which a team's hitters appear at home plate during a game.

Beanball: A pitch that is deliberately thrown to hit the batter.

Bees: The sting a batter feels when he hits a pitch off-center, usually felt in cold weather.

Bench: What players sit on while they are in the dugout. Players who are benched, are grabbing some bench, or have been forced to ride the pines, have been indefinitely removed from a team's starting lineup.

Bench jockey: A player, usually a sub who rarely appears in games, who hurls insults from the dugout at opposing players on the field to break their concentration.

Big Bill: A ground ball's final hop (it bounces as high as the bill on a crouched fielder's cap).

Big leagues: The major leagues.

Bingle: A softly hit single.

Bird dog: A part-time baseball scout.

Black, The: The outer edges of home plate. Balls that are "on the black" are strikes and difficult to hit squarely. Control pitchers like Greg Maddux or Jimmy Key are often said to "paint the black" with their pitches.

Bleachers: The most inexpensive seats in the park. Located behind the outfields of most major league parks.

Bleeder: A base hit, usually one that barely makes it through the infield. It can also be a weak pop fly that falls in front of an outfielder.

Bloop: Or blooper. A weakly hit fly ball that just makes it over the infield. Also known as a *dying quail* or *Texas Leaguer.*

Blue darter: A hard hit, low line drive.

Bonehead Play: A mental error. A typical boner by a player who rarely made one: Babe Ruth made the final out of the 1926 World Series when he was caught trying to steal second with the score 3-2.

Bonus baby: A young prospect, usually a college player, who signs for a large bonus before proving himself as a professional.

Book, The: A mythical compendium of traditional baseball strategies. Managers who "go by the book" play to tie in the ninth at home, bring in left-handed relievers to get out left-handed hitters, and have their pitchers bunt with none (and often one) out and runners on base. The best managers often go against The Book.

Boot: A fielding error. Also known as a *muff.*

Box score: The statistical record of a baseball game.

Breaking pitch: Any ball that curves.

Brushback: A pitch aimed at a batter not to hit him (though they sometimes do, often to the pitcher's chagrin) but to move him off the plate. Also known as a *purpose pitch* or *chin music.*

Bug on the rug: A ball that eludes outfielders by bouncing about on the turf (artificial grass).

Bullpen: The area where pitchers warm up before entering a game. In most stadiums, it is located behind the outfield fence. In other parks, the bullpens can be found in foul territory along the left and right field lines.

Bunt: An offensive weapon in which the hitter holds his bat in the hitting zone and lets the ball make contact with it. If he is bunting for a hit, the batter tries to get to first before an infielder fields the softly hit ball and throws him out. If he is bunting to move a baserunner up a base, the hitter only needs to push the ball to a spot where a play at first base is the infielder's sole option.

Bush: Any amateurish action or behavior. Publicly criticizing a teammate for a failed but honest effort is considered *bush.*

Butcher: A poor fielder.

Call: The umpire's declaration of safe or out, ball or strike, fair or foul.

Called game: A game that has been terminated by the umpire-in-chief before its completion. Umpires usually call games due to inclement weather or curfews.

Can of corn: An easy fly-ball out.

Catch: The act of a fielder getting secure possession of the ball in his glove or hand. Whether you have secure possession is sometimes obvious, but it is often a subjective call by an umpire.

Checked swing: A swing that is terminated before a batter breaks his wrists. Whether the hitter went around too far is the umpire's subjective call.

Choke: Failing to produce in a crucial situation.

Choke hitter: A hitter who grips the bat at least an inch or two from its handle. Using an extreme version of this grip (four inches or more) sacrifices power for contact.

Circus catch: A spectacular, unusually acrobatic fielding play.

Cleanup: The number four hitter in your lineup. He is expected to "clean" the bases by driving in runs.

Closed stance: A hitting stance in which the batter's front foot is nearer to the plate than the back one.

Closer: The relief pitcher who finishes games, usually in save situations. Mariano Rivera, Randy Myers, Rod Beck, and John Franco are all considered premier closers.

Clubhouse lawyer: A player who is outspoken and critical about club, league, or union policy.

Clutch: A situation when the outcome of a game or series is on the line. It often occurs in the late innings of an important ball game.

Collar: From "horse collar" (which resembles a large 0). A batter who doesn't get a hit in a game is *wearing the collar.*

Come-backer: A ball hit back to the pitcher.

Corked bat: A bat with a deep hole drilled into the center of its barrel. The perpetrator (corked bats are illegal) fills the hole with cork, shredded rubber, or mercury, and then plugs it with glue and sawdust to make the bat appear normal. Reducing the bat's weight gives the hitter a faster swing.

Count: The numbers of balls and strikes called on a hitter during a time at bat. The balls are always listed first. A 2-1 count means the batter has two balls and one strike.

Cousin: A pitcher who can't get a particular hitter out with any regularity, as in "Edgar Martinez hits (fill in the name of any New York Yankee pitcher) as if he were his cousin."

Cup of coffee: A brief stay in the major league. A minor league player who fills in for an injured major leaguer for a few weeks and is then sent back down has been up for "a cup of coffee."

Cycle: When a hitter hits a single, double, triple, and home run in the same game. Of these four, the triple is hardest to collect (unless you are a hitter like Chicago Cubs outfielder Lance Johnson, who rarely homers but annually leads his league in triples).

Dead ball: A ball which the umpire has ruled is no longer in play because play has been suspended. (A baserunner is *dead* when he is thrown out by a fielder.)

Dead from the neck up: A phrase used to describe a player who is gifted physically but is intellectually challenged. A similar phrase: "He's a $50 million airport with a $100 control tower."

Defensive indifference: An undefended stolen base. The defensive team makes no attempt to throw out the base stealer.

Defensive interference: Any act by a fielder that interferes with a batter's swinging at a pitch.

Designated hitter (DH): The hitter in the American League lineup who bats without having to take the field. He always bats in place of the pitcher, though the rules state he may bat in any position in the batting order.

Diamond: A baseball field (more correctly, the *infield*).

Dish: Home plate.

Double: A two-base hit.

Double play: A single defensive play that produces two outs; it usually occurs in the infield.

Double steal: Two baserunners attempting to steal on the same pitch.

Doubleheader: Two consecutive games played between the same teams on the same day.

Ducks on the pond: Baserunners.

Earned run: Any run charged to the record of the pitcher. These runs can score as the result of a hit, a sacrifice fly, a fielder's choice, a walk, a hit batsman, a wild pitch, or a balk. Runs that score as the result of an error, passed ball, or catcher's interference are *unearned*. (See Chapter 14 for how to figure a pitcher's earned run average, or ERA.)

Error: A defensive misplay.

Even stance: A hitting stance in which both of the batter's feet are equidistant from the plate.

Fair ball: A batted ball that settles in fair territory between home plate and first base or first base and third. Or, a ball that is on or over fair territory when it goes into the outfield past first or third.

Fair territory: The part of the playing field between and including the first and third base lines, from home base to the outfield fences.

Farm system: A major league team's system of minor league clubs.

Fielder's choice: When a fielder handles a ground ball and attempts to throw out a baserunner other than the hitter.

Fireman: A relief pitcher, usually one who is brought into a precarious situation. He is there to put out the fire.

Five-tool player: A player who runs the bases quickly, fields his position expertly, demonstrates a strong, accurate throwing arm, and hits for both power and average. Ken Griffey, Jr., Barry Bonds, and Larry Walker are five-tool players.

Fly ball: A ball hit into the air on an arc.

Force out: When a batted ball forces a runner to advance to another base and the fielder possessing the ball tags that base before the runner reaches it.

Foul pole: The yellow poles along the outfield walls that mark the end of the foul lines. They indicate whether a ball hit into the seats is foul or a home run. Balls hit to the left of the left field foul pole are foul, as are balls hit to the right of the right field pole. A ball that hits either pole is, for reasons no one understands, called fair. (That being the case, why don't they call it the fair pole?)

Foul territory: The section of the playing field outside the first and third base lines.

Foul tip: A batted ball that careens sharply toward the catcher's mitt and is caught. It is a foul tip *only* if it is caught. Any foul tip is also a strike. The ball is in play. If the catcher catches a foul tip with two strikes on the batter, the batter has struck out. If a foul tip is not caught (in which case it remains a foul ball), the pitch is called a strike if the batter has less than two strikes. With two strikes on the batter, the count holds and the at-bat continues.

Franchise player: A star player, usually young, around whom management can build a team. Boston's Nomar Garciaparra and Montreal's Vladmir Guererro are both franchise players. When the young Tom Seaver was leading the New York Mets out of oblivion in the '60s, he was nicknamed "The Franchise."

Free agent: A player who is not contracted to play for any team. He is free to negotiate with any club interested in his services.

Full count: When the pitcher has three balls and two strikes on the batter.

Fungo: A long, thin bat used by a coach or player to hit grounders or flies during fielding practice. The hitter tosses the ball into the air before striking it. A ball hit in this manner is also called a fungo.

Gamer: A player who thrives in pressure situations, handles adversity well, or has a high threshold of pain. Also, the bat a hitter uses during a game. Out of every dozen bats he orders, the average major leaguer usually finds three or four gamers. He uses the other bats during batting practice or gives them away as souvenirs.

Gap: The area between the left fielder and center fielder or the right fielder and center fielder. *See* alley.

Gap shot: An extra-base hit that lands in the gap and usually rolls or bounces to the wall. Also called a *tweener*.

Glove: The padded leather covering that protects a fielder's hand and makes it easier for him to catch a baseball. All fielders use gloves — except the catcher and first baseman who wear mitts. (The difference between a mitt and a glove? Mitts have more padding.)

Glove man: An expert fielder.

Goat: A player who makes a glaring mistake that contributes to a defeat. It's a term used almost exclusively by reporters and fans.

Gold Glove: The annual award given in the major leagues (AL and NL) to the best fielding player at each position.

Gopher ball: A pitch that is hit for a home run.

Grand slam: A home run with the bases loaded (the popular phrase "grand slam home run" is a redundancy). Also known as a *grand salami* (a term popularized by New York Mets broadcaster Tim McCarver).

Green light: Not an actual sign. When a player has his manager's "green light," he has permission to steal a base whenever he chooses, or to "swing away" on 3-0 and 3-1 counts.

Ground ball: A batted ball that rolls or bounces on the ground. Also known as a *grounder.*

Ground-rule double: A fair ball that goes over the outfield fence on a bounce. The runners take two bases.

Gun: A fielder's strong throwing arm. The term is usually applied to an outfielder or catcher. Texas catcher Ivan Rodriguez has a gun behind home plate.

Gun shy: Being fearful of getting hit by a pitch.

Handcuffed: What sometimes happens to an infielder when a ball is hit so hard that he can't handle it, even though it was hit right at him.

Handle: The end of the bat gripped by the hitter. It is the thinnest part of the bat. However, in the *bottle bat* (which is rarely used today), the difference in thickness between handle and barrel is almost imperceptible.

Hanging curve: A curveball that breaks little except a pitcher's heart. Hanging curves don't hang for very long; hitters usually quickly deposit them into the upper decks for home runs.

Headhunter: A pitcher who throws at hitter's heads.

Heat: An above-average fastball. Also known as *cheese, high cheese, smoke, gas, high heat,* and *hummer.* St. Louis Cardinals closer Dennis Eckersley used to call his fastball a *yakker.* Want to flash some retro-cool? Try on a term popularized by the Cincinnati Reds pitchers during the mid-1960s. That hard-throwing lot — they led the National League in strikeouts four times in five years — measured their fastballs by how much *hair* they had. The faster the pitcher, the more hair he had on the ball. ("Did I have much hair out there today?" — "You were positively shaggy, son.")

Hill: The pitcher's mound.

Hit: A ball batted into fair territory, which allows the hitter to reach base safely without benefit of a fielding error or a fielder's choice.

Hit by pitch: A plate appearance that results in the hitter getting hit by a pitch. He is awarded first base. It's also known as *taking one for the team.*

Hit-and-run: An offensive strategy called by a manager with a runner on first. As the pitcher winds up, the runner takes off for second base. The batter must make contact so that the runner can safely take second on an out or go for extra bases on a hit.

Hitch: The term used to describe a hitter's bad habit of dropping his hands just prior to swinging his bat. It disrupts the timing of most batters, though for some players like slugger Cecil Fielder, a hitch is part of their timing mechanism.

Hole: In fielding, an area deep and to the far right of the shortstop. In hitting, when a pitcher has a ball-strike advantage over a hitter, the batter is said to be *in a hole.* "Clemens has Buhner in an 0-2 hole." Also, a batter who doesn't make contact often is said to have a lot of *holes in his swing.*

Home plate: Home plate is a 17-inch (43cm) square with two of its corners removed to leave a 17-inch long edge, two 8^1/$_2$-inch (21.5cm) adjacent sides, and two 12-inch (30.5cm) long sides angled to a point. The result is a five-sided slab of white rubber with black borders. A runner scores by safely rounding all bases and touching home plate.

Home run: A fair fly ball that travels over the outfield fence. An inside-the-park home run doesn't leave the playing field; it is a fair ball that eludes fielders for so long that the hitter is able to circle the bases before a play can be made on him. Other terms for the home run include *homer, dinger, jack, going yard, dial 8, long-ball, round-tripper, 'tater, four-bagger, going downtown,* and *clout.*

Home team: The host team in a baseball team. Mutual agreement determines who will be the home team when a game is played on neutral ground.

Hoover: An expert infielder who fields or "vacuums" ground balls. It was also the nickname of third baseman Brooks Robinson, a perennial Gold Glove winner.

Hot corner: Third base.

Hot dog: A player who shows off (for example, a hitter who stands at home plate admiring his own home run). Players like Rickey Henderson, who field their positions with flamboyance, are often said to be *hot-dogging* or *cutting the pie.*

In jeopardy: A term that indicates the ball is in play and the offensive player can be put out.

Infield fly rule: With less than two out, a fair fly ball (that is neither a line drive nor an attempted bunt) that can be caught with ordinary effort by one of the infielders when first base and second base are occupied by runners (or when runners are on all the bases). This rule is called by the umpires. The batter is automatically out even if the fielder misses the ball. (This rule is designed to keep infielders from missing fly balls on purpose in order to make an unfair double play — with less than two out, runners don't try to advance if they think a ball is going to be caught!)

Inning: A unit of a baseball game consisting of a turn at-bat and three outs for each team. Regulation games consist of nine innings. A game can have fewer innings if it is called (canceled) by the umpire (due to inclement weather or some other circumstance) and more innings if the game is tied after the regulation nine.

Jamming: When a pitcher throws the ball inside and near the batter's hands, he is *jamming the batter.*

Journeyman: A serviceable player, rarely a star, who bounces around from club to club. The prototypical journeyman: right-handed pitcher Robert Miller, who was traded or sold 12 times to 10 different teams.

Junk: Off-speed pitches such as the change-up, the slow curve, the palmball, and the knuckleball. Relief pitcher Stu Miller was a renowned junkballer during the 1960s. He was said to throw at three speeds: slow, slower, and slowest.

K: Another term for a *strikeout.*

Keystone: Second base. A team's shortstop and second baseman are known as the *keystone combination* for their double-play collaboration.

Laugher: A lopsided victory, as in "The Braves won an 11-1 laugher." Also known as a *blowout.*

Lead-off hitter: The hitter who bats first in the batting order. Also, the hitter who bats first in any inning.

Left-handed specialist: A reliever who is usually brought in solely to get out one to three tough left-handed hitters.

Leg hit: What a hitter earns when he gets a single on a batted ball that doesn't travel beyond the infield. Also, an *infield hit.*

Line drive: A ball that is hit, usually hard, on a straight line. Also known as a *bullet* or *frozen rope.*

Lineup: The nine players (or ten if you are using a designated hitter) who start a game.

Live ball: A ball that is in play.

Long reliever: A relief pitcher who enters in the early innings after a starter has been bombed or injured. Also known as the *long man,* he usually pitches three innings or more.

Lord Charles: Uncle Charlie has long been a nickname for the curveball. Lord Charles is the *curveball maximus.* It doesn't merely break, it dives and is as fast as most pitchers' sliders.

Magic number: You hear this term mentioned frequently as the season winds down. The number represents any combination of wins and losses by the first- and second-place teams that clinches the top spot in the standings for the first-place club. For example, the Atlanta Braves lead the National League East with a record of 100-60; the Florida Marlins are in second at 99-61. With only two games left in the 162-game season, Florida cannot possibly win more than 101 games. Therefore, the magic number for the Braves is two; if Atlanta wins both of its remaining games, it will have 102 wins, a total Florida cannot reach. Atlanta can also clinch by winning one game while Florida loses once because the Braves would have 101 victories while the Marlins could not win more than 100.

Middle reliever: Usually enters in the fifth or sixth inning of a close game.

Mop-up man: You don't want to see him pitching too often for your favorite team. Mop-up men pitch when their team is losing by a lopsided score.

No-hitter: A nine-inning complete game in which a pitcher does not allow a hit to the opposing team. The opposition can have baserunners through fielding errors or walks. (*See* Perfect game.)

Obstruction: A call made by the umpire when a fielder who neither possesses the ball nor is about to field the ball, impedes the progress of the runner.

Offensive interference: Any act by the offensive team that interferes with or confuses a fielder attempting to make a play, such as if a baserunner deliberately runs into the second baseman while he is fielding a ground ball.

On-deck circle: The circle between the dugout and home plate where a player awaits his turn at-bat.

Open stance: A hitting stance in which the front foot is farther away from the plate than the back foot.

Out: One of the three required retirements of an offensive team during its half-inning turn at bat.

Out pitch: A pitcher's best pitch; the one he is most likely to throw to get an out or finish off a hitter.

Overslide: The act of a baserunner sliding past and losing contact with a base.

Payoff pitch: A pitch thrown on a full count.

Peg: A fielder's throw.

Pennant: The flag awarded to the champion of each league.

Pepper: A fast-moving (soft) hitting and fielding game designed to improve a player's reflexes. The fielder and hitter stand 20 feet apart. The hitter hits the ball to the fielder, who catches it and immediately pitches it back. The hitter hits that offering, and play continues.

Perfect game: A complete game in which the pitcher does not hit any batter with the ball and does not allow any hits, walks, or errors.

Phantom double play: A double play called by the umpire, even though the second baseman or shortstop did not step on second base for the force out.

Pick it: Catching a ball. Players who can "really pick it" are good fielders.

Pick-off: A throw by a pitcher or catcher to nab a runner off base.

Pinch hitter: A hitter who substitutes for a teammate in the batting order. Managers often ask this hitter to come through "in a pinch" or crucial situation.

Pinch runner: A runner who substitutes for a teammate on the bases.

Pine tar: A dark, viscous substance spread on the bat handle so that a hitter can get a better grip.

Pitchout: When a pitcher intentionally throws the ball outside the strike zone so that his catcher has a better chance to catch a baserunner trying to steal.

Plate appearance: Any trip to the plate by a hitter. Plate appearances include at-bats, walks, sacrifices, interference calls, and hit-by-pitches.

Platoon: A system in which players are alternated at a position. It is usually based on what side of the plate batters swing from. Left-handed platoon hitters generally start against right-handers; their right-handed counterparts usually take the field against lefties.

"Play!" or "Play Ball!": The umpire's order to start the game or to resume play following a dead ball.

Play-by-play: Any verbal or written account of every play that occurs in a given game. Also, a broadcaster's verbal description of a ball game broadcast on TV or radio.

Player-manager: A player who also acts as his team's manager. No one has held that title in the major leagues since the Cincinnati Reds' Pete Rose in 1986.

Portsider: A left-handed pitcher.

Productive out: Any out that advances a runner, or, even better, scores a run. Productive outs are at their most productive in close ball games. Whitey Herzog's St. Louis Cardinals were perennial leaders in this unofficial category during the mid-1980s.

Protest: Managers play games "under protest" when they believe an umpire has made a call that contradicts the rule book. No one can protest an umpire's judgment call. Managers must announce their protests to the umpire immediately following the disputed action, before the next play begins. The league office is the arbiter of all protests. Protests are rarely allowed.

Pull: To hit the ball early enough so that the bat meets the ball in front of the hitter. Right-handed hitters pull the ball to the left side; left-handers pull to the right. Pull hitters usually hit for power.

Pull the string: To throw an off-speed pitch.

Punch-and-Judy hitter: A batter who sprays softly batted hits to all fields.

Punchout: A strikeout. Also called a *whiff* or a *K*.

Quality start: Any game in which the starting pitcher works six or more innings while allowing three or fewer runs.

Quick pitch (or quick return): A pitch made before the batter is set. A judgment call by the umpire who must decide whether the batter was set; the pitch is illegal.

Rabbit ears: Any player, manager, or umpire who is hypersensitive to criticism.

Radar gun: The device used by baseball scouts to measure the speed of pitches, also know as the *Jugs gun*. Scouts refer to them as "fast" or "slow," depending on the make and how it records speed.

Regular season: In the major leagues, the 162-game season that determines each division's final standings and playoff participants.

Regulation game: A baseball game that is played to its completion.

Release: A pink slip. What a player reluctantly obtains when he is permanently cut from a team's roster.

Relief pitcher (reliever): Any pitcher who enters a game after the *starter* (the starting pitcher) has been removed.

Retouch: The act of a runner returning to a base.

Rookie: A first-year player.

Rubber: A 6-x-24-inch (15.5cm x 61cm) rubber slab on top of the pitcher's mound.

Rubber game: The third game of a three-game series in which the opposing teams have split the first two contests.

Run: A scoring unit posted by an offensive player who touches first, second, third, and home plate in that order.

Run Batted In (RBI): A batter is credited with a run batted in when he drives a runner home (helps him score a run) via a hit, a sacrifice bunt or fly, a walk, a hit batsman, a fielder's choice, or on an error if the official scorer rules the run would have scored had the error not been made. (For example, a runner scores from third with less than two out on a long, catchable fly ball that is dropped by the center fielder. The center fielder is charged with the error. However, the official scorer credits the batter with a run batted in after deciding that the runner would have scored on a sacrifice fly had the ball been caught. Had the ball been hit to shallow center, and the scorer ruled it was not hit far enough to score the runner without the error, the batter would not receive an RBI.) You would also credit a batter with an RBI if he drives himself in with a home run. Batters do not get *ribbies* when they drive runners while grounding into double plays.

Run-down: Members of the defense chasing a runner back and forth on the basepaths in an attempt to put out the runner.

Runner: An offensive player who is advancing toward, returning to, or occupying a base.

Sacrifice bunt: When the hitter willingly bunts into an out in order to advance a baserunner.

Sacrifice fly: A ball hit deep enough to score a runner from third base.

Save: The statistical credit awarded to a reliever who finishes a game on the victorious side but does not get the win. (To discover how saves are calculated, see Chapter 14.)

Scatter arm: A pitcher or fielder who throws wildly.

Score: The graph that allows you to track every play in a game, inning by inning.

Scoring position: A runner on second or third base, where he can score on almost any hit to the outfield. Exceptions: Sluggers like Mark McGwire, Ken Griffey Jr., and Frank Thomas; you could say they are in scoring position the minute they step in the batter's box.

Scout: The person who evaluates talent for a professional baseball organization. Most scouts scour the high schools, colleges, and minor leagues for players. Advance scouts monitor other major league clubs to pinpoint opposing players' strengths and weaknesses.

Season tickets: Tickets for an entire season of home games.

Seeing-eye grounder: A ground ball that barely eludes an infielder for a base hit.

Set position: The position the pitcher takes on the pitching rubber just before going into the wind-up.

Set-up man: A relief pitcher who usually arrives in the seventh or eighth inning, preferably when his team is winning. He sets up the ninth inning for the closer.

Seventh-inning stretch: A brief pause in the action between the top and bottom of the seventh inning. It allows time for fans to stand and stretch their legs.

Shoestring catch: A running catch made at the top of a fielder's shoes.

Show, The: The major leagues. A term popularized in the film *Bull Durham,* starring Kevin Costner.

Shutout: A pitcher's complete game victory in which the opposition doesn't score.

Signs: Managers, coaches, and players use these coded signals to pass information to each other during a game.

Single: A one-base hit. Also known as a *knock.*

Slugfest: A high-scoring game.

Slugger: A hitter who is usually among the home run leaders. Mark McGwire is the quintessential slugger.

Solo homer: A home run with the bases empty.

Southpaw: A left-handed pitcher.

Spectator interference: What an umpire should call when a fan reaches out of the stands or enters the playing field and touches a ball that's still in play.

Squeeze play: When a hitter attempts to score a runner from third with a bunt. If the runner leaves third before the hitter makes contact with the ball, it is called a *suicide squeeze;* if the hitter misses the pitch, the runner is dead. In the *safety squeeze,* the runner waits for the hitter to make contact before racing toward home.

Starting rotation: A team's group of regular starting pitchers who pitch in sequence.

Strawberry: A pinkish abrasion on the hip or leg, usually caused by sliding.

Stretch drive: The final lap of a horse race, or the final weeks of a season when teams are driving toward the pennant.

Strike: What occurs when a) a batter swings and misses, b) the batter hits a foul ball (unless he already has two strikes on him), c) the ball crosses the plate in the strike zone and the batter doesn't swing, or d) the players' union and the major league baseball owners can't reach an agreement and the players refuse to come to work.

Strike zone: The area a ball must pass through to be called a strike by an umpire. According to the rules, this zone is the width of home plate and extends from the bottom of the kneecap to the uniform letters across a player's chest. In practice, it varies, sometimes widely, from umpire to umpire.

Strikeout: An out made by a batter who accumulates three strikes during an at-bat.

Striking out the side: Perhaps the most misused phrase in baseball. To strike out the side, a pitcher must strike out every batter he faces in an inning rather than merely strike out three batters in an inning. If the pitcher allows a baserunner of any kind during the inning, the phrase does not apply.

Suspended game: A game that is called, but is scheduled to be completed at some future date.

Sweet spot: The best part of the bat to hit the ball. The sweet spot is a few inches from the end of the barrel.

Switch-hitter: A batter who hits from both sides of the plate.

Tag: The act by which a fielder retires a baserunner. The fielder either touches a base with his body or the ball before the fielder arrives, or the fielder touches the runner with the ball (which can be in the fielder's glove or hand) before the runner reaches the bag.

Take: To let a pitch go by without swinging.

Tape-measure home run: A long home run, usually one that travels 450 feet or more. Mark McGwire and Juan Gonzalez regularly hit tape-measure shots. The term was first applied to the long home runs hit by Mickey Mantle in the 1950s.

"Time": The umpire's declaration that interrupts play. The ball is dead.

Tools of ignorance: The catcher's equipment. The term implies that one has to be lacking intelligence to want to wear them. Actually, the converse is true. A good catcher is usually one of the smartest people on a team.

Trade: An exchange of players between two or more teams.

Triple: A three-base hit.

Triple play: Any defensive play that produces three outs on the same batted ball. In an *unassisted* triple play, one fielder records all three outs.

Twin killing: A double play.

Umpire: The on-field baseball official who declares whether a batter is safe or out, a pitch is a ball or a strike, or a batted ball is foul or fair. He also interprets the rule book on all plays.

Umpire's interference: An act by the umpire that obstructs a catcher as he's attempting to throw out a base stealer. This call is also made when a fair ball strikes an umpire in fair territory before passing a fielder. The ball is dead.

Uniforms: What players wear on the field.

Utility player: A player, usually a substitute, who has the versatility to play more than one position. Though it rarely happens, utility players can get enough plate appearances at their various positions to qualify as regulars. Billy Goodman started at six different positions for the 1950 Boston Red Sox and won an American League batting title.

Walk: When a hitter receives four balls during a plate appearance, he is entitled to take first base. All other baserunners advance if they are forced in by the walk. *See* Base on balls.

Warning track: A dirt path in front of the outfield fences, it warns the outfielders of their proximity to the walls.

Waste pitch: A pitch deliberately thrown outside the strike zone in the hope that the batter will chase it. Pitchers usually throw them if they are ahead of the batter in the count (on 0-2 or 1-2 counts). This pitch really is a waste if you throw it to a bad-ball hitter who will probably hammer it for extra bases.

Wheelhouse: A hitter's power zone, an area that is usually waist-high and over the heart of home plate.

Wheels: A player's legs.

Whitewash: A shutout.

Wild pitch: A pitched ball that is thrown so far from the target that it gets past the catcher. If the official scorer decides the catcher should have caught the pitch, he can rule it a *passed ball*. Wild pitches and passed balls are charged only when they advance a baserunner or allow a batter to reach base safely on a third strike.

Winter league: A baseball league that plays during the winter months. Most winter leagues are based in Florida, Arizona, or Latin America. Many Latin American big leaguers play winter ball for their hometown teams as a matter of local pride. American major leaguers usually play in these leagues to sharpen their skills after an injury-plagued season or learn a new position.

Worm-burner (worm-killer): A ground ball that rolls over the infield without taking a bounce.

Baseball Career Years

Player	Active Years
Cy Young	1890–1911
Honus Wagner	1897–1917
Christy Mathewson	1900–1916
Ty Cobb	1905–1928
Walter Johnson	1907–1927
Babe Ruth	1914–1935
Rogers Hornsby	1915–1937
Lou Gehrig	1923–1939
Lefty Grove	1925–1941
Jimmie Foxx	1925–1945
Satchel Paige	1926–1965
Josh Gibson	1930–1945
Joe Dimaggio	1936–1951
Bob Feller	1936–1956
Ted Williams	1939–1960
Stan Musial	1941–1963
Warren Spahn	1942–1965
Yogi Berra	1946–1965
Jackie Robinson	1947–1956
Whitey Ford	1950–1967
Willie Mays	1951–1973
Mickey Mantle	1951–1968
Ernie Banks	1953–1971
Hank Aaron	1954–1976
Sandy Koufax	1955–1966
Roberto Clemente	1955–1972
Brooks Robinson	1955–1977
Frank Robinson	1956–1976
Curt Flood	1956–1971
Bill Mazeroski	1956–1972
Luis Aparicio	1956–1973
Bob Gibson	1959–1975
Willie McCovey	1959–1980
Maury Wills	1959–1972
Juan Marichal	1960–1975
Carl Yastrzemski	1961–1983
Lou Brock	1961–1979
Pete Rose	1963–1986
Rusty Staub	1963–1985
Joe Morgan	1963–1984
Steve Carlton	1965–1988
Nolan Ryan	1966–1993
Tom Seaver	1967–1986
Johnny Bench	1967–1983
Bill Lee	1969–1982
Mike Schmidt	1972–1989
Ken Griffey, Sr.	1973–1991
Keith Hernandez	1974–1990
Ozzie Smith	1978–1996

Appendix B
Major League Records

Games played

Most Games Played
NL: 3,562, Pete Rose (Cincinnati, Philadelphia, Montreal, 1963–86)
AL: 3,308, Carl Yastrzemski (Boston, 1961–83)

Most Consecutive Games Played
AL: 2,478, Cal Ripken (Baltimore 1982 through 1997)
NL: 1,207, Steve Garvey (Los Angeles, San Diego, September 3, 1975–July 29, 1983)

Hitting

Highest Batting Average
Career (10-year minimum)
AL: .367, Ty Cobb (Detroit, Philadelphia, 1905–28)
NL: .359, Rogers Hornsby (St. Louis, New York, Boston, Chicago, 1915–33)

Season (130-game minimum)
NL: .424, Rogers Hornsby (St. Louis, 1924)
AL:.422, Napoleon Lajoie (Philadelphia, 1901)

Most Years Leading the League in Batting Average
AL: 12, Ty Cobb, (Detroit, 1907–15, 1917–19)
NL.: 8, Honus Wagner (Pittsburgh, 1900, 1903–04, 1906–09, 1911),
Tony Gwynn (San Diego Padres, (1984, 1987–89, 1994-97)

Lowest Batting Average by a Batting Champion
AL: .301, Carl Yastrzemski (Boston, 1968)
NL: .313, Tony Gwynn (San Diego, 1988)

Highest Slugging Average
Career (15-year minimum)
Major Leagues: .690, Babe Ruth (Boston Red Sox, New York Yankees, Boston Braves, 1914-35)
AL:.692, Babe Ruth (Boston, New York 1914–34)
NL: .578 Rogers Hornsby (St. Louis, New York, Boston, Chicago 1915–33)

Season (130-game minimum)
AL: 847, Babe Ruth (New York, 1920)
NL:.756 Rogers Hornsby (St. Louis, 1925)

Most Runs Scored
Career
AL: 2,245, Ty Cobb (Detroit, Philadelphia, 1905–28)
NL: 2,165, Pete Rose (Cincinnati, Philadelphia, Montreal, 1963–86)

Season (130-game minimum)
NL: 196, Billy Hamilton (Philadelphia, 1894)
AL: 177 Babe Ruth (New York, 1921)

Game
NL: 6, held by many
AL: 6, John Pesky (Boston, May 8, 1946), Spike Owen (Boston, August 21, 1986)

Most Home Runs
Career
Major Leagues: 755, Henry Aaron (Milwaukee NL, Atlanta NL, Milwaukee AL 1954–76)
NL: 733, Henry Aaron (Milwaukee, Atlanta 1954–74)
AL: 708, Babe Ruth (Boston, New York 1914–34)

Season
AL: ~~61, Roger Maris (New York, 1961)~~ *70, Mark McGwire, 1998)*
NL: 56, Hack Wilson (Chicago, 1930) *57, Ken Griffey Jr, 1998)*

Game
NL: 4, held by many
AL: 4, Lou Gehrig (New York, June 3, 1932), Pat Seerey (Chicago, July 18, 1948), Rocky Colavito (Cleveland, June 10, 1959)

Most Consecutive Home Runs
NL: 4, Bobby Lowe (Boston, May 30, 1894), Mike Schmidt (Philadelphia, April 17, 1976)
AL: 4, Lou Gehrig (New York, June 3, 1932), Rocky Colavito (Cleveland, June 10, 1959)

Most Consecutive Games, at Least One Homer Each Game
NL: 8, Dale Long (Pittsburgh, May 19–28, 1956, eight home runs)
AL: 8, Don Mattingly (New York, July 8–18, 1987, ten home runs),
Ken Griffey Jr. (Seattle, July 20–28, 1993, eight home runs)

Most Pinch-Hit Home Runs
Career
Major Leagues: 20, Cliff Johnson (Houston NL, New York AL, Cleveland AL, Chicago NL, Oakland AL, Toronto AL, 1974–86)
NL: 18, Jerry Lynch (Cincinnati, Pittsburgh, 1957–66)
AL: 16, Gates Brown (Detroit, 1963–75)

Season
NL: 6, Johnny Frederick (Brooklyn, 1932)
AL; 5, Joe Cronin (Boston, 1943)

Most Grand Slams
Career
AL: 23, Lou Gehrig (New York, 1923–39)
NL: 18, Willie McCovey (San Francisco, San Diego 1959–80)

Season
AL: 6, Don Mattingly (New York, 1987)
NL: 5, Ernie Banks (Chicago, 1955)

Game
AL: 2, held by many
NL: 2, Tony Cloninger (Atlanta, July 3, 1966)

Most Runs Batted In
Career
Major Leagues: 2, 297, Henry Aaron (Milwaukee NL, Atlanta NL, Milwaukee AL, 1954–76)
NL: 2,202, Henry Aaron (Milwaukee, Atlanta 1954–76)
AL: 2,192, Babe Ruth (Boston, New York, 1914–34)

Season
NL: 190, Hack Wilson (Chicago, 1930)
AL: 184, Lou Gehrig (New York, 1931)

Game
NL: 12, Jim Bottomley (St. Louis, September 16, 1924), Mark Whiten (St. Louis, September 7, 1993)
AL: 11, Tony Lazzeri (New York, May 24, 1936)

Most Singles
Career
NL: 3,215, Pete Rose (Cincinnati, Philadelphia, Montreal 1963–86)
AL: 3,052, Ty Cobb (Detroit, Philadelphia, 1905–28)

Season
NL: 202, Willie Keeler (Baltimore, 1898)
AL: 187, Wade Boggs (Boston, 1985)

Most Doubles

Career

AL: 793, Tris Speaker (Boston, Cleveland, Washington, Philadelphia, 1907–28)

NL: 746, Pete Rose (Cincinnati, Philadelphia, Montreal, 1963–1986)

Season

AL: 67, Earl Webb (Boston, 1931)

NL: 64, Joe Medwick (St. Louis, 1934)

Most Triples

Career

Major Leagues: 312, Sam Crawford (Cincinnati NL, Detroit AL, 1899–1917)

AL: 298, Ty Cobb (Detroit, Philadelphia 1905–28)

NL: 252, Honus Wagner (Louisville, Pittsburgh, 1900–1917)

Season

NL: 36, Owen Wilson (Pittsburgh, 1912)

AL: 26, Joe Jackson (Cleveland, 1912), Sam Crawford (Detroit, 1914)

Most Hits

Career

NL: 4,256, Pete Rose (Cincinnati, Philadelphia, Montreal 1963–86)

AL: 4,191, Ty Cobb (Detroit, Philadelphia, 1905–28)

Season

AL: George 257, (St. Louis, 1920)

NL: 254, Lefty O'Doul (Philadelphia, 1929), Bill Terry (New York, 1930)

Nine-Inning Game

NL: 7, Wilbert Robinson (Baltimore, June 10, 1892), Rennie Stennett (Pittsburgh, September 16, 1975)

AL: 6, held by many

Most Pinch-Hits

Career

NL:150, Manny Mota (San Francisco, Pittsburgh, Montreal, Los Angeles, 1962– 80, 1982)

AL: 107, Gates Brown (Detroit, 1962–75)

Season

NL: 28, John Vander Wal (Colorado, 1995)

AL: 24, Dave Philley (Baltimore, 1961)

Most Total Bases
Career
Major Leagues: 6,856, Henry Aaron (Milwaukee NL, Atlanta NL, Milwaukee AL, 1954–76)
NL: 6,591, Henry Aaron (Milwaukee, Atlanta 1954–76)
AL: 5,862, Ty Cobb (Detroit, Philadelphia, 1905–28)

Season
AL: 457, Babe Ruth (New York, 1921)
NL: 450, Rogers Hornsby (St. Louis, 1922)

Game
NL: 18, Joe Adcock (Milwaukee, July 31, 1954, 4 home runs, 1 double)
AL: 16, held by many

Batting streaks

Most Consecutive Games Batting Safely
AL: 56, Joe DiMaggio (New York, May 15–July 16, 1941)
NL: 44, Wee Willie Keeler (Baltimore, April 22–June 18, 1897), Pete Rose (Cincinnati, June 14–July 31, 1978)

Most Consecutive Hits
AL: 12, Pinky Higgins (Boston, June 19–21, 1938), Walt Dropo (Detroit, July 14–15, 1952
N.L: 10, held by many

Most Consecutive Times Reaching Base Safely
AL: 16, Ted Williams (Boston, September 17–23, 1957)
NL: 14, Pedro Guerrero (Los Angeles, July 23–26, 1985)

Most Consecutive Pinch Hits, Season
NL: 8, Dave Philley (Philadelphia, September 9–28, 1958), Daniel "Rusty" Staub, (New York, June 11–26, 1983)
AL: 7, Bill Stein (Texas, April 14–May 25, 1981), Randy Bush (Minnesota, July 5–August 19, 1991)

Stealing

Most Stolen Bases
Career
Major Leagues: 1,165, Rickey Henderson (Oakland, New York, Toronto, San Diego, Anaheim, 1979 through 1997)
AL: 1,165, Rickey Henderson (Oakland, New York, Toronto, Anaheim, 1979 through 1997)
NL: 938, Lou Brock (Chicago, St. Louis, 1961–79)

Season
AL: 130, Rickey Henderson (Oakland, 1982)
NL: 118, Lou Brock (St. Louis, 1974)

Game
NL: 7, Billy Hamilton (Philadelphia, August 31, 1894)
AL: 6, Eddie Collins (Philadelphia, September 11, 1912, and September 22, 1912)

Most Consecutive Steals before Getting Caught
NL: 50, Vince Coleman (St. Louis, 1985)
AL: 40, Tim Raines (Chicago, July 23 1993–August 4, 1995)

Most Stolen Bases without Getting Caught During the Season
NL: 21, Kevin McReynolds (New York, 1988)
AL: 20, Paul Molitor (Toronto, 1994)

Most Steals of Home
Career
AL: 50, Ty Cobb (Detroit, Philadelphia 1905–28)
NL: 33, Max Carey, (Pittsburgh, Brooklyn 1910–29)

Season
AL: 8, Ty Cobb (Detroit, 1912)
NL: 7, Pete Reiser (Brooklyn, 1946)

Bases on balls and strikeouts

Most Bases on Balls
Career
Major Leagues: 2,056, Babe Ruth (Boston AL, New York AL, Boston NL, 1914–35)
AL: 2,036, Babe Ruth (Boston, New York 1914–34)
NL: 1,799, Joe Morgan (Houston, Cincinnati, San Francisco, Philadelphia, 1963–83)

Season
AL: 170, Babe Ruth (New York, 1923)
NL: 151, Barry Bonds (San Francisco, 1996)

Game
NL: 6, Walt Wilmot (Chicago, August 22, 1891)
AL: 6, Jimmie Foxx (Boston, June 16, 1938)

Most Intentional Walks
Career
Major Leagues: 293, Henry Aaron (Milwaukee NL, Atlanta NL, Milwaukee AL 1954–76)
NL: 289, Henry Aaron (Milwaukee, Atlanta 1954–74)
AL: 229, George Brett (Kansas City, 1973–93)

Season
NL: 45, Willie McCovey (San Francisco, 1969)
AL: 33, Ted Williams (Boston, 1957), John Olerud (Toronto, 1993)

Most Strikeouts by a Hitter
Career
AL: 2,597, Reggie Jackson (Kansas City, Oakland, New York, California, 1967–87)
NL: 1,936, Willie Stargell (Pittsburgh, 1962–82)

Season
NL: 198, Bobby Bonds (San Francisco, 1970)
AL: 186, Rob Deer (Milwaukee, 1987)

Nine-Inning Game
NL: 5, held by many
AL: 5, held by many

Fewest Strikeouts
Career (14-year minimum)
AL: 113, Joe Sewell (Cleveland, New York 1920–33)
NL: 117, Lloyd Waner (Pittsburgh, Boston, Cincinnati, Philadelphia, Brooklyn, 1927–45)

Season (150-game minimum)
AL: 4, Joe Sewell (Cleveland, 1925, 155 games), Joe Sewell (Cleveland, 1929, 152 games)
NL: 5, Charles Hollocher (Chicago, 1922, 152 games)

Pitching

Most Games Pitched
Career
Major Leagues: 1,070, Hoyt Wilhelm (New York NL, St. Louis NL, Cleveland AL, Baltimore AL, Chicago AL, California AL, Atlanta NL, Chicago NL, Los Angeles NL 1952–1972)
NL: 1,050, Kent Tekulve (Pittsburgh, Philadelphia, Cincinnati, 1974–89)
AL: 807, Sparky Lyle (Boston, New York, Texas, Chicago, 1967–80, 1982)

Season
NL: 107, Mike Marshall (Los Angeles, 1974)
AL: 90, Mike Marshall (Minnesota, 1979)

Most Starts
Career
Major Leagues: 818, Cy Young (Cleveland NL, St. Louis NL, Boston AL, Cleveland AL, Boston NL, 1890–1911)
NL: 677, Steve Carlton (St. Louis, Philadelphia, San Francisco, 1965–86)
AL: 666, Walter Johnson (Washington 1907–1927)

Season
NL: 74, Will White (Cincinnati, 1879)
AL: 51, Jack Chesbro (New York, 1904)

Most Relief Appearances
Career
NL: 1,050, Kent Tekulve (Pittsburgh, Philadelphia, Cincinnati, 1974–89)
AL: 807, Sparky Lyle (Boston, New York, Texas, Chicago 1967–1980, 1982)

Season
NL: 106, Mike Marshall (Los Angeles, 1974)
AL: 89, Mike Marshall (Minnesota, 1979, Note: Marshall also started one game in 1979), Mark Eichhorn (Toronto, 1987)

Most Consecutive Relief Appearances
NL: 13, Mike Marshall (Los Angeles, June 18–July 3, 1974)
AL: 13, Dale Mohorcic (Texas, August 6–August 20, 1986)

Most Complete Games
Career
Major Leagues: 751, Cy Young (Cleveland NL, St. Louis NL, Boston AL, Cleveland AL, Boston NL, 1890–1911)
NL: 557, Pud Galvin (Buffalo, Pittsburgh, St. Louis, 1879–1886, 1887–88, 1891–92)
AL: 531, Walter Johnson (Washington, 1907–1927)

Season
NL: 74, Will White (Cincinnati, 1879)
AL: 48, Jack Chesbro (New York, 1904)

Most Innings Pitched
Career
Major Leagues: 7,377, Cy Young (Cleveland NL, St. Louis NL, Boston AL, Cleveland Al, Boston NL, 1890–1911)
AL: 5,924, Walter Johnson (Washington, 1907–27)
NL: 5,246, Warren Spahn (Boston, Milwaukee, San Francisco, New York 1942, 1946–65)

Season
NL: 683, Will White (Cincinnati, 1879)
AL: 464, Ed Walsh (Chicago, 1908)

Most Wins
Career
Major Leagues: 511, Cy Young (Cleveland NL, St. Louis NL, Boston AL,
Cleveland AL, Boston NL, 1890–1911)
AL: 416, Walter Johnson (Washington, 1907–27)
NL: 373, Christy Mathewson (New York, Cincinnati, 1900–1916),
Grover Alexander (Philadelphia, Chicago, St. Louis, 1911–1930)

Season
NL: 60, Charles "Old Hoss" Radbourn (Providence, 1884)
AL: 41, Jack Chesbro (New York, 1904)

Most Consecutive Games Won
Career
NL: 24, Carl Hubbell (New York, July 17, 1936–May 27, 1937)
AL: 17, John Allen (Cleveland, September 10, 1936–September 30, 1937),
Dave McNally (Baltimore, September 22, 1968–July 30, 1969)

Season
NL: 19, Tim Keefe (New York, June 23–August 10, 1888), Rube Marquard
(New York, April 11–July 3, 1912)
AL: 16, Walter Johnson (Washington July 3–August 23, 1912), Smokey Joe
Wood (Boston, July 8–September 15, 1912), Lefty Grove (Philadelphia,
June 8–August 19, 1931), Schoolboy Rowe (Detroit, June 15–August 25, 1934)

Highest Winning Percentage
Career (200-decision minimum)
AL: .690, Whitey Ford (New York 1950, 1953–65)
NL: .665, Christy Mathewson (New York, Cincinnati, 1900–16)

Season (35 or more decisions)
AL: .886, Lefty Grove (31-4, Philadelphia, 1931)
NL: .833, Charles "Old Hoss" Radbourne (60-12, Providence, 1884)

Season (20 or more wins)
AL: .893, Ron Guidry (25-3, New York, 1978)
NL: .880, Fred Goldsmith (22-3, Chicago, 1880), Preacher Roe (22-3, Brooklyn,
1951)

Most Games Lost

Career

Major Leagues: 313, Cy Young (Cleveland NL, St. Louis NL, Boston AL, Cleveland AL, Boston NL, 1890–1911)

AL: 279, Walter Johnson (Washington, 1907–1927)

NL: 268, Pud Galvin (Buffalo, Pittsburgh, St. Louis, 1879–85, 1887–88, 1891–92)

Season

NL: 48, John Coleman (Philadelphia, 1883)

AL: 26, Jack Townsend (Washington, 1905), Bob Groom (Washington, 1909)

Most Consecutive Games Lost

Career

NL: 27, Anthony Young (New York, May 6, 1992–July 24, 1993)

AL: 19, Jack Nabors (Philadelphia, April 28–September 28, 1916)

Most Saves

Career

Major Leagues: 473, Lee Smith (Chicago NL, Boston AL, St. Louis NL, New York AL, Baltimore AL, California AL, Cincinnati NL, Montreal NL, 1980–97)

NL: 342, Lee Smith (Chicago, St. Louis, Cincinnati, Montreal 1980–97)

AL: 323, Dennis Eckersley (Cleveland, Boston, Oakland, 1975–84)

Season

AL: 57, Bobby Thigpen (Chicago, 1990)

NL: 53, Randy Myers (Chicago, 1993)

Most Games Won in Relief

Major Leagues: 124, Hoyt Wilhelm (New York NL, St. Louis NL, Cleveland AL, Baltimore AL, Chicago AL, California AL, Atlanta NL, Chicago NL, Los Angeles NL 1952–1972)

NL: 96, El Roy Face (Pittsburgh, Montreal, 1953, 1955–1969)

AL: 87, Sparky Lyle (Boston, New York, Texas, Chicago 1967–1980, 1982)

Season

NL: 18, El Roy Face (Pittsburgh, 1959)

AL: 17, John Hiller (Detroit, 1974), Bill Campbell (Minnesota, 1976)

Most Games Lost in Relief

Season

NL: 16, Gene Garber (Atlanta, 1979)

AL: 14, John Hiller (Detroit, 1974), Darold Knowles (Washington, 1970), Mike Marshall (Minnesota, 1970)

Lowest Earned Run Average (all ERA records before 1912 are not official)
Career (2,500-inning minimum)
AL: 1.82, Ed Walsh (Chicago, 1904–1916)
AL: 2.37, Walter Johnson (Washington, 1913–1927)
NL: 2.06, Mordecai Brown (St. Louis Chicago, Cincinnati. 1903–13, 1916)
NL: 2.33, Tim Vaugh (Chicago, 1913–1921)

Season (300-inning minimum)
NL: 1.12, Bob Gibson (St. Louis, 1968)
AL: 1.14, Walter Johnson (Washington, 1913)

Season (200-inning minimum)
AL: 1.00, Dutch Leonard (Boston, 1914)
NL: 1.12, Bob Gibson (St. Louis, 1968)

Most Strikeouts
Major Leagues: 5,714, Nolan Ryan (New York NL, California AL, Houston NL, Texas AL, 1966, 1968–93)
NL: 4,000, Steve Carlton (St. Louis, Philadelphia, San Francisco 1965–1986)
AL: 3,508, Walter Johnson (Washington, 1907–27)

Season
NL: 411, Charles "Old Hoss" Radbourn (Providence, 1884)
AL: 383, Nolan Ryan (California, 1973)

Nine-Inning Game
AL: 20, Roger Clemens (Boston, April 29, 1986), Roger Clemens (Boston, September 18, 1996)
NL: 19, Charles Sweeney (Providence, June 7, 1884), Steve Carlton (St. Louis, September 15, 1969), Tom Seaver (New York, April 22, 1970), David Cone (New York, October 6, 1991)

Extra-Inning Game
AL: 21, Tom Cheney (Washington, September 12, 1962, 16 innings)
NL: Less than the regulation game record

Most Consecutive Strikeouts
NL: 10, Tom Seaver (New York, April 22, 1970)
AL: 8, Nolan Ryan (California, July 9, 1972), Nolan Ryan (California, July 15, 1973), Ron Davis (New York, May 4, 1981), Roger Clemens (Boston, April 28, 1986)

Most Shutouts Won
Career
AL: 110, Walter Johnson (Washington, 1907–27)
NL: 90, Grover Alexander (Philadelphia, Chicago, St. Louis, 1911–30)

Season
NL: 16, George Bradley (St. Louis, 1876), Grover Alexander (Philadelphia, 1916)
AL: 13, Jack Coombs (Philadelphia, 1910)

Most Consecutive Shutouts Won
NL: 6, Don Drysdale (Los Angeles, 1968)
AL: 5, Guy (Doc) White (Chicago, 1904)

Longest Complete Game Shutout
NL: 18 innings, Monte Ward (Providence, August 1882, Ward won 1-0), Carl Hubbell (New York, July 2, 1933, Hubbell won 1-0)
AL: 18 innings, Ed Summers (Detroit, July 16, 1909, 0-0 tie), Walter Johnson (Washington, May 15, 1918, Johnson won 1-0)

Consecutive Scoreless Inning Streak
NL: 59, Orel Hersheiser (Los Angeles, 1988)
AL: $55^2/_3$, Walter Johnson (Washington, 1913)

Most Scoreless Innings Pitched, One Game
NL: 21, Joe Oeschger (Boston, May 1, 1920)
AL: 20, Joe Harris (Boston, September 1, 1906)

Most 1-0 Victories
Career
AL: 38, Walter Johnson (Washington, 1907–27)
NL: 17, Grover Alexander (Philadelphia, Chicago, St. Louis, 1911–30)

Season
AL: 5, Reb Russell (Chicago, 1913), Walter Johnson (Washington, 1913 and 1919), Joe Bush (Boston, 1918), Dean Chance (Los Angeles, 1964)
NL: 5, Carl Hubbell (New York, 1933)

Most 1-0 Losses
Career
AL: 26, Walter Johnson (Washington, 1907–27)
NL: 13, Lee Meadows (St. Louis, Philadelphia, Pittsburgh, 1915–29)

Season
AL: 5, Bill Donovan (Detroit, 1903), Jack Warhop (New York, 1914)
NL: 5, George McQuillan (Philadelphia, 1908), Roger Craig (New York, 1963), Jim Bunning (Philadelphia, 1967), Ferguson Jenkins (Chicago, 1968)

Most No-Hitters Pitched
Career
Major Leagues: 7, Nolan Ryan (California AL, 1973 two, 1974, 1975, Houston NL 1981, Texas AL 1990, 1991)
AL: 6, Nolan Ryan (California 1973, 1973 two, 1974, 1975, Texas 1990, 1991)
NL: 4, Sandy Koufax (Los Angeles 1962, 1963, 1964, 1965)

Season
NL: 2, Johnny Vander Meer (Cincinnati, June 11, June 15, 1938), Jim Maloney (Cincinnati, June 14, August 10, 1965)
AL: 2, Allie Reynolds, (New York, July 12, September 28, 1951), Virgil Trucks (Detroit, May 15, August 25, 1952), Nolan Ryan (California, May 15, July 15, 1973)

Most Consecutive No-Hit Games
NL: 2, Johnny Vander Meer (Cincinnati, June 11, June 15, 1938)
AL: 0

Most Home Runs Allowed
Career
Major Leagues: 505, Robin Roberts (Philadelphia NL, Baltimore AL, Houston NL, Chicago NL 1948–66)
NL: 434, Warren Spahn (Boston, Milwaukee, San Francisco, New York, 1942, 1946–65)
AL: 422, Frank Tanana (California, Boston, Texas, Detroit, New York, 1973–93)

Season
AL: 50, Bert Blyleven (Minnesota, 1986)
NL: 46, Robin Roberts (Philadelphia, 1956)

Game
NL: 7, Charlie Sweeney (St. Louis, June 12, 1886)
AL: 6, Al Thomas (St. Louis, June 27, 1936), George Caster (Philadelphia, September 24, 1940)

Inning
NL: 4, held by many
AL: 4, held by many

Most Walks Allowed
Major Leagues: 2,795, Nolan Ryan (New York NL, California AL, Houston NL, Texas AL, 1966, 1968–93)
AL: 1,775, Early Wynn (Washington, Cleveland, Chicago, 1939, 1941–44, 1946–63)
NL: 1,717, Steve Carlton (St. Louis, Philadelphia, San Francisco, 1965–86)

Season
NL: 276, Amos Rusie (New York, 1890)
AL: 208, Bob Feller (Cleveland, 1938)

Nine-Inning Game
NL: 16, Bill George (New York, May 30, 1887), George Van Haltren (Chicago, June 27, 1887)
AL: 16, Bruno Haas (Philadelphia, June 23, 1915)

Fewest Walks Allowed, Season (250-inning minimum)
NL: 18, Babe Adams (Pittsburgh, 263 innings, 1920)
AL: 28, Cy Young (Boston, 380 innings, 1904)

Most Consecutive Innings without Allowing a Walk
AL: 84^1/$_3$, Bill Fischer (Kansas City, August 3–September 30, 1962)
NL: 68, Christy Mathewson (New York, June 19–July 18, 1913), Randy Jones (San Diego May 17–June 22, 1976)

Most Hit Batters
Career
AL: 206, Walter Johnson (Washington, 1907–1927)
NL: 195, Emerson Hawley (St. Louis, Pittsburgh, Cincinnati, New York, 1892–1900)

Season
NL: 41, Joe McGinnity (Brooklyn, 1900)
AL: 31, Chick Fraser (Philadelphia, 1901)

Game
NL: 6. John Grimes (St. Louis, 1897)
AL: 4, held by many

Most Wild Pitches
Career
Major Leagues; 277, Nolan Ryan (New York NL, California AL, Houston NL, Texas AL, 1966, 1968–93)
AL: 206, Jack Morris (Detroit, Minnesota, Toronto, Cleveland, 1977–94)
NL: 200, Phil Niekro (Milwaukee, Atlanta 1964–83, 1987)

Season
NL: 64, Bill Stemmyer (Boston, 1886)
AL: 26, Juan Guzman (Toronto, 1993)

Game
NL: 10, Johnny Ryan (Louisville, 1876)
AL: 5 Charlie Wheatley (Detroit, September 27, 1912), Jack Morris (Detroit, August 3, 1987)

Most Balks
Season
AL: 16, Dave Stewart (Oakland, 1988)
NL: 11, Steve Carlton (Philadelphia, 1979)

Game
NL: 5, Bob Shaw (Milwaukee, May 4, 1963)
AL: 4, Vic Rashi (New York, May 3, 1950), Bobby Witt (Texas, April 12, 1988), Rick Honeycutt (Oakland, April 13, 1988), Gene Walter (Seattle, July 18, 1988), John Dopson (Boston, June 13, 1989)

Appendix C
Baseball Organizations

The Major Leagues

Office of Major League Baseball
350 Park Avenue
17th Floor
New York, New York 10022
Phone: 212-339-7800
Fax: 212-758-8660

American League
350 Park Avenue
18th Floor
New York, New York 10022
Phone: 212-339-7600
Fax: 212-593-7138

National League
350 Park Avenue
New York, New York 10022
Phone: 212-339-7700
Fax: 212-935-5069

Major League Players Association
12 East 49th Street
New York, New York 10017
Phone: 212-826-0808
Fax: 212-752-3649

Major League Umpires Association
23712 Birtcher Drive
Lake Forest, California 92630
Phone: 714-458-7600
Fax: 714-458-9454

National Baseball Hall of Fame and
Museum
25 Main Street
Cooperstown, New York 13326
Phone: 607-547-7200
Fax: 607-547-2044

Major League Alumni Association
3637 4th Street North
St. Petersburg, Florida 33704
Phone: 813-822-3399
Fax: 813-822-6300

Negro Leagues Baseball Museum
1601 East 18th Street, Suite 110
Kansas City, Missouri 64108
Phone: 816-221-1920
Fax: 816-221-8424

Media

Baseball Writers Association of America
78 Olive Street
Lake Grove, New York 11755
Phone: 516-981-7938
Fax: 516-585-4669

National Association of Baseball Writers
and Broadcasters
P.O. Box A
St. Petersburg, Florida 33131
Phone: 813-822-6937
Fax: 813-821-5819

Publications

Baseball America
P.O. Box 2089
Durham, North Carolina 27702
Phone: 919-682-9635
Fax: 919-682-2880
E-mail: ba@interpath.com

Baseball Digest
990 Grove Street
Evanston, Illinois 60201
Phone: 847-491-6440
Fax: 847-491-0867

The Sporting News
10176 Corporate Square Drive
St. Louis, Missouri 63132
Phone: 314-997-7111
Fax: 314-997-0765

Sports Illustrated
Time & Life Building
1271 Avenue of the Americas
New York, New York 10020
Phone: 212-522-1212
Fax: 212-522-4543

Street and Smith's Baseball Yearbook
342 Madison Avenue
New York, New York 10017
Phone: 212-880-8698
Fax: 212-880-4347

Total Baseball
205 Main Street
Westport, Connecticut 06880
Phone: 203-454-2451
Fax: 203-454-8761

USA Today Baseball Weekly
1000 Wilson Boulevard
Arlington, Virginia 22229
Phone: 703-558-5630
Fax: 703-558-4678

Statistics and Research

Elias Sports Bureau
500 Fifth Avenue
New York, New York 10110
Phone: 212-869-1530
Fax: 212-354-0980

Howe Sports Data International
Boston Fish Pier, West Bldg. #2
Suite 306
Boston, Massachusetts 02210
Phone: 617-951-0070
Stats Service: 617-951-1379
Fax: 617-737-9960

STATS, Inc.
8131 Monticello Avenue
Skokie, Illinois 60076
Phone: 847-676-3322
Fax: 847-676-0821

Society for American Baseball Research
P.O. Box 93183
Cleveland, Ohio 44101
Phone: 216-575-0500
Fax: 216-575-0502

American League Teams

Anaheim Angels
2000 Gene Autry Way
Anaheim, California 92806
Phone: 714-940-2000
Fax: 714-940-2205

Baltimore Orioles
333 West Camden Street
Baltimore, Maryland 21201
Phone: 410-685-9800
Fax: 410-547-6272
www.theorioles.com

Boston Red Sox
4 Yawkey Way
Boston, Massachusetts 02215
Phone: 617-267-9440
Fax: 617-236-6797
www.redsox.com

Chicago White Sox
333 West 35th Street
Chicago, Illinois 60616
Phone: 312-674-1000
Fax: 312-674-5116
www.chisox.com

Cleveland Indians
2401 Ontario Street
Cleveland, Ohio 44115
Phone: 216-420-4200
Fax: 216-420-4396
www.indians.com

Detroit Tigers
2121 Trumbull Avenue
Detroit, Michigan 48216
Phone: 313-962-4000
Fax: 313-965-2138
www.detroittigers.com

Kansas City Royals
1 Royal Way
Kansas City, Missouri 64129
Phone: 816-921-2200
Fax: 816-921-5775
www.kcroyals.com

Minnesota Twins
34 Kirby Puckett Place
Minneapolis, Minnesota 55415
Phone: 613-375-1366
www.mntwins.com

New York Yankees
Yankee Stadium
161st Street and River Avenue
Bronx, New York 10451
Phone: 718-293-4300
Fax: 718-293-8431
www.yankees.com

Oakland Athletics
7677 Oakport Street, Suite 200
Oakland, California 94621
Phone: 510-638-4900
Fax: 510-568-3770
www.oaklandathletics.com

Seattle Mariners
83 South King Street
Seattle, Washington 98104
Phone: 206-628-3555
Fax: 206-628-3340
www.mariners.org

Tampa Bay Devil Rays
1 Tropicana Drive
St. Petersburg, Florida 33705
Phone: 813-825-3137
Fax: 813-825-3300
www.devilray.com

Texas Rangers
1000 Ballpark Way
Arlington, Texas 76011
Phone: 817-273-5222
Fax: 817-273-5206
www.texasrangers.com

Toronto Blue Jays
1 Blue Jays Way, Suite 2000
Toronto, Ontario M5V 1J1
Phone: 416-341-1000
Fax: 416-341-1250
www.bluejays.ca

National League Teams

Arizona Diamondbacks
400 North Fifth Street, Suite 1100
Phoenix, Arizona 85004
Phone: 602-514-8500
Fax: 602-514-8599
www.azdiamondbacks.com

Atlanta Braves
755 Hank Aaron Drive
Atlanta, Georgia 30312
Phone: 404-522-7630
Fax: 404-614-1391
www.atlantabraves.com

Chicago Cubs
1060 West Addison Street
Chicago, Illinois 60613
Phone: 773-404-2827
Fax: 773-404-4129
www.cubs.com

Cincinnati Reds
100 Cinergy Field
Cincinnati, Ohio 45202
Phone: 513-421-4510
Fax: 513-421-7342
www.cincinnatireds.com

Colorado Rockies
2001 Blake Street
Denver, Colorado 80205
Phone: 303-292-0200
Fax: 303-312-2319

Florida Marlins
2267 NW 199th Street
Miami, Florida 33056
Phone: 305-626-7400
Fax: 305-626-7428
www.flamarlins.com

Houston Astros
8400 Kirby Drive
Houston, Texas 77054
Phone: 713-799-9500
Fax: 713-799-9562
www.astros.com

Los Angeles Dodgers
1000 Elysian Park Avenue
Los Angeles, California 90012
Phone: 213-224-1500
Fax: 213-224-1269
www.dodgers.com

Milwaukee Brewers
210 South 46th Street
Milwaukee, Wisconsin 53201
Phone: 414-933-4114
Fax: 414-933-7323
www.milwaukeebrewers.com

Montreal Expos
4549 Pierre-de-Coubertin Avenue
Montreal, Quebec H1V 3N7
Phone: 514-253-3434
Fax: 514-253-8282
www.montrealexpos.com

New York Mets
123-01 Roosevelt Avenue
Flushing, New York 11368
Phone: 718-507-6387
Fax: 718-565-6395

Philadelphia Phillies
3501 South Broad Street
Philadelphia, Pennsylvania 19101
Phone: 215-463-6000
Fax: 215-389-3050
www.phillies.com

Pittsburgh Pirates
600 Stadium Club Circle
Pittsburgh, Pennsylvania 15212
Phone: 412-323-5000
Fax: 412-323-9133
www.piratesball.com

St. Louis Cardinals
250 Stadium Plaza
St. Louis, Missouri
Phone: 314-421-3060
Fax: 314-425-0640
www.stlcardinals.com

San Diego Padres
8880 Rio San Diego Drive
San Diego, California 92108
Phone: 619-881-6500
Fax: 619-497-5454
www.padres.org

San Francisco Giants
3Com Park at Candlestick Point
San Francisco, California 94124
Phone: 415-468-3700
Fax: 415-467-0485
www.sfgiants.com

The Minor Leagues

National Association
210 Bayshore Drive SE
St. Petersburg, Florida 33701
Phone: 813-822-6937
Fax: 813-821-5819

American Association
6801 Miami Avenues, Suite 3
Cincinnati, Ohio 45243
Phone: 513-271-4800
Fax: 513-271-7887

International League
55 S. High Street Suite 202
Dublin, Ohio 43017
Phone: 614-791-9300
Fax: 614-791-9009

Pacific Coast League
2345 South Alma School Road, Suite 110
Mesa, Arizona 85210
Phone: 602-838-2171
Fax: 602-838-2741

Mexican League
Angel Pola #16
Col. Periodista, Mexico D.F. CP 11220
Phone: 011-525-557-2454
Fax: 011-525-395-2454

Eastern League
511 Congress
Portland, Maine 04101
Phone: 207-761-2700
Fax: 207-761-7064

Southern League
One Depot Street
Marietta, Georgia 30060
Phone: 770-428-4749
Fax: 770-428-4849

Texas League
2442 Facet Oak
San Antonio, Texas 78232
Phone: 210-545-5297
Fax: 210-545-5298

California League
2380 S. Bascom Avenue
Campbell, California 95008
Phone: 408-369-8038
Fax: 408-369-1409

Carolina League
1806 Pembroke Road
Greensboro, North Carolina 27408
Phone: 910-691-9030
Fax: 910-691-9070

Florida State League
103 East Orange Avenue
Daytona Beach, Florida 32114
Phone: 904-252-7479
Fax: 904-252-7495

Midwest League
1118 Cranston Road
Beloit, Wisconsin 53511
Phone: 608-364-1188
Fax: 608-364-1913

South Atlantic League
504 Crescent Hill
Kings Mountain, North Carolina 28086
Phone: 704-739-3466
Fax: 704-739-1974

New York-Penn State
1629 Oneida Street
Utica, New York 13501
Phone: 315-733-8036
Fax: 315-797-7403

Northwest League
5900 North Granite Reef Road, Suite 105
Scottsdale, Arizona 85250
Phone: 602-483-8224
Fax: 602-443-3450

Appalachian League
283 Deerchase Circle
Statesville, North Carolina 28677
Phone: 704-873-5300
Fax: 704-873-4333

Pioneer League
812 West 30th Street
Spokane, Washington 99203
Phone: 509-456-7615
Fax: 509-456-0136

Arizona League
5900 North Granite Reef Road, Suite 105
Scottsdale, Arizona 85250
Phone: 602-483-8224
Fax: 602-443-3450

Gulf Coast League
1503 Clower Creek Drive, Suite H–262
Sarasota, Florida 34231
Phone: 941-966-6407
Fax: 941-966-6872

Dominican Summer League
Avenue John F. Kennedy, No. 3
Santo Domingo, Dominican Republic
Phone: 809-563-3233 ext. 5020
Fax: 809-563-2455

Independent Leagues

Atlantic League
227 Fourth Avenue
Bayshore, New York 11706
Phone: 516-665-5655
Fax: 516-665-7277

Big South League
4300 North State Street
Jackson, Mississippi 39206
Phone: 601-982-5544
Fax: 601-982-8166

Frontier League
P.O. Box 2662
Zanesville, Ohio 43702
Phone: 614-452-7400
Fax: 614-452-2999

Heartland League
3582 Canterbury Drive
Lafayette, Indiana 47905
Phone: 765-474-5341
Fax: 765-474-6462

North Atlantic League
823-C North Highway
Southampton, New York 11968
Phone: 516-287-0557
Fax: 516-283-2252

Northeast League
1306 Davos Pointe
Woodbridge, New York 12789
Phone: 914-434-7262
Fax: 914-434-4806

Northern League
524 South Duke Street
Durham, North Carolina 27701
Phone: 919-956-8150
Fax: 919-683-2693

Prairie League
427 Lark Bay North
Regina, Saskatchewan S4Y 1H7
Phone: 306-522-7575
Fax: 306-522-7539

Texas-Louisiana League
401 Cypress Street, Suite 300
Abilene, Texas 79601
Phone: 915-677-4501
Fax: 915-677-4215

Western League
P.O. Box 80381
Portland, Oregon 97280
Phone: 503-203-8557
Fax: 503-203-8438

Arizona Fall League
10201 South 51st Street
Phoenix, Arizona 85044
Phone: 602-496-6700
Fax: 602-496-6384

Hawaii Winter Bare ball
905 Makahiki Way Unit C
Honolulu, Hawaii 96826
Phone: 808-973-7247
Fax: 808-973-7117

Foreign Leagues

Australian Baseball League
48 Atchison Street, Level 2
St. Leonards, NSW 2065, Australia
Phone: 011-61-2-9437-4622
Fax: 011-61-2-9437-4155

Japanese Leagues
Imperial Tower
7F, 1-1-1 Uchisaiwai-cho, Chiyoda-ku
Tokyo 100, Japan
Phone: 011-03-3502-0022
Fax: 011-03-3502-0140

Pacific League (Japan)
Asahi Building
9F, 6-6-7, Ginza, Chuo-ku
Tokyo 104, Japan
Phone: 03-3573-1551
Fax: 03-3572-5843

Central League
Asahi Building
3F, 6-6-7, Ginza, Chuo-ku
Tokyo 104, Japan
Phone: 03-3572-1673
Fax: 03-3571-4545

Chinese Professional Baseball League
14 F, No. 126, Section 4
Nanking East Road
Taipei, Taiwan
Phone: 886-2-577-6992
Fax: 886-2-577-2606

Korean Baseball Organization
946-16 Dokok-Dong, Kangnam-Gu
Seoul, South Korea
Phone: 011-82-2-557-7887~9
Fax: 011-82-2-557-7800

Caribbean Baseball Confederation
Frank Feliz Miranda No. 1 Naco
P.O. Box 21070 y 21416
Santo Domingo, Dominican Republic
Phone: 809-562-4737 or 562-4715
Fax: 809-565-4654

Dominican League
Estadio Quisqueya
Santo Domingo, Dominican Republic
Phone: 809-567-6371
Fax: 809-567-5720

Mexican Pacific League
Pesqueira No. 401-R
Navojora, Sonora, Mexico
Phone: 52-642-2-3100
Fax: 52-642-2-7250

Puerto Rican League
P.O. Box 1852
Hato Rey, Puerto Rico 00919
Phone: 787-765-6285
Fax: 787-767-3028

Venezuelan League
Avenida Sorbona
Edif, Marta Piso 2 No. 25
Urbanizacion Colinas de Bello Monte
Caracas, Venezuela
Phone: 011-58-2-751-2079 or 752-6897
Fax: 011-58-2-751-0891

College Baseball

National Collegiate Athletic Association
6201 College Boulevard
Overland Park, Kansas 66211
Phone: 913-339-1906
Fax: 913-339-0026

National Association of Intercollegiate
Athletics
6120 South Yale Avenue, Suite 1450
Tulsa, Oklahoma 74136
Phone: 918-494-8828
Fax: 918-494-8841

National Jr. College Athletic Association
P.O. Box 7305
Colorado Springs, Colorado 80933
Phone: 719-590-9788
Fax: 719-590-7324

Community College League of California
2017 O Street
Sacramento, California 95814
Phone: 916-444-1600
Fax: 916-444-2616

American Baseball Coaches Association
108 South Univeristy Avenue, Suite 3
Mount Pleasant, Michigan 48858
Phone: 517-775-3300
Fax: 517-775-3600

High School Baseball

National Federation of State High School
Associations
11724 NW Plaza Circle
Kansas City, Missouri 64153
Phone: 816-464-5400
Fax: 816-464-5571

National High School Baseball
Coaches Association
P.O. Box 12354
Omaha, Nebraska 68112
Phone: 402-457-1962
Fax: 402-457-1962

National Classic High School Tournament
El Dorado High School
1651 North Valencia Avenue
Placentia, California 92870
Phone: 714-993-5350
Fax: 714-524-2458

Sunbelt Baseball Classic Series
505 North Boulevard
Edmond, Oklahoma 73034
Phone: 405-348-3839

National Amateur All-Star Baseball
Tournament
400 North Michigan Avenue
Chicago, Illinois 60611
Phone: 800-622-2877
Fax: 312-245-8088

Eastern U.S. Baseball Showcase
P.O. Box 2126
Chapel Hill, North Carolina 27514
Phone: 919-962-2351

NCAA Summer Baseball
6201 College Boulevard
Overland Park, Kansas 66211
Phone: 913-339-1906
Fax: 913-339-0026

Alaska League (Summer College League)
1625 Old Steese Highway
Fairbanks, Alaska 99701
Phone: 907-451-0095

Alaska Central League
P.O. Box 318
Kenai, Alaska 99611
Phone: 907-283-7133
Fax: 907-283-3390

Arizona Collegiate League
995 East Baseline Road, Suite 1024
Tempe, Arizona 85283
Phone: 602-949-4225
Fax: 602-949-4225

Atlantic Collegiate League
26 Eric Trail
Sussex, New Jersey 07461
Phone: 201-702-1755
Fax: 210-702-1898

Cape Cod League
Tabor Academy
Marion, Massachusetts 02738
Phone: 508-748-0337
Fax: 508-748-0552

Central Illinois Collegiate League
RR 13, Box 369
Bloomington, Illinois 61704
Phone: 309-828-4429
Fax: 309-828-4429

Clark Griffith Collegiate League
4917 North 30th Street
Arlington, Virginia 22207
Phone: 703-536-3252
Fax: 703-536-1729

Coastal Plain League
4900 Waters Edge Drive, Suite 201
Raleigh, North Carolina 27606
Phone: 919-852-1960
Fax: 919-852-1973

Great Lakes League
24700 Center Ridge, Suite 10
Westlake, Ohio 44145
Phone: 216-871-8100
Fax: 216-871-4221

Jayhawk League
South Adams Place
Halstead, Kansas 67056
Phone: 316-755-2361
Fax: 316-755-1285

New England Collegiate League
57 Steuben Street
Meriden, Connecticut 06451
Phone: 203-238-4111
Fax: 203-238-4111

Northeastern Collegiate League
3148 Riverside Drive
Wellsville, New York 14895
Phone: 716-593-3923
Fax: 716-593-3923

Northwest Collegiate League
16077 Bales Way
Sherwood, Oregon 97140
Phone: 503-725-5634
Fax: 503-725-5610

Northwoods League
5145 Colbert Road
Lakeland, Florida 33813
Phone: 941-644-4022
Fax: 942-644-1238

Pacific International League
504 Yale Avenue North
Seattle, Washington 98109
Phone: 206-623-8844
Fax: 206-623-8361

San Diego Collegiate League
948 Jasmine Court
Carlsbad, California 92009
Phone: 619-438-0347

Shendandoah Valley League
Route 1, Box 189J
Staunton, Virginia 24401
Phone: 540-886-1748
Fax: 540-885-7612

Senior Leagues

Men's Senior Baseball League
One Huntington Quadrangle
Mellville, New York 11747
Phone: 516-753-6725
Fax: 516-753-4031

Men's Adult Baseball League
One Huntington Quadrangle
Mellville, New York 11747
Phone: 516-753-6725
Fax: 516-753-4031

National Adult Baseball League
3900 East Mexico Avenue, Suite 330
Denver, Colorado 80201
Phone: 303-639-9955
Fax: 303-753-6804

Roy Hobbs Baseball
1864 Deepwood Drive
Akron, Ohio 44313
Phone: 330-940-2008
Fax: 330-940-2008

Youth Baseball

USA Baseball
Hi Corbett Field
3400 East Camino Campestre
Tuscon, Arizona 85716
Phone: 520-327-9700

All American Amateur Baseball
Association
331 Parkway Drive
Zanesville, Ohio 43701
Phone: 614-453-8531

Amateur Athletic Union
The Walt Disney World Resort
P.O. Box 10000
Lake Buena Vista, Florida 32830
Phone: 407-363-6170

American Amateur Baseball Congress
118-119 Redfield Plaza
P.O. Box 467
Marshall, Michigan 49068
Phone: 616-781-2002

American Legion Baseball
National Americanism Commission
P.O. Box 1055
Indianapolis, Indiana 46206
Phone: 317-630-1213

Babe Ruth Baseball
1770 Brunswick Pike
P.O. Box 5000
Trenton, New Jersey 08638
Phone: 609-695-1434

Continental Amateur Baseball Association
82 University Street
Westerville, Ohio 43081
Phone: 614-899-2103

Dixie Baseball
P.O. Box 193
Montgomery, Alabama 36101
Phone: 334-241-2300

Dizzy Dean Baseball
902 Highway 9 North
Eupora, Mississippi 39744
Phone: 601-258-7626

Hap Dumont Baseball
P.O. Box 17455
Wichita, Kansas 67217
Phone: 316-721-1779

Little League Baseball
P.O. Box 3485
Williamsport, Pennsylvannia 17701
Phone: 717-326-1921

National Amateur Baseball Federation
P.O. Box 705
Bowie, Maryland 20718
Phone: 301-262-5005

National Association of Police Athletic
Leagues (PAL)
Suite 201
618 U.S. Highway 1
North Palm Beach, Florida 33408
Phone: 561-844-1823

PONY Baseball
P.O. Box 225
Washington, Pennsylvania 15301
Phone: 412-225-1060

Reviving Baseball in Inner Cities (RBI)
350 Park Avenue
New York, New York 10022
Phone: 212-339-7800

T-Ball USA Association
Suite 1901
915 Broadway
New York, New York 10010
Phone: 212-254-7911 or 800-741-0845

Youth Baseball Athletic League
567 Alger Drive
Palo Alto, California 94306
Phone: 800-477-9225

Index

• *Numbers* •

3-6-3 double play, 145-146
3Com Park: San Francisco
    Giants, 280–281

• *A* •

Aaron, Hank, 306, 342
ace, 351
adjudged, 351
Alfonzo, Edgardo, 337
All American Amateur
    Baseball Association, 229
alley, 351
All-Star Game, 263
Alomar, Roberto, 332
aluminum bats, 19–20
Amateur Athletic Union,
    228–229
American Amateur Baseball
    Congress, 229
American Association, 232
American League. *See also*
    Major League Baseball
    franchises, 249
    stadiums, 281–285
    team organizations, 380–381
American Legion Baseball, 229
Anaheim Stadium: Anaheim
    Angels, 281
Anderson, Sparky, 241–243
Aparicio, Luis, 331
appeal, 351
appeal play, 31, 351
Arizona Diamondbacks Web
    site, 289
Arizona Fall League, 238
around the horn, 351
Asian baseball, 237
assists, 273, 351
Astrodome: Houston Astros,
    277–278
at 'em ball, 351
Atlanta Braves Web site, 289
Australian Baseball League
    (ABL), 238

• *B* •

Babe Ruth League, 228
backhand play, 160
bad hops, 351
bad-ball hitters, 351
bags. *See* bases
Bagwell, Jeff, 314
bailing out, 91
balks. *See also* pitchers
    avoiding, 166
    defined, 351
    record, 378
The Ballpark At Arlington:
    Texas Rangers, 284
ballparks. *See also* stadiums
    behind home plate view, 269
    bleacher view, 269
    etiquette at, 270
    first base view, 268
    foul ball seating, 269
    seat selection at, 268–269
    third base view, 268
    upper deck view, 269
    visiting, 267
Ballparks by Munsey &
    Suppes Web site, 289
balls (pitched), 16, 351
Baltimore chop, 352
Baltimore Orioles Web site,
    289
bandbox, 352
bang-bang play, 352
banjo hitter, 352
Bank One Park: Arizona
    Diamondbacks, 281
base on balls, 352
    See also walks
base stealers. *See also* stealing
    aggressiveness of, 196
    good, 192, 193
    studying pitcher and, 193
baseball
    Asian, 237
    careers, 364
    Caribbean Baseball Confed-
        eration (CBC), 237–238
    collegiate, 230
    Cuban, 239

in cyberspace, 287–290
    fantasy, 295–301
    history of changes in,
        343–347
    Japanese, 235–236
    leagues, 227–229
    Major League, 247–249
    objective of, 9
    in print, 292–293
    roots of, 9
    strike (1994), 347
    on TV, 290–292
Baseball America, 233, 293
Baseball Canada, 227
Baseball Digest, 293
Baseball - The Early Years, 249
Baseball - The Golden Years,
    249
baseball mud, 352
Baseball Server, 288
Baseball Weekly, 299, 300
Baseball Writers Association
    of America, 15
baseballs. *See also* equipment
    characteristics of, 17
    charging, 120, 126
    defined, 352
    in dirt, 135–136
    illustrated, 18
    purchasing, 18
    RIF (Reduced Injury Factor),
        18
    synthetic leather, 19
    toy, 19
baseline, 12, 31
baserunners
    advancement on ground
        balls, 181
    baseline and, 31
    collision with catcher at
        home plate, 191–192
    defined, 361
    in double plays, 154
    first baseman playing
        behind, 144
    holding on first base,
        143–144, 163–164
    outfielders and, 172

(continued)

baserunners *(continued)*
  picking off, 139, 150, 164–166
  retiring, 31
  rules for, 30–31
  tagging, 181
  third baseman and, 157
  throwing out, 137
  tracking, 273–275
baserunning, 175–197
  See also leads
  from batter's box, 176–177
  coaches and, 183–184
  for double play prevention,
    190–191
  on ground balls, 176
  hit-and-run, 184
  importance of, 175
  mental game of, 182
  sliding and, 184–190
bases
  advancing on, 14
  defined, 11, 352
  getting on, 30
  most total record, 369
  rounding, 182
  running, 31
  tagging, 30–31
bat around, 352
bat speed
  defined, 352
  developing, 67
  power and, 62
batboy/batgirl, 352
bats. *See also* equipment;
    hitting
  aluminum, 19–20
  arms and, 64–66
  barrel of, 352
  body and, 64
  ceramic, 20
  characteristics of, 19
  choosing, 18–19, 61–62
  corked, 354
  defined, 13, 352
  graphite, 20
  handle, 356
  holding, 62–66
  holding for bunting, 84–85
  illustrated, 19
  labels, 63
  lead, 67
  shapes of, 62
  windmilling, 65
  wood, 19, 20
batters

at-bats, 16
  defined, 13, 352
  designated hitter (DH), 30
  hit by pitches, 94
  leaving without permission,
    28
  pinch hitter, 30, 95–96, 246,
    359
  rules for, 28–30
batter's box, 66–68
  deep in, 68
  defined, 352
  front of, 67
  middle of, 68
  running from, 176–177
battery, 352
batting
  See also bunts; hitting
  average, 252, 341, 365
  cage, 352
  choking up, 63, 77, 354
  eye, 352
  grip, 62–63
  helmets, 23, 95, 352
  order, 13, 352
  records, 369
  tee, 91
batting gloves
  choosing to wear, 62
  defined, 23, 352
  manufacturer, 23
batting practice. *See also*
    hitting
  getting the most out of,
    89–90
  long ball and, 90
  for pinch hitters, 95
  pitcher, working with, 90
  swinging at strikes during, 78
  tips, 91–92
  troubleshooting, 92–95
beanball, 353
*Beckett's Baseball Card
    Monthly,* 293
bees, 353
bench, 353
bench jockey, 353
Bench, Johnny, 131–138,
    140, 329
bench press. *See also* weight
    training
  close grip, 54
  defined, 53
  dumbbell, 54
bent-leg slide, 185–186
best fielders (all-time)

Aparicio, Luis, 331
Bench, Johnny, 329
Clemente, Roberto, 329–330
Flood, Curt, 328–329
Griffey, Ken Jr., 330
Hernandez, Keith, 330
Mays, Willie, 328
Mazeroski, Bill, 329
Robinson, Brooks, 330
Smith, Ozzie, 328
best fielders (current)
Alomar, Roberto, 332
Bonds, Barry, 331
Caminiti, Ken, 333
Edmonds, Jim, 333
Griffey, Ken Jr., 331
Johnson, Charles, 332
Larkin, Barry, 333
Ordonez, Rey, 333
Rodriguez, Ivan, 332
Vizquel, Omar, 332
best pitchers (all-time)
Carlton, Steve, 319–320
Gibson, Bob, 321
Grove, Lefty, 319
Johnson, Walter, 318
Koufax, Sandy, 320–321
Marichal, Juan, 322
Mathewson, Christy, 319
Paige, Satchel, 322
Seaver, Tom, 320, 321
Spahn, Warren, 318
Young, Cy, 318
best pitchers (current)
Clemens, Roger, 323
Cone, David, 324
Fernandez, Alex, 325
Glavine, Tom, 323
Hentgen, Pat, 324
Johnson, Randy, 323
Maddux, Greg, 322–323
Martinez, Pedro, 324
Mussina, Mike, 325
Smoltz, John, 324
best players (all-time)
Aaron, Hank, 306
Clemente, Roberto, 310
Cobb, Ty, 307–308
DiMaggio, Joe, 310
Gibson, Josh, 310
Mantle, Mickey, 308
Mays, Willie, 306
Robinson, Frank, 309
Robinson, Jackie, 310–311
Ruth, Babe, 306, 307
Williams, Ted, 311–312

best players (current)
Bagwell, Jeff, 314
Bonds, Barry, 312
Gonzalez, Juan, 315
Griffey, Ken Jr., 312, 313
Gwynn, Tony, 314
McGwire, Mark, 315
Piazza, Mike, 314
Thomas, Frank, 313
Vaughn, Mo, 315
Walker, Larry, 314
big Bill, 353
big leagues, 353
bird dog, 353
Black Sox scandal, 345
black, the, 353
bleachers, 353
bleeder, 353
blocking the ball, 148
blocking the plate, 138–139,
192
blue darter, 353
Bonds, Barry, 312, 331
bonehead play, 353
bonus baby, 353
book, the, 353
boot, 353
Boston Red Sox Web site, 289
Boudreau Shift, 81
box jump, 47
box score, 353
brushback, 353
bug on the rug, 353
bullpen, 353
bunts. *See also* hitting
catcher and, 140–141
defined, 82, 353
drag, 86, 87, 88
dump, 86
faking, 87–88
fielding, 140–141, 144
first baseman and, 144
grip, 84
for hits, 86
pitchers and, 82
pivot stance, 83
push, 86
sacrifice, 85, 217, 218, 361
squared-stance, 83–84
squeeze play and, 86–87
stance, 83–85
third baseman and, 156–157
Busch Stadium: St. Louis, 279
bush, 353
butcher, 353

butterfly stretch, 45

• C •

called game, 14, 354
Caminiti, Ken, 155–158, 333
can of corn, 354
caps, 23
Caribbean Baseball Confederation (CBC)
defined, 237
leagues, 237–238
telecasts, 292
Carlton, Steve, 319–320
Cartwright, Alexander Joy, 9,
344
catcher
abbreviation for, 10
arm strength of, 116–117, 130
blocking plate, 138–139
characteristics of, 116–118,
130
collisions with baserunners,
191–192
in double/triple down left
field line plays, 209, 213
in double/triple down right
field line plays, 212, 216
in double/triple to left center
field gap plays, 210, 214
in double/triple to right
center field gap plays,
211, 215
equipment, 21–22
force outs and, 141
knee position, 131
leg strength of, 116
low-center of gravity of, 118
mental toughness, 117–118
mitt, 20, 117
obstructing swing, 30
pain and, 116
pick-offs, 139
pitchouts and, 139
playing, 130–141
in pop fly plays, 221, 222, 223
readying to receive pitch,
133–134
in sacrifice bunt plays, 217,
218
setup, 131–132
signs, 130, 132–133
in single to center plays, 201,
204, 207
in single to left plays, 200,

203, 206
in single to right plays, 202,
205, 208
stance, 131, 133
target, 134
throwing, 136–137
in wheel play, 219
in wheel play fake, 220
catches
basket, 352
circus, 354
defined, 354
shoestring, 123, 361
catching
balls in dirt, 135–136
bunts, 140–141
glove placement for, 134
receiving pitch and, 135
tracking errant pitches and,
135–136
center field
defined, 12
double/triple to left gap
plays, 210, 214
double/triple to right gap
plays, 211, 215
pop fly play, 223
single to, plays, 201, 204, 207
center fielder. *See also*
outfielders
abbreviation for, 10
arm strength of, 121
characteristics of, 121
in double/triple down left
field line plays, 209, 213
in double/triple down right
field line plays, 212, 216
in double/triple to left center
field gap plays, 210, 214
in double/triple to right
center field gap plays,
211, 215
glove, 117
in pop fly plays, 221, 222, 223
in sacrifice bunt plays, 217,
218
in single to center plays, 201,
204, 207
in single to left plays, 200,
203, 206
in single to right plays, 202,
205, 208
in wheel play, 219
in wheel play fake, 220

changes, history of, 343–347
  baseball strike (1994), 347
  Black Sox scandal (1920), 345
  color line shattered (1946), 346
  Dodgers/Giants go west (1957), 346–347
  first farm system (1920), 345
  first major league formed (1871), 344
  first night game (1935), 346
  Messersmith-McNally decision (1975), 347
  pitcher's mound moved (1893), 344–345
  rules codified (1845), 344
change-up. *See also* pitches
  circle, 110–111
  three-fingered, 110
charging the ball, 120, 126
cheat, 194
checked swing, 354
Chesbro, Jack, 341
chest pass (medicine ball), 48, 49
Chicago Cubs Web site, 290
Chicago White Sox Web site, 290
choke hitter, 354
choking up, 63, 77, 354
chopping, 92–93
Cincinnati Reds Web site, 290
Cinergy Field: Cincinnati Reds, 276
circle change-up, 110–111
circus catch, 354
Classic Sports Network, 292
cleanup, 354
Clemens, Roger, 323
Clemente, Roberto, 310, 329–330
Cleveland Indians Web site, 290
close grip bench press, 54
closed stance
  defined, 69, 354
  illustrated, 70
  shoulders in, 70
closer, 354
clubhouse lawyer, 354
clutch, 354
coaches. *See also* coaching
  baserunning and, 183–184
  defined, 14
  first base, 14, 183–184

function of, 12, 14
  managers working with, 245
  third base, 14, 184
  visits to the mound, 32
coache's box, 12
coaching. *See also* coaches; managers
  bench players and, 243
  criticism, 245
  elements of wining team and, 243–244
  first five innings and, 244
  knowing players and, 242–243
  perspective, 245
  pinch-hitters and, 246
  responsibilities of, 241–242
  spring training and, 244
Cobb, Ty, 307–308
collar, 354
collegiate baseball, 230, 385–386
collisions, catchers/baserunners at home plate, 191–192
come-backer, 354
Comiskey Park: Chicago White Sox, 282
The Complete Baseball Record Book, 263
Cone, David, 324
contact, making, 75–76
Continental Amateur Baseball Association, 229
Coors Field: Colorado Rockies, 277
corked bat, 354
count, 354
County Stadium: Milwaukee Brewers, 277
cousin, 354
cross-seam grip, 170
crouch, 71
Cruz, Jose Jr., 336
Cuban baseball, 239
cup of coffee, 354
curl to press, 55
curveball. *See also* pitches
  defined, 109
  follow-through, 110
  hanging, 356
  illustrated grip, 110
  Lord Charles, 358
  reverse, 112

cut-off plays
  first baseman and, 144–145
  second baseman and, 152
cycle, 354

• D •

daylight pick-off plays, 150
dead ball, 354
dead from the neck up, 354
decisions, pitching, 256
defense, 115–173
  See also playbook
  catcher, 130–141
  first base, 141–146
  fly ball, 128–129
  gloves and, 117
  good hands, 116
  ground ball, 126–127
  line drive, 128
  outfield, 166–173
  positioning for, 127–128
  second base, 146–155
  shortstop, 158–162
  third base, 155–158
defensive indifference, 354
defensive interference, 355
defensive team, 10
delayed steals, 196
delivering a pitch, 13
designated hitter (DH), 30, 355
Detroit Tigers Web site, 290
diamond. *See* infield
digging in, 72
DiMaggio, Joe, 310, 340
dinking, 81
dip splits, 45–46
dish, 355
Dixie Baseball, 228
Dizzy Dean Baseball, 229
Dodger Stadium: Los Angeles Dodgers, 278
Dominican League, 237
double plays
  3-6-3, 145–146
  benefit of, 152
  getting lead runner and, 146
  phantom, 359
  pivot for, 153
  preventing, 190–191
  quickness of, 153
  runner and, 154
  second baseman and, 119, 152–154
  shortstop and, 154, 161

starting, 161
third baseman and, 157
double steal. *See also* stealing
defined, 355
derailing, 137
executing, 196–197
doubleheader, 355
doubles
defending against, 209–216
defined, 13, 355
ground-rule, 356
record, 368
drag bunts, 86, 87, 88
drop step, 168
ducks on the pond, 355
dugouts
defined, 12
fielders stepping into, 28
dumbbell bench press, 54
dump bunts, 86

• E •

earned run average (ERA)
calculating, 255
career record, 342
defined, 255
lowest record, 375
earned runs, 355
Edmonds, Jim, 333
equipment
baseballs, 18–19
bats, 19–20
batting gloves, 23
caps, 23
catcher's, 21–22
gloves, 20–22
helmets, 23
jock strap/protective cup, 24
purchasing, 17–19, 25
shoes, 22
sweatbands, 23
uniforms, 23–24
errors
aggressiveness and, 125
defined, 30, 355
fear of, 126
getting on base with, 30
hidden, avoiding, 126
mental, 126
reaction to, 125–126
ESPN, 291
Estes, Shawn, 338
even stance, 69, 70, 355
extra-base hits, 89

• F •

fair balls, 355
fair territory, 13, 29
faking
bunts, 87
steals, 197
throw during run-downs, 151
wheel play, 220
Fall Classic. *See* World Series
fantasy baseball, 295–301
administrative tasks, 299
defined, 295–296
four category players, 301
information on, 296
leagues, staring, 296–297
playing, 296–300
reserves, 298
roster, filling out, 298
scoring categories, 296
scoring example, 300
statistics, 299
supply and demand in, 301
teams, drafting, 297
teams, managing, 298–299
tips for success, 300–301
winning at, 299–300
farm system
defined, 355
first, 345
fastball. *See also* pitches
four-seam, 106–107
slider, 108
split-fingered, 108–109
two-seam, 107
Fenway Park: Boston Red Sox,
282
Fernandez, Alex, 325
field. *See* infield; outfield;
playing field
fielders. *See also specific*
positions
best (all-time), 327–331
best (current), 331–333
defined, 14
fielder's choice, 355
fielding
bunts, 140–141, 144
fly balls, 128–129
ground balls, 126–127
line drives, 128
pop-ups, 140
fielding average, 256
fireman, 355
first base

coach, 14, 183–184
leading off, 177–179
pick-offs at, 194
pitcher covering, 145, 163
rounding, 183
running through, 176
second baseman covering,
151
first baseman
in 3-6-3 double play, 145–146
abbreviation for, 10
bad throws and, 143
balance, 142
ball handling, 142
body position of, 142–143
bunts and, 144
catching throws, 142–143
characteristics of, 118
cut-off plays and, 144–145
in double/triple down left
field line plays, 209, 213
in double/triple to left center
field gap plays, 210, 214
in double/triple to right
center field gap plays,
211, 215
footwork, 142
holding runners, 143–144
mitt, 20, 117
playing as, 141–146
playing behind runner, 144
in pop fly plays, 221, 222, 223
in sacrifice bunt plays, 217,
218
in single to center plays, 201,
204, 207
in single to left plays, 200,
203, 206
in single to right plays, 202,
205, 208
in wheel play, 219
in wheel play fake, 220
first pitches, 79
five-tool player, 355
Flood, Curt, 328–329
Florida Marlins Web site, 290
fly balls
calling for, 129
catching, 170–171
collisions over, 129
coming in on, 171
defined, 355
fielding, 128–129, 170–172
going out on, 171–172
infield, 129
leads on, 179
positioning for, 128

follow-through
  hitting, 77–78
  pitching, 104
force outs
  catcher and, 141
  defined, 181, 355
  safe because of, 30
  tagging for, 181
forearm stretch, 42–43
foreign leagues, 385
forward bend, 39, 40
forward leg bend, 40–41
foul lines, 12
foul pole, 355
foul territory, 29, 355
foul tips, 355
four-seam fastball, 106–107
Fox Broadcasting, 291
franchise players, 356
free agents, 356
free weights. *See* weight
    training
full count, 356
fungo, 356
future stars
  Alfonzo, Edgardo, 337
  Cruz, Jose Jr., 336
  Estes, Shawn, 338
  Garciaparra, Nomar, 336
  Guerrero, Vladimir, 335–336
  Jeter, Derek, 337
  Jones, Andruw, 337
  Perez, Neifi, 338
  Rodriguez, Alex, 336
  Rolen, Scott, 337

• *G* •

gamers, 356
games
  consecutive played record,
    342
  finishing before nine full
    innings, 10–11
  night, first, 346
  official, 14
  records, 365
  regulation, 360
  suspended, 362
  thrown out of, 33
  umpires calling (ending), 14
gap, 356
gap shots, 356
Garciaparra, Nomar, 336
Gibson, Bob, 100, 102–108,
    114, 321

Gibson, Josh, 310
Glavine, Tom, 323
glove man, 356
gloves. *See also* equipment
  batting, 23
  caring for, 22
  catcher's, 20, 117
  defined, 356
  fielder's, 20
  first baseman's, 20, 117
  illustrated, 21
  open, 160–161
  outfielder's, 117
  second baseman's, 117
  shortstop's, 117
  specifications for, 20
  third baseman's, 117
  webbing, 21
goat, 356
Gold Glove, 356
Gonzalez, Juan, 315
good hands, 116
gopher ball, 356
green light, 356
Griffey, Ken Jr., 312, 313,
    330, 331
Griffey, Ken Sr., 167–172
grips
  batting, 62–63
  bunting, 84
  circle ch ange-up, 111
  cross-seam, 170
  curveball, 110
  four-seam fastball, 107
  knuckleball, 113
  palmball, 112
  slider, 108
  split-fingered fastball, 109
  three-fingered change-up,
    111
  for throwing, 122–123
ground balls
  baserunner advancement
    and, 181
  baserunning on, 176
  calling, 148
  catching by outfielders,
    172–173
  charging, 126
  defined, 356
  double play and, 161
  errors on, 125
  fielding, 126–127
  positioning for, 127
  seeing-eye, 361
  staying down on, 127

ground-rule doubles, 356
Grove, Lefty, 319
Guerrero, Vladimir, 335–336
gun, 356
gun shy, 356
Gwynn, Tony, 314

• *H* •

Hall of Fame, 15
hammer curls, 55
handcuffed, 356
hand-eye coordination, 92
hanging curve, 356
Hap Dumont Baseball, 229
Hawaii Winter League, 238
head-first slide. *See also*
    sliding
  defined, 186
  illustrated, 187, 188
  minimizing risk of, 187
headhunter, 356
heat, 357
helmets, 23
Hentgen, Pat, 324
Hernandez, Keith, 330
high pitches, 77, 85
high school baseball organiza-
    tions, 386–387
hill. *See* mound
hip toss (medicine ball), 50
hit by pitch, 357, 378
hit-and-run play, 88
  baserunner in, 184
  defined, 357
  timing in, 184
hitch, 93, 357
hits
  defined, 357
  extra-base, 89
  leg, 358
  most record, 368
hitting, 59–97
  See also batting practice;
      swing
  adaptability and, 61
  against the shift, 81
  aggressiveness in, 94
  to all fields, 79–80
  arms during, 64–66
  bailing out and, 91
  from batting tee, 91
  body during, 64
  bunting, 82–88
  contact and, 75–76

courage and, 61
crouch, 71
difficulty of, 59–60
digging in and, 72
elbows during, 64–65
fine-tuning and, 76–77
first pitch and, 79
focus and, 60
follow-through, 77–78
geometry of, 59–60
hit-and-run play and, 88
hunger, 61
off heels, 92
to opposite field, 79, 80
pinch, 30, 95–96, 359
pitch types and, 60
for power, 62
practice tips, 90–92
pull, 79, 80
records, 365–369
reflexes and, 60
requirements for, 60–61
run-and-hit play and, 88–89
self-awareness and, 79
slumps, 97
stance, 69–70
stepping up to home plate
    and, 66–68
streak record, 340
stride, 72–74
strike out fear and, 94–95
strike zone and, 61, 78–79
troubleshooting, 92–94
upper body strength and, 61
vision and, 60
hole, 357
home plate
    blocking, 138–139, 192
    defined, 357
    dimensions, 12
    illustrated, 13
    stealing, 195
    stepping up to, 66–68
    umpire, 14
home runs
    career record, 342
    defined, 13, 30, 357
    grand slam record, 367
    inside-the-park, 13
    most allowed record, 377
    most consecutive record,
        366
    most scored record, 366
    ratio, 254

solo, 361
    tape-measure, 362
home team, 357
hook slide. *See also* sliding
    avoiding injury with, 189
    defined, 188
    illustrated, 189, 190
    to left, 188
    to right, 189
    risks, 189
hoover, 357
Hornsby, Rogers, 341
hot corner, 357
hot dog, 357
Houston Astros Web site, 290
Hubert H. Humphrey
    Metrodome: Minnesota
    Twins, 283

• I •

*The Imperfect Diamond: A
    History of Baseball's
    Labor Wars,* 249
in jeopardy, 357
independent leagues, 384–385
infield
    defined, 11
    dimensions, 11
    flies, 129
    fly rule, 129, 357
innings
    bottom of, 10
    defined, 10, 358
    extra, 11
    first five, 244
    outs in, 13
    top of, 10
inside pitches, 77
inside-the-park home runs, 13
interleague play, 247
International League, 232

• J •

Jacobs Field: Cleveland
    Indians, 283
jamming, 358
Japanese baseball
    format for, 235–236
    history of, 235
    leagues, 235
    players, 236

quality of, 236
Jeter, Derek, 337
jock straps, 24
jogging knee lifts, 38
Johnson, Charles, 332
Johnson, Randy, 323
Johnson, Walter, 318
Jones, Andruw, 337
journeyman, 358
The Joy of Keeping Score, 175
jump and run, 47
jump pivot, 137
jumps (medicine ball), 50
junk, 358

• K •

Kansas City Royals Web site,
    290
Kauffman Stadium: Kansas
    City Royals, 283
keystone, 358
Kingdom: Seattle Mariners,
    284
knee pulls, 43, 44
knuckleball, 112–113
Koufax, Sandy, 320–321

• L •

Larkin, Barry, 158–162, 333
lateral raise, 56
laugher, 358
lead-off hitter, 358
leads. *See also* baserunning
    on catchable fly balls, 179
    from first base, 177–179
    primary, 177, 178, 179, 180
    from second base, 179–180
    secondary, 178
    stationary, 194
    for stealing, 194
    from third base, 180–181
    two-way, 178
    walking, 194
League Championship Series
    (LCS)
    defined, 260
    expansion and, 260
    National (NLCS), 259
    wild cards and, 260–261

leagues
  All American Amateur
    Baseball Association, 229
  Amateur Athletic Union,
    228–229
  American Amateur Baseball
    Congress, 229
  American Association, 232
  American Legion Baseball,
    229
  Arizona Fall League, 238
  Asian, 237
  Australian Baseball League
    (ABL), 238
  Babe Ruth League, 228
  Continental Amateur
    Baseball Association, 229
  Cuban, 239
  Dixie Baseball, 228
  Dizzy Dean Baseball, 229
  Dominican League, 237
  first formed, 344
  foreign, 385
  Hap Dumont Baseball, 229
  Hawaii Winter League, 238
  independent, 384–385
  International League, 232
  Japanese, 235–236
  Little League Baseball, 228
  Mexican League, 232
  Mexican-Pacific League,
    237–238
  minor, 231–235
  National Amateur Baseball
    Federation, 229
  National Association of
    Police Athletic Leagues,
    229
  Pacific Coast League, 232
  PONY Baseball, 229
  Puerto Rican League, 238
  Reviving Baseball In Inner
    Cities, 229
  senior, 387
  types of, 227
  U.S. Amateur Baseball
    Association, 229
  Venezuelan League, 238
  Winter, 363
  Youth Baseball Athletic
    League, 229
Lee, Bill, 100, 109–113, 162–166
left field

defined, 12
double/triple down line
  plays, 209, 213
double/triple to gap plays,
  210, 214
pop fly play, 222
single to, plays, 200, 203, 206
left fielder. *See also*
  outfielders
  abbreviation for, 10
  characteristics of, 120
  charging the ball and, 120
  in double/triple down left
    field line plays, 209, 213
  in double/triple down right
    field line plays, 212, 216
  in double/triple to left center
    field gap plays, 210, 214
  in double/triple to right
    center field gap plays,
    211, 215
  glove, 117
  in pop fly plays, 221, 222, 223
  in sacrifice bunt plays, 217,
    218
  in single to center plays, 201,
    204, 207
  in single to left plays, 200,
    203, 206
  in single to right plays, 202,
    205, 208
  in wheel play, 219
  in wheel play fake, 220
left-handed pitchers, 194, 358
leg hits, 358
line drives
  defined, 358
  fielding, 128
lineups, 13, 358
Little League Baseball, 228
live ball, 358
loaded bases, 141, 206
long ball, 90
long retriever, 358
Lord Charles. *See* curveball
Los Angeles Dodgers Web site,
  290
low pitches, 77, 85
lunges
  free weight, 54–55
  medicine ball, 51
  warning, 55
lying triceps extension, 56–57

• M •

McCovey, Willie, 141–146
McGwire, Mark, 315
Maddux, Greg, 322–323
magic number, 358
Major League Baseball
  American League, 248, 249
  business, 247
  franchises, 248–249
  games played in, 247
  interleague play, 247
  National League, 248
  number of teams in, 247
  organizations, 379
  Players Association, 248
  rosters, 249
  today, 247–248
managers. *See also* coaching
  defined, 14
  incompetent, 242
  player-manager, 359
  responsibilities of, 242
  visits to the mound, 32
  working with coaches, 245
Mantle, Mickey, 308
Marichal, Juan, 322
Martinez, Pedro, 324
Mathewson, Christy, 319
Mays, Willie, 306, 328
Mazeroski, Bill, 329
media organizations, 379
medicine ball. *See also*
  training
  basic toss, 49
  chest pass, 48, 49
  hip toss, 50
  jumps, 50
  lunges, 51
  rotation pass, 48, 49
  toe push, 50
mental errors, 126
Messersmith-McNally decision
  (1975), 347
Mexican League, 232
Mexican-Pacific League,
  237–238
middle reliever, 358
Milwaukee Brewers Web site,
  290
Minnesota Twins Web site,
  290
minor leagues. *See also*
  leagues

Class A, 233
Class AA (Double A), 233
Class AAA (Triple A), 232
defined, 231
lower, 233
organizations, 383–384
stars of, 234
MLB@Bat, 287–288
Montreal Expos Web site, 290
mop-up man, 358
Morgan, Joe, 146–154
mound. *See also* pitching
before walking onto, 113
conferences, 130
defined, 13
manager/coach visits to, 32
moved back 15 feet (1893), 344–345
Mussina, Mike, 325

• *N* •

National Amateur Baseball Federation, 229
National Association of Police Athletic Leagues, 229
National Baseball Hall of Fame, 15, 288
National Collegiate Athletic Association (NCAA), 230
National League. *See also* Major League Baseball
Championship Series (NLCS), 259
expansion, 262
franchises, 348
stadiums, 275–281
team organizations, 381–382
NBC, 291
Negro Leagues Baseball Museum, 288
New York Yankees Web site, 290
night games, first, 346
Nine Sides of the Diamond: Baseball's Great Glove Men On the Art of Defense, 173
no-hitters, 358, 376–377

• *O* •

Oakland Alameda County Coliseum: Oakland Athletics, 284
Oakland Athletics Web site, 290
obstruction, 359
October Heroes, 263
offensive interference, 359
offensive team
defined, 10
statistic measurements, 251–254
official games, 14
official scorers, 15–16
The Official T-Ball USA Family Guide to T-Ball Baseball, 228
Olympic Stadium: Montreal Expos, 278
on-base percentage, 253
on-deck circle, 12, 359
one arm dumbbell row, 54
open stance. *See also* stance
defined, 69, 359
illustrated, 70
shoulders in, 70
opponents' batting average, 255–256
Ordonez, Rey, 333
organizations
American League team, 380–381
college baseball, 385–386
foreign league, 385
high school baseball, 386–387
independent league, 384–385
Major League Baseball, 379
media, 379
minor league, 383–384
National League team, 381–382
publication, 379–380
senior league, 387
statistics and research, 380
youth baseball, 388
Oriole Park at Camden Yards: Baltimore Orioles, 281
out pitch, 359
outfield

center field, 12, 201, 204, 207, 210–211, 214–215, 223
defined, 12
left field, 12, 200, 203, 206, 209–210, 213–214, 222
playing, 166–173
right field, 12, 202, 205, 208, 211–212, 215–216, 221
shaded, 182
outfielders
ball trajectory and, 169
balls in the gap and, 170
catching balls and, 170
center, 10, 117, 121
coming in on balls and, 171
going out on balls and, 171–172
ground balls and, 172–173
left, 10, 117, 120
limitations of, 168
movement on fly balls, 169
playing as, 166–173
positioning of, 168
right, 10, 117, 121
runners on base and, 172
setup, 167–168
sound of hit balls and, 169
stance, 168
warm-ups for, 169
outs
defined, 359
in inning, 13
productive, 360
situations for, 28–29
outside pitches, 77
overslide, 359
overstride, 73, 74

• *P* •

Pacific Coast League, 232
Paige, Satchel, 322
palmball, 111–112
payoff pitch, 359
peg, 359
pennant, 359
pepper, 91–92, 359
Perez, Neifi, 338
perfect game, 359
performance
improving, 53–57
measuring, 251–257

phantom double play, 359
Philadelphia Phillies Web site, 290
Piazza, Mike, 314
pick it, 359
pick-offs
  balks and, 166
  catcher and, 139
  daylight play, 150
  defined, 359
  at first base, 194
  pitcher and, 164–166
  at second base, 165, 194
  second baseman and, 150
  at third base, 165
  time play, 150
pinch hits record, 368
pinch hitters
  advice, 95–96
  batting practice for, 95
  choosing, 246
  defined, 30, 359
  emotional strength of, 95
  platoon, 246
  studying pitchers and, 96
pinch runners, 359
pine tar, 359
pitchers
  abbreviation for, 10
  aggressive fielding for, 163
  analyzing, 82
  balks, 32, 166, 351, 378
  base stealing and, 193–194
  batting practice, working
    with, 90
  best (all-time), 317–322
  best (current), 322–325
  bunting and, 82
  characteristics of, 121–122
  covering first base, 145, 163
  as defensive players,
    121–122, 162–166
  defined, 13
  in double/triple down left
    field line plays, 209, 213
  in double/triple down right
    field line plays, 212, 216
  in double/triple to left center
    field gap plays, 210, 214
  in double/triple to right
    center field gap plays,
    211, 215
  familiar, facing, 79
  fielding position, 104, 162
  hitting batters, 94
  holding runners on first

base, 163–164
  keeping notes on, 82
  left-handed (stealing on), 194
  motion of, 72
  pick-offs and, 164–166
  in pop fly plays, 221, 222, 223
  relief, 360
  right-handed (stealing on),
    194
  rules for, 32–33
  in sacrifice bunt plays, 217,
    218
  in single to center plays, 201,
    204, 207
  in single to left plays, 200,
    203, 206
  in single to right plays, 202,
    205, 208
  stance after pitch, 162
  stealing on, 193–194
  warming up, 32
  in wheel play, 219
  in wheel play fake, 220
pitches, 106–113
  circle change-up, 110–111
  curveball, 109–110
  delivering, 13
  doctored, 33
  errant, tracking, 135–136
  first, 79
  four-seam fastball, 106–107
  half-hearted, 113
  high, 77, 85
  inside, 77
  knuckleball, 112–113
  low, 77, 85
  moving towards, 73
  out, 359
  outside, 77
  palmball, 111–112
  payoff, 359
  pulling, 79
  purpose, 353
  quick, 360
  receiving, 135
  recognizing, 75
  screwball, 112
  slider, 108
  spitball, 33
  split-fingered fastball,
    108–109
  taking, 79
  three-fingered change-up,
    110
  toughest to hit, 68
  two-seam fastball, 107

two-strike, 77
  waste, 363
  wild, 363, 378
pitching, 99–114
  arm angle, 103
  arsenal, 106–113
  decisions, 256
  follow-through, 104
  hard, 114
  leg kick, 100, 101
  measurements, 254–256
  motion, 100–104
  pivot foot, 100, 103
  records, 340, 341, 342,
    371–378
  release, 103–104
  release point, 114
  stance, 100
  striding foot, 102
  target, 134
  from the stretch, 105
  thrust, 102–103
  wind-up, 100–101
pitching rubber
  defined, 360
  dimensions, 12
  distance to home plate, 12
  illustrated, 13
  pivot foot touching, 100
pitchouts, 139, 359
Pittsburgh Pirates Web site,
    290
pivot foot (pitchers), 100, 103
plate appearances, 359
platoon, 359
"Play Ball!," 359
playbook, 199–223
  double/triple down left field
    line: bases empty, 209
  double/triple down left field
    line: runners on base,
    213
  double/triple down right
    field line: bases empty,
    212
  double/triple down right
    field line: runners on
    base, 216
  double/triple to left center
    field gap: bases empty,
    210
  double/triple to left center
    field gap: runners on
    base, 214
  double/triple to right center
    field gap: bases empty,
    211

double/triple to right center
field gap: runners on
base, 215
pop fly to shallow center
field, 223
pop fly to shallow left field,
222
pop fly to shallow right field,
221
sacrifice bunt: runner on
first, 217
sacrifice bunt: runners on
first and second, 218
single to center: bases
empty, 201
single to center: runners on
first/first and third, 204
single to center: runners on
second/first and second/
bases loaded, 207
single to left: bases empty,
200
single to left: runners on
first/first and third, 203
single to left: runners on
second/first and second/
bases loaded, 206
single to right: bases empty,
202
single to right: runners on
first/first and third, 205
single to right: runners on
second/first and second/
bases loaded, 208
wheel play, 219
wheel play fake, 220
play-by-play, 359
player-manager, 359
players
abbreviations for, 10
active years, 364
bench, 243
best (all-time), 305–312
best (current), 312–315
five-tool, 355
franchise, 356
list of, 10
in playing field illustration,
11
utility, 363
playing field
dimensions, 12
illustrated, 12

illustrated with players, 11
structure of, 12
playoffs. *See* League Championship Series
plays
appeal, 31, 351
backhand, 160
bonehead, 353
called dead, 28
cut-off, 144–145, 152
hit-and-run, 88
pick-off, 139, 150
run-and-hit, 88–89
PONY Baseball, 229
pop-up slide, 185, 186
pop-ups
fielding, 140
to shallow center field play,
223
to shallow left field play, 222
to shallow right field play,
221
portsider, 360
postseason baseball. *See*
League Championship
Series; World Series
primary lead, 177, 178, 179,
180
print, baseball in, 292–293
Pro Player Stadium: Florida
Marlins, 277
productive out, 360
protective cups, 24
protest, 360
publication organizations,
379–380
Puerto Rican League, 238
pull the string, 360
pulling the ball, 79, 80, 360
Punch-and-Judy hitter, 360
punchout, 360
push bunts, 86
pylometrics. *See also* training
box jump, 47
defined, 46
drills, 47–48
jump and run, 47
jumping form, 47
padded box for, 46
side-to-side jumps, 48
warm ups, 46

• Q •

Qualcomm Stadium: San Diego
Padres, 279
quality start, 360
quick hands, 116
quick pitch, 360

• R •

rabbit ears, 360
radar gun, 360
records
bases on balls, 370–371
batting average (.424)
Rogers Hornsby, 341
batting streak, 369
career ERA (1.82) Ed Walsh,
342
career home runs (755) Hank
Aaron, 342
career slugging percentage
(.690) Babe Ruth, 340
career strikeouts (5714)
Nolan Ryan, 341
career wins/losses (512/313)
Cy Young, 340
consecutive games-played
streak (2478 and
counting) Cal Ripken,
342
consecutive no-hitters (2)
Johnny Vander Meer, 341
games played, 365
hitting, 365–369
hitting streak (56-games) Joe
DiMaggio, 340
most wins in a season (41)
Jack Chesbro, 341
pitching, 371–378
stealing, 369–370
strikeout, 371
Reduced Injury Factor (RIF)
baseballs, 18
reflexes, hitting and, 60
regular season, 360
regulation game, 360
release, 360
release point, 114
relief pitchers, 360
retired, 31
retouch, 360
Reviving Baseball In Inner
Cities, 229

Rickey, Branch, 345, 346
right field
    defined, 12
    double/triple down line
        plays, 212, 216
    double/triple to gap plays,
        211, 215
    pop fly play, 221
    single to, plays, 202, 205, 208
right fielder. *See also*
        outfielders
    abbreviation for, 10
    characteristics of, 121
    in double/triple down left
        field line plays, 209, 213
    in double/triple down right
        field line plays, 212, 216
    in double/triple to left center
        field gap plays, 210, 214
    in double/triple to right
        center field gap plays,
        211, 215
    glove, 117
    in pop fly plays, 221, 222, 223
    in sacrifice bunt plays, 217,
        218
    in single to center plays, 201,
        204, 207
    in single to left plays, 200,
        203, 206
    in single to right plays, 202,
        205, 208
    in wheel play, 219
    in wheel play fake, 220
right-handed pitchers, 194
Ripken, Cal, 342
Robinson, Brooks, 330
Robinson, Frank, 309
Robinson, Jackie, 310–311, 346
rock and throw, 137
Rodriguez, Alex, 336
Rodriguez, Ivan, 332
Rolen, Scott, 337
rookies, 360
rotation pass (medicine ball),
        48, 49
Rotisserie League Baseball,
        296, 298, 299
rounding the bag, 182, 183
rules, 27–34
    batter, 28–30
    designator hitter (DH), 30
    double-play breakup, 191
    modification of, 34
    pitcher, 32–33
    "Play," 27–28

runner, 30–31
umpire, 33–34
web site for, 34
weight training, 53
The Rules of Baseball, 34
run-and-hit play, 88–89
run-downs
    defined, 150, 361
    faking throw and, 151
    fielders during, 150–151
runners. *See* baserunners
runs
    defined, 360
    most batted in record, 367
    most scored record, 366
    scoring, 13
Runs Batted In (RBI), 360
Ruth, Babe, 306, 307, 340
Ryan, Nolan, 341

● *S* ●

sacrifice bunts
    defined, 85, 361
    placement of, 85
    plays, 217, 218
sacrifice fly, 361
*Sadaharu Oh and the Zen Way
        of Baseball,* 240
St. Louis Cardinals Web site,
        290
San Diego Padres Web site,
        290
San Francisco Giants Web site,
        290
saves, 361
scatter arm, 361
The Science of Hitting, 79
score, 361
scorekeeping
    abbreviations, 272–273
    codes, 272–273
    color coding and, 275
    diamonds, 273–274
    player numbers, 272
    scorecards, 270–271
    tracking the runner and,
        273–275
scorer, official, 14–16
scoring position, 361
scouts, 361
screwball, 112
season tickets, 361
seated groin stretch, 43
Seattle Mariners Web site, 290

Seaver, Tom, 320, 321
second base
    leading off, 179–180
    pick-offs at, 165, 194
    tagging up from, 183
second baseman
    abbreviation for, 10
    blocking the ball, 148
    characteristics of, 118–119
    communication with
        shortstop, 149
    covering first base, 151
    cut-offs and, 152
    defense against steals, 149
    double plays and, 119,
        152–154
    in double/triple down left
        field line plays, 209, 213
    in double/triple down right
        field line plays, 212, 216
    in double/triple to left center
        field gap plays, 210, 214
    in double/triple to right
        center field gap plays,
        211, 215
    glove, 117
    improvisation of, 155
    pick-offs and, 150
    play depth, 148
    playing as, 146–155
    in pop fly plays, 221, 222, 223
    relays and, 152
    run-downs and, 150–151
    in sacrifice bunt plays, 217,
        218
    setup, 146–148
    in single to center plays, 201,
        204, 207
    in single to left plays, 200,
        203, 206
    in single to right plays, 202,
        205, 208
    stance, 146, 147
    tagging and, 151
    throwing to first, 149
    in wheel play, 219
    in wheel play fake, 220
secondary lead, 178
seeing-eye grounder, 361
senior league organizations,
        387
set position, 361
set-up man, 361
seventh-inning stretch, 361
shaded outfield, 182
Shea Stadium: New York Mets,
        278–279

shifts
  destroying, 81
  hitting against, 81
  impact of, 81
shoes, 22
shoestring catches, 123, 361
short hops, 116
shortstop
  abbreviation for, 10
  arm strength of, 120
  backhand plays, 160
  calling ground balls, 148
  characteristics of, 119–120
  cheating steps at, 159
  communication with second
    baseman, 149
  diving, 159
  double plays and, 154, 161
  in double/triple down left
    field line plays, 209, 213
  in double/triple down right
    field line plays, 212, 216
  in double/triple to left center
    field gap plays, 210, 214
  in double/triple to right
    center field gap plays,
    211, 215
  fielding balls at, 159
  glove, 117
  as mirror of second
    baseman, 158
  open glove and, 160–161
  playing as, 158–162
  in pop fly plays, 221, 222, 223
  range of, 119
  in sacrifice bunt plays, 217,
    218
  setup, 158–159
  in single to center plays, 201,
    204, 207
  in single to left plays, 200,
    203, 206
  in single to right plays, 202,
    205, 208
  throwing from, 159
  in wheel play, 219
  in wheel play fake, 220
shoulder roll, 41, 42
show, the, 361
shrugs, 55–56
shutouts, 361, 375–376
side-to-side jumps, 48
signs
  defined, 361
  flashing, 132
  importance of, 130

physical, 133
  with pump system, 133
  stolen, 133
  take, 241
singles
  defending against, 200–208
  defined, 13, 361
  record, 367
skipper. *See* manager
skipping leg extensions, 38, 39
SkyDome: Toronto Blue Jays,
  284
slider, 108
sliding
  bent-leg slide, 185–186
  blocking the plate and,
    138–139
  head-first slide, 186–188
  hook slide, 188–190
  pop-up slide, 185, 186
  practicing, 184
  straight-leg side, 185, 191
slow rollers, 156–157
slugfest, 361
sluggers, 361
slugging average, 253, 365–366
slugging percentage record,
  340
slumps, 97
Smith, Ozzie, 328
Smoltz, John, 324
Society for American Baseball
  Research (SABR), 250
*The Society of American
  Baseball Research's
  Minor League Baseball
  Stars,* 239
solo homers, 361
southpaw, 361
Spahn, Warren, 318
spectators
  ball park and, 267–270
  interference by, 361
  scorekeeping, 270–275
  TV and, 270
spitballs, 33
split-fingered fastball, 108–109
The Sporting News, 292
Sports Illustrated, 292
The Sports Network (TSN),
  292
Sports Network Web site, 289
spray hitters, 79
spring training, 244
sprinting. *See also* training
  for home, 51–52
  hurdles, 51, 52
  importance of, 51

square stance, 69
squats, 54
squeeze play, 86–87, 361
stadiums. *See also* ballparks
  3Com Park: San Francisco
    Giants, 280–281
  American League, 281–285
  Anaheim Stadium: Anaheim
    Angels, 281
  Astrodome: Houston Astros,
    277–278
  The Ballpark At Arlington:
    Texas Rangers, 284
  Bank One Park: Arizona
    Diamondbacks, 281
  Busch Stadium: St. Louis, 279
  Cinergy Field: Cincinnati
    Reds, 276
  Comiskey Park: Chicago
    White Sox, 282
  Coors Field: Colorado
    Rockies, 277
  County Stadium: Milwaukee
    Brewers, 277
  Dodger Stadium: Los Angeles
    Dodgers, 278
  Fenway Park: Boston Red
    Sox, 282
  Hubert H. Humphrey
    Metrodome: Minnesota
    Twins, 283
  Jacobs Field: Cleveland
    Indians, 283
  Kauffman Stadium: Kansas
    City Royals, 283
  Kingdom: Seattle Mariners,
    284
  National League, 275–281
  Oakland Alameda County
    Coliseum: Oakland
    Athletics, 284
  Olympic Stadium: Montreal
    Expos, 278
  Oriole Park at Camden
    Yards: Baltimore Orioles,
    281
  Pro Player Stadium: Florida
    Marlins, 277
  Qualcomm Stadium: San
    Diego Padres, 279
  Shea Stadium: New York
    Mets, 278–279
  SkyDome: Toronto Blue Jays,
    284
  statistics for, 285–286
  Three Rivers Stadium:
    Pittsburgh Pirates, 279,
    280

(continued)

stadiums *(continued)*
Tiger Stadium: Detroit Tigers, 283
Tropicana Field: Tampa Bay Devil Rays, 284–285
Turner Field: Atlanta Braves, 276
Veterans Stadium: Philadelphia Phillies, 279
Wrigley Field: Chicago Cubs, 276
Yankee Stadium: New York Yankees, 283–284
stance
bunting, 83–85
catching, 131, 133
closed, 69, 70, 354
even, 69, 70, 355
knees and, 71
open, 69, 70, 359
outfielder, 168
pitcher (after pitch), 162
pitching, 100
pivot, 83
second baseman, 146, 147
square, 69, 83–84
third baseman, 155
starting rotation, 362
stationary lead, 194
statistics
base-on-balls percentage, 253
batting average, 252
defensive measurements, 256
earned run average (ERA), 255
fielding average, 256
home run ratio, 254
lowdown on, 257
offensive measurements, 251–254
on-base percentage, 253
opponents' batting average, 255–256
organizations, 380
pitching measurements, 254–256
pitching winning percentage, 254–255
slugging average, 253
stolen base percentage, 254
strikeout ratio, 254
team measurements, 256–257
won-lost percentage, 256–257
Staub, Rusty, 95–96, 167–172
stealing. *See also* base stealers
benefits of, 192
catcher throw and, 136–137
delayed, 196
double, 137, 196–197
faking, 197
home plate, 195
leads and, 194
left-handed pitchers and, 194
records, 369–370
second baseman prevention against, 149
studying pitcher for, 193
successful, percentage of, 192
third base, 179, 194–195
when to say no to, 196
step and throw, 137
stepping in the bucket, 94
stolen base percentage, 254
Stolen Season, 239
The Story of Minor League Baseball: A History of the Game of Professional Baseball in the United States, 240
straight-leg slide, 185, 191
strawberry, 362
Street & Smith's Baseball, 293
stretch drive, 362
stretch, pitching from, 105
stretches. *See also* training
benefits of, 38
breathing and, 39
butterfly stretch, 45
dip splits, 45–46
forearm and wrist stretch, 42–43
forward bend, 39, 40
forward leg bend, 40–41
holding, 39
knee pulls, 43, 44
performing, 39
seated groin stretch, 43
shoulder roll, 41, 42
torso twist, 39, 40
triceps stretch, 41, 42
V-stretch, 43, 44
stride. *See also* hitting; swing
beginning, 74
importance of, 72
length of, 73
looking before, 72–73
overstride, 73, 74
troubleshooting, 73–74
strike zone
defined, 16, 362
hitting, 78–79
illustrated, 16
judgment, 61
learning, 78–79
strikeouts
consecutive record, 375
defined, 362
fear of, 94–95
hitter records, 371
pitcher record, 375
ratio, 254
record, 341
strikes
defined, 16, 362
third, getting past catcher, 30
umpire's calling of, 78
striking out the side, 362
suicide squeeze, 86
suspended game, 362
sweatbands, 23
sweet spot, 362
swing. *See also* hitting
checked, 354
chopping and, 92–93
eyes during, 70
fine-tuning, 76–77
follow-through, 77–78
in front of mirror, 91
head bobbing and, 94
head during, 70
hitching and, 93
lead bats, 67
locking front hip and, 93
lunging and, 93
shoulders during, 70
slightly down approach, 74–75
slightly up approach, 74–75
stepping in the bucket and, 94
stride and, 72–74
uppercutting and, 93
swinging bunts, 87
switch-hitter, 362

● *T* ●

tagging
defined, 362
execution, 151
for force out, 181

tagging up, 182–183
take sign, 241, 362
Tampa Bay Devil Rays Web site, 290
tape-measure home run, 362
T-Ball, 227–228
team organizations, 380–382
television
  Caribbean leagues, 292
  Classic Sports Network, 292
  ESPN, 291
  Fox Broadcasting, 291
  NBC, 291
  The Sports Network (TSN), 292
Temple Cup, 262
Texas Rangers Web site, 290
third base
  coach, 14, 184
  leading off, 180–181
  stealing, 179, 194–195
  tagging up from, 183
third baseman
  abbreviation for, 10
  anticipation by, 155–156
  arm strength of, 120
  baserunners and, 157
  bunts and, 156–157
  characteristics of, 120
  checking park, 156
  double plays and, 157
  in double/triple down left field line plays, 209, 213
  in double/triple down right field line plays, 212, 216
  in double/triple to left center field gap plays, 210, 214
  in double/triple to right center field gap plays, 211, 215
  glove, 117
  playing as, 155–158
  in pop fly plays, 221, 222, 223
  in sacrifice bunt plays, 217, 218
  in single to center plays, 201, 204, 207
  in single to left plays, 200, 203, 206
  in single to right plays, 202, 205, 208
  slow rollers and, 156–157
  stance, 155
  throws, 158
  in wheel play, 219

in wheel play fake, 220
Thomas, Frank, 313
Three Rivers Stadium: Pittsburgh Pirates, 279, 280
three-fingered change-up, 110
thrown out of games, 33
throws
  aiming, 124
  arm warm-up for, 122
  catcher, 136–137
  delivering, 123–125
  to first baseman, 142–143
  grip for, 122–123
  hardness of, 125
  jump pivot, 137
  overhand, 124
  rock and, 137
  shortstop, 159
  sidearm, 124
  step and, 137
  from third baseman, 158
  trajectory of, 197
  wrist snap, 125
Tiger Stadium: Detroit Tigers, 283
time pick-off plays, 150
toe push (medicine ball), 50
tools of ignorance, 362
Toronto Blue Jays Web site, 290
torso twist, 39, 40
toss (medicine ball), 49
Total Baseball, 249, 288–289
trades, 362
training, 37–57
  medicine ball, 48–51
  pylometric, 46–48
  sprinting, 51–52
  stretching, 38–46
  warm up, 38
  weight, 52–57
triceps stretch, 41, 42
triple play, 362
triples
  defending against, 209–216
  defined, 13, 362
  record, 368
Tropicana Field: Tampa Bay Devil Rays, 284–285
Turner Field: Atlanta Braves, 276
turning two, 119
twin killing, 362

two-seam fastball, 107
two-strike pitches, 77
two-way lead, 178

● *U* ●

Ultimate Baseball Book, 295
umpires
  authority of, 14
  calling games, 14
  calling "Play," 27–28, 359
  calling "Time," 14, 362
  calls, 354
  defined, 14, 362
  home plate, 14, 33
  interference, 362
  positions of, 14
  rules for, 33–34
uniforms
  caps, 23
  defined, 362
  how to wear, 24
  manufacturers, 24
U.S. Amateur Baseball Association, 229
uppercutting, 93
upright row, 55
USA Baseball, 227
USA Today, 292
utility players, 363

● *V* ●

Vander Meer, Johnny, 341
Vaughn, Mo, 315
Venezuelan League, 238
Veterans Stadium: Philadelphia Phillies, 279
Vizquel, Omar, 332
V-stretch, 43, 44

● *W* ●

Walker, Larry, 314
walking lead, 194
walks
  aggressive, 89
  defined, 363
  percentage, 253
  records, 370–371, 377–378
Walsh, Ed, 342
warm-ups, 38
warning track, 363

waste pitch, 363
Web sites
  Ballparks by Munsey &
    Suppes, 289
  Baseball Server, 288
  major league team, 289, 290
  MLB@Bat, 287–288
  National Baseball! Hall of
    Fame, 288
  Negro leagues, 288
  Sports Network, 289
  Total Baseball, 288–289
weight training. *See also*
    training
  balancing with other
    training, 53
  bench press, 53
  benefits of, 52
  caution, 53
  close grip bench press, 54
  curl to press, 55
  dumbbell bench press, 54
  hammer curls, 55
  lateral raise, 56
  lunges, 54–55
  lying triceps extension,
    56–57
  one arm dumbbell row, 54
  pitfalls, 53
  rules, 53
  shrugs, 55–56
  spotter, 53
  squats, 54
  upright row, 55
wheel play
  defined, 219
  fake, 220
  player positions for, 219
wheelhouse, 363
wheels, 363
whitewash, 363
Who's Who In Baseball, 293
wild pitches, 363, 378
Williams, Ted, 25, 59, 311–312
winning
  elements of, 243–244
  at fantasy baseball, 299–300
  percentage (pitching),
    254–255
Winter league, 363
won-lost percentage, 256–257
wood bats, 19, 20
World Series
  first, 261
  history of, 261–263

records of, 263
worm-burner, 363
Wrigley Field: Chicago Cubs,
  276
wrist stretch, 42–43

• Y •

Yankee Stadium: New York
  Yankees, 283–284
Young, Cy, 318, 340
Youth Baseball Athletic
  League, 229
youth baseball organizations,
  388

IDG BOOKS WORLDWIDE BOOK REGISTRATION

Register This Book and Win!

We want to hear from you!

Visit **http://my2cents.dummies.com** to register this book and tell us how you liked it!

- ✔ Get entered in our monthly prize giveaway.
- ✔ Give us feedback about this book — tell us what you like best, what you like least, or maybe what you'd like to ask the author and us to change!
- ✔ Let us know any other ...*For Dummies*® topics that interest you.

Your feedback helps us determine what books to publish, tells us what coverage to add as we revise our books, and lets us know whether we're meeting your needs as a ...*For Dummies* reader. You're our most valuable resource, and what you have to say is important to us!

Not on the Web yet? It's easy to get started with *Dummies 101*®: *The Internet For Windows*® *95* or *The Internet For Dummies*®, 4th Edition, at local retailers everywhere.

Or let us know what you think by sending us a letter at the following address:

...*For Dummies* Book Registration
Dummies Press
7260 Shadeland Station, Suite 100
Indianapolis, IN 46256-3945
Fax 317-596-5498

BUSINESS AND
**GENERAL
REFERENCE
BOOK SERIES
FROM IDG**

**COMPUTER
BOOK SERIES
FROM IDG**